About Island Press

Island Press is the only nonprofit organization in the United States whose principal purpose is the publication of books on environmental issues and natural resource management. We provide solutions-oriented information to professionals, public officials, business and community leaders, and concerned citizens who are shaping responses to environmental problems.

In 1994, Island Press celebrated its tenth anniversary as the leading provider of timely and practical books that take a multidisciplinary approach to critical environmental concerns. Our growing list of titles reflects our commitment to bringing the best of an expanding body of literature to the environmental community throughout North America and the world.

Support for Island Press is provided by Apple Computer, Inc., The Bullitt Foundation, The Geraldine R. Dodge Foundation, The Energy Foundation, The Ford Foundation, The W. Alton Jones Foundation, The Lyndhurst Foundation, The John D. and Catherine T. MacArthur Foundation, The Andrew W. Mellon Foundation, The Joyce Mertz-Gilmore Foundation, The National Fish and Wildlife Foundation, The Pew Charitable Trusts, The Pew Global Stewardship Initiative, The Rockefeller Philanthropic Collaborative, Inc., and individual donors.

About The Global Development And Environment Institute

The Global Development And Environment Institute (G-DAE) was founded in 1993 to combine research and curricular development activities of two ongoing programs at Tufts University: the Program for the Study of Sustainable Change and Development in the School of Arts and Sciences, and the International Environment and Resource Policy Program at the Fletcher School of Law and Diplomacy. The combination creates a center of expertise in economics, policy, science, and technology.

G-DAE works toward understanding actual and possible past and future trajectories of economic development, emphasizing the relation between social and economic well-being on the one hand, and ecological health on the other. It develops an improved theoretic understanding of economic systems as they are embedded in the physical contexts of history, politics, ethics, culture, institutions, and human motivations and goals. Finally, it assists the public and private sectors of nations at different stages of development to develop policies that promote sustainability. G-DAE pursues its goals through research, publication projects, curriculum development, networking, and policy work.

THE
CONSUMER
SOCIETY

FRONTIER ISSUES IN ECONOMIC THOUGHT
VOLUME 2
NEVA R. GOODWIN, SERIES EDITOR

THE CONSUMER SOCIETY

Edited by
Neva R. Goodwin,
Frank Ackerman,
and David Kiron

The Global Development
And Environment Institute
Tufts University

ISLAND PRESS

Washington, D.C. ■ Covelo, California

Library of Congress Cataloging-in-Publication Data

The consumer society/edited by Neva R. Goodwin, Frank Ackerman, and David Kiron
       p. cm.—(Frontier issues in economic thought series)
    Includes bibliographical references and index.
    ISBN 1-55963-485-5 (cloth).—ISBN 1-55963-486-3 (pbk.)
       1. Consumer behavior—Social aspects—United States.
    2. Consumption (Economics)—Social aspects—United States.#. I. Goodwin, Neva. II. Ackerman, Frank. III. Kiron, David. IV. Series
    HF5415.33.U6C66   1997
    306.3'4—dc20   96-22627
                                          CIP

Printed on recycled, acid-free paper ✪

Manufactured in the United States of America

10 9 8 7 6 5 4 3 2 1

To Tibor Scitovsky,
who has raised so many of the critical questions

Note to the Reader

In general, the summaries presented here do not repeat material from the original articles verbatim. In a few instances it has seemed appropriate to include in the summaries direct quotations from the original text ranging from a phrase to a few sentences. Where this has been done, the page reference to the original article is given in square brackets. The complete citation for the article always appears at the beginning of the summary. References to other books or articles appear in endnotes following each summary.

Contents

PART III

Family, Gender, and Socialization

PART VI
Critiques and Alternatives in Economic Theory

PART VIII
Consumption and the Environment

PART IX
Globalization and Consumer Culture

PART X
Visions of an Alternative

Authors of Original Articles

George A. Akerlof Dept. of Economics, University of California, Berkeley, California

Russell W. Belk Dept. of Consumer Studies, University of Utah, Salt Lake City, Utah

Raymond Benton, Jr. Dept. of Marketing, Loyola University, Chicago, Illinois

Fred Block Dept. of Sociology, University of California at Davis, Davis, California

Samuel Cameron Dept. of Social and Economic Studies, University of Bradford, West Yorkshire, England

Colin Campbell Dept. of Sociology, University of York, Haslington, England

Edward Canda Dept. of Sociology, University of Iowa, Iowa City, Iowa

Mario Cogoy Dept. of Economics, University of Trieste, Italy

David A. Crocker Dept. of Philosophy, Colorado State University, Fort Collins, Colorado

Gary Cross Dept. of History, Pennsylvania State University, University Park, Pennsylvania

Mihaly Csikszentmihalyi Dept. of Psychology, University of Chicago, Chicago, Illinois

Herman Daly School of Public Affairs, University of Maryland, College Park, Maryland

Helga Dittmar Dept. of Psychology, University of Sussex, Falmer, Brighton, England

S.A. Drakopoulos Dept. of Economics, University of Aberdeen, Aberdeen, Scotland

James S. Duesenberry Dept. of Economics, Harvard University, Cambridge, Massachusetts

Alan Durning Director, Northwest Environment Watch, Seattle, Washington

Richard Easterlin Dept. of Economics, University of Southern California, Los Angeles, California

Duane Elgin Director, Choosing Our Future, Larkspur, California

Paula England Dept. of Sociology, University of Arizona, Tucson, Arizona

Ben Fine Dept. of Economics, School of Oriental and African Studies, University of London, Russell, England

A. Fuat Firat Dept. of Marketing, Arizona State University West, Glendale, Arizona

Robert H. Frank Dept. of Economics, Cornell University, Ithaca, New York

John Kenneth Galbraith Dept. of Economics, Harvard University, Cambridge, Massachusetts

David B. Hamilton Dept. of Economics, University of New Mexico, Albuquerque, New Mexico

Mary Beth Haralovich Dept. of Media, University of Arizona, Tucson, Arizona

Fred Hirsch (deceased)

Jeffrey James Dept. of Economics, Tilburg University, Netherlands

Noreene Janus President, Counterparts Incorporated, Arlington, Virginia

Rhys Jenkins University of East Anglia, Norwich, Norfolk, England

Sut Jhally Dept. of Communications, University of Massachusetts, Amherst, Massachusetts

Harry G. Johnson (deceased)

Joel Jay Kassiola Dean, School of Behavior and Social Sciences, San Francisco State University, San Francisco, California

Nathan Keyfitz Dept. of Sociology and Demography, Harvard University, Cambridge, Massachusetts

John Maynard Keynes (deceased)

Stephen Kline Dept. of Communications, Simon Fraser University, Burnaby, British Columbia, Canada

Robert Kubey Dept. of Communications, Rutgers University, New Brunswick, New Jersey

Rudi Laermans Dept. of Sociology of Religion and Culture, Catholic University of Leuven, Leuven, Belgium

Kelvin Lancaster Dept. of Economics, Columbia University, New York, New York

Robert E. Lane Dept. of Political Science, Yale University, New Haven, Connecticut

T.J. Jackson Lears Dept. of History, Rutgers University, New Brunswick, New Jersey

Martyn J. Lee Cultural and Communication Studies, Coventry University, England

Harvey Leibenstein (deceased)

William Leiss Eco-Research Chair in Environmental Policy, School of Policy Studies, Queens University, Kingston University, Ontario, Canada

Ellen Leopold Cambridge, Massachusetts

Staffan B. Linder Stockholm School of Economics, Sweden

Mark A. Lutz Dept. of Economics, University of Maine, Orono, Maine

Kenneth Lux Clinical Psychologist, Penobscot, Maine

J. Fred MacDonald Dept. of History, Northeastern Illinois University, Chicago

Grant McCracken Dept. of Ethnography, Royal Ontario Museum, Toronto, Ontario, Canada

Neil McKendrick Gonville and Caius College, Cambridge, England

Daniel Miller Dept. of Anthropology, University College, London, England

David Morley Dept. of Media and Communications, Goldsmits College, University of London, New Cross, England

Chandra Mukerji Dept. of Communications, University of California, San Diego

Ragnar Nurkse (deceased)

Richard Pollay Dept. of Marketing, University of British Columbia, Vancouver, Canada

Clive Ponting University College of Swansea, University of Wales

Marsha Richins Dept. of Marketing, College of Business and Public Administration, University of Missouri, Columbia, Missouri

Aaron Sachs Worldwatch Institute, Washington, D.C.

Mark Sagoff Dept. of Philosophy and Public Policy, University of Maryland, College Park, Maryland

Marshall Sahlins Dept. of Anthropology, University of Chicago, Chicago, Illinois

Allan Schnaiberg Dept. of Sociology, Northwestern University, Chicago, Illinois

Juliet Schor Director of Studies, Women's Studies, Harvard University, Cambridge, Massachusetts and Professor of Economics of Leisure, Tilburg University, Netherlands

Tibor Scitovsky Professor of Economics Emeritus, Stanford University, Palo Alto, California

Jerome M. Segal Dept. of Philosophy, University of Maryland, College Park, Maryland

Carole Shammas Dept. of History, University of California at Riverside, Riverside, California

David E. Shi President, Furman University, Greenville, South Carolina

Leslie Sklair Reader in Sociology, London School of Economics and Political Science, London, England

Alladi Venkatesh Graduate School of Management, University of California at Irvine, Irvine, California

Paul Wachtel Dept. of Psychology, City University of New York, New York

Thomas Walz Dept. of Sociology, University of Iowa, Iowa City, Iowa

Alan Warde Dept. of Sociology, University of Lancaster, England

Susan Willis Dept. of English, Duke University, Durham, North Carolina

John E. Young Worldwatch Institute, Washington, D.C.

Viviana Zelizer Dept. of Sociology, Princeton University, Princeton, New Jersey

Foreword

On no matter is economics more in contradiction with itself than in its view of consumer behavior and motivation and the consumer-oriented society. With increasing consumer well-being, it is held, the urgency of consumer goods production does not diminish. There is no concept of enough or more than enough. In technical terms, while the marginal utility of the particular product does decline, that of goods in general and specifically the money income that procures them are broadly regarded as constant. Systematically ignored is the evident fact that above a certain level of income it is also expected that some part will be saved and—greatly in the public interest—will be invested for more production.

Equally, perhaps even more strenuously, resisted is the notion that consumer wants are, in any substantial measure, created by the firms that supply them. It is commonly known that with the production of goods goes the persuasion that assures their purchase. Advertising, as in several essays here told, is an essential feature of the economic process. But this economic reality has long been denied. In the orthodox view consumer sovereignty reigns supreme. Questioning this some years ago, I was powerfully assailed in textbooks for failing to note that the Ford Motor Company had once produced a vehicle, the Edsel, which consumers, exercising that sovereign choice, chose not to buy. That quite a few other models were successfully promoted went unmentioned. Economists, one could only conclude, did not (still do not) watch television.

From the foregoing come two consequences of especially urgent effect. As the need for goods in the modern consumer economy lessens and becomes more contrived, the economic system achieves its importance, even urgency, not for the goods and services it produces but for the work and income it provides. The modern politician, quite regardless of party or political faith, never speaks of the need to produce more goods and services. Plenitude is here assumed. Reference is always to the jobs provided. Everyday political expression corrects the basic economic theory, emphasizing not the goods created, or the service rendered, but the employment provided; not the wants satisfied but the income made available.

Related is the way in which the modern consumer economy is locked into the social need for steadily expanding output. Absent this expansion, there is stagnation, recession, depression, unemployment, and, perhaps, acute political and social tension. The stable or reduced supply of goods and services causes no pain, no deprivation; it is the reduced flow of income, the unemployment, the effect on business income and solvency that is cited and feared. The modern consumer economy is tied in unrelenting fashion to the need for steadily expanding production. Consumption, once the purpose of economic life, has now a supporting role. One can suffer a shortage of income; one never, in all ordinary circumstances, suffers a shortage of goods to buy.

A further point—speaking of the market economy. In the modern society there is also the role of the state. Essential functions—a safety net for the poor, education, low-income housing, essential regulation, and much else—come from government. Private goods and services have enormous and costly promotional support: the advertising and salesmanship of the market sector. Public services, especially those for the poorer citizens, enjoy no such promotion. As a result, the modern economy has an inherently unequal and unsocial distribution of resources between its private and public sectors—wonderfully expensive television programs, poor schools; spacious, handsomely furnished houses, filthy streets; abundant automobiles, dense traffic jams and poor public transportation.

With the development, perhaps one should say exploitation, of the modern consumer economy has come a marked change in social concern as regards consumer products. There was once the consumer movement—a determined investigation of, and report on, the value and utility of various consumer products and supporting public regulation and education. This continues but with a diminished sense of social urgency. The poor still need guidance on what they buy, including protection against consumer scams. For the more affluently supplied there is no similar urgency. There is no social need for according guidance on the purchase of a Cadillac or a Mercedes Benz. Or for that matter, designer jeans or a vast range of other affluent products. As consumer necessity yields to fashion and persuasion, concern for consumer protection and choice inevitably recedes. This is recognized in part, but far from fully, in either public discourse or practice.

But enough. The foregoing will tell why I am attracted to this book as, I trust, will be many others. It is a diverse, technically competent, and intellectually compelling look at the modern consumer economy. It brings the modern consumer economy into focus in all its many aspects, including the highly important question of environmental effects. The consumer society, it makes clear, is peculiarly the good fortune of the fortunate. Were it at a similar level of production and resources use for all the people of all the poor lands, life on the planet would be endangered, perhaps impossible. Pollution would be insufferable; so also the use of space and, as noted, the depletion of natural resources. The Dalai Lama, a friend of mine from my India days, put the matter with wonderful precision in conversation a few weeks ago: " What would the world be like if everyone drove a motor car?"

In recent years, Tufts University, long a place of diverse interests, wisely has added to its distinction by its teaching, research, and outward education on pressing social concerns at home and abroad. This has included and indeed emphasized environmental issues but also much else of urgent public concern. A committed, articulate, and distinguished group of scholars has come together for this effort, as this, and the series of studies of which it is a part, amply reveal. As I have made sufficiently clear, the matters here discussed have long reflected my particular interest. But that is a small part of the present effort. This (and companion volumes to come) is work of breadth, depth, and diversity, displaying a strong sense of social responsibility. For all concerned with the urgent questions of modern economic life, this volume is to be read, admired, and, I trust, made a source of strong comment and national and international motivation.

John Kenneth Galbraith
Harvard University

Acknowledgments

The writing of this book has been enormously aided by the generous assistance of individuals who have thought deeply about the issues raised herein. We sought, and received, comments and suggestions from many people. We hope that the following list is complete; however the responsiveness of friends and colleagues was such that there is a danger we will have forgotten to include some who should be mentioned.

Throughout the process there have been a few people whom we have called on repeatedly for their wisdom, knowledge, and inspiration. We wish to pay special tribute to Alan Durning, John Kenneth Galbraith, Vicki Robin, Juliet Schor, and Tibor Scitovsky for their intellectual leadership; we also feel privileged to regard them as friends.

During the time we were working on this book we were fortunate to be invited to several conferences on closely related subjects. To mention just three: David Crocker, at the University of Maryland, brought together a splendid group of people whose papers and discussions have made significant contributions to the topic. A conference convened by Betsy Taylor, Director of the Merck Family Fund, established important links between academic understanding and consideration of what actions should and can be taken in response to the growing influence of the consumer society. Betsy Taylor has provided critical leadership in recognizing and articulating the salience of these issues. Donella Meadows and the Balaton Group over which she presides held a fascinating international conference in Hungary titled "Sustainable Consumption."

In addition to individuals already listed, we benefited greatly from meetings with Brendt Blackwelder, Barbara Brandt, Daniel Faber, Sheldon Krimsky, Robert Kuttner, Bruce Mazlish, and S.M. Miller.

At a number of points along the way we were grateful to receive comments on our evolving table of contents from Allan Hoben, Paul Joseph, Howard Solomon, and Susan Strasser. Others who provided helpful and generous bibliographical guidance include Amy Agigian, John Applegath, Russell Belk, Colin Campbell, Gary Cross, Hazel Henderson, Jeffrey James, Peter Johnson, Mark Sagoff, Leslie Sklair, Alladi Venkatesh, Paul Wachtel, Thad Williamson, and the E.F. Schumacher Society.

The preparation of a Frontiers volume requires a tremendous commitment of time to survey the literature, read them (about a thousand were read carefully for the final selection of approximately 90 represented in this book), write and edit the summaries, and organize the summaries into coherent sections with introductions. Aside from the names on the cover of this volume, and the signed introductory essays for each section, a number of individuals have contributed importantly to the effort.

- In conjunction with writing her Tufts master's thesis "Beyond Consumer Culture," Elisa Blanchard spent nearly a year researching literature in the field while the rest of the Frontiers group was still primarily involved with Volume 1. She continued as one of the two lead researchers for this volume, contributing a valuable perspective and deep knowledge of the area.

- Kevin Gallagher, the other principal researcher for the Frontiers project during this book, has played two roles—adding that of project manager—and has done both with high ability and effectiveness. He and Elisa also wrote some of the summaries.

- Rajaram Krishnan was the Project Director at the time that we turned from Volume 1 (*A Survey of Ecological Economics*) to Volume 2. He contributed some of the summaries in this book and played a role in the early process of shaping and conceptualizing it.

- Miranda Kaiser contributed some summaries.

- Sy Bellin has volunteered his time as a member of our team, participating very helpfully in discussions and decisions.

- Kristen Bishop has done an excellent job as our in-house copy editor.

- Tufts undergraduates Jim Bures, Jeanie McDevitt, and Shea O'Neil have brought intelligence, energy, and good humor to library searches, copying, and other tasks.

Staffing and supporting an endeavor of this scope is costly. It would not have been possible without the recognition, by several foundations, of the importance of bringing to the attention of economists and others the centrality, in modern socioeconomic life, of the issues we have defined as on the frontiers of economic thought. We are extremely grateful to have received support for this volume from the MacArthur Foundation, Merck Family Fund, Rockefeller Brothers Fund, Island Foundation, and Bauman Foundation.

Tufts University has provided a stimulating environment within which the Global Development and Environment Institute (G-DAE) has worked on the Frontiers program, along with a number of other projects. We are especially grateful to the Fletcher School of Law and Diplomacy and the Graduate Department of Urban and Environmental Policy, which jointly administer G-DAE, providing us with friends, colleagues, and a good institutional home.

Volume Introduction

Neva R. Goodwin

Studies of the consumer society are valuable for the light they shed on two apparently opposed phenomena: affluence and poverty. Many of the earliest and loudest critics of such a society come from the side of affluence; their most general complaints are that they have been led to desire something (a lifestyle, a collection of goods) that does not bring them the promised satisfaction, or that leads them (or other people) away from development of their better, higher potential.

Less is currently being written in defense of the consumer society, in part because those who uphold the pillars on which it rests feel that they have a very strong position. They present it, implicitly, in the question: Then would you rather be poor? But this is an oversimplification. Poverty is not the only conceivable alternative to a consumer society. However the affluence of modern industrialized countries as they are currently organized does depend upon a cultural, institutional, and economic "package" of industrial society of which consumerism is a part. It is not always clear how to remove one part of this package and still enjoy the benefits of the rest.

Consumer Society and Poverty: Solution or Cause?

Is a consumer society a good society? Does it achieve real human well-being? One way to approach these questions draws on the view of consumerism as part of an *industrial package,* and asks whether this package represents a good, or the best available, solution to the age-old human problem of poverty.

Consider the following passage from a book written by the American economist George Katona in the early 1960s:

> Today in this country minimum standards of nutrition, housing, and clothing are assured, not for all, but for the majority. Beyond these minimum needs, such former luxuries as homeownership, durable goods, travel, recreation and entertainment are no longer restricted to a few. The broad masses participate in enjoying all these things and generate most of the demand for them.
>
> What is known all over the world as the American standard of living does not consist of luxurious living by the wealthy. Prosperity by a thin upper class would be neither new nor envied by millions abroad. What is

new is the common man's sharing in the ways of living that in the past were reserved for the few. The common man's ability to use some of his money for what he would like to have rather than for what he must have represents the revolutionary change. [1]

This statement, accompanied by perhaps a more arguable assertion that "higher living standards in turn appear to set the stage for, rather than to impede, cultural aspirations," leads Katona to conclude: "There is much cause to be grateful for the fact that ours is a consumer-oriented society." [2] Since most of the world agrees with this conclusion—or would like to be able to have such cause for gratitude in their own societies—it is hardly one to be dismissed offhandedly. It is not, however, a point of view that is much represented in this book. Why not?

One reason is precisely that it *is* the majority opinion, not only in the discipline of economics, but in the world—and the purpose of the Frontiers series is to give exposure to alternative ways of understanding economic issues within the context of their social and physical environments. In justifying the investigation of alternative perspectives on consumption, the question we must address is the following: Given the widely accepted humanitarian importance of a rapid increase in output and consumption in much of the developing world, as well as improved living conditions for the truly poor in the industrialized world, why do we think it is worthwhile to focus on the negative side of the consumer society?

Different authors will answer this question differently and we, the editors and researchers associated with this book, do not agree with every one of the (sometimes mutually contradictory) critiques of the consumer society that we have summarized. Nevertheless, there are some broad statements that can be made to explain why it is not necessarily contradictory to wish to alleviate poverty, and even to promote a decent standard of comfort, while at the same time finding fault with the consumerist ethos that is so closely associated with many of the prevailing approaches to economic growth.

One way of doing this is to analyze the industrial package that was implicitly presented in George Katona's work, cited earlier. Critical aspects of that package include: (1) higher output per worker, achieved by (2) technological and institutional innovations, along with (3) increased energy use and material inputs, accompanied by (4) higher average purchasing power, and supported by (5) a consumerist mentality which assures that the things produced will be purchased.

Of these factors, the environmental critique of the consumer society tends to focus on increased energy use and material inputs, an important part of the rising labor productivity that is the root of modern affluence but also is a source of concern because of its impacts on the natural world. The optimistic response to the environmentalists ignores this in favor of technological and institutional innovations, which represent other major sources of increased labor productivity.

To the extent that improved technology, along with improved management and the accumulation of human, physical, and information capital, can increase the productivity of energy and materials at the same time as it raises labor productivity—reducing throughput (the total flow of materials and energy through the economic system)—the technological optimists have a strong argument. It is weakened, however, by the observation that rising per capita consumption has, so far, stayed well ahead of any reduction in materials or energy per unit of output. Thus, throughput has continued to rise, with dangerous implications and impacts on the natural world. The bottom line of the environmental position is that it does not seem possible, based on any known technology, for the people of China, India, or other large populations in the developing world to imitate the consumption patterns of the North.

This assertion raises a number of important questions; for example, what are the possibilities for future technological breakthroughs that will dramatically decrease the environmental impact of consumption? How far can we reduce the material and energy elements in the consumer's market basket without reducing the associated satisfaction? What does such a trend (i.e., toward service industries) do to the work experience? What does such a trend imply for the distribution of consumer products and power? Is it in fact true that there are environmental limits to how much the human race can consume; if so, how will these limits make themselves felt; and when will they have been surpassed—or have they been already?

There do not appear to be answers to these questions that will convince both sides—the environmental pessimists and the technological optimists. (We will address many of these questions in more detail in future volumes of the Frontiers series.) To the extent that the environmentalists are correct, there is a direct link between present high consumption and future, and some present, poverty. This link demonstrates the fact that an important effect of reduced environmental quality is a reduction in the amount of output that can be produced with a given amount of input. This suggests that environmental degradation will cause a rolling back of the successes of the industrial model, with reductions in the overall availability of consumption goods.

Meanwhile, however, the pressure for development continues, in most places, to mean pressure for "the good life" as exemplified by the high-consumption North. This brings us to another major critique, focusing on point five of the industrial package outlined above: the consumerist mentality that assures that the things produced will be purchased.

A variety of specific connections have been suggested by thinkers who see the ethos of the consumer society as exacerbating the fact, the effects, or the feelings of poverty. For example, poverty is created by a desire for more (Marshall Sahlins, Part I); poor people and poor countries make inappropriate decisions on what to consume, and reduce their savings and investment, because they are misled by seeing the consumption of richer people and nations (Ragnar Nurkse, Part V); and the driving force of profit-seeking capitalism creates pressures for poor countries and poor individuals to make and purchase commodities that respond to wants manufactured by consumer-society-dominated media, rather than putting their efforts and resources into serving true needs (Russell Belk and Nathan Keyfitz, Part IX).

In addition to these suggestions, that the consumerist ethos directly increases the fact or the pain of poverty, there is a much larger body of criticism aimed at the effect of this ethos on those who have achieved affluence. We will now turn to that subject.

Consumer Society and Affluence: Theoretical Predictions for an Optimal Outcome

A salient characteristic of a consumer society is that it is one in which a principal focus of leisure or nonwork time is the spending of money. These leisure activities may be both active and passive, including shopping, window-shopping, daydreaming about possessions, and purchasing and displaying possessions. A consumer society promotes the belief that ownership of things and activities that require spending money—and the spending of money itself—are the primary means to happiness. A subtext in such a society is the assumption that happiness is the single real goal in life. (See the introductory essay to Part I for more definitions of consumption and a consumer society.)

A curious fact that has been alleged about consumer societies by a number of writers represented in this book is that the ostensible functions of the things purchased—their announced uses—become less and less important, as compared to nonutilitarian or symbolic functions. The latter include the provision of novelty and status; provision of a basis for personal relationships of comparison, sharing, envy, or social ranking; and provision of a sense of identity.

It is interesting to speculate, as an economist, on what forces might operate to bring about such a society. Who gains from it? Are there any losers? An obvious group of gainers in the microeconomy are the producers who, through the advertising and media promotion of consumerist behavior, generate markets for the products and services they sell. As to the losers, that issue is less obvious and harder to approach. Many (though by no means all) of the writings summarized in this volume will take the position that the consumers themselves are losing out.

It is hard for this idea even to be considered within economics. It is difficult for mainstream economics to confront the possible welfare implications of the notion that the consumer society, as it appears to be evolving, may not bring about the welfare maximization that was supposed to result from the discipline's assumption of an economy driven by consumer wishes.

Mainstream economics today views production as valuable primarily as a means to satisfy the needs and wants of consumers, but has taken a simple —some say, simplistic—approach to identifying those needs and wants. In fact, the desire to turn this issue into one that can be answered with objective, quantifiable data has caused the economics profession to accept, as the goal of the consumer, not his or her well-being, but the maximization of his or her consumption.

We may, for example, find this conclusion emerging from the following logic. In the neoclassical economic paradigm, the single overt value (aside from money values) is efficiency, but efficiency is only a means. When pressed to name the end to which efficiency is a means, neoclassical economists offer "the maximization of utility." However, in practice, most economic writings admit that utility is undefinable, and therefore use as a proxy goal the maximization of consumption (and therefore of production) within feasibility constraints. Thus the dominant economic paradigm has accepted a goal of increasing consumption, with no built-in concept of "enough."

The motivation of economics to be scientific, dealing with objective, quantifiable data, has dovetailed nicely with an important historical aspect of the creation of our present society. One of the most dramatic aspects of modern industrial experience has been the continuing increase in labor productivity. Growth in labor productivity means higher output for the same number of labor hours; each person, on average, produces more, so each person, on average, can consume more. The snag is that, for this to work, society as a whole *must* consume more—even if the things being consumed happen not to add to anyone's well-being, or to address genuine needs.

The theoretical bias of economics, coinciding with this core reality of industrialization, creates a logic that elevates the virtues of *competitiveness* and *profit maximization* (these characteristics are valued because they lead to efficiency, which we just discussed, as a means to an uncertain end). The forces that we have come to associate with these characteristics may result in loss of jobs or degradation of the work experience, but they are still desirable because they efficiently maximize output and, therefore, the possibilities for consumption.

Economic Goals in Theory and in the World

We thus have a set of assumptions and facts which tie together in a tight circle of consumption, production, and competition. Out of the assumption that consumer satisfaction is the ultimate goal of economic activity comes the use of productive and allocative efficiency as the ultimate standard for judging the success of an economic system. Where efficiency is the standard, the theory implicitly contains an evolutionary mechanism in which perfect competition is the system most likely to succeed. However, the competition for profits drives a system whose real-world effects, while they maximize consumption, may not maximize the well-being of consumers.

This disturbing possibility is all the more consequential when we remind ourselves that the identity of the consumer is, after all, an artificial one. Most adult human beings are both consumers and producers, as well as being a number of other things, such as citizens, parents, and so on. When we think about the well-being of the whole person we must include all of these avatars. This realization adds to our reasons to question the announced goal of the neoclassical economics paradigm. That goal, remember, is to maximize consumer well-being. Does our experience in the real world suggest that this goal—when it is not defined simply as consumption—is being met? Are consumers in fact getting what they *really* want? And is what (they think) they want really "good for them"?

We can launch ourselves into these issues by imagining that it is possible for a group of people, acting in one of their social roles specifically, as marketers, to influence what the majority of the society (including themselves in another role as consumers) believe they want. Now we know, for example, when people are persuaded to want drugs (for their thrill, for an escape from mundane reality, or a cool image), society agrees that this is not in their best interests—this want should not be encouraged. But what if it were possible to persuade people not just to want some particular thing that will lessen their well-being, but to adopt a lifestyle that will continually offer temptations for short-term satisfactions while taking them ever further from a form of well-being that they would prefer if they actually experienced it?

The image here is of a situation in which a rather questionable good is the enemy of the best good—in which people live in a topology where the loudest voices suggest they climb the nearest, easiest hills; and these drown out the voices that suggest it is better to look over the whole terrain to find and strive toward the global maximum.

To make this image more concrete, the amount spent annually on advertising in the United States is about $150 billion. This is approximately equal to the total spent in the nation on higher education. By the time they are eighteen, most children will have spent more time watching television than they will have spent in school. [3] Children learn many things in school. They learn how to perform tasks that they will need in jobs and to survive in a highly complex society. Schools also devote some time (though this may have decreased over recent decades) to teaching children things that will make it possible for them to receive some of the more complex and demanding satisfactions in life, satisfactions that require the active and educated engagement of the mind or body in, for example, arts, literature, sports, science, and informed discourse.

The voice of formal education that teaches people how to live a good life by these standards is relatively small compared to the voice of commercialism. The results sought by the commercial interests are immediate, allowing very efficient feedback and fine-tuning of messages, while the results sought from formal education are spread over decades and affected by many forces. Also, as noted, schools teach many things, but the commercial interests have, basically, one message: shop! purchase! consume! What if that strong voice, dominating more and more of our society, is, in fact, leading people to accept a lifestyle that is, in important ways, inferior to what is actually possible? To whom should such a possibility be a concern? Specifically, should economists worry about it? Should producers worry about it? If the issue is only relevant to "citizens," what about the citizens who are also economists or producers?

Neoclassical economics, the current mainstream theory, leaps to a conclusion on many of these issues, for it contains core assumptions which state that, even without taking the difficult route of asking people to explain their actions, we can infer the answers to our questions by collecting certain simple data about behavior. These critically convenient core assumptions are: (1) most people are rational and (2) rational behavior implies making decisions that will bring about the desired results.[4]

Buried in assumption #2 is a set of less well-examined beliefs. For it to be true that rational decisions will bring about the desired results it is necessary that people possess a high degree of understanding of the relationships between actions and their consequences. This implies complete knowledge about the circumstances that relate causes and effects. Moreover, if we include in "the desired results" a state of satisfaction with the consequences, this presumes that people will be glad, after the fact, that they have achieved what they set out to achieve. To put this another way, it assumes that the final goals which motivate action—e.g., the achievement of security, comfort, honor, and amusement[5]—are actually reached by the consumption decisions that are taken for those ends.

The beliefs implied in the neoclassical assumption—that rational behavior implies making decisions that will bring about the desired results—are at the heart of most debates over whether the consumer society is "a good thing." Beyond the environmental questions, of how much economic activity, and of what kind, the earth can support, is the issue of whether this economic activity is what we really want. That accompanies another very large question: Does the industrial package we described above have to be taken as a whole? If there were a way of eliminating the generation of a consumerist mentality by media and advertising, so that people were left alone to consume what they want, and not persuaded (as many of the authors in this book believe they are persuaded) to consume much that they do not really want, what would happen to the economy?

This line of questioning expands our subject into major philosophical, social, and cultural, as well as, macroeconomic issues. It is similar to the task awaiting any systems-minded economist who inquires whether our economy has shaped itself into a form that is less than optimal for consumers, or for people in general. Enormous questions are then opened, such as: to what alternative—real or hypothetical—should we compare our economic system? Or, if we cannot imagine a full alternative, but don't like the direction in which we are going, what different direction should we head? And how shall we go about changing our course?

We will not pursue these questions here. Some of them will be explored—though not as far as we might wish—in the concluding section of this volume. For now it is sufficient to note that the topic of the consumer society turns out to be a Pandora's box: Open it and you may end up reexamining everything.

The Scope of This Book and Its Place Within Academic Thought

This book, like the other volumes in the *Frontier Issues in Economics Thought* series is designed for a variety of readers. We expect it to be of interest and use to mainstream economists, nonstandard economists, other social scientists, and activists, students, and other citizens—who are concerned with the environmental, moral, and other social implications of a consumer society or of consumerist lifestyles. The projected Frontiers volumes obviously do not attempt to represent all possible alternative views:

Instead we have selected topics that seem of special salience, where there is a strong emerging body of writing providing alternatives that deserve to be taken seriously.

When we first conceptualized the "frontier areas" that would be examined in this series, we expected, in this volume especially, we would be defining a field that had not been seen as such by anyone else. By the time we had finished writing Volume 1 and started work on *The Consumer Society* we found (on the whole, with more pleasure than chagrin) that the salience of this topic had not only been recognized by many individual authors, but was being organized in a number of very useful ways. A leader in defining the field is Colin Campbell, who in 1991 published an article called "Consumption: The New Wave of Research in the Humanities and Social Sciences." It is worth quoting at length from his opening paragraph:

> Occasionally a special combination of events causes a topic or field of study to spring into prominence in several disciplines at approximately the same time. This is indeed what has happened over the past decade with respect to 'consumption'. Previously deemed unworthy of much serious interest by academics within the social sciences or the humanities and hence largely the preserve of those in such applied fields as marketing or consumer affairs, it has quite suddenly become a major topic of academic study. Not surprisingly, this has been accompanied by a considerable inter-disciplinary exchange of ideas with scholars often feeling that they have more in common with researchers in other disciplines who are studying the same topic than with their erstwhile colleagues. [6]

In emphasizing the importance of interdisciplinary exchange, Campbell also notes that economics, which tends to ignore the other disciplines, has deprived itself of the richness of social and cultural analysis that is necessary for an appreciation of this topic. Economics has therefore lagged behind the other social sciences in broadening its understanding of consumption and the consumer society.

The same point, about the relatively slower, more constricted movement of economics into this area, is made in an essay by Ben Fine, "From Political Economy to Consumption," which recently appeared in *Acknowledging Consumption*. Edited by Daniel Miller, this collection provides an excellent overview of the field, surveying the literature within such disciplines as sociology, history, and anthropology. We are glad to be able to point out the ways in which Miller's book and our book complement, rather than compete with, one another.

Each of the essays in *Acknowledging Consumption* provides a careful annotated bibliography of the literature in one area of study, along with thoughtful general reflections on the academic development of the topic.

Where our methodology is different from Miller's—and is, indeed (as far as we know), unique within any scholarly context—is in presenting relatively lengthy *summaries* of each article or chapter of a book that we finally select as one of the critical writings to define the field under review. We are aware, of course, that in most (not quite all) cases a summary, in its abbreviations, must give the reader less to think about than the original. We hope, and assume, that use of the Frontiers volumes will encourage readers to seek out the original works that especially match their interests. An important function of our work is to make it easier for others to identify such works.

While we would, ideally, wish to have been totally comprehensive in the literature we reviewed for this book, it is important to state what our boundaries are. First of all, we have limited ourselves to reading what is available in English. This is a decision that was driven simply by practicality. However, with regard to *The Consumer Society* we do feel that there is a particular justification for concentrating on U.S. material because of the special role played by this country in defining and setting the pace for our subject. (Note will be taken of the areas where we would especially have liked to have found more material than we did on non-U.S. aspects of the topic.)

In the definition of our topic we have accepted several limitations that we thought useful, not only because they helped us avoid the temptation to include everything, but also because they fit with accepted economic theory.

- We have defined *consumption* as something that happens after the point of sale. We have limited ourselves to summarizing writings on the consumption of *final goods,* leaving out the large topic of the use by firms of intermediate materials that are made into goods for final sale. We have also excluded consumption by government, focusing, instead, upon the standard definition of the consumer as an individual or a household.

- Our focus has been micro- rather than macroeconomic. That means that we have not paid much attention to such Keynesian or aggregate concepts as consumption functions, aggregate propensities to consume, and so on. Thus we focus on the causes, interpretations, and effects of consumer behavior, rather than on the economic relationships among consumption, savings, taxes, and investment.

- Finally, we have paid very little attention to the consumer protection movement. Our reason for doing so was initially that we felt this movement did not stand outside of the consumer society; rather, it seemed to accept the goals of maximizing consumption, merely concerning itself with assisting consumers to get the most and the best for their money, while restraining the blind forces of competitive production only far enough to protect consumers from physical hazards. A closer look at the literature in this area, along with more recent trends in this country and elsewhere in the world, suggests that this characterization was not quite fair, ignoring the diversity of consumer protection movements and the philosophical subtlety behind some of them. Nevertheless, the literature in this area did not seem central to our effort to find writings that could enrich economic theory while informing noneconomists about the best thinking on a topic of everyday significance.

It should be noted in this connection that the word *consumerism* is ambiguous, referring, as it does, both to the general ethos of the consumer society and to a vigorous consumer protection movement, not only in the United States, but in Japan, France, and other mostly developed parts of the world. For this reason, we have tried wherever possible to avoid using this word.

In addition to areas where we intentionally limited the research on the consumer society, there are also a number of aspects of the topic that we would have liked to include, but we were disappointed in not being able to find writing that advanced knowledge enough to warrant its inclusion. We would have liked to represent more work dealing with the effects on the poor living in a consumer society; with the interactions between gender and consumption; and with technology and consumption. We would also have liked to find more grounded, empirical work on related international issues, especially from economists. Newspapers are full of comments on the role and effect of Western culture and Western goods in other cultures, but we did not manage to find as many academic papers on these issues as we had expected.

A final point has to do with the language in which the Frontiers summaries are written. As noted at the outset, this series is designed to be used by a variety of audiences, including both economists and noneconomists. As we have written the summaries that constitute the larger part of each book in the series, we have tried to avoid professional jargon. We might, for example, say that "twice as much of a good provides twice as much of each of its characteristics" when, if we had been writing only for an audience of economists we could have said "consumption activities are linearly homogeneous." Since the two statements amount to almost exactly the same thing, we hope our economist readers will not mind the use of more ordinary terms.

Notes

1. George Katona, *Mass Consumption Society* (New York: McGraw Hill Book Company, 1964) pp. 5–6.

2. Ibid, p. 4. The text of this Introduction will not note all of the arguments that could be marshalled against Katona's optimistic view. While I believe that Katona's view of our society has much justification, I do want to argue against three points that he specifically makes: (1) In the 1960s there was good reason to cite growing equality as one of the virtues of the American model. This trend has been strongly reversed in the last fifteen years, in the United States and to varying degrees in other industrialized countries. The dissatisfaction associated with inequality is one of the themes appearing repeatedly in critiques of consumer society. (2) Many of the economic motivators on the producers' side in consumer societies seem to push toward a lowering, rather than a raising, of cultural standards. (3) The largest base for dispute is Katona's conflation of consumer society with the achievement of higher living standards. This relationship will be examined—though by no means resolved—in the following text.

3. Michael F. Jacobson and Laurie Ann Mazur, *Marketing Madness [A Survival Guide for a Consumer Society]* (Westview Press, Boulder, 1995) pp. 16 and 22.

4. For a thoughtful argument that the assumption of economic rationality alone has almost no observable implications, see Kenneth J. Arrow, "Economic Theory and the Hypothesis of Rationality," in *The New Palgrave: The World of Economics* eds., John Eatwell, Murray Milgate, and Peter Newman (New York: Norton, 1991).

5. This is a list of universal human aspirations that was provided by anthropologist Allan Hoben (in conversation, 1993).

6. Published in a special issue of the *Journal of Social Behavior and Personality*, vol. 6, no. 6, pp. 57–74. The above quotation is from p. 57. This article is summarized in Part I.

THE
CONSUMER
SOCIETY

PART I
Scope and Definition

Overview Essay

by Neva R. Goodwin

The scope of this volume must depend, in part, on how we define the subject with which we are grappling. What is a Consumer Society? Let us start with a smaller part of that question: What is consumption?

Economic and Other Views on Consumption

In the Introduction to this volume we said that we would restrict our exploration to the economic concept of "final" consumption, most often associated with households (as distinct from, for example, the consumption or use of materials by firms or by governments). This accords with most economic theory and modeling, which is concerned with the consumption of goods and services that have been purchased from a "producer" and are then in some way used by the "consumer." In the conventional view, consumption in economics is a simple, individual, readily quantified process of satisfying well-defined needs. This part will consider some alternative views that have recently gained prominence, diverging from mainstream economic theory in two directions.

The "sociological view" (held by others as well as sociologists) emphasizes the social and symbolic meanings of consumption. The "environmentalist view" emphasizes the material implications of consumption, in light of potential ecological limits to growth.

One starting point for the sociological view has come from economics. Kelvin Lancaster pointed out that what we seek when we set out to make a purchase is not a good itself, but rather its *characteristics*. Along similar lines, Harry Johnson has noted that what we actually *consume* may or may not be the good, but will, in any case, be the *"service"* that the good can provide.[1] For example, when we buy a hat we are seeking the characteristics of style, warmth, rain or sun protection, and so on. We won't actually consume the hat, but will consume the services contributed by its charac-

1

teristics (the feelings we receive from wearing a stylish hat, the protection and warmth it provides, and so forth). The hat can continue to provide some of these services as long as it holds together; others may be used up more quickly. For example, if "newness" is an important characteristic, that will soon wear off.

Some recent writers have extended the Lancaster/Johnson approach, moving even farther away from the actual thing (or service) that is purchased and used by the consumer. Daniel Miller and Alan Warde are two writers who especially focus on the postpurchase activities in which the consumer distances herself from the impersonality of the market transaction, actively incorporating the thing into a world of her own creation.

This contrasts with the approach of the environmentalists, who emphasize the material starting point of the whole economic process. Most consumption activities can be traced back to some extraction and use of natural resources—the environmentalists' special concern. This is expressed by Herman Daly, a leading ecological economist, when he states that "consumption is the disarrangement of matter, the using up of value added that inevitably occurs when we use goods. Consumption is the transformation of natural capital into manmade capital and ultimately to waste."[2]

Essential Characteristics of a Consumer Society

Now we are ready to attempt a broader definition of the consumer society. One of the motives for the recent focus on this topic comes from the environmentalists' concern with the physical entropy that arises in all stages of the economic process, from extraction through production, distribution, use, and disposal, with entropy usually increased at each of these stages. Nevertheless, the environmentalists' concern for what happens to material resources is not the central feature of the prevailing definitions of the consumer society. Two quotations will give the general flavor:

> A consumer society is one in which the possession and use of an increasing number and variety of goods and services is the principal cultural aspiration and the surest perceived route to personal happiness, social status, and national success.[3]
>
> A consumerist society makes the development of new consumer goods and the desire for them into a central dynamic of its socioeconomic life. An individual's self-respect and social esteem are strongly tied to his level of consumption relative to others in the society.[4]

An apparently necessary, though not sufficient, characteristic of a consumer society is that "people obtain goods and services for consumption through exchange rather than self-production."[5] The things whose consumption characterizes a consumer society are not those that are needed for subsistence, but are "valued for non-utilitarian reasons, such as status seeking, envy provocation, and novelty seeking."[6]

One of the most common themes is that a consumer society relates individual identity to consumption, so that our judgments of ourselves and of other people relate to the "lifestyle" that is created by consumption activities. Thus Raymond Benton, Jr. defines "consumerism" as "the acceptance of consumption as the way to self-development, self-realization, and self-fulfillment,"[7] and Anderson and Wadkins contrast consumption-oriented societies with production-oriented ones, noting that, in the former, "[a]n individual's identity is tied to what one consumes rather than in a production culture where an individual's identity is more tied to what one produces."[8]

Throughout these definitions we may see that the characteristics of a consumer society include issues to do with:

(a) *Commodity characteristics* and the *symbols* associated with them.

(b) The interlinked *behaviors* of producers (who, through advertising, etc., attempt to increase their sales) and of consumers (whose behavior is often seen as manipulated by producers).

(c) *Attitudes* toward commodities and toward commodity-oriented behavior.

All of these issues are engaged, for example, in the attention that has been paid to mass production. The characteristics of mass-produced items (the fact that they arrive on the market in large numbers, all alike, and are produced at a relatively low marginal cost) make it possible—and necessary—for producers to induce most members of a society (not just the elite) to become habituated to consuming purchased items, and to purchasing more than they need for bare subsistence. The behavior of producers and consumers are to some degree shaped by this necessity. Cultural attitudes have been called into play—some may, indeed, have been called into being—to support the behavior that is a necessary basis for a socioeconomic system much of whose activity is oriented to the production and sale of mass-produced commodities.

If Consumption Is the Means, What Is the End?

The preceding paragraph laid out one picture of the consumer society, presenting a complex relationship—with some hints as to the directions of causality—among commodity characteristics, cultural attitudes, and socioeconomic behaviors. Is this an accurate picture of our society? Is it more accurate than other, different pictures? Many of the writers represented in this book grapple with the questions of what is an accurate description of our society, and of the roles played in our society by consuming behavior and by attitudes toward consumption. These authors offer a variety of different descriptions, even though by no means all views will be directly represented. We will find that the attempt to describe our world as it is will be complicated by the strong normative (value-related) views of the authors. These views are necessarily interrelated with debates over positive (objective, fact-based) analysis. For example, the issue of whether greater consumption brings greater happiness involves both the interpretation of survey results (positive analysis) and also perceptions about social and environmental norms and values.

Durning's article—the first one summarized in this section—makes a critically important point with respect to this issue when he says:

> In the end, the ability of the earth to support billions of human beings depends on whether we continue to equate consumption with fulfillment. (Durning, 157)

The implication here—one that deserves to be spelled out explicitly—is that human beings have some choice in how we define success (or happiness, or well-being, or whatever word we use for our goals). That definition depends partly, to be sure, on our biological needs, but it also contains a large cultural component—a component that probably becomes relatively more dominant as the wealth of societies expands beyond what is needed for the simple maintenance of life.

It is increasingly recognized that even what we think of as basic, essential needs are human constructs; culture is even more so. No individual can, alone, create a culture, but each of us participates in its ongoing construction. The statement quoted from Durning suggests that, as we continue this process, if we are wise we will accept guidance from the realities presented to us by ecologists, replacing a shortsighted, throw-away culture that is severely damaging to our environment with "a culture of permanence."

Durning speaks of the "correlation between ability to consume and happiness." From the perspective just described, this is not a given. Our sense of well-being depends in an important way on our *definition* of well-being. That definition is a variable which we might choose to try to affect if we are persuaded that it is necessary to do so in order to preserve something of value. Are the "facts" about the impact of consumption on the natural world, as described by environmentalists, more scientific, less subjective, than the way we ourselves are affected by our consumerist lifestyle? We are seeing the early stage of the development of a strong body of research about, for example, the likelihood of global warming, the health effects of agricultural chemicals, even perhaps the human psychological dependence on certain aspects of nature. All of these issues continue to be hotly debated, and human values, wishes, and practical interests play a large role on each side of the debate.

The second summary in this section is of an article by David Crocker, which takes the value issues head-on. He raises the questions:

> To what extent, if any, is our current consumption good for us? Bad for us? Would some other level or kind of consumption be better? What evaluative criteria should we employ to assess the impact on our lives of our present consumption and to evaluate alternatives? (Crocker, 3)

Crocker identifies the important theme of means and ends that is carried through a number of other papers summarized here, especially those by Marshall Sahlins and William Leiss. Sahlins says that "Scarcity is not an intrinsic property of technical means. It is a relationship between means and ends." (Sahlins, 4–5) In other words, your goals can be so defined that what you have is enough; or they may be differently defined, "causing" scarcity.

The idea that scarcity is not given to us as a fixed fact, but depends on the level of our wants, is not new to much of Eastern philosophy. It is, however, diametrically opposed to two basic premises of modern neoclassical economics, which assumes that (1) wants are exogenous to the economic system (they are not influenced within it), and (2) wants are insatiable.

Many commentators in this century have accepted the second assumption at the expense of the first, as the evolution of economic logic made it necessary to choose between the two. (For example, the appearance of insatiability is in effect derived from the fact that new wants arise in response to evolving economic possibilities; thus wants must be seen as endogenous to the system.) This theoretic choice was partly the result of an image of human nature that emphasizes the driving forces of emulation and envy, along the lines laid out by Thorstein Veblen in *The Theory of the Leisure Class* (published in 1899). A related tendency of human nature that is described, in various forms, by many different writers, is that whatever we get seems less appealing than it was before we got it. Colin Campbell (in a book partially summarized in Part VII) emphasizes the creative role of the imagination, which can daydream a better world than any we are likely to encounter. Other authors find other reasons to anticipate, as Leiss does, that "no matter how wealthy and productive our society might become, we would always require higher levels of production and greater quantities of goods." (Leiss, 24) A result, as Crocker concludes, is that "American consumerism seems more productive of dissatisfaction than contentment." (Crocker, 24)

These observations about inherent tendencies in human nature and the resulting state of dissatisfaction have been offered as statements of fact. It would be nice if we could turn to the discipline of psychology for clear and undisputed evaluations of their truth. Unfortunately, none of these issues have been comfortably settled.

The Roads to Happiness

Emulation and the tendency to want more than we possess have been observed at least since Aristotle's time. This century's communist regimes conducted some grand (largely unsuccessful) social experiments in controlling wants or in redirecting emulation to nonmaterial goals. There is still little agreement on the extent to which these characteristics are inevitable, how large a role they play, or what cultural controls might be effective in reducing their impact.

There have been many studies on the issues of how happy people are and what makes them happy. As this is a topic which will have a prominent place in the next Frontiers volume (*Human Well-Being and Economic Goals*), we have not gone into it in depth here, only summarizing the single article that seemed to best represent the state of knowledge as it applies, particularly, to the consumer society. Richard Easterlin's 1974 article, "Does Economic Growth Improve the Human Lot? Some Empirical Evidence"[9] has been widely cited, discussed, and argued over for two decades. His recent article, "Will Raising the Incomes of All Increase the Happiness of All?," summarized in this part, brings the debate up to the present.

Recognition of the imponderable effects of cultural differences, along with attention to methodological and other criticisms, have caused Easterlin to reduce the importance he had earlier placed on international comparisons. At least on a within-country basis, however, his essential conclusion remains: Happiness is relative; a person's sense of well-being depends less on the objective reality of material affluence than on how his or her position compares to the reference group. At any point in time, wealthier people as a group are much happier than poorer members of the same society. However, careful research over a period of decades in many developed countries has shown that even substantial economic growth and increases in average incomes lead to no increase in average happiness for society as a whole.

The authors summarized in the rest of this volume, whether or not they address these questions openly, almost all seem to make some assumptions about their answers. Most of these writers accept some version of the Easterlin conclusion—namely, that the part of happiness which depends on material well-being is a function of how one interprets one's achievements; and that, in turn, is determined by the expectations raised by the material achievements of one's reference group. Only a few of the writers represented in this book accept the hypothesis that there is some absolute dependence of well-being upon material success. That is, however, the dominant assumption in neoclassical economics writings.

There is, thus, a division between economics, on the one hand, with its implicit assumption that maximizing well-being and maximizing material wealth are the same thing, and, on the other hand, the findings of researchers in the Easterlin tradition, who find that this correlation is weak or even nonexistent *when it is measured over time*. Within a consumer society the economic view has a strong consonance with popular beliefs.

The rise of the twentieth-century consumer society has been an integral aspect of the continuing evolution of Western culture. At any point in time the majority of such a population appears to look at those with higher consumption levels as models for a better, happier way of life. The small elite who are at the top of the heap, with no one to look up to as a model for how to spend more, still strive for more because they want to stay ahead of the pack. It is difficult for people to adjust their immediate wishes to the little-known fact that, as the tide raises all boats together, those who maintain the same relative position to others will not feel better off—even though they have achieved higher consumption. Even those who guess that this might be so often stay in the rat-race in the hope that their relative, as well as their absolute, position will improve.

It is almost impossible, within such a culture, to imagine the lack of desire for durable goods and the distaste for differentiation of which we catch glimpses in some anthropological reports. Sahlins is especially valuable for his projection of an alternative way of living and thinking. (Another very accessible image of a nonconsumerist mind-set was the 1960s movie *The Gods Must be Crazy*, with its beautiful, funny, and perhaps accurate depiction of neolithic attitudes.)

Our embededness in the consumer society makes it important, but very difficult, to answer a set of critical questions concerning not what people want, but what actually supports well-being—namely: (1) Is there some optimum level of consumption, after which more consumption is far less likely to contribute to more well-being? (2) If so, how is that level defined—apart from comparison with a reference group? (3) Would an "optimum level of consumption" be pretty much the same throughout humanity, or does it depend strongly on cultural definitions of success, happiness, and so on? (4)

If the latter, what are the options for affecting those cultural definitions? (Again, Frontiers Volume 3 will summarize writings that address some of these questions.)

In attempting to get at the aspects of well-being that are *not* dependent on norms and the related forces of emulation and envy, it may be that in our culture there is at present no way of defining an optimal consumption limit. While there are few places in the world today that are not strongly affected by this culture, it seems perfectly plausible that there have been and could be other societies in which people know how to define "enough." However, if we are to take seriously Durning's quest for a society that can ask and answer that question, it appears that the best way to achieve this will be to go forward and discover some never-before-seen, perhaps postindustrial, very distant relative of Sahlins' "original affluent society."

Neoclassical Theory and Consumer Society: A Confluence of Critiques

The foregoing discussion makes it evident why the scope of this book is best expressed in the title, "the consumer *society*." While a study of this topic makes it necessary to look closely at the three narrower subjects suggested earlier—the *behaviors* and *attitudes* of consumers and producers, and the *characteristics* of the commodities over which they meet—ultimately our topic is the whole society whose options for how to live well are at present shaped by a consumption-oriented culture.

The thinkers who in one way or another address this broadly-defined topic are generally impelled to do so because they perceive a problem. By contrast, those—like the mainstream economists—who take our socioeconomic system as given, or who do not feel that it should be regarded as problematic, have less reason to write about it. (An exception is Stanley Lebergott's book, *Pursuing Happiness: American Consumers in the 20th Century*, which was written as a defense of the consumer society, responding to the mounting chorus of complaint against it.)

Among the most creative and thoughtful authors in our field are the three summarized in this part who directly take on the whole system as a problem: Alan Durning, Allan Schnaiberg, and Juliet Schor. The first two of these focus especially on environmental issues, where there is more hard evidence for the belief that the consumer society is riding for a fall. While Durning sees the resolution of this problem as a cultural issue ("The challenge before humanity is to bring environmental matters under cultural controls"—Durning, 167), Schnaiberg finds a different approach to social definition. Reflecting on whether the creation of the consumer society is driven by consumers themselves or by producers (an issue that will recur in Part IV), he comes down strongly on the latter side, concluding that the central fact of a modern industrialized society is that "Consumption in the aggregate must be kept high to maintain the economic structure." (Schnaiberg, 167) In his view American products are designed to accommodate, not the consumer, but the methods of production and distribution and the profit maximization and market positioning of the producers. The producers have the power to limit consumer sovereignty by creating and directing a culture of wants. The solution to the problem, therefore, must be found on the production side.

Schor's approach to a solution starts from the vision that was to be found a hundred years ago, before the consumer society had fully taken hold, when "the alternative to 'work and spend' was leisure time and public culture." (Schor, 7) She and Schnaiberg both remind us that the consumer is normally also a worker and a citizen. Schor emphasizes the hope that the full person (worker-consumer-citizen) can be brought to see the desirability of adopting a practical combination of less work/less income/less consumption.

Schor urges a positive (as opposed to a normative) critique of the standard economic assumptions, based on continued study of the question of how consumption is related to well-being. Colin Campbell, the last author summarized in this section, reviews the ability of academic writers from a variety of fields to respond to this call. His knowledgeable survey provides another, more succinct introduction to a range of writings in the field (including many that are summarized in this book and many that have not been included). The special value of his article is that it relates different aspects of the work currently being done on the consumer society, showing how ideas are being exchanged and built upon across disciplines.

According to Campbell, the simple perspective of neoclassical economic utility theory, developed in conjunction with assumptions of general equilibrium and perfect competition, is no longer a dominant part of the broader discussion of consumption. Indeed, he asserts, the discussion has even moved beyond a protest against this unrealistic approach. At the same time, the flurry of largely normative critiques of the consumer society (as distinct from critiques of neoclassical consumer theory) has laid the groundwork for a different turn for the debate. Yet economics, as Campbell notes, has remained apart from this broader discussion.

The Introduction and several other essays introducing parts of this book examine and critique the neoclassical claim that a social optimum can be achieved by the socioeconomic system expressed in the consumer society. The editors of this volume, along with virtually all of the authors summarized herein, accept that this system, as a whole, deserves further scrutiny.

How is such an examination to be organized? In this book we have not tried to cover all possible issues. However, our list of issues is quite broad; it includes what we believe to be most of the critical dimensions of the topic—for example, the meanings and effects of consumption in affluent societies; the impact of a consumer culture on families, on gender definitions, and on the socialization of children; the history of the consumerist ethos; foundations and critiques of economic theories of consumption; the way the creation of wants (through media and advertising) perpetuates the consumer culture; the impacts of consumption on the environment; and the global spread of consumer culture.

The last part of this book will summarize and discuss some visions of an alternative to the consumer society, allowing a return to a number of the questions raised in this essay.

Notes

1. See Part VI for the Muth/Becker use of this concept and for the summary of Lancaster's article.

2. Herman Daly, "Consumption, Value-Added, Physical Transformation and Welfare," in *Getting Down to Earth: Practical Applications of Ecological Economics,* eds. R. Costanza, O. Segura, and J. Martinez-Alier (Washington, DC: Island Press, 1996).

3. Paul Ekins, "A Sustainable Consumer Society: A Contradiction in Terms?" *International Environment Affairs,* vol. 4, no. 4 (Fall 1991), 244.

4. Jerome Segal, "Alternatives to Mass Consumption," in *Philosophy and Public Affairs,* special issue on "Ethics of Consumption," vol. 15, no. 4 (Fall 1995), 27–29, 276.

5. Kathleen Rassuli and Stanley Hollander, "Desire—Induced, Innate, or Insatiable?" *Journal of MacroMarketing* (Fall 1986), 5.

6. Russell Belk, "Third World Consumer Culture," in *Marketing and Development* (Greenwich: JAI Press, 1988), 105.

7. "Work and the Joyless Consumer," in *Philosophical and Radical Thought in Marketing,* eds. A. Firat, N. Dholakia, R. Bagozzie (Lexington: Heath, 1987), 245.

8. Laurel Anderson and Marsha Wadkins, "Japan—A Culture of Consumption?" *Advances in Consumer Research* (1991), 18: 129.

9. Published in *Nations and Households in Economic Growth,* eds. Paul David and Melvin Reder (New York: Academic Press, 1974), 89–121.

Summary of

Asking How Much Is Enough

by Alan Durning

[Published in *State of the World* (New York: Norton, 1991), 153–170.]

Increasing consumption levels around the world threaten our natural resource base and diminish our overall quality of life. As consumerism has become entrenched in industrial countries, material standards of success have come to dominate traditional nonmaterial values. As a result, more and more societies are pursuing material goals that lead to global environmental degradation. This summary argues that a global consumer society, based on the continuing spread of the richest countries' high consumption lifestyles, is unsustainable, while the lifestyle of the "global middle class" is more ecologically benign. It identifies factors driving society toward ever-higher consumption; the author advocates a culture of permanence as an alternative to consumerism (see Durning summary in Part X of this volume).

The Consuming Society

Evidence that consumption is increasing around the globe is available on almost any consumption-based indicator. While consumption among America's wealthy classes continues to rise, Japanese and Western European consumption patterns have come to parallel those of the United States. Even poor societies such as China and India and Eastern European countries are beginning to adopt the consumer lifestyle of the West.

The costs of global consumerism are too high for this planet and its human inhabitants. The biosphere cannot support a global consumer lifestyle like that of the United States. Too many natural resources would be required and too much pollution and waste would be produced to sustain a livable environment. Not only are ecological costs high, but consumerism does not seem to promote human happiness. Despite spending twice as much per capita as they did in 1957, Americans have shown no increase in the number of those who report being "very happy." In addition, cross-cultural studies show little difference between self-reports of happiness in rich and poor countries. Since pursuit of high consumption levels is both unsustainable and does not promote high levels of personal fulfillment, our social goals should be redefined.

In Search of Sufficiency

The notion of sufficiency applies to two distinct areas. The first concerns consumption levels that can be supported by the biosphere. The second involves personal consumption levels that are sufficient for human satisfaction.

The ecological impact of the global economy is determined by the size of the population, average consumption, and technologies that provide goods and services. Technological advances may decrease burdens on the environment that are caused by increases in population and consumption. But without a reduction of consumer demand, environmental benefits from technological innovation will likely be inadequate to stop the resultant environmental degradation.

Obviously, average consumption levels vary within the global population, but it is only the world's affluent who consume at rates that are too much for the biosphere. The global population may be divided into three groups or classes that differ in their rates of consumption. The affluent class is responsible for consumption of 80 percent of the world's resources, but comprises only one-fifth of the world's population. The global middle class is associated with moderate or sustainable consumption levels, and comprises three-fifths of the world's population. The lower class, another one-fifth of the world, lives in absolute deprivation. An examination of the most important ecological consumption patterns (those involving transportation, diet, and use of raw materials) indicates that the middle class is a model for consumption levels that can be supported by the biosphere, while the more affluent class is not. (Table 1 outlines the types of consumption associated with each class.)

As consumption of automobiles, red meat, and packaged goods increases, so does waste and natural resource depletion. Excessive use of automobiles by the affluent depletes the ozone layer, pollutes the air, and contributes to acid rain. Meat consumption, almost all by the affluent, takes 40 percent of the world's grain supply for feed, contributes to the greenhouse effect, and wastes energy in the long-distance transport of agricultural goods. Processing and packaged goods support a throw-away economy in which disposability and obsolescence are merchandisable qualities. If all countries were to adopt this affluent level of consumption as their model, there would be no hope for the biosphere.

In contrast, members of the global middle class characteristically ride bicycles or take public transportation, eat the healthiest diets of grains and vegetables, and use less than one-tenth the amount of raw materials of their affluent counterparts. The global poor have a negligible ecological impact and are forced to depend on unproductive ecosystems because of popula-

Table 1. The World's Three Socioecological Classes

Overconsumers	Sustainers	Marginals
1.1 billion	3.3 billion	1.1 billion
> $7,500 per capita	$700–$7,500 per capita	< $700 per capita
(cars-meat-disposables)	(living lightly)	(absolute deprivation)
Travel by car and air	Travel by bicycle and public surface transport	Travel by foot, maybe donkey
Eat high-fat, high-calorie meat-based diets	Eat healthy diets of grains, vegetables, and some meat	Eat nutritionally inadequate diets
Drink bottled water and soft drinks	Drink clean water plus some tea and coffee	Drink contaminated water
Use throw-away products and discard substantial wastes	Use unpackaged goods and durables and recycle wastes	Use local biomass and produce negligible wastes
Live in spacious, climate-controlled, single-family residences	Live in modest naturally ventilated residences with extended/multiple families	Live in rudimentary shelters or in the open; usually lack secure tenure
Maintain image-conscious wardrobe	Wear functional clothing	Wear second-hand clothing or scraps

This chart is based on Durning's work, but was compiled by David Korten, "Sustainability and the Global Economy Beyond Bretton Woods," address to the Environmental Grant-makers Association in October 5, 1994.

tion pressures and landlessness caused by the overconsumption of the global rich. Examination of these consumption patterns suggests that modest consumption levels can provide modern comforts and are supportable by the biosphere.

The Cultivation of Needs

The modern consumer society employs five cultural factors to promote the desire to consume: social pressures, advertising, shopping, government, and the mass market.

(1) As pecuniary measures have replaced traditional virtues (e.g., integrity, honesty, and skill) as indicators of social worth, social status is determined primarily by consumption-based comparisons with others.

However, status seeking through consumption becomes unsatisfying and fruitless when individuals keep trying to outconsume each other.

(2) The expansion of advertising into every aspect of our daily lives promotes ever-increasing consumption. Advertising infests not only radio, television, and print media, but also classrooms, doctors' offices, "telemarketing" calls in our homes, and more. Growth in total global advertising expenditures has outpaced global economic output.

(3) Shopping culture, as exemplified in mall design, encourages acquisitive impulses and draws commerce away from local merchants. Mall sales account for more than half of all retail sales in the United States; the country has more shopping centers than high schools. Shopping itself has become a primary cultural activity.

(4) Government economic policies promote high consumption levels through taxes and policy. In Britain, for example, automobile consumption is supported by tax breaks for companies that buy fleets of company cars. Globally, government policies undervalue renewable resources, ignore ecosystems, and underprice raw materials. Worst of all, such policy goals, based on the assumption that "more is better," misinterpret the ecological havoc of overconsumption as healthy growth.

(5) Convenient, disposable, mass-market products overwhelm household and local community enterprises. Household purchases are geared toward items that save time but contribute to waste and ecological burdens.

These factors fail to promote human satisfaction and tear away at the fabric of local economies. They promote social values that are not grounded in local communities and that dominate nonmaterial measures of success. In addition, they create a false impression that there is a positive relationship between the ability to consume and happiness.

Summary of

Consumption, Well-Being, and Virtue
by David A. Crocker

[Paper delivered at conference on "Consumption, Global Stewardship, and the Good Life" (University of Maryland, September 29–October 2, 1994.)]

How should we evaluate current U.S. consumption patterns? Alan Durning asks, "How much is enough?" But the question is incomplete. We must ask, "How much of *what?*" "Enough for *whom?*" and "Enough for *what purpose?*" In search of answers to such basic questions, this summary analyzes the consumerist ideal and three philosophical visions of the good life—utilitarianism, basic-needs ethics, and the capabilities ethic.

American Consumerism

The "shop 'til you drop" ethos pervades our popular culture. One of the essential features of consumerism is the production of new consumer goods and the desire for them. Americans find meaning and self-esteem in buying and having an ever-changing ensemble of consumer goods.

However, even in a consumerist society most people want possessions not just for their own sakes, but also because of what they bring the consumer—including physical well-being, creature comforts, pleasure, and fantasy. Consumption choices express meaning and personal identity. However, if commodities are the means to, rather than the meaning of, well-being, we must ask again, What is worth achieving for its own sake?

Utilitarianism

Following Amartya Sen's approach,[1] utilitarianism may be described as a philosophy that identifies human well-being, welfare, and utility with the mental state of happiness or the satisfaction of preferences. From a utilitarian perspective, and looking only at the individual, whatever maximizes individual happiness is best. This need not always mean that more is better; consuming the wrong things, or too many things that are enjoyable in moderate quantities, could be less satisfying than consuming less. However, it tends to endorse an open-ended process of accumulation of consumer goods.

Is utilitarianism the answer? Should we identify happiness or preference satisfaction with well-being? While happiness is an intrinsic part of well-being, it is not alone sufficient. Almost everyone, no matter how wealthy or destitute, finds some reasons to be happy at times; happiness can camouflage and distort objective deprivation such as malnutrition and morbidity. On the other hand, discontent and frustration often motivate genuine achievement and the fulfillment it brings.

Basic Human Needs

A second normative perspective starts from the assumption that there is a fundamental difference between real needs and "false needs," or mere desires. But what needs are basic? Indispensability for biological survival, as in the provisions needed for famine relief, sets an extremely low threshold. Basic-needs theorists often include many further goals concerning physical and mental health, social development, and others. If the list becomes too long, however, it loses its moral urgency. An extensive list of basic needs must be defended in terms of a conception of well-being or the good life. The distinction between natural and artificial needs is problematic, and conceptions of what is "natural" vary widely. The needs that seem "basic" to many people vary over time, and often past luxuries come to be treated as necessities.

Although the basic-needs perspective is an improvement over utilitarianism, it remains incomplete. It suffers from conceptual unclarity about what needs are and the means to meet or satisfy them; it tends toward a static perspective that overlooks changing perceptions of needs; it often fails to be clear about why it is important to meet "basic" needs, beyond minimal biological survival levels.

The Capability Ethic

A third approach answers the question, How much is enough for *what?*, with the response, "For human virtue." Such an approach is perhaps best represented by the neo-Aristotelian approaches of philosopher Martha Nussbaum and economist Amartya Sen.[2] For Nussbaum, virtues are the capabilities to perform valuable human "functions" or activities; to have a virtue is to be able to be and act in valuable ways.[3] Nussbaum's long list of valuable capabilities may be grouped into three categories, with a few examples noted in each case: bodily virtues (good health, nourishment, escaping avoidable morbidity and premature mortality); individuality virtues (ability to have pleasurable experiences, function cognitively, make autonomous choices, enjoy self-respect); and social virtues (ability to engage in friendship, recreation, participation in family, communal, and political life). Sen defines an individual's well-being as her own valuable bodily, individual, and social functions or activities as well as the capabilities to perform those activities.

The neo-Aristotelian virtue ethic differs from the stoic ideal of the good life. Rather than renunciation of goods and desires, the Aristotelian argues that we realize our greatest achievements by satisfying *certain* desires, meeting human needs, pressing against limits, and coping with misfortune. Consumption is unjustified when it weakens the prospects for realizing our valuable capabilities.

One advantage of the capabilities approach is that it recognizes individual and social variation in the level of consumption needed to achieve desired objectives. The same level of nutrition may require different types and amounts of food for different individuals; the virtue of being able to appear in public without shame requires different clothing in different times and places. Participation in a more affluent society inevitably requires greater affluence, a point missed by some proponents of the simple life.

American Consumption and Human Virtues

Suppose a consensus were to evolve around a core of fundamental human virtues such as Sen's and Nussbaum's list. What evaluation of current American consumption is implied by that consensus? A brief examination suggests that many Americans have too much of some things, and not enough of others, for their own good.

In relation to "bodily virtues" of health, nourishment, and shelter, the poor often cannot afford minimally acceptable physical functioning, while those with economic advantages are under pressure to work longer and harder, sometimes "working themselves to death." Turning to "individuality virtues," dissatisfaction and discontent with consumer society are widespread; compulsive or addictive consumption is common, fueled in part by advertising and fashion. Rational discussion is more common about topics such as cars and sports than about political life. Social virtues are undermined by the pressures to work and earn money for consumption. Middle-class Americans are so pressed for time that they often cannot be very good spouses, parents, friends, citizens, or environmental trustees. Even the available leisure time becomes commodified, as days off from work become opportunities for shopping.

Toward Conscientious Consumption

"Conscientious consumption is consumption that is good for the consumer, fair to other people, and sustainable with respect to the environment. . . . The neo-Aristotelian approach in virtue ethics has emerged as the most promising way to conceptualize human well-being and the good life and assess current American consumption. It provides us with a persuasive and explicit vision of human well-being. Conscientious consumption is consumption that promotes, secures, and expresses the diverse constituents—both self- and other-regarding—of a good human life." [26–27]

Notes

1. A. Sen, "The Standard of Living," in *The Standard of Living*, ed. Geoffrey Hawthorn (Cambridge: Cambridge University Press, 1987), 1–19.

2. D. Crocker, "Functioning and Capability: The Foundations of Sen's and Nussbaum's Development Ethic," *Political Theory* 20 (1992): 584–612; "Functioning and Capability: The Foundation of Sen's and Nussbaum's Development Ethics, Part 2," in *Women, Culture and Development: A Study of Human Capabilities*, eds. M. Nussbaum and J. Glover (Oxford: Clarendon Press, 1995), 153–199.

3. M. Nussbaum, "Non-Relative Virtues: An Aristotelian Approach," in *The Quality of Life*, ed. M. Nussbaum and A. Sen. (Oxford: Clarendon Press, 1993), 242–276.

Summary of

The Original Affluent Society
by Marshall Sahlins

[Published in *Stone Age Economics* (Chicago: Aldine and Atherton, 1972), 1–39.]

> There are two possible courses to affluence. Wants may be "easily satisfied" either by producing much or desiring little. . . . [There is] a Zen road to affluence, departing from premises somewhat different from our own: that human material wants are finite and few, and technical means unchanging but on the whole adequate. [1–2]

A long-standing tradition in economics, dating back at least to the time of Adam Smith, views preagricultural societies of hunters and gatherers as desperately poor populations engaged in a continual, exhausting struggle to survive. This dismal portrait provides the backdrop for the long narrative of historical progress, as first agriculture and then industry increased productivity and allowed the satisfaction of more and more individual desires. But in contrast to the traditional view, both historical and anthropological evidence show that many hunter-gatherer societies obtained an adequate diet with surprisingly little labor, and enjoyed substantial leisure time. This summary presents the evidence for "Stone Age affluence," and discusses its significance for contemporary economics.

Sources of the Misconception

Prejudice against hunting may be as old as agriculture. It is echoed in the biblical story of Jacob, the successful farmer, and Esau, the hunter who lost his birthright. But low opinions of the hunting-gathering economy involve more than "neolithic ethnocentrism." A newer, bourgeois ethnocentrism may be at work: Modern capitalism views economic life as organized around scarcity, and takes it for granted that earlier, less technological societies suffered from even greater scarcity.

> Having equipped the hunter with bourgeois impulses and paleolithic tools, we judge his situation hopeless in advance. Yet scarcity is not an intrinsic property of technical means. It is a relationship between means and ends. We should entertain the empirical possibility that hunters are in business for their health, a finite objective, and that bow and arrow are adequate to that end. [4–5]

Recent observation of existing hunters and gatherers has tended to distort our understanding in two ways. First, the remote and exotic environments of hunter-gatherer societies are inhospitable to agriculture or urban life, and the foods found there include items deemed repulsive and inedible by outsiders; the naive observer naturally wonders "how anyone could live in a place like this." Second, the surviving hunter-gatherer societies have been pushed into resource-poor environments by the expansion of more advanced economies, and do not enjoy the richer opportunities that were available when their way of life was universal.

"A Kind of Material Plenty"

In many accounts, however, hunters and gatherers are described as acting as if they felt affluent—working short hours, sharing everything they have freely with others, and showing no interest in storing or accumulating resources. They own few tools, utensils, or items of clothing, and pay little attention to preserving those they do have, as new ones can always be made from readily available materials when the need arises. In a nomadic society, mobility is a condition of success, and material wealth is a burden. The hunter appears to be an "uneconomic man," with scarce wants and plentiful resources, the reverse of the textbook model. "It is not that hunters and gatherers have curbed their materialistic 'impulses'; they simply never made an institution of them." [13–14]

But the crucial question is, how hard do they work at gathering food? Careful observation of two groups of native Australians in Arnhem Land in 1948 found that both men and women spent an average of only four to five hours a day on all food-related activities. Both groups enjoyed an adequate diet and had plenty of opportunities for daytime resting, sleeping, visiting and talking, and other leisurely activities. Similar findings emerge from a study of !Kung Bushmen of the Kalahari Desert in Botswana. It must be noted that these are studies of people living in marginal environments;

fragmentary historical accounts suggest that life was even easier for hunters and gatherers in resource-rich regions of Africa and Australia before they were driven out by the European conquest of these areas. When the choice is available, some contemporary hunters and gatherers have rejected agriculture precisely in order to preserve their leisure. As a Bushman reportedly said, "Why should we plant, when there are so many mongomongo nuts in the world?" [27]

The assumption of ongoing abundance in food supplies, combined with the need for mobility, explains the failure of hunters and gatherers to store their occasional surpluses of food for future use. Although food storage was often technically feasible, it would tie the group to a fixed geographic area, in which they would likely exhaust the local food supplies. As such, they opted to eat the surplus when it was available and thus remain free to move on to richer areas as the need arose; nature's food storage exceeds what humans could set aside in diversity as well as amount. Occasional periods of hunger are the price they pay for such freedom.

Rethinking Hunters and Gatherers

The real handicap of hunting and gathering societies is not the low productivity of labor, but rather the imminence of diminishing returns. The food available within a convenient range of camp is always declining, and the need for mobility is unending. This not only limits the level of material culture to that which can easily be shouldered, but also imposes harsh demographic constraints. Individuals, as well as things, that inhibit movement must at times be shed; infanticide and euthanasia are, as hunters tell it, sometimes sadly necessary. The larger a group grows the more often it must move, so groups must remain small, especially in today's inferior hunting-gathering environments. In such societies, people spend most of the year in small, widely spaced groups, isolated from other human contact.

"But rather than the sign of underproduction, the wages of poverty, this demographic pattern is better understood as the cost of living well." [34] Hunters typically worked 20 to 35 hours per week; the rise of agriculture probably meant that people on average began to work much harder. Although hunters and gatherers sometimes experience a few days without food due to the whims of nature, dependence on agriculture has subjected people everywhere to famine in times of drought or crop failure. The proportion of the earth's population that goes to bed hungry every night is undoubtedly higher today than in the Old Stone Age.

This paradox reflects the two contradictory movements of economic evolution. On the one hand, technology has increased the availability of goods and services and brought increased freedom from environmental constraints. The development of agriculture created enough of a food surplus in one place to allow stable social life, which in turn is the foundation of all later cultural development.

On the other hand, the same processes have created scarcity and poverty. Technological development has also allowed discrimination in the distribution of wealth and differentiation in styles of life.

> The world's most primitive people have few possessions, *but they are not poor*. Poverty is not a certain small amount of goods, nor is it just a relation between means and ends; above all it is a relation between people. Poverty is a social status. As such it is the invention of civilization. It has grown with civilization, at once as an invidious distinction between classes and more importantly as a tributary relation—that can render agrarian peasants more susceptible to natural catastrophes than any winter camp of Alaskan Eskimo. [37–38, emphasis in original]

Finally, it should be borne in mind that this discussion takes modern hunters and gatherers as historically typical, accepting them as an evolutionary base line. Yet in the days when their way of life held sway throughout the world's richer environments, who knows what greater heights of culture, now vanished without record, may have characterized the original affluent society?

Summary of

The Limits to Satisfaction: Examination
by William Leiss

[Published in *The Limits to Satisfaction: An Essay on the Problem of Needs and Commodities* (London: Boyars, 1978), 1–45.]

The market economy of affluent societies is characterized by the provision of many technologically sophisticated commodities to large numbers of people. This high-intensity market setting is governed by the principle that the economy should expand steadily and the concern that sufficient resources be available for this purpose. This summary argues that the systematic orientation of all needs toward commodities within such markets makes it difficult to determine and satisfy individual desires, intensifies the experienced scarcity of goods, and promotes a dangerously shortsighted view of the ability of the environment to absorb the resource costs of mass production.

The Individual

In an expanding marketplace, the individual consumer faces a number of insurmountable problems. Since many mass-produced goods require complex production processes, consumers often do not have the knowledge or the time to make informed decisions that avoid the physiological and psychological dangers that accompany consumption of some commodities. Ideally, consumer choices are informed by an intimate understanding of the goods that will achieve their desired ends. This is the kind of knowledge that is applied in craft skills. For example, a cook who carefully prepares a sauce knows which ingredients and pans are most useful.

In a mass market nobody can possibly have craft knowledge of more than a few products. Without craft knowledge, individual choice amounts to little more than a grand arbitrary experiment in matching goods with needs and wants. One consequence is that most actual consumer decisions reflect a choice among the messages or images associated with different commodities, rather than among the commodities themselves. Many product images create short-lived impressions of indispensability that reflect the shallowness of most consumer wants.

A consumer's health may be endangered in a number of ways by ignorance of the nature and effects of commodities. In a high-intensity market setting, the number and variety of goods depend on the incorporation of materials that have untested long-term physical effects on people and the environment. Hyperactivity in children, poor nutrition, and drug dependencies are but a few of the many physical problems that have been associated with the consumption of some modern products.

Psychologically, a significant health issue arises with attempts to satisfy the multitude of needs generated by advertising. Advertising fragments genuine social needs into many other needs, each of which is associated with a particular commodity and message. For example, the consumer need for an acceptable external appearance is broken into smaller and smaller needs by compartmentalizing the body into different parts, each of which requires separate products. Thus, for example, a variety of deodorants and other chemical mixtures are designed to enhance the smells and appearance of different body parts. The consumer who is hooked on addressing needs through consumption will spend more and more time consuming in order to maintain a sense of self.

In *The Harried Leisure Class*, summarized in Part II of this volume, Staffan Linder argues convincingly that the value of time spent consuming goods increases with productivity gains in the labor sector of the economy. He raised the important point that leisure will become increasingly oriented toward activities that utilize consumer goods. As a result, activities that do not depend on consumption will become less important to consumers bent on optimizing the yield on their time. The urge to optimize leisure time is exemplified by the packaged tour, which allows travelers to see as much as possible in the least amount of time. Unfortunately, experiencing efficiency is not the same as experiencing different cultures. The planned menus, bus trips, and guided tours effectively insulate the traveler from contact with other cultures.

The appeal of the packaged tour and its seeming "efficiency" to the harried consumer raises questions concerning the meaning of the phrase "satisfaction of wants."

> In the high intensity market setting . . . both the states of feeling that are incorporated in an individual's wants and the multidimensional aspects of commodities are highly complex; the complexity of the interplay between needs and commodities increases exponentially as a result. It is far too simplistic to adopt the conventional description of this process as one in which "new" wants emerge attendant upon the "satisfaction" of previously existing ones. In this setting wants become less and less coherent, and their objectives less clear and readily identifiable, as individuals continually reinterpret their needs in relation to the expanding market economy. [27]

If it is true that consumers are often unable to relate goods to their perceived desires, this calls into question the usefulness of the notion that human wants are insatiable. Wants cannot be continuously generated and satisfied when it is difficult to say when and whether any particular want is satisfied.

Society

Early proponents of an expansionist market economy believed that the scarcity of goods results from limited productivity and that problems related to the elimination of scarcity represent the central concerns of economic systems. This notion of scarcity implies a relation between wants and available resources, but fails to recognize that scarcity has an experiential component that cannot be addressed or eliminated by increasing production. "If we view scarcity as the disparity between our wants and our capacities, we can understand the possibility that scarcity might increase simultaneously with rising social wealth and productivity." [30] For instance, in any society respect from others is not easy to obtain, so it has a scarcity value. When scarce commodities are associated with respectability, the experienced scarcity of respect is compounded. Consequently, it is possible for individuals living in a society of wealth and limitless resources to have intense experiences of scarcity. The threat of scarcity is a socially manufactured, permanently entrenched characteristic of any society that connects the satisfaction of needs to consumption of goods, and this threat will not be diminished by increases in the supply of goods.

The threat of scarcity has returned as a significant economic issue as mismanagement of industrial waste products begins to pose global environmental threats. Multinational corporations avoid pollution restrictions in industrial societies by producing in countries that accept environmental hazards for economic benefits. The export of industrial waste threatens global resources while political and economic pressures place the burden of proof on environmentalists to show that environmental problems will result from a given activity or policy. Consequently, the dangers of uncertain, long-term environmental costs are underplayed to keep costs down and sustain short-term product development for the consumer.

Nonhuman Nature

To understand the character of human needs in a high-intensity market setting it is essential to appreciate the nature of our dependence on the natural environment, the ultimate source of consumed goods. The modern day realization that industrial wastes burden a limited resource base has been slow to address the prevailing philosophical view that nature exists to serve man's purposes. This perspective can be traced back at least as far as Sir Francis Bacon, who believed that human nature is distinct from that of nonhuman nature and that nonhuman nature has no inherent purpose. This belief provided the moral foundation for exploiting the environment for whatever purposes humans deemed appropriate. In Bacon's view, conquering non-human nature could allow humans to release their innate, destructive passions without hurting anyone. "Nonhuman nature 'pays the price' for achieving peace and serenity in human society." [42]

The idea that the rational control of nature through science and technology could be accomplished by a species that does not have control over its own nature is fundamentally paradoxical. In exploiting resources to manufacture goods to satisfy needs, we avoid careful examination of the nature of our material interests and ignore the basic confusions and ambiguities that exist in the complex relationship between needs, their satisfaction, and commodities.

Summary of

Will Raising the Incomes of All Increase the Happiness of All?

by Richard Easterlin

[Published in *Journal of Economic Behavior and Organization* 27 (1995), 35–48.]

In his widely cited 1974 article on income and subjective well-being,[1] Easterlin drew three major conclusions from a review of empirical evidence: First, within a country rich people are happier than poor people at any point in time; second, increases in average income over time do not lead to increases in average happiness; and finally, people in rich countries are no happier, on average, than those in poor countries. This summary returns to the subject of income and happiness, finding that an additional twenty years of data and analysis have strengthened support for the first two conclusions but rendered the third problematical.

Theoretical Model

For most people, judgments of their own economic well-being depend on the incomes and living standards of others. If your income is unchanged while everyone else receives an increase, you will probably feel poorer. In formal terms, happiness varies directly with one's own income and inversely with the incomes of others, as suggested by Duesenberry's model of interdependent preferences (see summary in Part V). This model predicts that income and happiness are positively correlated at any point in time, as is actually observed. It predicts that increases in everyone's income need not make anyone happier, since the increase in happiness from one's own gains is offset by the effect of everyone else's success. This, too, is consistent with observation.

A more realistic model would also take account of habit formation: The utility resulting from one's current income depends in part on habits and expectations, based on past income. This should diminish the correlation between income and happiness: The rich have high expectations, reducing the satisfaction they get from large incomes; the poor have low ones, increasing the satisfaction they experience from small incomes. If spending habits and expectations were all that mattered, there might be no relationship between current income and happiness. More realistically, the combination of interdependent preferences and habit formation predicts some connection between income and happiness, though less than that which would prevail in the absence of habit formation.

Empirical Evidence

Numerous studies from the United States, Europe, and Japan confirm that increasing per capita incomes do not result in increasing happiness. In the United States, real incomes rose substantially between the 1940s and the 1970s; new, detailed studies of that period have confirmed Easterlin's 1974 finding that happiness peaked in the late 1950s and then declined. From 1972 through 1991, a period when per capita income after tax rose by one-third, annual survey data from the National Opinion Research Center likewise show no upward trend in happiness.

Surveys of life satisfaction in nine European countries from 1973 through 1989 show a slight upward trend in two countries, a slight downward trend in two, and no trend in the remaining five; during those years real per capita gross domestic product (GDP) rose from 25 to 50 percent in the nine countries. A study of Japan found no increase in subjective well-being from 1964 to 1981, despite the fact that real per capita GDP more than doubled.

Other survey evidence shows that people's expectations and standards for a given level of satisfaction rise at about the same rate as incomes. The income requirements for being "completely happy" move upward over time, as do the much lower standards for "minimum comfort." One historical study found that minimum comfort standards, over a long period of time, were a roughly constant percentage of per capita gross national product.

The evidence for a positive relationship between income and happiness at any point in time is also extensive. Some analysts have pointed out that the statistical relationship is a weak one if other factors such as educational level are controlled; however, these other factors may be mechanisms through which income produces its effects.

For international comparisons of happiness, theoretical predictions are unclear, as is the evidence. It has been established that there are durable cultural differences between countries in the tendency to answer questions positively or negatively. Similarly, there are differences in the tendency to answer moderately or extremely. One attempt at international comparison found that Brazilians were among the most satisfied, but also among the most worried and dissatisfied, on a range of measures; the likely explanation is that Brazilians are among the most immoderate in their responses. Such difficulties underscore the importance of single-country studies for analysis of the relationship between subjective well-being and economic development.

Conclusion

Rich people are happier than poor people in the same country at the same time. However, raising the incomes of all does not increase the happiness of all. Despite the obvious relevance of such findings for economic theory, economists have, with few exceptions, ignored the issue. A survey of more than 200 studies on the measurement and determinants of subjective well-being found only two in economics journals. The reluctance of economists to consider new research on subjective well-being doubtless reflects, in part, the continuing commitment to utilitarianism, and the often-stated commitment to positive rather than normative analysis. Recently there have been encouraging signs of an emerging interest in normative economics. "An economics that is engaged actively and self-critically with the moral aspects of its subject matter cannot help but be more interesting, more illuminating, and ultimately more useful than one that tries not to be." [2]

Notes

1. Richard Easterlin, "Does Economic Growth Improve the Human Lot?," in Paul David and Melvin Reder, eds., *Nations and Households in Economic Growth: Essays in Honor of Moses Abramovitz* (New York: Academic Press, 1974), 89–125.

2. Daniel Hausman and Michael McPherson, "Taking Ethics Seriously: Economics and Contemporary Moral Philosophy," *Journal of Economic Literature* 31 (1993), 723, quoted in Easterlin.

Summary of

The Expansion of Consumption

by Allan Schnaiberg

[Published in *The Environment: From Surplus to Scarcity* (New York & Oxford: Oxford University Press, 1980), 157–204.]

In the final analysis, then, consumption cannot be the leading factor in the expansion of production. Increased consumption may permit expanded production, but it does not generally cause it. Wage income shifts typically follow production changes, marketing typically follows production shifts, and consumption follows all three of these factors. Consumer resistance, though, can and does occur, where it is permitted. Some products die because of it, but few are born solely because of consumer wants or needs, independent of the production structure. [192]

In recent decades, environmental degradation has followed increases in material consumption by consumers and producers. According to neoclassical economic theory, changes in consumer behavior will be sufficient to ameliorate or negate the harmful effects on the environment. This summary argues that in industrialized countries' consumption levels are determined primarily by producers and that changes in production are essential to reversing or reducing environmental degradation.

In industrialized economies, high aggregate consumption levels are necessary to maintain profits. To maintain high production and profit levels, producers work to stimulate demand for products that can be mass produced. Once wages are high enough to permit innovations in consumption, producers shift their investment patterns to create products in new areas, thereby creating new avenues for consumer demand.

Advanced industrialization has brought about a broad panoply of environmental problems through increases in material consumption. Consumption levels have risen dramatically despite the fact that services now constitute a growing proportion of total consumption. This suggests that demand for services is closely tied to goods consumption:

> Consumption of services, therefore, exists in a variety of relationships to the goods produced by the primary/secondary industrial sectors. First, service industries are consumers of many of the products of these sectors (energy and paper, especially). Second, they stimulate a variety of demands for production goods by other consumers: industrial, government, and private ones. Third, they provide the mechanisms by which consumption of these producer goods can continue—through delivery and repair. [171]

As consumers, the service industries have had a devastating impact on the environment (for example, waste production, use of land for waste disposal, and air/water pollution).

Of course, an expanding service sector is not the only perpetrator of environmental harm; the nonservice sectors extract ever increasing amounts of natural resources to support high volumes of production without adequately replenishing or compensating disrupted ecosystems.

The view that environmental degradation can be effectively stopped by changing consumption patterns is represented by the neoclassical model of the *sovereign consumer.* Consumers are said to be sovereign in the sense that individual preferences, formed and acted upon with very little influence from producers, govern the decisions of producers. This model is compelling in that it provides for a simple solution to consumption-based environmental problems. If the population is controlled and consumption per capita is decreased, then the impact on the environment will be reduced. One significant problem with the sovereign consumer model is that it provides an inadequate account of the dynamic connections between consumption and production processes.

Consumer Demand and Production Expansion

The view that consumers are sovereign is untenable in light of the pressures that producers are under to ensure that consumer demand stays high. Generally, the sovereign consumer model fails in two important respects. It does not account for the influence of external, political forces on the formation of consumer preferences; and it suggests falsely that consumer behavior is essentially autonomous. In fact, consumers do not freely determine their preferences, and they are not always self-determining in their attempts to satisfy their preferences.

According to the consumer sovereignty model, individual consumers prioritize desires and producers then develop products to satisfy them. However, producers are much more proactive in developing consumer preferences than this model allows. For instance, advertising is often used to heighten consumer awareness of unmet needs and to argue that such needs can be satisfied through the purchase of its products. By persuading consumers of the importance of certain desires, advertising influences the way individual wants are prioritized.

The consumer sovereignty model also implies that each consumer choice is independent of the next. Consumption of certain goods necessitates the consumption of many other types of goods. For example, buying a house in a suburb often involves increased consumption of automobiles, electricity, and land. Once a lifestyle is chosen, consumers are confined to the limited choices made available by producers; for example, suburban consumption patterns are often energy inefficient with respect to the provision of many family services. "Rather than thinking about demand for a given type of product, then, we must think of clusters of related demands, contingent upon an initial consumer choice or consumer response to extensive supply structures." [181]

Consumer choices are heavily influenced by the range of available public goods and services since these can be effective substitutes for large volumes of private goods and services. The large political influence wielded by businesses has prevented any such substitution. Consumers may appear to freely choose suburbia over other locations, but the public policies that make it easy to do so are supported by businesses rather than consumers.

> The political processes underlying the shift to more environmentally costly transportation have been far afield from any model of consumer sovereignty. Although consumers, in some organized groups, have made inputs that relate to contingent demands (e.g., arising from past suburbanization), the decision making for such policies has been heavily weighted in favor of producer groups. Little of this decision making has occurred in open public debate, with informed public representatives present. Organized interest groups have been predominantly (and at times, almost exclusively) auto-truck related industries, the so-called highway-automobile complex. No extension of the consumer demand model can be stretched to cover such decision making. Yet the inevitable consequence has been the shift to totally different patterns of transportation. [182]

For example, in the middle third of this century, United States political policies that supported the expansion of public transportation were replaced by business-influenced government programs that favored the development of a national roadway infrastructure, suburbanization, and the subsidization of truckers.

Constraints on Consumer Actions

Even if autonomy is not compromised in the formation of consumer preferences, it is constrained by a number of factors once these preferences are formed. The wealthiest groups exercise disproportionate control over what is produced; the more a consumer spends, the greater his voting power in the marketplace. Producers react to the needs and priorities of big spenders, not just any consumer; buying trends are set by those with money to spend on novelties. The effective demand of wage-earners is constrained by collective bargaining arrangements and government policies that are, for the most part, independent of the "autonomous" consumer.

The sovereign consumer model implies that consumer purchases reflect reasoned choices, but this cannot be true, considering how little consumers often know about their purchases. For example, the technology and manufacturing processes that underlie many products are concealed from most consumers. It is the producers who have the power to influence the processes employed in goods production. When alternatives, such as automobiles of different sizes or running on different fuels, are not offered by producers, consumers have no ability to "choose" them.

Shifts in consumption patterns are the end result of changes in income, production, and marketing. Consequently, any efforts to reduce environmental degradation must focus on the production system and the role of politics, rather than on consumer behavior.

From a social structural perspective, there is no theoretical basis for treating consumers as distinct from the multiplicity of roles they play in society, for consumption seems to be an outcome of these other roles. That is, consumers are not organized per se, except in the sense of a consumer movement, which has its roots in other political and economic roles of participants quite often. But consumers are typically workers, or dependents of workers, and as such are immediately tied to the production system. They are also citizens, and thereby linked to the political structure. [191]

Summary of

New Analytic Bases for an Economic Critique of Consumer Society
by Juliet Schor

[Paper delivered at conference on "Consumption, Global Stewardship, and the Good Life" (University of Maryland, September 29–October 2, 1994).]

In contrast to scholars in other fields, economists have contributed relatively little to the emerging critiques of consumer society. This summary reviews the arguments offered by economists in the past, criticizes the treatment of consumer choice in conventional economic theory, and identifies four bases on which a new economic approach to consumerism could be grounded.

Thorstein Veblen's classic critique, *The Theory of the Leisure Class* (1899), had a tremendous but transitory influence on economic thought. A more sanguine approach to consumption ultimately triumphed within the discipline of economics, for example, that was exemplified by Simon Patten's *The Consumption of Wealth* (1889). Patten argued that society was emerging from an age of scarcity to an age of abundance, and that it was ethically desirable to embrace the new consumer society.

Optimists such as Patten had to overcome not only Veblenesque critiques, but also the long-standing fear that society might not generate sufficient consumer demand to grow and prosper. Many economists believed that, as wages rose, people would find their needs for goods satisfied and reduce their hours of work.

Nevertheless, Patten's views did triumph. In the 1920s, economists such as Hazel Kyrk, Theresa McMahon, and Constance Southworth argued that a new type of consumer was (and should be) emerging. The possibility of unlimited wants appeared in their writings, and was soon taken for granted in business and marketing circles as well as in economic theory.

Debates about the nature of consumption and the quality of life virtually disappeared from economics after World War II. With a few notable exceptions, economists accepted neoclassical general equilibrium theory and its presumption that the relationship between goods and satisfaction was unproblematic and uninteresting. By the last quarter of the century, concern about underconsumption and stagnation was replaced with worries about insufficient savings. The turn away from studying consumption and home economics also constituted a shift away from studying women's economic behavior, and contributed to the marginalization of women within the economics profession.

In the general equilibrium model, competition ensures that workers and consumers find their preferences validated in the market. Workers' and consumers' sovereignties are crucial to the demonstration that market outcomes are optimal. If consumers want something else, they can change their buying patterns; if workers want either more or less leisure, they can change their working patterns. Consumer wants are assumed to be insatiable, and independent of other individuals' behavior. Economists have rarely done research that tested these assumptions.

Even a largely empirical defense of consumer society, in Stanley Lebergott's *Pursuing Happiness: American Consumers in the Twentieth Century* (1993), rests on economic theory at a crucial point. The fact that consumers buy new goods, for Lebergott, implies that the new goods yield more "worthwhile" experiences. "But the critique of consumer society is not about older versus newer goods, so much as it is about consumer society versus alternative ways of living." [6]

Market (and Other) Failures:
Four Bases for a Critique of Consumerism

There are four theoretical bases for a critique of consumer society. First, market failure in the labor market undermines the presumption of worker sovereignty. If most workers cannot choose their hours of work,[1] then there is no sense in which the current trade-off between leisure and income, or leisure and consumption, is optimal. In the neoclassical model, sovereign workers/consumers "get what they want." But workers who are constrained to work more than they would choose, and become habituated to spending the resulting income, end up "want[ing] what they get."

Second, the failure of environmental or natural capital to be priced and incorporated into the market results in the underpricing of goods and services. This means that there is "excess" consumption of goods and services compared to the optimal level that would exist in the absence of external effects.

Third, some critics argue that consumerism undermines community. Robert Putnam has shown that strong community ties yield substantial benefits in terms of efficient government, law-abidingness, and quality of life. However, the decline of free time outside the workplace diminishes opportunities to maintain community ties.

Finally, social interaction affects consumption, as shown by James Duesenberry as well as by Veblen. Duesenberry argued that what matters to consumers is not their absolute level of income, but their income relative to those around them. One of the few economists to follow up on this insight, Robert Frank, has shown that if leisure has lower status than consumer goods, then an optimal outcome (less money and less work) can only be reached by cooperation, not by competition.

Some past critiques of consumerism have been aesthetically based and elitist. Environmental critiques, on the other hand, often rely largely on moral appeals. The centrality of consumer goods in American society blunts the effectiveness of such appeals; structural limitations make it difficult for most consumers to respond to ethical persuasion. A new critique should be positive, arguing "in favor of a better way of organizing the economy and society. It should stress the *costs* of consuming—in terms of environment, time, community, and quality of social interaction. It should offer people an appealing vision of an alternative society." [14]

Note

1. As argued in Schor's research, summarized in Part II.

Summary of

Consumption: The New Wave
of Research in the Humanities and Social Sciences
by Colin Campbell

[Published in *To Have Possessions: A Handbook on Ownership and Property*, special issue of *Journal of Social Behavior and Personality* 6 (1991): 57–74.]

Recent years have seen a marked upsurge of interest in the topic of consumption both in the social sciences and in the humanities. This summary surveys leading contributions to consumption research from a wide range of disciplines.

Several factors have contributed to the outburst of recent research on consumption. Historians have recognized that characteristics of a consumer society can be found in preindustrial societies, giving rise to studies of the role of consumption before and during industrialization. A group of neo-Marxist writers has adapted Marxist ideas, formerly focused on production, to the analysis of modern consumer societies. Trends in cultural analysis have led to a deeper understanding of the nature and meaning of consumer culture. Urban sociology has focused on collective consumption. Feminism and women's studies have given prominence to such topics as fashion, the body, diet, advertising, shopping, and housework. Effects of these and related changes are seen throughout the social sciences and humanities.

Social Sciences

Until recently, traditional analyses of consumption in the social sciences, such as those of Veblen, Marx, Weber, and others, were largely neglected in fields other than anthropology. Anthropology emphasizes social systems, structures of interaction, and kinship. This focus has led to concerns for property rights, inheritance, and consumption practices within the context of large systems of social relations. In 1978, Douglas and Isherwood's book, *The World of Goods*,[1] was an isolated contribution to the understanding of consumption. More recent anthropology has focused on "material culture" with a consequent interest in exchange and commodities.

Within sociology, the neo-Marxist Jean Baudrillard has been influential in drawing on semiotics to analyze the "commodity sign" rather than the commodity. For Baudrillard, commodities are valued for their symbolic meanings rather than for their use; in many cases, only the meanings are consumed. Neo-Marxist thinker, Daniel Miller, blends Simmel, Hegel, and Marx to develop a theory in which consumption in modern industrial societies is alienating, but at the same time allows the possibility of an escape from alienation. Other new wave writers, not all of them Marxists, tend to echo the theme that there is the potential for liberation within modern consumption.

The recent revival of urban sociology has included a focus on collective consumption. Peter Saunders draws on this and other areas of sociology to develop a theory in which consumption plays a central role, analogous to the role of production in classical Marxism; his work has predictably been controversial. The most important recent sociological work, attributed to Bourdieu, relates semiotics to neo-Marxist thought; but perhaps it is understood best as a development and extension of Veblen's work. Like Veblen, Bourdieu sees the role of consumption, and the development of socially differentiated tastes, as central to the creation of hierarchy. He differs in stressing the individual's possession of symbolic or cultural capital that can be used to display taste, rather than material goods per se.

"Economics remains the one social science discipline in which least progress has occurred with respect to the study of consumption." [64] Despite the writings of Veblen, Keynes, and Galbraith, little has been done. Important works, none of them current, include Nurkse on the international demonstration effect, and Hirsch and Scitovsky on the inadequacies of conventional theories of demand.

Research on consumption in psychology appears less prominent than it did in the past, although there are signs of stirring and new approaches. The work of Csikszentmihalyi and Rochberg-Halton on the meaning and symbolic significance of material objects has been influential; their work is compatible with the approaches to consumption in other fields as well as in psychology.

Humanities

In history the role of consumption in the Industrial Revolution, and its significance in "early" or "premodern" societies, has been studied by a growing number of historians. The pathbreaking works are those of Fernand Braudel, especially *Capitalism and Material Life 1400–1800*.[2] McKendrick, Brewer, and Plumb have argued that a consumer revolution was a necessary part of England's eighteenth-century revolution in production. Numerous other historians have examined other aspects of European consumption before and during industrialization, all emphasizing the vital contribution that consumption made to the emergence of modern society.

In philosophy, the debates over the concept of "need," and the associated distinction between "necessity" and "luxury," have been important to economic theory in the past and to social theory today. Simple distinctions between "true" and "false" needs are generally untenable, while there are still significant questions relating to the distinction among needs, wants, desires, and interests. However, these questions no longer occupy their earlier prominence in social theory.

Semiotics, which emphasizes communication and symbolic meanings, has influenced the discussion of consumption. In the absence of detailed case studies of eighteenth- and nineteenth-century consumption, theorists have sometimes turned to fiction of the period as a source of descriptive narratives.

Conclusion

An early phase of research on consumption, dominated by critiques of the conventional utilitarian approach of economics and appeals for the development of new methods, is coming to an end. The "pre-paradigmatic" stage of consumption studies is nearly complete, although it is not yet clear what the new theoretical paradigm will be, or where the boundaries of the emerging field of study will lie.

Several concluding observations may be hazarded about the further development of the field.

> [First,] the tendency, prevalent in economics, to see consumption as an end of human activity has . . . given way to a presumption that it is indeed better understood as a means to some further end. . . . [Second,] the assumption that consumption refers specifically to the selection, purchase and use of material objects has increasingly been questioned . . . because of a growing awareness that it is not so much objects as their meanings which are indeed consumed. . . . Third and finally, one might predict that the study of consumption will slowly free itself from its present close involvement with cultural theory . . . [and] debates over postmodernism . . . [71]

Notes

1. M. Douglas and B. Isherwood, *The World of Goods: Toward an Anthropology of Consumption* (New York: Norton, 1978).

2. Fernand Braudel, *Capitalism and Material Life 1400–1800* (London: Weidenfeld and Nicolson, 1973).

PART II

Consumption in the Affluent Society[1]

Overview Essay

by David Kiron

In industrialized countries, the costs of affluence are coming into focus. In 1989, the average American consumed much more than his or her counterpart in 1969, while the average worker labored 160 more hours—equivalent to an extra month of full-time employment.[2] The expectation that productivity increases would eventually translate into a life of leisure for the masses has not been realized. As communities become more fragmented, status consumption has intensified rather than diminished. The fruits of economic growth—more consumption, a growing strain on the natural environment, but no more happiness all around—raise serious questions for our economic agenda.

This part analyzes rising consumption levels in affluent societies during the twentieth century and their effect on both the public sector and the experience of consumers. The summarized articles address various aspects of the relationship between production and consumption. The first five summaries focus on the relation among work life, consumption, and issues of personal identity. The next four look at the social impact of increasing consumption levels.

The American Dream

The relationship between producers and consumers is essential to understanding consumption in the affluent society. One of the most influential writings on this topic is John Kenneth Galbraith's *The Affluent Society*.[3] Galbraith questioned one of the basic tenets of neoclassical economic theory: the assumption of consumer sovereignty, which implies that tastes are exogenous to the economic system. His concern was that creating and satisfying wants through the market would not lead to greater well-being. The issue of consumer sovereignty subsumes a number of questions about the nature of choice in industrialized societies. Did individuals choose to work longer hours in order to afford the good life promised by marketers, or were they lashed to the work wheel by their employers for the sake of competition, costs, and profits? Is it possible for consumers to create for themselves a strong sense of self through consumption if creative work is unavailable? Has interest in maintaining the public sector waned because people have chosen to meet an increasing number of wants and needs through the market, or is it that pressures to support public goods are not as strong as those that support the provision of private goods?[4]

This list of questions contains a notable omission. After an exhaustive search, our research turned up few articles since the 1970s that examine the effects of consumer culture on the poor. A number of recent authors point out the existence of a problem and suggest that it is growing in scale, but no one seems to have focused on this topic. What happens to consumers who cannot afford the standard of respectable membership that is set by a consumer society? Many cultural critics have taken issue with the role of status consumption among the middle class, but the impact of status goods is felt nowhere more strongly than among poor urban teens who have been murdered for their fashionable jackets and sneakers. Many of the manufacturing jobs that once allowed movement out of poverty have vanished, leaving the poor with a drive to consume but with few legitimate routes to incomes that support higher consumption levels.

During the 1920s, pressures to consume were harnessed and given expression through images of the American Dream, a producer-inspired vision that included a single-family detached house in the suburbs, an automobile, a radio (and later, a television), and various household appliances. The Great Depression and World War II delayed the active pursuit of this image, though during the war the government prepared Americans for a big splurge with messages of imminent mass distribution of abundance. After the war, the GI bill and subsidization of a suburban infrastructure laid the groundwork for widespread, middle-class home ownership. More homes with more room for more stuff were crucial elements of the push toward higher consumption levels. A consumerist consensus emerged, reaching something of a zenith in 1950s when more people rated themselves as "very happy" than at any time before or since.[5]

Clearly, the interests of both producers and consumers have contributed to changes in consumer behavior over the course of the twentieth century. The elaboration of the American Dream by mass producers in the 1920s was in part a response to uncertainty over whether consumers would buy enough to sustain economic growth. At the same time, consumer demand that was pent-up during a successful war effort in World War II was unleashed during the euphoria that followed in the postwar decades.

In the heyday of the postwar boom (the 1950s), labor was more interested in higher wages than in more free time, but today the reverse is true. Contemporary workers are willing to give up career advancement in order to spend more time with their families.[6] The use and value of time in the affluent society have followed a complicated trajectory since union efforts in the early part of the century won a standard eight-hour work day. In the first article summarized in this part, Gary Cross argues that the consumerist tendencies that emerged after World War II had their roots in the Depression, which left many workers disillusioned with free time and intensely concerned with economic and job security. Work and higher wages appeared much more attractive since they delivered to wage earners what leisure could not: status, stability, and security.

Is economic insecurity or adaptation to progressively higher living standards the central force behind consumption in contemporary affluent society? Answers to this question acknowledge that, for most people, jumping off the work-spend cycle is an option that has been given little support within the current economic system. Full-time employment rather than shorter hours and shared work has always been preferred by business. As capital has become more mobile and global, firms have turned to cheap overseas labor and domestic temporary services.[7] Corporate downsizing has become commonplace as competitive pressures leave fewer top jobs and create greater economic insecurity for all. In the second summary in this section, Juliet Schor analyzes this trend, arguing that middle-class wage earners have been trapped in a cycle of work and spend, having become habituated to greater levels of affluence and lacking part-time employment alternatives that could preserve living standards at fixed levels. In opposition to the neoclassical assumption that workers get the hours they want, Schor contends that in reality firms set the work schedules, and workers wind up having to accept the terms they are offered.

Schor brings into relief a problem with our freedom to choose that echoes the voices of critics like Andrew Bard Schmookler. Schmookler argues that greater choice among goods comes at the expense of choice in other more important areas of life.[8] Whether the choice is between work time and leisure time, or this good or that, the market assumes that if you do not like something, you can show your disapproval by not choosing it or not buying it. As Michael Schudson suggests, "We learn to dissent by exit rather than by voice. We are instructed in choice but not in living with or against the choices we make."[9] That we are steeped in an ideology of choice, but do not structure the agenda within which choices are made, is a theme that reverberates throughout Schor's book.

Consumption as a Source of Meaning

Jobs that provide meaningful work are becoming more scarce. Education is no longer a guaranteed ticket to better, more interesting jobs. Mass production requires a form of labor participation that makes it difficult to value work as one of the most important sources of meaning in life. It is ironic that the noted decline of a work ethic has coincided with people being forced to work longer hours. Can the lack of meaningful work be fully countered through consumption? Raymond Benton, Jr. says no, in a summarized article that extends Hannah Arendt's critique of the routine labor process that underlies much of mass production. Benton argues that mass consumption cannot be a satisfying goal of an economy, especially one dependent on labor that produces primarily throw-away goods.

Anthropologist Daniel Miller argues the opposite position, contending that it is possible to counter the alienated conditions of the workplace through consumption practices. In doing so, Miller develops a thesis that reflects a growing consensus among academicians in fields other than economics, namely that consumption plays an important role in the cultivation of a sense of self. He rejects the view that consumption is an activity that is primarily about tastes. Miller is skeptical of the contemporary relevance of an analytic tradition that originated with Thorstein Veblen's seminal *Theory of the Leisure Class*,[10] which framed much of this century's sociological research on consumption. Veblen, and more recently Bourdieu,[11] observed that taste is a function of the ability to distance oneself from work. Where Veblen demonstrated that conspicuous consumption among American social elites in the late nineteenth century established a standard of emulation that trickled down through the classes, Bourdieu analyzes the pluralism of tastes that abound among French subcultures, citing education and position in the production process as the central determinants of taste. In recognizing that many consumption activities, such as hobbies, enable identity-building projects that may be either individualistic or social, Miller challenges those sociologists who view consumption as a function of taste.[12]

Alan Warde represents a new breed of sociologists who, like Miller, view consumption as a process that is much more complex than is recognized by the field of economics. "No longer is it possible to think of consumption in a simple, one-dimensional way. It is not just something that happens within the household contributing to the reproduction of labor power, nor can it be reduced to the distribution of assets, nor simply treated as an area of choice."[13] Warde presents an analytic framework for understanding both the experience of consumption and the role of production in the consumption process.

Social Impacts of Consumption

Two of the more notable social consequences of higher private consumption levels are the decline of free time and a deterioration in the quality of public goods and services. It is curious that the most important economic writings on the former were produced before the 1980s. Among the authors represented here, Harry Johnson, Staffan Linder, and Fred Hirsch each argue that economic growth creates pressures to economize on time outside of work. Johnson provides theoretical support for Schor's contention that people really do not want to be working as much as they are. He notes that, with increasing affluence, individuals will want to spend less time at work to enjoy their growing collection of goods.

Staffan Linder points out that productivity increases make time more valuable at work, and, since leisure time and work time are substitutes for one another, the price of leisure time should rise correspondingly. Both Linder and Hirsch point out the consequences of economizing leisure time by increasing the number of goods consumed. Linder emphasizes that less time may be spent with each good. Hirsch extends the point to sociability, arguing that if we spend more time with goods, especially time-saving goods that require individual usage, less time will be spent with other people. In a society with greater social mobility, we run a greater risk that acts of friendliness and social obligations will be unreciprocated or unfulfilled.[14]

With consumer interest directed toward spending more time with more private goods, it is perhaps unsurprising that less effort is directed toward promoting and sustaining public goods and services. Contemporary resistance to the allocation of resources to the public sector supports Hirsch's view that deterioration in the public sector stems from the economics of individualistic demand. With rising affluence, more people have access to status goods that are valued for their exclusive qualities, a category that Hirsch calls "positional goods" (discussed further in Part VI). If a vacation home with a private beach is affordable and desirable, why go to a public beach or be interested in paying taxes that support one? Greater competition for positional goods, which requires an unequal distribution of resources, is a zero-sum game that eventually diminishes the interest in and quality of public goods.

It used to be that the desirability of automobile use and suburban living was linked to the ideals of escape and freedom. But as more people acquired access to suburbia, roads became crowded, time traveling to work increased, and overall time pressures mounted. When looking at the social geography of America, it is apparent that Hirsch's analysis has gone unheeded. In the final article summarized in this part, Alladi Venkatesh examines recent trends in consumer culture in Orange County, California, and finds that the legacy of postwar suburbanization has taken on a life all its own. Suburbia is no longer exclusively residential, quiet, and white. In the new suburbia, busy, dual-income families from different classes and ethnic backgrounds come together at restaurants, shopping malls, and in front of the television, when they come together at all.

In 1991, Venkatesh could not have foreseen that bankruptcy was ahead for Orange County, one of the wealthiest metropolitan regions in the country and well known for its conservative values, status consumption, and revolt against higher taxes. Orange County typifies a national political trend toward downsizing the federal government and cutting its social programs: a movement that reflects both the desire to preserve income and a concern with the efficient resolution of issues related to a growing underclass. Part of the motivation for preserving income is due to the economically sanctioned pursuit of an ever-expanding vision of the good life. Yet this goal seems to be achieved at the expense of increasing socioeconomic stratification, which is widely believed to promote social ills. Consequently, reshuffling public spending will not solve the persistent social problems that are created by high levels of private consumption in certain economic sectors.

Notes

1. The title of this section reflects the distinction between consumer societies like the United States, where affluence is widespread, and those in developing countries where affluence is concentrated among elites and a growing middle class.

2. Juliet Schor, *The Overworked American* (New York: Basic Books, 1992).

3. First published in 1958; this is partially summarized in Part V.

4. Underlying each question is the idea that the meaning of consumption is inextricably linked to both the types of goods consumed and the purposes of consumption. For instance, What makes a good an item of necessity or luxury? What aspects of goods are actually consumed? Are goods consumed primarily for their status qualities or other reasons? Does the consumption of certain goods have an impact on the quality of their future use? The economic view that consumption relates only to the satisfaction of preferences or generation of utility is systematically challenged by the works collected here.

5. Richard Easterlin, "Does Economic Growth Improve the Human Lot? Some Empirical Evidence," in *Nations and Households in Economic Growth*, eds. Paul David and Melven Reder (New York: Academic Press, 1974), 85–125.

6. Juliet Schor, *The Overworked American* (New York: Basic Books, 1992).

7. Jackson Lears' summary in Part VII suggests that this trend is responsible for

corporations leaving their base of mass consumption in national locales. With mass consumption readily available in the global market, there is less pressure to maintain high wages at home to buy their products.

8. Andrew Bard Schmookler, *The Illusion of Choice: How the Market Economy Shapes Our Destiny* (Albany: SUNY Press, 1993).

9. Michael Schudson, "Delectable Materialism," *American Prospect* 1991.

10. Thorstein Veblen, *The Theory of the Leisure Class* (London: Unwin Books, 1899).

11. Pierre Bourdieu, *Distinction: A Social Critique of the Judgement of Taste* (Paris, 1979).

12. Miller also rejects Jean Baudrillard's view that contemporary consumption has little to do with the functional uses of goods. As a critic of modern consumer society, Baudrillard's analysis of the symbolic role of goods has been very influential among semioticians and postmodernists; however, his turgid writing makes his work difficult for the lay person.

13. Alan Warde, "Notes on the Relationship Between Production and Consumption," in *Consumption and Class,* eds. Burrows and Marsh (New York: St. Martin's, 1992), 13–32.

14. In a recent work, Daniel Miller critiques a caricature of this objection to sociability, missing the thrust of Hirsch's argument. In describing a sequence of myths raised by critics of the consumer society, Miller identifies the objection from sociability in the following terms: "consumption is opposed to sociality since it is premised on a concern for goods which replaces a previous concern for people." (*Acknowledging Consumption*, New York: Routledge, 1995, p. 23) This "myth" is a red herring since it fails to acknowledge the role of time, which is at the heart of Hirsch's argument.

Summary of

Traumas of Time and Money in Prosperity and Depression
by Gary Cross

[Published in *Time and Money: The Making of Consumer Culture* (London: Routledge, 1993), 128–154.]

At the end of World War I workers in America, Britain, and France fought for shorter work days and work weeks. It appeared for a time that productivity gains might be shared with workers in the form of reductions in hours as well as increases in pay. Yet the movement for shorter hours soon lost its momentum, and the equation of productivity gains with wage increases became widely accepted, allowing the creation of a mass consumer culture. This summary analyzes the forces that blocked further reductions in hours of work in the 1920s and 1930s, while another paper by the same author, entitled "The Consumer's Comfort and Dream" (see Part IV in this volume), argues that working people actively participated in the formation of the consumer society during the interwar years.

Choice and Discipline in the Interwar Years

Unions were relatively strong at the end of World War I, and many strikes demanded an eight-hour day or other reductions in hours. But organized labor had an ambiguous attitude toward the choice between time and money. It was more difficult to win reductions in work time than increases in wage rates because of the increased training and benefit costs, reduced flexibility in scheduling, and weakened labor discipline involved with shorter hours. When the labor movement grew weaker after 1919 as a result of recession and political opposition, the demand for shorter hours was dropped. During the 1920s, church and business reformers rather than unions continued the pressure for the eight-hour day in industry.

Lacking organized support for alternatives such as increased leisure, individual workers could only pursue advancement through wage gains and the accompanying increase in consumption. In the United States, by far the wealthiest country of the era, there was one car on the road for every 1.3 families by 1929, most of them paid for on the installment plan. Yet, by later standards, the consumer culture was barely under way; it was economic insecurity and the absence of an alternative, more than creeping consumerism, that drove the bias toward money.

That bias was intensified during the Depression as unemployment became a source of misery and social isolation. The trauma of job insecurity

> [T]ended to diminish the value of free time while it reinforced the attractions of money and the goods that it could purchase. Unemployment disrupted routines and made free time something more to dread than to long for. It intensified the linkage of status with work, wages, and the goods that money could buy. [136]

Traumas of Joblessness and the Declining Value of Free Time

Unemployment undermined the value of free time because it destroyed the routines of work and play. This loss of a work routine was recognized as significant by government and philanthropic groups. Work relief programs in the United States and occupational clubs in Britain were developed with the objective of preserving the self-respect and manual skills of the jobless, while providing a structure for their time. These programs and clubs did achieve their objectives to a certain extent, but proved to be inadequate substitutes for work.

Unemployment left many with unstructured free time and the feeling that they had no right to participate in public leisure time. Existing social networks and institutions were inadequate to provide for people's needs, and so many withdrew into their homes and families. Men found themselves thrust into the traditionally female sphere of housework and domesticity, often resulting in conflict or discomfort for both husbands and wives. The lack of work routines heightened the awareness of status differences and reinforced the commitment to the values of work and the things that wages could buy.

Was There Love on the Dole?

Economic hardship was very unevenly distributed during the Depression, and daily exposure to the co-existing affluent society only increased the humiliation of poverty. Prices dropped faster than hourly wages, so that those who remained steadily employed were actually better off. Luxury consumption did not fall as quickly as national income; in America sales of new appliances such as refrigerators continued to grow. Working-class leisure consumption had an escapist character, including spending on gambling, sensational films, and cheap magazines.

Spending money was psychologically liberating while its absence was devastating. Resentment of affluence was tempered by identification with those who could still afford to buy. For men, the lack of money often signified an inability to play the role of provider; joblessness undermined the traditional masculine role and sometimes even led to psychosomatic illness. Yet the sexual division of labor within the household was rarely reversed, even when married women held jobs while their husbands did not. Families struggled, often against immense odds, to maintain established images of respectability and propriety.

The fact that unemployment led to humiliation rather than political activism or creative self-realization

> [W]as inevitable in a society where, especially for men, free time was a compensation for work and leisure was inherently dependent upon income beyond subsistence. Not only was the value of free time diminished and money endowed with special social power, but commitment to work was reinforced. [152]

Summary of

The Insidious Cycle of Work and Spend
by Juliet Schor
[Published in *The Overworked American* (New York: Basic Books, 1992), 107–137.]

To afford the "good life" of materialism, Americans must work long hours. Traditional economic analysis suggests that Americans have freely chosen to work longer to afford high consumption levels. This summary argues that the traditional analysis is incorrect and that a causal relationship exists between increasing levels of consumption and the inability of workers to freely choose their schedules.

Shop 'Til You Drop

Today the average American is consuming twice as much as she did forty years ago. Increasingly, when people are not at work, they are shopping. Leisure activities, like visiting museums or national parks, which used to be free of shopping opportunities are now consumer destinations. Computers, televisions, and telephones have made households into veritable retail outlets, where the desire to buy can be instantly gratified. In conjunction with such technological innovations, the option to buy on credit has made consumption easy, accessible, and in some cases dangerous to consumers (e.g., to those who become debt-ridden shopping addicts).

The United States as a whole has become a wealthier nation in the past forty years. However, during the 1980s, the material standard of living rose for the wealthy and dropped substantially for the poor. For those in the middle, longer hours at work became necessary to maintain their living standards. The average worker's real hourly wages declined, so that in the absence of longer hours of work his/her annual earnings would have bought less than at the beginning of the 1980s.

Most important, the pursuit of ever higher material standards of living has eroded the desire for leisure time. Economic growth has resulted in less leisure time to pursue the "higher" life. Instead, the American worker has sought meaning and satisfaction through increased consumption.

While consumption increases have improved the material aspects of the quality of life (especially for poor households), it is not clear that consumption has increased the overall quality of life. For example, the quality of public life in the areas of safety, education, and community has diminished. Forty years of increasing consumption has not made the population any happier than it was in the 1950s; nevertheless, attachment to consumption and consumerist values has intensified. In fact, since there are always more desirable goods to be had, consumerism seems to result in dissatisfaction with the standard of living at every income level. Even people who make six-figure salaries complain that they feel poor.

Capitalism's Squirrel Cage

The crucial period for the formation of modern American consumerism was in the 1920s, when manufacturers confronted the possibility that once basic needs were met mass consumption might not follow mass production and rising productivity levels. In response, business helped create the "American Dream," a materialistic image of success to which everyone might aspire. But for many families, this dream was a moving target, always out of reach. Households would aspire to one level of material affluence, attain it and become habituated to it, and then aspire to the next level. The role of business in promoting this cycle of aspiration and habituation is essential to understanding the cycle of work-and-spend.

Through advertising, consumer credit, and the concept of the American dream, business developed the means for its own survival and success. Since consumer behavior was no longer directed only at satisfying basic needs, business could fill the American dream with a never-ending supply of luxury needs. For each socioeconomic class, goods were linked by advertising to needs for self-esteem, status, friendship, and love. As a result, people's psychological and social identities were associated with the possession of goods. Consumption of goods brought short-lived satisfactions, since new and improved products were continually being developed. For instance, the business strategy of planned obsolescence promoted consumer dissatisfaction by creating desirable new products that left consumers unhappy with current possessions.

Trade unionists and social reformers objected unsuccessfully to business's campaign to bind the American consumer to the satisfaction of unlimited wants. These groups recognized that increased consumption levels would require more income, achieved through more work time, so they argued that the benefits of productivity increases should be offered in the form of leisure time so that workers could pursue cultural and spiritual development. However, business came to be adamantly opposed to conceding increases in leisure time, preferring long hours and growth in output. Eventually, the economic and political power of business prevailed over labor interests.

Pitfalls of Consumerism

Consumerism has two significant problems. First, consumerism cannot bring about long-term satisfaction for all because it promotes the value of relative consumption. Suppose you buy a large-screen television that is the first on the block and find it very satisfying for that reason. Your satisfaction with the television diminishes when large screen televisions become commonplace on your block. Relative consumption concerns the satisfaction derived from comparing what you consume with what others in your socioeconomic group consume. "Keeping up with the Joneses" is fruitless because Jones is keeping up with you at the same time. Even if you were to jump far ahead into a different income bracket, you would find a higher income incarnation of Jones with whom to compete.

The second significant problem with consumerism is that consumption-based satisfactions are short-lived. Rotary telephones were an improvement over previous phones, but soon became unsatisfying when touch-tone phones came on the market. Now simple touch-tone phones are becoming obsolete as numbers can be preprogrammed into newer phones and "dialing" requires only the press of one button. Luxuries are taken for granted as we become habituated to the roles they occupy in our daily lives. This process of habituation explains, in part, why even the wealthy are unsatisfied with their lot.

Causes of the Work-and-Spend Cycle

Employer reaction to productivity growth drives the work-and-spend cycle. When productivity increases, employers offer higher wages and/or longer hours, rather than leisure time. Increases in wages then initiate consumption cycles. As workers become accustomed to more income and habituated to new spending patterns, their standards of living change. As a result, exchanging income for leisure time becomes undesirable. Thus, attitudes toward consumption come to be determined by the interdependent process of earning and consuming.

Neoclassical economic theory assumes that workers have control over their work schedules and that they freely choose higher wages over increases in leisure time. In this view, firms are passive and *workers get what they want*. In contrast, various studies show that workers do not have free choice concerning their work time. By having their schedules dictated to them, workers become habituated to certain spending patterns that do not reflect freely chosen behaviors. In effect, *workers want what they get*, rather than get what they want. In a 1978 Department of Labor study, 84 percent of workers were willing to trade off some or all of future increases in income for additional free time. Yet average hours of work have continued to increase since then.

The Social Nature of Work-and-Spend

Social and market forces make it difficult to break out of the work-and-spend cycle. Those who seek part-time work suffer harsh economic penalties, loss of benefits, social alienation, and fewer employment opportunities. Men and women are bound differently to the cycle of work-and-spend. Since there are few part-time jobs available for men, most males will be unable to obtain managerial, professional, or administrative positions that provide benefits and high pay. Men cannot leave well-paid full-time employment for slightly lower paying part-time jobs because there are none. For women, the transition to part-time labor is less traumatic because women are already discriminated against in full-time work. But women's part-time work offers few avenues to career advancement.

Traditional economics represents human beings through the theoretical construct of *homo economicus*—a rational individual whose every action is designed to maximize his well-being, and whose preferences are organized around the principle that more is always better than less. Unfortunately, homo economicus is trapped in a never-ending, vicious cycle of acquisition because the only way he can think about becoming satiated is to acquire more goods, and these acquisitions soon leave him dissatisfied and wanting more. This results in perpetual economic growth, which has dire effects on the planet's limited resources. The answer lies in reducing our desires and limiting our preferences to items that are durable, do not harm the environment, and promote a sense of well-being that is not dependent on trends and fashions.

> Instead of craving novelty in consumer goods, we could cultivate attachments to possessions that were high-quality and long-lasting, from clothes to automobiles to gadgets. We would use things until they wore out, not until they went out of fashion or we just grew tired of them. Foresight would be necessary, to avoid new products that ultimately leave us no better off. Maybe the Joneses and the Smiths could even cooperate rather than compete. If they were less concerned about acquiring, the two families could share expensive household items that are used only intermittently. [138]

Summary of

Work, Consumption, and the Joyless Consumer
by Raymond Benton, Jr.
[Published in *Philosophical and Radical Thought in Marketing,*
eds. A. Fuat Firat, Nikhilesh Dholakia, and Richard P. Bagozzi
(Lexington: Lexington Books, 1987), 235–249.]

[T]here is little that marketing can do to enhance the quality of life as long as it is primarily concerned with maximizing the market's consumption of goods and services. Indeed, marketing might be expected to decrease, rather than increase, the quality of life in direct proportion to the vigor with which it pursues that traditional purpose. [247]

This summary was written as a corrective to the philosophical narrowness of the marketing field. It seeks to remind members of the marketing profession that "economic growth and goods consumption is not necessarily correlated with the feeling of well-being by the people who participate in the process," [235] and argues that consumerism has developed in response to the lack of meaningful work in contemporary American society.

On Work and Consumption: The Theoretic

The distinction between labor and work is crucial for understanding the theoretical relationship between "work" and mass consumption. The etymological roots of *labor* connote pain and trouble, while those of *work* connote creativity. Labor produces goods that satisfy bodily needs and are quickly consumed, whereas work produces goods that are long-lasting and purposeful. Thus, the animal and human dimensions of "work" are represented, respectively, by *animal laborans* who is responsible for providing the means of human survival, while *homo faber* produces goods that contribute to a purpose beyond that of material necessity.

Throughout history, humans have struggled to emancipate themselves from the labor required to satisfy the material necessities of life. While ancient Greeks used human slaves for this end, the modern industrial approach was intended to render labor obsolete through the mass production of basic goods. Emancipation through abundance has required the fragmentation of production into highly regimented, mechanized, and laborious processes. Mass production employs on a grand scale the labor skills of *animal laborans,* rather than the craft work of *homo faber*. As a result, mass production fails to achieve freedom from the labor required for material necessity.

Since labor rather than work is the source of mass-produced goods and *labor* produces goods that are intended for quick consumption, the current addiction to consumption follows naturally from an abundance of labor-produced goods. Unfortunately, the relative paucity of craft goods lends itself to a growing disrespect for durable objects (such as furniture), which are now consumed almost as quickly as foodstuffs.

The Primacy of Work Over Consumption

Every person is both a producer and a consumer; however, neoconservative economic analyses give a central role to the consumer in each of us. Witness Adam Smith's comment that consumption is the sole end of all production. This type of view stands in stark contrast to the belief expressed by all religions that production or work is more important than consumption. For example, the Roman Catholic Church distinguishes between objective and subjective work goals. The objective aim of work—the production of necessary goods—is the one alluded to by Smith. But the more important aim of work is the subjective development of oneself and the achievement of one's humanity. In the Church's view, work is a fundamental dimension of human existence and a vehicle for self-fulfillment. Similarly, Protestantism asserts that work is a duty to the community and a service to God.

The American work ethic combines the views on work embodied by Protestantism and the Roman Catholic Church. People want and expect work to be a source of autonomy and creativity, an arena of self-development, and a process that is itself meaningful. In other words, Americans want to be craftpersons who have control over their work and can see the relation between their exertions and a finished product.

Historical Aspects of Work and Consumption

In contrast to opportunities available in preindustrial economies, the contemporary mass-production workforce holds jobs that limit workers' input to the formulation and adjustment of tasks and goals. The reduction of work to a meaningless, industrialized routine led to new forms of labor discipline to compensate for low motivation and to the introduction of institutions that encourage consumption as the route to life's satisfactions and meaning. Increasing consumption levels required abandonment of the Protestant ethic of frugal living. This involved the education (if not creation) of the American consumer through advertising, the introduction of credit financing, and the development of a novel cultural definition of achievement.

> The old value pattern that defined achievement as doing and making, and in which people displayed their character in the quality of their work, was intentionally and systematically replaced by a value pattern in which achievement was redefined to emphasize status and taste. The importance of doing was replaced by the importance of having as the citizen-craftsperson was replaced by the citizen consumer. In a very real sense, a culture of production and creation was replaced by a culture of consumption. [247]

Unfortunately, consumption pales in comparison to work as a means of achieving happiness and fulfillment.

To understand consumption patterns we must gain a historical perspective that reaches beyond the restricted sphere of consumption to include the moral and psychological milieu in which consumer culture developed. Efforts to transform our consumer society into one that serves distinctively human aspirations require first and foremost a change in the nature of work.

Summary of

The Study of Consumption, Object Domains, Ideology, and Interests
and
Toward a Theory of Consumption
by Daniel Miller[1]

[Published in *Material Culture and Mass Consumption* (Oxford: Basil Blackwell, 1987), 147–217.]

Consumption is important to various social functionings, but it also represents an avenue through which individuals can express themselves and combat the contradictions of modern culture. These summaries critique prior sociological analyses of consumption represented by the works of Veblen, Bourdieu, Marcuse, and Baudrillard, and then argue for a theory that vindicates consumption's greater role in society.

Consumption as Social Differentiation

Thorstein Veblen's classic, *The Theory of the Leisure Class* (1899), may almost be credited with initiating the study of consumption as a social phenomenon.

Veblen clarified the two major means by which the relatively small leisure class extended influence over society through its tastes. First, "refined" or "cultivated" taste became associated with distance from the world of work; objects suggesting practical necessity could be dismissed as "cheap." Second, the process of emulation, by which each group seeks to copy those above itself, extends upper-class standards throughout society.

Pierre Bourdieu's recent book, *Distinction* (1984), also locates the source of tastes in distance from work and sees such tastes as the key dimension controlling the significance of goods. In addressing the formation of preferences, Bourdieu analyzes Kant's concept of the aesthetic as contemplation that transcends the immediacy of experience. This detached, abstract aesthetic is only one of several possible perspectives—specifically, that of the dominant class, which can distance itself from work and necessity.

Bourdieu contrasts this with the "anti-Kantian" aesthetic of popular culture, which prefers immediate entertainment, and sensual and representational styles of art. The "anti-Kantian" tastes of working people derive from the immediacy of their work experience and the pressure imposed by their needs and insecurities. In contrast, those brought up in the abstractions of education and capital, secure in their economic position, can cultivate "Kantian" tastes.

Education is increasingly used to develop tastes that support current social differences, since it generates distinctions based on learning rather than birth or wealth. Education gives rise to what Bourdieu terms "cultural capital"—certain kinds of knowledge, such as knowledge of the classics or memorizing football scores. Education emphasizes the importance of, and provides the means to decode, the abstract and esoteric subjects of high culture. The differing tastes of social groups can be seen not only in the arts but also in areas such as food, with nouvelle cuisine as the analogue to abstract art and avant-garde theater.

Bourdieu clearly intends to expose the pretensions of middle- and upper-class taste, but his account is limited by his exclusive reliance on a questionnaire, rather than surveys of actual practice; his neglect of the influence of marketing; and his lack of a historical perspective on consumption. Ultimately, Bourdieu implies the same romantic preference for the work ethic and antipathy toward abstraction as Veblen.

Material Ideology

Bourdieu and others assume that differences in consumption practices correspond to differences between predefined social groups. An alternative approach allows that consumption of particular groups of commodities need not be associated with a given social group. Several illustrations can be drawn from consumption patterns in contemporary Britain.

For example, the widespread council (public) housing is a powerful expression of the ideals of communality, technology, and modernism. However, it is created by architects, builders, developers, and other members of the professional middle class. These professionals do not choose council housing for themselves, but rather prefer suburban, semidetached, or detached houses, which can be seen as part of an opposition to elements of modernity and urbanization. The same group of people sustain the image of individualism and opposition to modernity when acting as consumers, yet construct the very image of community and modernity when acting as producers. As a result, the image they create as producers appears to be the image of those who have been excluded from decision making, namely the tenants of council housing.

The Limits of Objectivism

Objectivist analyses—those that downplay the subject- or agency-centered perspective—have tended toward a totalizing approach, subsuming the whole spectrum of commodities under a notion of cultural dominance. Examples of this approach include Marcuse, the earlier work of Lukacs, Barthes, Lasch, Ewen and Ewen, and Haug. An example of what appears to be the inevitable result of objectivism can be seen in the study of the commodity by the French social theorist Baudrillard. Beginning with a symbolic analysis of modern mass consumption, Baudrillard was concerned to critique the concepts of utility in mainstream economics and use value in Marxian theory. While initially creative, this critique eventually led to the contention that objects not only did not signify use value, but in fact did not signify anything outside of themselves. The result is typical of poststructuralist thought; one is left with objects without meaning, signs without signification.

All analyses based on strong objectivism tend to reproduce what has been called the mass culture critique, in which the objects of mass consumption today are treated as so tainted, superficial, and trite that they could not possibly be worth investigating. In Bourdieu's terms, this rejection of popular taste, in the form of esoteric academic critiques, can be seen as closely aligned with the avant-garde arts as a type of cultural capital.

Recontextualization

Extreme objectivism, expressing an image of overarching class interest or subsuming discourse linked to production or to capitalism in general, eliminates the possibility of dominated groups as arbiters of cultural form. In the case of building style, this is a viable approach; but other examples suggest an alternative conclusion.

For example, a study of candies purchased by British children themselves, as opposed to those purchased by adults for them, reveals a pattern of symbolically "inedible" colors and shapes, particularly ghoulish representations of corpses, blood, vampires, and death. Here a dominated group, children, clearly asserts a perspective of opposition to the interests of the dominant group, adults. This suggests a degree of autonomy in cultural production on behalf of dominated groups. While the candies are mass produced, it is hard to believe that industry has chosen the forms that are popular with their customers; rather, there is the emergence, over time, of a children's culture, and a mutually constituted relationship between the interests and self-images of industry and its young customers.

A balance between objectivism and subjectivism can be seen as a balance between the weight assigned to production and consumption. The two are constantly interactive, not largely autonomous as implied by Bourdieu. Despite enormous efforts made through advertising, profits are always dependent on the reciprocal ability of marketers to interpret changes in the way goods are used in social relations.

This point is underlined by another example, a study of the changing meaning of the motor scooter. The scooter was originally developed and marketed in Italy as the feminine alternative to the more macho motorcycle. Later, the scooter fit into the emergent polarities in British youth culture, being adopted by the "mods" as part of a softer, continental style, rather than the "rockers," who preferred motorcycles for their harder, American image. No longer tied to gender, the British meaning of the scooter is consistent with, but not determined by, the original image created by the industry.

The three examples, all drawn from contemporary British consumption patterns, lend themselves to different theoretical perspectives. It is no coincidence that they differ markedly in size, and hence in related properties as well. Buildings are enormous, expensive, highly visible, and highly durable objects; the result is extensive involvement of the state and opportunities for conspicuous consumption. In contrast, "portable industrial artifacts," of which scooters are only one of many examples, are cheaper, less durable, and therefore more amenable to short-term fashion; while not attracting state involvement, they are the subject of mass marketing and experience dynamic interplay between the worlds of business and consumption. Finally, there are goods such as candies, which are so small, cheap, and transient that little research is likely to be put into active promotion of new forms determined by industry; the producer may be reduced to relatively passive response to apparent shifts in demand. In sum, the nature of material culture itself may be a much underestimated factor in accounting for the patterns and relationships of modern style.

The complexity of the relationship between producer and consumer interests is further illustrated by the case of advertising in women's magazines, which merges with and often overwhelms the articles. Do readers merely put up with the advertising to read the incidental articles? A more plausible view is that readers want the advertising as a guide to socially acceptable or fashionable consumption, which they look forward to as a reward for and relief from time spent in unpleasant labor. The fact that advertising may have nothing to do with the material and functional nature of the product is beside the point, if consumers are buying a product for its social (or humorous, moral, or sexual) meaning.

Unlike architecture and art, where professionals impose the image of another class on consumers, fashion offers the possibility of mass participation in which images provide groups with a vehicle for appropriating and utilizing cultural forces themselves. The fantasy involved in fashion may or may not mystify the objective facts of women's oppression; but like religion, it is a world of idealized morals and possibilities, of outrageous alternatives to everyday life—and as such, it has attractions of its own for the consumers.

The complexity of, and differences among, the examples discussed here calls for a recognition of the pluralism of consumer culture. In certain circumstances, segments of the population are able to appropriate industrial objects and utilize them in the creation of their own image. In other cases, people are forced to live in and through objects created by a different and dominant section of the population. As in the case of motor scooters, the meaning of a good may be transformed by consumers after it is produced.

Unhappy Consciousness

The feeling of anomie experienced in modern society is due to the contradictions that inhere in modern industry, state, and culture. These contradictions embrace both the conveniences of modern life and the negative aspects of their cumulative impact on modern conditions.

Industry's autonomous interests in their products as vehicles for capital expansion conflict with consumer interests in products as a means of self-creation. This contradiction is evident in the role played by money. Ostensibly, money gives the consumer freedom to choose goods, while industry is interested in capital accumulation—profit. Since successful industry is determined by profitability rather than by the impact of its products, consumers may suffer when industrial interests are left unbridled.

The state is the only force large enough to limit industry's excessive pursuit of profits. But state intervention to ensure equitable distributions of capital may conflict with its interest in cultural diversity, especially if it becomes an autonomous institution that seeks equality at the expense of pluralism. Finally, the growth of cultural modernism leads not only to the advance of science and social innovation, but also to the rise of sterile art and architecture, and other factors contributing to the sense of modernism as alien abstraction.

Postmodernist critics view consumption and the consumer through the narrow lenses of the commodity-form and the process of commodity acquisition, respectively. This approach fails to appreciate that historical changes in labor conditions (for example, contemporary laborers work fewer hours) have led to an overall increase in hours spent in consumption, transforming the dynamics of consumption. The extra time for consumption allows the consumer to personalize goods in a manner that overwhelms their alienated origins in the process of mass production. At the moment of purchase or allocation the consumer begins to integrate the good into a process of self-construction, transforming the good from a condition of alienation to one of inalienation. "This is the start of a long and complex process, by which the consumer works upon the object purchased and recontextualizes it, until it is often no longer recognizable as having any relation to the world of the abstract and becomes its very negation, something which could be neither bought nor given." [190]

Modern Consumption and Equality

While individualism and social inequality are often linked to mass-consumption practices in capitalist systems, the global diversity of mass-consumption societies suggests that consumption is expressed in a range of forms. The central problem for modern consumption practices is that goods are often consumed vicariously for individualistic reasons. When goods are consumed for purposes of class oppression and social climbing, consumption promotes inequality. Alternatively, consumption may promote equality when goods are consumed for the purposes of creating strong social networks. Different goods lend themselves to these alternative purposes. In consumption lies the promise for social equality, but this potential can only be achieved when the demand for greater material advantage represents the demand for sociability, close social peer groups, and normative order.

Consumption practices have become a form of self-production: witness the return to gardening, home brewing, and do-it-yourself activities. Such

productive consumption challenges traditional dichotomies between production and consumption as well as Bourdieu's view that all consumption
is social differentiation. Bourdieu overlooks the possibility that consumption may be used by all social groups to confront alienation.

> Mass goods represent culture, not because they are merely there as the en-
> vironment within which we operate, but because they are an integral part
> of that process of objectification by which we create ourselves as an in-
> dustrial society: our identities, our social affiliations, our lived everyday
> practices. The authenticity of artifacts as culture derives, not from their re-
> lationship to some historical style or manufacturing process . . . but rather
> from their active participation in a process of social self-creation in which
> they are directly constitutive of our understanding of ourselves and others.
> [215]

Note

1. Miller's discussion of consumption is motivated by his view that a better world
will be organized around a form of socialism. Progress toward a progressive socialist state can only arise when the alienating effects of mass production are offset by
consumption-based activity in which consumers create themselves through modern
goods. This summary does not focus on the political implications of Miller's work.
Also, the summary starts in the middle of chapter 8, on p. 147.

Summary of

Notes on the Relationship Between Production and Consumption
by Alan Warde

[Published in *Consumption and Class: Divisions and Change* eds. Roger Burrows
and Catherine Marsh (New York: St. Martin's Press, 1992), 15–31.]

> No longer is it possible to think of consumption in a simple, one-dimen-
> sional way. It is not just something that happens within the household
> contributing to the reproduction of labor power, nor can it be reduced to
> the distribution of assets, nor simply treated as an area of choice and taste.
> [28]

Research on the sociology of consumption has recently challenged the traditional view that consumption is simply a consequence of production.
Even so, current sociological views lack a coherent approach to the multifaceted character of consumption. This summary argues for an analytical

framework that develops "a set of concepts for understanding consumption in all spheres that can support a sociological appreciation of production and the experience of consumption." [17]

Recent sociological approaches to consumption have focused on consumerism, consumption sector cleavages, and household dynamics. Each type of analysis, however, oversimplifies its intended subject matter. For example, analyses connected with consumerism address taste formation, status, and consumption experience but fail to elaborate on the relationship between production and consumption. Alternatively, some British analyses examine the "cleavage" in consumption of services such as health care—the differential social advantage gained from access to private market goods rather than from the provision of state services. While this approach acknowledges the importance of the mode of provisioning goods and services, it fails to adequately address the role of domestic allocation. The significance of household dynamics is elaborated by feminist scholars who assert that an understanding of power distribution within households must be part of any adequate theory of consumption.

Conceptual Synthesis

There are three sorts of values that people seek in consumption. Exchange value, or price, is important when buying something that may later be resold, such as a house or an antique. Use values are achieved in the process of "final consumption," as when food is eaten or services are delivered. Finally, identity value is provided by styles and status-oriented consumption, when an object or activity places the consumer in a desired social circle. These are irreducible, distinct values; analysis of consumption should concern the ways in which people achieve the three types of values.

Consumption is best understood as a process in which functional values are obtained from goods and services. The process is characterized by modes of provision, or "distinctive ways of producing the good which embodies the value to be obtained at the end of any [consumption] episode and by the social relations governing access to the fruits of labor." [19] In contemporary society, market, domestic, state, and communal provision are the principal modes, typically governed "by relations of market exchange, familial obligation, citizenship right and reciprocity. It is because services are provided under distinctive conditions and access to them is regulated accordingly, and because this subsequently has consequences for their enjoyment, that the substitution of services between modes is so important socially and politically." [19] The shift between modes that has attracted the most attention is that from state to market provision; however, services have also moved from the state to the household (e.g., British community care policies) and from the household to the market (e.g., child care services).

Production and consumption occur in cyclical episodes that include four distinct phases: the process of production, the conditions of access, the manner of delivery, and the environment in which final consumption is experienced. Changes in the mode of provision of goods and services can affect all four phases, with important implications for the values derived from consumption. For example, a meal can be produced by an employee of a private firm (restaurant), oneself or a family member, or a public sector employee; access can be based on payment, family membership, or status in a public or communal institution; delivery, even within the category of marketed meals, can range from cafeteria self-service to impersonal fast-food service to highly personal table service in a fancy restaurant; and the social environment for final consumption—the company at the table—exerts a separate influence on the enjoyment of a meal.

Enjoyment: Analyzing the Experience of Consuming

Final values are obtained from goods through the creation of use and identity values during the consumption experience. Research in this area has attempted to understand consumption as pleasure, examining exceptional consumption events such as carnivals and tourism. However, this approach has little to offer for analyses of average consumer behavior. Interestingly, Hirschman suggests that only nondurable goods are sources of pleasure. For example, the pleasure of eating when hungry can be constantly recreated, while durable goods such as housing cannot change as often as one's wants and are therefore prone to induce disappointment. This perspective makes sense of the increased interest in packaged experiences such as theme parks and package tours: The experience of pleasure is ephemeral, and often depends on the presence of crowds; hence it is potentially profitable to reproduce the experience for another crowd tomorrow.

Consumers, as suggested above, may seek use value, exchange value, or identity value in consumption. All three may be provided at once, as with the purchase of a house in a fashionable neighborhood. On the other hand, many everyday acts of consumption yield no exchange (or resale) value; perishable foods and most services fall into this category. Can items of consumption lack the other two values? Youth subcultures have been known to give distinctive identity values to a wide range of mundane objects; nothing is intrinsically too humble for this role. However, purely routine consumption items and low-status state services may be lacking in identity value. Finally, while it is of course possible to purchase status symbols that are devoid of use value, it is rare. Far more common is the expression of identity value through carefully chosen purchases of items that have a use value as well, such as clothing, cars, and home furnishings.

Discussion

Examining consumption in this way emphasizes its complex, multifaceted nature. It demonstrates that work is involved in every episode of consumption; often the work is informal, voluntary, or domestic, and happens outside of formal employment relations. The disaggregation of consumption episodes makes it clear that production and consumption form a cycle, involving many values and objectives in addition to maximization of consumer satisfaction.

The categorization of modes of provision and phases of consumption episodes establishes a framework against which existing theories can be evaluated. Most can be seen to have omitted one or more of the central issues. For example, debates about state versus market provision of services typically overlook the role of domestic provisioning. Accounts of housing problems that focus only on housing production overlook the importance of the ways in which people gain access to, and derive pleasure from living in, various types of dwellings. The separation of use, exchange, and identity values allows a more integrated appreciation of the role of consumption in social changes such as gentrification.

Above all, the approach suggested here mitigates against one-sided and partial theoretical accounts of consumption.

Summary of

The Political Economy of Opulence
by Harry G. Johnson
[Published in *Money, Trade and Economic Growth*
(Cambridge: Harvard University Press, 1967), 164–177.]

This is a summary of the eighth chapter in Harry Johnson's book in which the author summarizes and further develops some of John Kenneth Galbraith's central points regarding consumption and the economic difficulties that relate to it.

John Kenneth Galbraith argues in *The Affluent Society* that many Western countries have solved the problems of scarcity that concerned classical economic theorists. However, as productivity and output rose, so did a new set of economic difficulties that were related to a change in the nature of consumption.

Consumption has been transformed by opulent societies, and the economic theory of demand must be expanded to embrace these changes. Galbraith's objection to modern economic policies provides us an analytical point of departure for his critique of classical demand theory. In Johnson's words, Galbraith argues that:

> [C]lassical economics was formed in and shaped by an atmosphere of grinding poverty for the mass of the population. In that environment, the economic problem appeared as a tripartite one: the inadequacy of production, which expressed the prevalence of poverty and the grimness of the human lot; the inequality of distribution, which accentuated the insufficiency of production to provide more than a miserable standard of living for the masses; and the insecurity of income, which reinforced the misery of inadequacy . . . [S]ince scarcity of resources was the apparent cause of poverty . . ., the need to increase production placed severe limits on the pursuit of policies aimed directly at overcoming inequality and insecurity.
>
> Production, inequality, and insecurity were the economic problems of the nineteenth century. But, Galbraith argues, these problems are no longer with us . . .
>
> But the solution of the economic problems of the nineteenth century through expansion of production raises new problems, because this solution involves our economic society in a rat-race in which people have to be persuaded by high-powered advertising and hidden persuasion to buy the goods which the business men think up to produce. Real scarcity has been succeeded by contrived scarcity, and the successful functioning of the economy depends on reiterating the contrivance . . . [T]he necessity of, and insistence on, sustained expansion of production carries with it a number of attitudes inimical to sensible economic policy. . . . Luxurious living, which drives the whole machine, becomes the necessary cost of production, so that the margin of resources available for social uses such as defense is unduly small in relation to national income. In particular, the assumption that it is private consumption that counts, together with the emphasis on the scarcity of resources and the need for efficiency, creates strong resistance to the provision of public services and collective consumption goods by tax-financed governmental activity. [165–166]

Thus, according to Galbraith our economy has achieved many essential economic goals and there are built-in structures (such as the institutionalization of capital accumulation and technical progress in the modern corporation) that perpetuate economic growth. If this view of the economy is correct, what implications might be drawn for revisions in traditional economic doctrine, and for the creation of what might be called the *political economy of opulence?*

The Nature of Opulent Consumption

Current demand theory originated with Alfred Marshall but has strayed far from its historical roots. Contemporary theory reduces the concept of demand to the logic of isolated choices: It assumes an individual with a given income and preferences, choosing between commodities in the market, and from this derives the demand curves for individual products. Marshall understood that economic progress changes the nature of demand and that the purpose of economic organization may eventually be oriented toward the development of wants rather than merely satisfying wants:

> . . . although it is man's wants in the earliest stages of his development that give rise to his activities, yet afterwards each new step upwards is to be regarded as the development of new activities giving rise to new wants, rather than of new wants giving rise to new activities.[1]

Economic progress results in the development of new wants that are a function of the improvement or education of taste. Although tastes may be shaped and facilitated by the advertising industry, the creation and satisfaction of new wants by advertising may produce social gain if it is possible to distinguish superior from inferior products and to thwart flagrant exploitation of consumers.

Consumption and Demand

In an age of opulence, created wants are typically satisfied by the services of consumer capital—the services provided by goods like televisions—rather than the consumption of perishable or nondurable commodities. Wants satisfaction via consumption is increasingly accomplished by substituting capital-intensive for labor-intensive methods. For example, household purchases of goods that provide labor-saving services are on the rise.

There are two significant implications of this change for economic theory. First, Marshall's rejection of the distinction between short-run and long-run demand curves should be reconsidered. The price of consumer durables has both a short-run effect on the optimal life of the existing stock of goods and a long-run effect on the desired level of stocks. The importance of consumer durables implies that the consumer has the same problem of short-run rigidity as the producer; response to a change in the price of consumer durables will not be complete until stocks have been adjusted to the new optimal level. Once the consumption of the services of capital is recognized as a structural component of an opulent economy, it becomes clear that the nature of demand will change over time.

Second, conventional conceptions of consumer choice must be expanded to embrace choice with respect to the use of one's time. In opulent societies, the value of an individual's use of time increases relative to the value accorded to commodities. As a result, as people become wealthier they will care more about their working conditions than they will about their financial rewards. People will want to spend less time at work so as to enjoy more fully the services of their consumer goods. Leisure activities will become increasingly capital-intensive as the equipment necessary to participate in travel and sport increasingly requires expensive capital equipment. Thus, choice in the use of time becomes a significant factor in economic decisions in the political economy of opulence.

Note

1. Alfred Marshall, *Principles of Economics, 8e* (London: MacMillan, 1920), 89; cited by Johnson, 168.

Summary of

The Increasing Scarcity of Time
by Staffan B. Linder

[Published in *The Harried Leisure Class*
(New York: Columbia University Press, 1970), 1–15.]

Roy Harrod once proposed that we may one day find ourselves unable to consume more goods simply because we will have no time to service and maintain them. His "consumption maximum" contrasts starkly with the long-standing belief that economic growth advances the development of mind, spirit, and culture. This summary argues that economic growth leads people to optimize the use of time they spend consuming goods by increasing the amount of goods consumed and decreasing the amount of time spent with each.

Modern affluent societies are characterized by an increasingly hectic pace of living, growth-oriented economic policies, and wasteful service economies. In wealthy countries, economic growth rather than cultural advancement continues to be a central policy goal even though general welfare has advanced to the point where most people can satisfy their basic material needs. This is paradoxical since the historical image of an affluent society is one in which the satisfaction of basic needs leads to individual and cultural development. The increasing scarcity of time is the root cause of this paradox.

Time as a Scarce Commodity

A commodity becomes scarce when demand for it exceeds available supply. Like other economic resources, there exists a certain supply of and demand for time in either leisure- or production-oriented activities. Obviously, work takes time just as experiencing the pleasures of a good cup of coffee requires time. In an affluent society, the demand for time is often much greater than the available supply of time.

As a scarce commodity, time is subject to the principles of economic laws that assert the importance of optimizing the use of one's time. The economic strategy for optimizing one's time is analogous to the manner in which one tries to get the most for one's money.

> When spending money, one presumably tries to balance one's expenditures in such a way as to obtain the best possible yield. This means that one will probably refrain from spending all one's assets on a single commodity. One will instead distribute one's expenditure over a variety of different goods and services. The optimum situation will have been reached when it is impossible to increase satisfaction by reducing expenditure in one field and making a corresponding increase in another. A more technical description of this condition of equilibrium would be to say that the marginal utility of one dollar must be the same in all different sectors of expenditure.
>
> In the same way, one tries to economize with one's time resources. They must be so distributed as to give an equal yield in all sectors of use. Otherwise, it would pay to transfer time from an activity with a low yield to one with a high yield and to continue to do so until equilibrium had been reached. [3]

Time use optimization is a common practice; for example, if reading this summary seems like a waste of time, the reader will spend his or her time elsewhere.

The Increasing Scarcity of Time

In periods of economic growth, increases in worker productivity raise the yield from time spent at work. Time spent in leisure activities must then also produce a higher yield to keep pace with the increased yield on time at work. For example, socializing may be oriented toward meeting business contacts, or reading could be directed toward self-improvement. Another method for raising the yield on time spent in consumption (that is, consumption time) is to increase the amount of goods consumed per unit of time. If this method is chosen, then less time must be spent on each good to bring the yield on consumption time in line with that of the increased yield on production time.

A Basic Problem in Social Science

The increasing scarcity of time has broad implications for our attitudes toward many social problems and behaviors, but these issues are not systematically explored by any social science. Psychologists recognize that some human disorders may be related to the effects of living under severe temporal constraints. Sociologists describe how individuals or groups allocate their time in and out of work. Anthropologists examine the attitudes toward time in different cultures.

No theoretical explanation of time allocation has been achieved by any of these disciplines because each fails to understand that the problem of time use and allocation is a problem of economizing an increasingly scarce resource. Surprisingly, economics—a science that is devoted to the study of the allocation of scarce resources—misses the significance of time as an economic resource. Typically, economics regards work time as a scarce resource and consumption as an instantaneous act that has no temporal extension:

> . . . when economists try to state the connection between the "utility" of a certain commodity and the amount of that commodity available, they never take into account the time an individual has at his disposal to consume the commodity in question. In economic theory, the pleasure an individual can be expected to derive from a couple of theater tickets is not taken to be dependent in any way on the time he can devote to playgoing . . . . The utility of theater tickets cannot be established without knowing whether or not the ticket holder has time to use them. [7–8]

This myopic view of time leads to two serious flaws in economic theory: the assumption that nonwork time is noneconomic time, and the belief that economic growth results in increasing amounts of free time.

Why This Neglect of Time Analysis?

Historical and conceptual factors explain why economic theory has avoided the analysis of consumption time as an economic resource, along with time analysis in general. With respect to history, early economists defined their field at a time when goods scarcity dominated all problems and time scarcity was not an issue. Changing circumstances have not brought about a change in scope.

Conceptually, the term "economic growth" conjures images of total affluence, where numerous economic opportunities grow simultaneously. These images contrast with the "partial" nature of economic growth, where a limited time supply is subject to growing demand. A different sort of conceptual mistake is the assumption that material well-being for all leads to the consumption of fewer goods and the cultivation of mind and spirit. This optimistic assumption continues to cloud our vision of an era in which time scarcity has led to increased goods consumption.

A Framework for Discussion

Time is not a homogenous entity that responds uniformly to economic growth. Time is used differently in various aspects of life, and, as one might expect, economic growth affects differently each sector of time use. The most important sector is *work time,* which is the amount of time spent in specialized production. Changes in the productivity of work time influence the supply, demand, and distribution of time in other activities. *Personal work time* is the amount of time spent on production of services and the maintenance of goods and of one's body. *Consumption time* is the amount of time spent consuming goods. *Culture time* is the amount of time spent cultivating the mind and spirit; the use of goods plays an incidental role if any in this time sector. The final category of time is *idleness time,* which is the amount of time spent being passive and experiencing a slow pace of life. If we take *work time* as a given, and since *personal work time* is a function of the goods we own and of our bodily needs, then the trade-offs on which we must focus are those in the last three categories: time used for consumption or for culture, or time that is simply allowed to go by.

Summary of

Social Limits to Growth: The Commercialization Bias
by Fred Hirsch

[Published in *The Social Limits to Growth*
(Cambridge: Harvard University Press, 1976), 70–113.]

(Key terms in these selected chapters are explained in the Hirsch summary in Part VI.)

> Commercialization in our economy, substituting explicit for informal exchange, is in some sectors not an efficient means of meeting individual preferences. It represents not what people want, choosing among all potential alternatives, but merely what they get when inadequate special provision is made for satisfying individual demands that the market is technically unsuited to fulfill. [94]

In economically advanced societies, social norms that influence sociability and friendliness are progressively strained by market forces. As individuals consume ever-increasing quantities of goods, time pressures mount, leaving less time to cultivate friendships.

Time pressures develop from increasing levels of consumption and the need for additional income. Linder (see summary in this part) argues persuasively that higher consumption levels require the consumer to economize on time, maximizing its use over an expanded consumption range. One economizing strategy is to substitute time-saving for time-intensive consumption goods.

This strategy affects consumer choice and national accounts measures. On the one hand, consumption of time-saving products or services is primarily instrumental to some final consumption goal. For example, a taxi's service may be purchased to save time in the pursuit of some other consumption activity. On the other hand, national accounts have no way of discriminating between time-saving/instrumental and time-intensive/final goal consumption. The taxi fare indicates, but does not itself constitute, increased welfare. To the extent that consumption levels reflect defensive consumption, or consumption undertaken in order to permit other forms of consumption, national accounts stray from indicating welfare.

Increased consumption needs (primarily defensive and positional) require more earnings, which often require longer hours at work, which in turn may increase the scarcity of time for nonwork activities. Since mass consumption of some goods tends to deteriorate the social conditions in which they are used (e.g., mass automobile consumption leads to congestion problems), more extensive defensive consumption is needed to maximize total consumption. As a result, the need for additional income biases the individual consumer against substituting nonmarket leisure for work.

The increasing scarcity of time permits an economic explanation for the common observation that sociability is diminished in modern marketized economies. In the economic context, social norms and casual, friendly behavior are similar to public goods, in that their costs and benefits cannot be appropriated by any one individual. As public goods, social norms and friendliness are susceptible to the vagaries of time pressures. Since friendliness is time consuming and any particular act of friendliness runs a great risk of being unreciprocated, the economizing consumer increasingly ignores social conventions supporting casual, friendly behavior.

Increasing time pressures as well as social mobility wreak havoc on the mutuality of exchange in friendships: It becomes difficult to trust that friends will pay back favors. The effects of the market on social relationships, specifically the effects on the perceived obligation to act according to social convention, are inappropriately excluded from the realm of economic discourse, just as pollution once was.

Friendly exchange approximates a private good when, for instance, a gesture today is reliably repaid tomorrow. However, in modern market economies, casual friendly exchanges cost a small amount of time, occur frequently, and may be reciprocated rarely and at unknown intervals by strangers. Consequently, motivation to participate in any particular casual friendly act is low, causing an underproduction of sociability. Both marketing and consumer protection groups sustain this situation by advocating the values of self-interest maximization.

> As the subjective cost of time rises, pressure for specific balancing of personal advantage in social relationships will increase. As long as the time cost is relatively low, whether because of fewer alternatives for use of leisure or because of fewer opportunities or pressures for additional work effort, the net cost of each specific time-absorbing activity connected with friendship or the social relationships will also be relatively low. In fact, it may not even be seen as a cost. Perception of the time spent in social relationships as a cost is itself a product of privatized affluence. The effect is to whittle down the amount of friendship and social contact to a level that leaves everyone wishing they had more at the expense of fewer material goods. This effect is doubly perverse since the relative value attached to friendship and other human relationships must be expected to increase as pressing material needs are increasingly met. [80]

Increasing productivity levels and increasing mobility tend to strengthen the public good characteristics of social behavior at the expense of its private good characteristics. The more social behavior resembles a public good, the more its benefit is diffused to others, the less responsive it is to individualistic demand. One effect is that increases in friendship will continue to be underproduced.

The New Commodity Fetishism

Economists neglect the social context in which individual acquisition of goods and services takes place and as a result are overly concerned with commodities as instruments of satisfaction. The market not only compromises social norms but also negatively affects the type of satisfactions derived from goods. Two factors are involved, which may be called the "commodity bias" and the "commercialization effect." The *commodity bias* is when excessive growth in the material sector of the economy leads to intensified positional competition, which channels a disproportionate amount of individual activity through the market. The *commercialization effect* refers to the impact on consumer satisfaction resulting from supplying commodities through the market rather than through some other mechanism (such as informal exchange or feelings of service or obligation).

Lancaster (see summary in Part VI) captures the commonsense notion that consumers derive satisfaction from the characteristics provided by goods, rather than from the goods themselves. By extension, utility derived from goods emerges from characteristics as well as the environmental conditions in which they are used. Mass automobile consumption may affect the satisfaction derived from consumption of a single automobile's transportation characteristics, as in the example of traffic congestion. Alternatively, the manner in which commodities are supplied may influence which characteristics are yielded by a given good or service. For instance, a doctor's services may improve a patient's health, but may also yield valuable characteristics that arise from strong doctor-patient relations (e.g., knowing and trusting the doctor). The commercialization effect on medical services has weakened doctor-patient relations and, as a result, has altered the characteristics that have traditionally been acquired from such services. Commercialization also affects the characteristics of other types of services, such as educational instruction, political or administrative leadership, and companionship.

Individual consumers may derive alternative satisfactions from the same product or service, depending on the motivation for its provision. A service that is provided to satisfy private wants may deliver a different set of characteristics from the same service when it is provided to satisfy societal needs. One unfortunate consequence is that commercialization of services diminishes expectations that obligations will be met without contracts. Such effects represent a deterioration in the characteristics of public goods.

The commercialization effect alters the social forces that influence individual behavior; social norms, mutually agreed upon, are replaced by privatized standards that are shaped by an individualistic ethos. As a result, weakened social norms increasingly fail to restrain individuals from maximizing short-term satisfaction at the expense of long-term objectives. But social norms are required for the pursuit of long-term goals when the effects of individual behavior are diffused and uncertain. Given the unpredictable effects of individual actions, even long-term self-interest will not always promote socially directed action. When individualistic attitudes prevail, the risk becomes too great that others will take a free ride on any altruistic act. Consequently, commercialization's debilitating effects on social norms become vicious.

People are usually prepared to take some risk that their sociability will not be reciprocated, but when the risk appears too high, behavior shifts toward securing fair exchange in any single transaction. Although the effects on social conventions are cumulative, the specific effects of each transaction are unnoticeable to any individual participant.

While the market tends to be inefficient at providing collective goods, it also tends to overproduce those private goods that it is efficient at producing. The resulting commodity bias provides the market with incentive to cater to demand that is amenable to commercialization. This means that the market has a structural incentive to privatize collective goods, effectively setting a price on access to them. The exclusionary nature of this practice may change the characteristics of the collective goods by affecting the manner in which they are acquired. Satisfaction derived from consumption of freely accessible common goods may no longer be possible for some. The poor who depend on public access will not benefit from collective goods that become costly to consume.

The market is well-equipped to satisfy piecemeal individual demand when the conditions of use are presumed fixed at present levels, but ill-equipped to satisfy individual demand when long-term ramifications on conditions of use are taken into consideration. The market bias toward the overproduction of commercial goods diminishes social welfare by neglecting its effect on the conditions in which characteristics are consumed.

The Hole in the Affluent Society

In sum, profit seeking corporations may excel in discovering what we individually want, within some given social context. They may even excel in executing our order for what we want. But where this is also what we cannot all have, this attention to our irreconcilable demands may be exactly the trouble. The corporations then do their jobs too well. Switching the order to the government sector will merely shift the locus of the misassignment. [109]

Any society that allocates its resources with the aim of satisfying individual wants is destined to have its efforts frustrated. Private goods have a social dimension that make it impossible for everyone to receive what each one wants. This is not a problem with distribution—rather it is an adding-up problem that exacerbates the disparity between the quality of private and public sector goods.

Economic growth was originally thought to redistribute wealth, eliminating gross disparities between rich and poor. The idea was that if everyone had more, everyone would be better off. However, economic growth has not brought about these changes because it has occurred primarily within only one sector of the economy, the material sector. The lack of growth in the positional sector has diminished public interest in redistributive transfers and forced all individuals to be overly concerned with their relative income levels. Intensified competition for positional goods and privatization of common access facilities have inhibited equitable resource distributions.

As Easterlin and others have observed, relative rather than absolute income plays an important role in making people happy. In contrast to Easterlin, the importance of relative income in determining happiness can be explained exclusively in terms of increased positional competition, rather than being based on social comparisons. A person who has seen his absolute income rise and has attempted to use this income to improve his lot by moving to the suburbs may derive a zero increase in happiness from the move because so many others have made the same move, causing congestion problems and leading to further increases in defensive consumption.

Galbraith correctly observed the imbalance between private affluence and public squalor, but mistakenly interpreted the problem in terms of a misallocation of resources. More accurately, the problem of social imbalance lies with the individualistic demand for public goods. "Goods and facilities provided directly or indirectly through the public sector fail to meet our individual demand partly because these cannot be met for all or most people together." [107] Consequently, expanding the public sector would fail to satisfy the individual demands of all. Contemporary frustration with the feeble returns from heavy public expenditures confirms this view. This frustration motivates individuals to increase their spending or demand more public spending.

Galbraith's observation of social imbalance can be explained in terms of market failure, that the price mechanism fails to reflect all available options.

Since the market caters only to demand that is susceptible to the commercialization effect, it does not offer alternatives that an individual might choose if they were available. Consumers desire the characteristics supplied by products in certain noncommercial conditions of use, but those conditions are not commonly supplied by corporations.

Summary of

Changing Consumption Patterns: The Transformation of Orange County Since World War II

by Alladi Venkatesh

[Published in *Postsuburban California: The Transformation of Orange County Since World War II*, eds. Rob Kling, Spencer Olin, and Mark Poster (Berkeley, Los Angeles, and Oxford: University of California Press, 1991), 142–164.]

This summary uses Orange County, an affluent county in southern California, as a case study of an area whose consumption patterns, credit dependency, diverse shopping environments, changing family patterns, and extensive use of information technologies typify current trends in consumer culture.

Many of the suburbs that once beckoned white, middle-class families to their sleepy, parochial neighborhoods in the 1950s are undergoing radical social and economic change. Unlike the suburbia of old, postsuburban areas mix different classes, races, industry, residential spaces, specialized services, and cultural activity. Consumerism is important to this transformation, especially in Orange County, where the prevalence of dual income, well-educated families, the proliferation of retail outlets, and readily accessible credit all contribute to a higher valuation of consumerist lifestyles.

The Roots of an Affluent Settlement Culture

Since World War II, migration to Orange County has led to cultural diversity, multilingualism, and economic stratification. Its diverse residents, however, share an openness to experimental consumption and a freedom from consumer traditions. Orange County's consumer culture is suggested both by its levels of affluence and the values of its citizens. As the sixteenth largest metropolitan area in the country, with a population of two million, its median annual family income of $43,000 in 1988 was the highest among the twenty most populated metropolitan regions. Orange County supports a significant market for retail trade, as well as for expensive, imported automobiles. The median price of a single-family home reached almost $250,000, one of the highest in the country.

Orange County's wealth resides more in its high consumption levels than in its civic concerns. Although its average income level is one of the highest in the country, 11 percent of its total population is at or below the poverty line. Many single-parent families and poor immigrants account for the fact that 35 percent of all households earn less than $25,000 annually. For the affluent majority, though, Orange County typifies a consumer region in the following respects:

> (1) The culture values consumption as a social accomplishment. (2) There are high levels and much distribution (as opposed to concentration) of wealth, which translates into buying power. (3) There is a nonhomogeneous marketplace, which results in highly differentiated consumer choice patterns. (4) There are high levels of education, which allow for market sophistication, market experimentation, and market innovation. [148–149]

Effects of Postsuburban Transformation

The opportunity to consume permeates every aspect of life in Orange County, and few choose to ignore the chance to indulge since consuming less could lead to social marginalization. Although the proliferation of shopping environments has set the stage for diverse consumption patterns, all are organized around the idea that consumption is entertainment, that shopping is a spectacle. Much of Orange County's affluent consumption is devoted simultaneously to entertainment and to the provision of social identity.

Orange County is fully serviced by shopping environments that can be found all over the United States, including neighborhood shopping centers, shopping malls, swap meets, and consumer warehouses. The "shopping experience" offers consumers adventure, novelty, and fantasy as well as a sense of community membership. Shopping malls have become tourist destinations, fantasy lands even for those who cannot afford many of the high-priced goods on sale there. Shopping has thus become less about choosing goods than about having certain experiences. Alternatively, swap meets offer personalized interactions and a market setting in which buyers can barter on their own terms, while consumer warehouses provide exclusive membership to consumers as they choose among low-priced goods.

Much of Orange County's affluence is due to the prevalence of dual-income families. Increasing levels of discretionary household income have followed women's increased labor participation and left many families with nontraditional, time-constrained spending patterns and consumption routines. Women's increased labor participation has affected "standards of living, shopping habits, types of products and services consumed, the use and quality of family time, and child rearing." [154] An increase in dining out is but one significant example of the new dual-income household consumption patterns. Another change is the increased participation of children in the household consumption decisions. Women's traditional sovereignty over consumption decisions in the household has been ceded to children and to external market forces. Marketers now recognize the decisive influence children have in many household consumption decisions and target them as the audience for many advertisements.

Affluent residents of Orange County have a great deal of buying power, which is extended by the widespread use and availability of credit. Orange County has a reputation for being one of the most credit-dependent regions in the country. Its average resident possesses more than three department-store credit cards. Households earning over $15,000 a year "receive an average of four credit card solicitations a month—three times the national average."[1] In the United States, installment debt as a percentage of annual income rose from 2 percent in 1945 to 18 percent in 1985. While much of this change is accounted for by the rising costs of home mortgages, credit-card purchases are the fastest growing aspect of this change. Orange County's heavy use of credit suggests that it is one of the leaders of a national trend toward greater credit dependency.

High levels of credit can lead to financial problems during economic downturns. But even in good years, increasing reliance on credit and the technology that serves it degrades an individual's right to privacy. Credit histories that should be private become publicly accessible, while it becomes impossible to function in a consumer economy without credit. "Without credit, the individual cannot participate in the consumer economy; with credit, he or she cannot escape it." [160] Whether this dilemma is a mere by-product of capitalism, an inevitability, or a chosen alternative, it is unlikely that Orange County's consumption patterns, tied so strongly to credit as well as to status and diminished privacy, represent a model for other regions to follow.

Note

1. S. Boyd, "Credit Overload," *Orange Coast* 15(8) (August, 1989): 122–123; cited by Venkatesh, 160.

PART III
Family, Gender, and Socialization

Overview Essay
by David Kiron and Seymour Bellin

With the rise in consumption levels following World War II, social relations—within the family, between genders, and among friends—have undergone enormous changes. Similarly, the development of markets aimed exclusively at children's interests has dramatically influenced the socialization of youth. Increasing consumption traditionally is welcomed as a sign of progress, but many of the accompanying changes have raised concerns about their impact on family, gender, and children. This part analyzes these effects and the influences of cultural trends and institutional forces such as government, technology, and commercialization. The summaries that follow offer telling evidence that consumer culture disrupts family stability and communities, promotes consumption as a significant arena in which to cultivate personal identity, and undermines certain aspects of child development.

The family, in some form, is a major socializing institution that assures the continuity and stability of any society. However, it is useful to distinguish between a society's ideal of the family and the diversity of actual family forms, which typically depart from the ideal. The nuclear family has been the prevailing normative ideal even though there has always been considerable departure from this ideal due to circumstances such as death, separation, or divorce. Since World War II, especially after the 1960s, divorce and separation have become much more common, as have never-married one-parent families. In recent years, even same-sex couple marriages and families have received legal recognition in some areas. However, a large majority of people have experienced a nuclear family form at some point in their lives. For purposes of our discussion we will focus on the nuclear family ideal, but take into account the reality of a trend toward an increasing diversity in family forms.

The Industrial Revolution wrought many changes in the family dynamic. With the emergence of the Industrial Revolution, the family changed in many important ways. In the preindustrial economy rural households were relatively self-sufficient as all members produced for their collective needs; but with urbanization and industrialization, households began to buy and consume more final goods from the market. The late nineteenth century witnessed the rise of the male breadwinner/female homemaker family, as men increasingly worked in industry, while domestic labor was often trivialized and left to women. As families acquired more capital, the distribution of money within the household became a contested matter between husband and wife, a major factor in marital instability that has continued to this day.

A Selective History of the Family

The first two summaries illustrate two consumption domains that influenced family stability and identity in the United States: domestic money transfers at the turn of the century and the mass introduction of television within the family context during the 1950s. Viviana Zelizer argues that between 1880 and 1930, monetary negotiations within the breadwinner/homemaker family were a source of conflict in every social class. In general, married men exercised control over family income, including the earnings of their wives and children. The mainstream method of domestic disbursements evolved during this period: At first, the husband allotted money as a gift or upon request and then according to an allowance schedule. Neither approach proved satisfactory, as the female homemaker continued to be a cashless household manager. It was not until the 1930s, when an egalitarian ideal of marriage began to take hold, that the idea of a joint account became an accepted means of allocating domestic monies. The breadwinner/homemaker family structure was deeply fractured by the onset of World War II, when many married and employed men went to war.

The period following World War II was marked by a series of events and government policies that have brought about significant changes in the family and mass consumption. Postwar government policy was predicated on two objectives. The first was to prevent mass unemployment following the demobilization of the large, conscript military forces that fought in the war. Those who served in the defense of the nation, it was believed, deserved to have the opportunity to return to the jobs they held at the time they enlisted or were called to service.[1] One route to this goal was to encourage women to leave industry, a policy consistent with the practices of many companies in industry and business. The exodus of women from industry not only solved the concern about massive unemployment but also restored traditional gendered family roles: the man as breadwinner and the woman as full-time housekeeper.

The second objective of postwar government economic policy was to promote suburbanization and single-family ownership. Toward this end, tax deductions were offered to home buyers; the government financed extensive highway construction, assuring convenient access from the suburbs to workplaces in the central city; and the Federal Housing Administration provided low-interest loans and mortgages.[2]

The years immediately following the War were unusual because of the disruptive influences of the War itself—delayed marriages, disrupted careers, and subsequent geographic mobility that separated extended families and uprooted people from their neighborhoods. Marriage rates reached a historical peak as did divorces and separations. By the early 1950s, however, there was a drop and leveling off in these rates, although divorce rates continued to rise. Despite the evidence of widespread marital distress, the decade of the 1950s continues to be viewed nostalgically as the "Golden Era" of the family: nuclear in form, stable, cohesive, and content.

Commercial television and family situation comedies (sitcoms) played an important role in reinforcing and validating normative ideals about the family during this period. In her article, Mary Beth Haralovich explores the idealization of the suburban family in an analysis of *Father Knows Best* and *Leave It To Beaver,* two popular family sitcoms of the 1950s, which seemed to represent model families. The joys of suburban living were exalted, while its familiar troubles were solved from show to show. The gendered space of the home was vividly portrayed; for example, husbands but not wives had private areas. Haralovich dramatizes the institutional forces that influenced the social construction of the homemaker role in suburban lifestyles. Consumer goods industries attempted to sell the female homemaker innovative, time-saving products as well as the idea of effortless home management. This sales pitch consolidated the images of good wife and good mother in the image of a good shopper and efficient household manager.

Televised images of family stability were important since families were moving much more frequently in the decade that followed the end of World War II. As businesses around the country expanded, one in five families moved annually and were uprooted from extended family, friends, and neighbors, important sources of information and advice (as well as social support). As a result, people faced an increasing need for information and advice on matters ranging from new household technologies and products to over-the-counter medications. Women, as the principal family consumer, turned to television and magazines for advice on personal and family matters.

In the 1950s, television was relatively new to the mass market. For the first time, families could see themselves, or what they wanted to see of themselves, reflected on the tube. Between 1950 and 1959, the percentage of households with at least one television exploded from 9 to 90 percent.[3] With its widespread appeal, the influence of commercial television extended far beyond its validation of certain family lifestyles. It transformed the use of time within the family dynamic, changing the dynamic of family life. For instance, as family viewing time rose from an average of four hours a day in the 1950s to an average of seven hours in the late 1980s, extended family dinners, which afford time for sociability and conversation, became less common. With the evolution of individualized frozen meals, many families stopped sharing a common meal. As families watched more television, they went to bed later and slept less. By the late 1980s, three out of four households owned more than one television set, which allowed for more private viewing.

The idea that people are engaging in more private consumption is a growing concern of researchers in various disciplines. Part of the concern stems from the idea that the pursuit of private pleasure has an isolating effect and social isolation is known to be connected with psychological depression. People who are embedded in a social network of family and friends are far less likely than those who are without such a support system to develop clinical depression in response to a major stress such as unemployment or the death of a loved one. Social disconnection both reflects and reinforces cultural trends toward self-interest, individualism, and the erosion of community commitments.

The trend toward more private consumption is described in the next summary by Robert Lane, who contends that television viewing, the modern shopping experience, and a rise in individualized consumption contribute significantly to social isolation, which exaggerates the risk of developing depression. And depression is on the rise. Lane cites evidence that people born after 1945 are ten times more likely to suffer from depression than those born earlier. Lane recognizes the difficulties in establishing causal relations among consumerism, social isolation, and depression, acknowledging that depression may lead to consumerist behavior just as consumerist behavior may lead to depression.

Lane's article also represents a more recent concern about the role of television in contemporary life.[4] Although television is discussed in more detail in Part VII, we note here that the controversy over the effects of television has now been extended to the civic domain. In a recent article that was published too late for consideration here, Robert Putnam offers television as a significant factor in the deterioration of civic participation and the quality of communities.[5] Putnam's work has made television into something of a lightning rod for controversy in the debate over civic vitality in the United States.

Gender and Consumer Culture

We are witnessing a major change in the role of work and consumption in shaping personal identity and meaning in the lives of men and women. Men are no longer constrained to find their identity solely in their work, nor women primarily in the home as wives and mothers. As more women enter the workforce, fewer women become full-time homemakers. Certainly some women continue to construct their identity as mother and wife through shopping and managing family consumption, but for many others consumption plays a larger role in defining aspects of self that are separate from the family context.

The next group of summaries discusses the intersection between cultural and institutional forces such as feminism and commercialization, and gender roles within the context of consumption. They reveal a dynamic interaction among gender stereotypes, the role of work, commodities, influences on the formation of preferences, and expressions of personal identity. Three key points emerge: (1) Stereotypes produced in the cultural arena may be embedded in goods exchanged in the market, permitting the reproduction of power relations that exists outside the marketplace; (2) commercialization contributes to the socialization of children through rituals and gendered toys that focus excessively on change rather than growth; and (3) since the 1950s, consumption has become an esteemed and valued project for both genders.

A. Fuat Firat analyzes the latter point, discerning a trend in which men no longer seek their identity solely in the workplace and look increasingly to consumption as a way of expressing themselves. They also suffer and share some of the same ailments and behaviors commonly associated with women: Men suffer from anorexia nervosa at highter rates, albeit at lower levels than women, and men spend millions of dollars a year on plastic surgery.[6] Similarly, working women have adopted some of the same consumer responses as men to occupational stress and hazards. They use tobacco, coffee, and alcohol at increasing rates, which has led to more incidences of lung cancer and heart disease. Firat also notes that the development of spheres of life outside of work and home (e.g., recreational, neighborhood, shopping) require both men and women to cultivate various personae, which depend on greater private consumption.

In affluent consumer societies, cultural assumptions about gender are incorporated into a vast array of products. The commodification of gender enables us to "buy into gender just as we buy into style."[7] Helga Dittmar and Susan Willis approach the consequences of this feature of life within twentieth-century capitalism in somewhat different ways, although both agree that gender stereotypes are perpetuated through goods, especially among children.

Dittmar offers evidence that men and women attach meanings to their most treasured possessions according to gender differences; men and women describe the importance of certain goods, even the same type of goods, in ways that reflect masculine and feminine attributes, respectively. She presents an interesting theoretical framework for understanding the transmission of gender stereotypes through goods. It states that the greater role of commodity consumption in everyday life has a stronger tendency to reproduce the power hierarchy that inheres in the gender status quo.

Willis emphasizes the impact of socializing children into consumer culture through goods that exaggerate differences between boys and girls. With the declining influence of feminism in the 1980s, rigidly gendered toys, such as He-Man dolls for boys, were reintroduced into the market, forcing a new generation of children to enter unwittingly into a gendered social order. From an early age, boys and girls are kept apart by marketing forces, in the types of toys, the kind of play prescribed by these toys, and even by the store aisles in which the toys are found.

Willis also contends that cultural and religious rituals that have traditionally marked the physical transition from childhood to adulthood have been marginalized with the broad acceptance of commercial birthday parties and action figure toys that link physical development with pleasure, fear, and control. The effect on a child's development and self-perception is significant. Birthday parties, certain toys, and superhero stories promote a magical view of inexplicable change, instead of promoting a sensible understanding of personal growth. Children are denied feedback and guidance about the meaning of the physical and emotional changes each gender experiences in the course of development. Willis points out that commercialism, or capitalism more broadly, offers girls and boys few opportunities to share in a gendering process; instead it relies on stereotyped images that promote separate gender development.

Children and Television

Commercial institutions influence the socialization of children on a number of levels. As storytellers, they entertain in order to produce profit. As producers of the stuff of children's material culture, they determine the badges of cultural participation. And as a significant source of time use by children, television structures daily routines. Some researchers have gone so far as to claim that television is the fifth institution of socialization beside family, peers, religion, and school. Since television consumption lies at the convergence of cultural, political, economic, and technological developments, few intradisciplinary studies have provided a broad view of the role of television and commercialization in children's socialization.[8]

In the final summary, Stephen Kline represents one successful effort to understand the growing intrusion of the marketplace within the context of child development. Kline voices a concern that is at the heart of many critiques of the relationship between consumer culture and children: "The marketplace will never inspire children with high ideals or positive images of the personality, provide stories which help them adjust to life's tribulations or promote play activities that are most helpful to their maturation."[9] The poignancy of Kline's remark is reinforced by the observation that commercial television has become one of the foremost storytellers to children in modern society. This is true even though many programs that children watch are not designed specifically for them. For example, only 8 percent of an average child's weekly television viewing occurs during Saturday mornings, when the concentration of children's shows is highest.[10] Still, these programs have the largest impact on children's culture. The characters, plots, toys, snacks, and clothes that the Saturday cartoons display contribute to the everyday conversations and interactions among children.

While the profit orientation of the children's entertainment industry is to be expected from a market economy, its unregulated expansion in the United States, during the 1980s especially, is rather uncommon among other industrialized countries. Although this arrangement is exactly what one might expect from a market democracy, other industrialized countries including Norway, Denmark, Sweden, Belgium, and the Canadian Province of Quebec have recognized the negative influence of television advertising on children and banned all of it. In Great Britain, where advertising is allowed but strictly regulated, only 30 percent of the toy market consisted of licensed toys (those tied to television characters) compared to 70 percent in the United States as of 1987. Legislative efforts to end advertising to children in the United States failed during the 1970s, and the few limits that were finally passed in 1974 were repealed in 1984, during the Reagan Administration.

Deregulation of commercial broadcasting to children in the 1980s ignored the fact that children under the age of six do not understand that the intent of television advertising is to sell goods. Many young children do not have the language skills to understand the meaning of disclaimers such as "batteries not included" or "partial assembly required," and have difficulty distinguishing between televised fantasy and real life. Although a great majority of children between the ages of three and seven sometimes watch television with a parent who could discuss or help interpret what is being viewed, few parents are patient enough or have enough time to watch Saturday morning cartoons, when children's advertising is most intense.[11]

In a different light, legislation in 1996 has taken seriously the potential negative effects on a child from watching violent programming, and has required that manufacturers incorporate into new televisions "V-chips," which would allow parents and guardians to more easily censor violent shows. Since frequent exposure to violence has been shown to exaggerate aggressive tendencies in children of various ages, V-chips may well benefit children who watch the new machines—if the shows are rated sensibly, and if parents use the chips' capabilities consistently, two important uncertainties. In any case only new televisions will be affected; V-chips will have little impact on the present generation of children growing up in chipless households.

Although children's television has great potential as an educational medium, there are few commercial incentives to take advantage of it. As a result, the simplistic moral messages to be found in most shows—good conquers evil—are bound up with commercial messages. For instance, Teenage Mutant Ninja Turtles is both a program whose plots often turn on saving the earth from evil and a marketing venue; there are "turtle" toys, foods, clothes, and movies. Kline develops the argument (one that is echoed by Willis as well) that action figure toys, such as Ninja Turtles, come with instruction, images, and scripts that describe, in detail, how to play with the toys. Such prefabricated play limits a child's imagination and stunts cognitive development.

Marketers take full advantage of children's interest in consuming and the fact that the average child spends 25 to 30 hours a week viewing television. Marketers have identified three distinctive and interconnected children's markets: (1) direct purchases by children with their own money—allowances, cash gifts, and earnings; (2) indirect purchases by parents for their children; and (3) future roles as consumers: children begin to be brand conscious as early as two years of age. Each market represents billions of dollars in potential sales. For instance, in 1992, children between the ages of 4 and 12 spent approximately $9 billion, while teenagers between 13 and 19 spent $93 billion.[12] Television advertising to children is focused primarily on a child's need for gratification and is limited in the kinds of goods it promotes. Studies have shown that the most heavily marketed snacks are the least nutritous. Finally, television marketing to children contributes to conflicts between children and their guardians over the appropriateness and desirability of certain goods.

Conclusion

A principal objective of this part is to describe the effects of consumerism on family, gender, and children. This essay reveals that answers to some of the most significant questions—where to live, who to live with, who works, what to own, where to play, how to play, who to play with, where to find meaning—have been transformed within a culture that exalts consumption. Researchers have identified at least five societal factors that have contributed to the rise of consumer culture: government policies, mass marketing of television, the development of consumption as an arena in which to seek and express personal identity, increasing rates of labor participation by women, and an expanded role of marketing to children. The negative effects of consumerism, some have argued, are intrinsic to capitalism. Others have argued that institutional opportunities exist within capitalism to diminish consumerist tendencies and their behavioral consequences.

The negative effects of consumerism include, but are not limited to, those of "too much" consumption. As children become consumers at earlier ages, more of their decisions are determined by commercial interests that exploit their need for gratification. As families become more harried, the appeal of the television as babysitter increases. As boys and girls learn to want through the gendered lens of commercial television, their desires are harnessed rather than developed. It is a worthy accomplishment to achieve greather choice in the domain of consumption, but if this achievement is brought about within a restricted range of marketing venues (more K-Marts, fewer neighborhood stores), valuable losses occur. From a social perspective, narrow consumption is at least as alarming as too much consumption.

Notes

1. For those who did not have jobs or whose education was interrupted, the G.I. Bill of Rights provided financial support to continue their education and help them realize the American Dream that they helped to preserve.

2. While these developments contributed greatly to the remarkable surge in consumption that occurred after the recession of 1948, it also had other long-term, less visible social consequences. To secure mortgages, the government worked with the real estate and banking industries to protect the property values in the new subur-

ban residential neighborhoods. This was accomplished by creating zoning regulations, "redlining" areas from which multidwelling and nonresidential buildings would be excluded. The net effect was the creation of homogeneous, white, middle-class communities, consisting primarily of young families. Excluded were ethnic, racial, and working-class families.

3. Robert Putnam, "Tuning In, Tuning Out: The Strange Disappearance of Social Capital in America," *PS: Political Science and Politics* (December, 1995), 664–683.

4. See Part VII and also Duane Elgin's article in Part X.

5. Putnam, ibid.

6. Gender roles and differences also vary across cultures. For example, in the United States, there is a tendency for women to seek to enlarge their breasts whereas in France, the opposite is true. See Lynn Payer, *Medicine and Culture: Varieties of Treatments in the United States, England, West Germany and France* (New York: Henry Holt and Company, 1988), 54.

7. Payer, 54.

8. For other views on the dynamics of children, advertising, and markets, see James McNeal, *Children as Consumers: Insights and Implications* (Lexington and Toronto: DC Heath and Company, 1987); Ellen Seiter, *Sold Separately: Children and Parents in Consumer Culture* (New Brunswick: Rutgers University Press, 1993); John G. Meyers, "Advertising and Socialization," in *Research in Marketing—Volume I* (Greenwich: JAI Press, 1978), 169–199. For a more critical perspective, see Michael F. Jacobson and Laurie Ann Mazur, *Marketing Madness: A Survival Guide for a Consumer Society* (Boulder, San Francisco, and Oxford: Westview Press, 1995).

9. Susan Willis, 23.

10. Kline, 350.

11. Although there is literature concerning the effects on children of adult programming and commercials, our research has focused on the effects of children's commercial television. However, this limitation is only part of what is not covered by the following discussion. There exists a massive, often contradictory literature on the effects of children's commercial television, including a long list of concerns that are only partly addressed here. There is even a long list of surveys of research into the effects of children's commercial television, each with different conclusions. We suggest that those interested in pursuing these ideas take a look at the bibliography at the end of Stephen Kline's book, *Out of the Garden*, which is partially summarized here.

12. *Marketing Madness*, op. cit., 21.

13. Aletha C. Huston, Dolf Zillmann, and Jennings Bryant, "Media Influence, Public Policy, and the Family," *Media, Children, and the Family: Social Scientific, Psychodynamic, and Clinical Perspectives* (Hillsdale, New Jersey: Lawrence Erlbaum Associates, 1994), 23.

Summary of
The Domestic Production of Monies
by Viviana Zelizer

[Published in *The Social Meaning of Money* (New York: Basic Books, 1994), 36–70.]

As the consumer economy multiplied the number and attractiveness of goods, while at the same time, the discretionary income of American households rose, the proper allocation and disposition of family income became an urgent and contested matter. Spending well became as critical as earning enough. [38–39]

Economic theory with its emphasis on market transactions has had little to say about the distribution of resources within the household. This summary examines the allocation, meaning, and uses of domestic money in the United States between the 1870s and 1930s, and how these aspects of household finance were affected by ideas about family life, gender relations, the presence of children, and by social class. Regardless of its sources, once money had entered the household, its distribution and function were subject to a set of changing domestic rules distinct from those of the market.

In the nineteenth century, the rise of the homemaker/breadwinner family coincided with industrialization, mass production, and the expansion of consumer markets. It also marked the beginning of a complicated struggle for control over family finances. As housewives became responsible for improving the family with their husbands' income, husbands maintained control over disbursements. This division of fiscal responsibilities led to a contradiction in women's economic life: They became cashless money managers, denied control over money, but expected to spend wisely. History reveals the strains of this dilemma on spousal relations: In 1811 a husband beat his wife to death for having taken four shillings from his pockets; in 1905 a man left a rat-trap in his trouser pockets to stop his wife from taking change; more affluent wives used various deception strategies to circumvent the husband's control of the purse.

As the consumer role of women expanded between 1880 and 1930, there were a succession of attempts to negotiate standards for resource allocation within the household. At first the breadwinner husband allotted monies without much structure, giving monies as gifts or upon request, less frequently according to an allowance plan. The dole method fell out of mainstream favor as pressure mounted to transform the homemaker's role from household mendicant and supplicant to something more formal and predictable. Advice journals criticized the inefficiency of providing for increasingly commercialized household needs through a beg and receive strategy. For example, a 1915 *Harper's Weekly* noted a rapid increase in the number of women who found it "unthinkable to ask another human being, *Please may I have another pair of shoes?*"(48) Eventually, it became unseemly for the husband to trust his honor, health, name, and children, but not household finance management, to his wife.

The preferred replacement, the allowance, led a short-lived existence, producing more questions about the uses and definition of household money than it answered. It represented neither an equitable share in the husband's income, which was often unknown to wives, nor a rejection of the supplicant image. In the 1920s Christine Frederick, "a leader of the popular household-efficiency movement, rejected the allowance as an un-businesslike scheme that undermined the modern goal of running the home as rationally as a factory or an office." [54] The allowance mixed confusingly the ideal of running the home as a business with the fact that allowances were neither performance based nor payment for services rendered.

Another significant problem with the allowance method was that it blurred the distinction between a married woman's personal and household monies. As individualized consumption patterns became more important, wives were often forced to obtain spending money through strategies of deception. Increasingly fathers, wives, and children all felt the pressures of wanting money for personal use and reacted by hiding monies from one another.

In the 1920s and 1930s the joint account became more fashionable as married women argued that domestic income and control ought to be shared, regardless of how the income was brought into the household. The *Ladies Home Journal* observed that the family purse should be a real partnership fund in which everything belongs to the home, not only to the father's interests. During this time, *American Magazine* described the good husband as one who splits his income with his wife, shares confidences with her, and plays fair. As a 1928 *Harper's* study indicates, movement to the joint account was slow; only a little more than a quarter of respondents to their questionnaire on marriage and money held a joint bank account.

Social class also influenced the nature of household money flows. In working-class families women had more control over finances than their upper-class counterparts. However, working-class wives maintained little overall discretionary control since there was seldom any money left over after purchasing for basic needs. In upper-class families, husbands were usually more secretive about their own income and permitted less equitable control over finances. Upper-class wives frequently had no money to call their own. In fact, until the early twentieth century, even if a married woman obtained money through her own market earnings, this income was viewed, from a legal perspective, as her husband's property.

The presence of children in the family also had a profound impact on the distribution and meaning of monies to every household member. A child's rightful share of family income was delivered in the form of an allowance, but its use was constrained by the view that it was essentially an educational tool for learning social, moral, and consumer skills. The consumer role of children expanded at the same time as child labor laws excluded them from the opportunity to obtain legal earnings. Children were put in a situation similar to their mothers: adopt consumerist patterns of behavior but without money of their own.

Thus, beginning in the 1870s, gender dynamics significantly influenced the use of the housewife's money, whether it was earned in the market or allocated by the husband. When a husband disbursed money in nonegalitarian marriages, gender influenced the timing, uses, and quantity of allocation. When a wife's money was earned in the market it was either collectivized, incorporated into the general household fund, or trivialized, treated as "gravy" or supplemental income.

In modern times, the prevailing sociological view is that when a family believes in a traditional gender ideology—the husband should provide—it matters little who brings in or how much money is brought into the household. "As long as couples adhere to the notion of the husband as the primary earner of income, it does not really matter how much a woman earns; her income will be treated as different, less significant, and ultimately dispensable." [69] It is only with the rejection of the male-provider ideology and the adoption of separate accounts that a wife's domestic power may be increased.

This view, however, narrowly conceives of gender dynamics as involving either an acceptance or rejection of a particular ideology without allowing for the possibility of interactions among ideology, behavior, and social relations. A broader and more accurate view is demonstrated by Kathleen Gerson, whose research shows that a wife's earnings will increase her domestic power only if this income is associated with her long-term career prospects. For example, a woman who is not engaged in a career, but earns money to supplement the household budget will more than likely have less of an impact on her domestic power than if she were drawing income actively pursuing a career. The changing dynamics of the family combine with an evolving set of social rules to reflect a broader mix of nonmarket rules that govern many perceptions of household monies. Finally, the author notes that ties to fellow employees, relatives, and financial institutions strongly affect the ways that household members organize the use of domestic money.

As we reach the turn of the twenty-first century, this domestication of legal tender still remains somewhat of a mystery. As households are being revolutionized by high divorce rates, as remarriage creates new kin networks, as single-parent units dramatically multiply while unmarried heterosexual or homosexual couples form new families, as women's paid employment expands and as home-based employment reappears, we barely know how it all shapes domestic monies. [67]

Summary of

Sitcoms and Suburbs:
Positioning the 1950s Homemaker
by Mary Beth Haralovich

[Published in *Private Screenings: Television and the Female Consumer,* eds. Lynn Spigel and Denise Mann (Minneapolis: University of Minnesota Press, 1992), 111–142.]

During the post–World War II period, gender roles within the middle-class family underwent a radical transformation as many women were forced out of paid employment and into suburban household management. The 1950s suburban family sitcom captured this change, creating an idealized, gendered household that became the focus of a growing consumer product industry. This summary argues that television programming, in parallel with marketing institutions and government policies, helped reproduce certain gender relations.

The middle-class female homemaker was both central and marginal to the economy. She was marginalized by her activities in what was deemed an unproductive sector, the household. On the other hand, as household manager she was the focus and foundation of the product design and marketing industries. Her marginalization was alleged to be a fair exchange: give up participation in work outside the household for the suburban promise of leisure and privacy. Marketers elaborated a vision of household life full of time-saving products that would free the homemaker from domestic work.

The creation of an ideal, middle-class domestic image was central to the reconstruction of the American family after World War II. Television programs like *Father Knows Best* and *Leave It To Beaver* represented this ideal, fostering normative images of domestic harmony and stability while simultaneously masking—and thus helping to reproduce—inequalities faced by the working class and minority groups. These shows also helped realign family gender roles, entrenching the suburban mother as homemaker and attractive object, and the father as breadwinner.

The realism of suburban-based family sitcoms dramatized a social and economic arrangement that was the cornerstone of the American social economy during the 1950s. Its appeal "derived not only from the traits and interactions of the middle-class family, but also from the placement of that family within the promises that suburban living and material goods held out for it." [113]

The middle-class suburban sitcom, such as *Father Knows Best* and *Leave It To Beaver*, contrasts in several ways with the urban working-class sitcom of the same era. While working-class sitcoms depended on the comedic virtuosity of individual characters such as Lucille Ball in *I Love Lucy* and Jackie Gleason in *Honeymooners*, the suburban sitcom appealed to the whole family and found humor within the family dynamic. The fictional American father was reconstituted from bumbling, technologically uncomfortable dolt living in cramped urban quarters to intelligent sovereign living in a spacious home with a beautiful wife and children. Domestic space was used in the suburban sitcom for family cohesion; in urban sitcoms, the home environment was used as the context for jokes.

Both housing design and suburban growth contributed to the definition of the modern family. Suburban architecture displayed class attributes. The commuter father and homemaker mother embraced the gendered domains of the suburban home: fathers to den and workroom; mothers to a modern kitchen and separate laundry. An open floor design fostered family togetherness.

The government viewed suburban growth as an important key to economic health, but implemented policies that created, intentionally or unintentionally, homogeneous communities with racial, ethnic, and class barriers to entry. These policies advanced two national priorities, the removal of women from the labor force and the construction of more housing. The Federal Housing Administration (FHA) promoted suburbanization through zoning practices that excluded multifamily dwellings and commercial property by redlining practices,

> in which red lines were drawn on maps to identify the boundaries of changing or mixed neighborhoods. Since the value of housing in these neighborhoods was designated as low, loans to build or buy houses were considered bad risks. In addition, the FHA published a technical bulletin titled "Planning Profitable Neighborhoods," which gave advice to developers on how to concentrate on homogeneous markets for housing. The effect was to "green-line" suburban areas, promoting them by endorsing loans and development at the cost of creating urban ghettos for minorities. [118]

Suburban growth focused on the affluent nuclear family, excluding minority men and women of all classes and ages, as well as elderly, working-, and lower-class white families and single white women.

The evolution of the suburban homemaker was central to the growth of and organization of the consumer product industry. The industry attempted to define the homemaker's interests and needs in creating a desirable home environment. It promised increased leisure, release from household drudgery, and a pleasing interior space. Interior designers sought to equate products with leisure, but were criticized for promoting class conformity by marginalizing other lifestyles and tastes.

By the late 1950s, intensified competition in the consumer product industry prompted market research into the alleged unconscious process of consumption. Market researchers discovered projective techniques that could elicit unconscious responses to market situations. The suburban shopping center began incorporating sales talk into packaging and product design as the shopping environment became less personalized.

Father Knows Best and *Leave It To Beaver* share characteristics that demonstrate cultural norms, involving interactions between class, gender, and the product design and marketing industries: Both shows obscure discrepancies among classes, extolling the virtues of white middle-class life while ignoring the working class and minorities; both share the same open floor plan, both center on either the family ensemble or the rearing of the younger child; for both, the narrative space is dominated by the home; they display similar tastes in wall decorations and furnishings; each home has a large living room with a fireplace; both fathers have their own private spaces, while the mothers have no equivalent; both confirm the sexuality of the mother through her dress and grooming; and each homemaker effortlessly maintains the domestic space of the home.

The latter characteristic diminishes the value of domestic labor by hiding its harsh realities and legitimizes consumer industry claims that middle-class life in the suburbs will be easier with its products. "By linking her identity as a shopper and homemaker to class attributes, the base of the consumer economy was broadened, and her deepest emotions and insecurities were tapped and transferred to consumer product design." [137]

Summary of

Gender as Commodity
by Susan Willis
[Published in *A Primer for Daily Life*
(New York and London: Routledge, 1991), 23–40.]

In late twentieth-century capitalism, gendering has invariably to do with commodity consumption. We buy into a gender in the same way we buy into a style. . . . To free gender from the commodity form requires seeing it as an ongoing expression of how we live our sexuality, something that emerges out of social relationships and in relation to larger social forces. Such a conceptualization of gender would be analogous to conceiving and creating objects in terms of use value alone. . . . To strive for gender as process as opposed to gender as commodity is to seek a basis for human variety and wholeness in a society where commodification equates wholeness with surfeit and variety with perversion. [23–24]

As the influence of feminism on American society waned in the 1980s, rigid gender roles reappeared in many parts of the culture. Nowhere was this more apparent than in the world of children's toys, where consumers learn at a tender age which ones are for boys and which ones are for girls. This summary examines the portrayal and perpetuation of gender roles through toys, arguing that gender-stereotyped toys offer children a caricatured interpretation of the meaning of adolescence, and that the popularity of superheroes among boys is a commercialized reflection of an ambiguity in the contemporary definition of masculinity.

Gender in the Toy Store

In an affluent capitalist society, gender roles are conveyed and delimited by the commodities we consume. This process begins at an early age: In any toy store the arrangement of the aisles recapitulates the strict distinction and separation of the sexes. Young children do not question the toy store's universe, nor do they understand how it is produced. Their apprehension of gender in the toy store is no different from the way in which adult consumers see commodities as autonomous. Just as banks, in the child's view, are windows that inexplicably dispense cash to those in need, toy stores dispense gendered information about how to play.

Among the most popular toys for four- to seven-year-olds are Barbie dolls for girls and a succession of muscular, mythic heroes such as He-Man and GI Joe for boys.

Clearly, Barbie and He-Man do not offer the child the possibility of prolonging polymorphous sexuality or developing an open notion about gendering. . . . Both toys play on the child's conscious and unconscious notions about adolescence. They focus the child's consumption of the transformations associated with adolescence in a singular fashion, and they suggest that change is somehow bound up in commodity consumption. [27]

In a society that has marginalized traditional rituals of coming of age (such as communion or bar mitzvah), the birthday party has become central to children's lives. It represents a magical moment of change; young children are often tense and apprehensive as the day draws near. Many ask to have their height measured on their birthdays, to see if they have grown overnight—demonstrating a conceptualization of and desire for bodily change. In adolescence, growth really does mean rapid change, a stage that younger children anticipate with a complex and confusing mixture of emotions. Toys such as Barbie and He-Man offer children a means to articulate notions about the transition to adolescence, albeit offering only a one-dimensional caricature of the external physical aspects of the transition.

No matter how deeply consumption is enmeshed in capitalism, it also includes utopian dimensions of social relationship, particularly for children.

> When a young girl buys Barbie or receives Barbie as a Christmas or birthday present, she experiences consumption in relation to a collectivity of young girls who have or want Barbies. The same group social practice that informs children's thoughts about their birthdays also conditions their acts of consumption. By comparison, most adults do not experience consumption as a form of reciprocal social practice. [32]

When children want the same toys as their friends, they may not be displaying greed or rivalry; rather, it may reflect their desire to share in each other's lives, as occurs when they play together or "sleep over" at friends' houses. Children at this stage have not yet learned the lesson that capitalism teaches adults: that alienation and commodities can be substituted for human relationships.

In a world in which all personal attributes and expressions are bound up with commodity consumption, how can we define gender in truly human terms? "The goal is to recognize in all our commodified practices and situations the fragmented and buried manifestations of utopian social relationships." [34]

Growth Versus Change

In terms of the messages about personal change that toys provide to children, it is particularly interesting to consider the "Transformers" and similar toys that became popular in the 1980s. These robots can be manipulated to become something quite different in appearance, such as vehicles or animals. While the notion of transformation suggests spontaneous change, the reality of the toy teaches preprogrammed outcomes and technological domination. Follow the instructions carefully, and one specific, remarkable transformation will occur; there is no possibility of conceptualizing change in any other way. Along similar lines, popular culture often conveys the desire for change combined with simultáneous fear of and need to control change, as in the tale of the sorcerer's apprentice (depicted in the movie *Fantasia*).

The desire for change characterizes twentieth-century mass culture. In contrast, nineteenth-century folk heroes such as Paul Bunyan or John Henry conveyed a solid, centered construction of masculinity, growing but never changing. Twentieth-century superheroes are just the opposite, changing but never growing, always articulating the moment of transformation. As Clark Kent becomes Superman or Peter Parker becomes Spiderman, they demonstrate a construction of masculinity as a duality, with the weak, bumbling, or even nurturing aspects somehow necessary to the emergence of the omnipotent form. Clark Kent always retains his boyish ineptitude, and Peter Parker never advances beyond an angst-ridden school career.

The He-Man toy and its story line, in which the hero, Prince Adam, suddenly gains a sword and equally suddenly relaxes afterward, invites a "vulgar Freudian" interpretation—but the notion of gender as a duality is deeper than that. Little boys are fascinated by both aspects of this story, demonstrating an appreciation of the boyish and nurturing side of the character as well as the sword and muscles.

> Uncovering the utopian aspects of the young boy's fascination with Prince Adam begs another, and with it a more radical, consideration: what about young girls? And what about girls and boys together? In a society dominated by mass culture and the commodity form, as ours is, is it possible to imagine a gendering process that boys and girls might experience reciprocally; or are there only Barbies and He-Men? [39]

Summary of

Gender and Consumption: Transcending the Feminine?
by A. Fuat Firat

[Published in *Gender Issues and Consumer Behavior*, ed. Janeen Arnold Costa (Thousand Oaks, London, New Delhi: Sage Publications, 1994), 205–229.]

This summary analyzes the relationship between consumption and gender within the Western capitalist system from historical and contemporary perspectives. The author argues that in the early periods of industrialization when production and consumption were separated and linked to the public and private spheres, respectively, the consumer role was simultaneously minimized and associated with feminine characteristics. More recently, consumption has supplanted production as the primary source of self-definition for both men and women, eliminating the historical feminization of consumption.

History of Consumption and Gender

Unlike preindustrial cultures in which work and leisure were merged, the industrial revolution separated the two domains and linked the home life with leisure, recreation, and consumption, activities requiring little expertise or important knowledge. Work in the male-dominated factory was prized much more highly than women's work or consumption in the home and was viewed as the primary source of value, creativity, and personal identity. Capitalism bestowed upon productive activity in the public domain an importance that did not exist in activities pursued in the privacy of home.

As women came to be associated with an increasingly trivialized private domain tied to consumption and men were associated more with the exalted public domain of production, feminine and masculine characteristics were linked to the separate spheres of consumption and production, respectively. Attaching discrepant values to public and private domains established a social order based on a normative picture of the modern family. These values perpetuated the myth that the domestic sphere was private even as domestic relations were determined increasingly from outside the family, by the politics and culture of the public domain as well as by the marketplace.

Market growth influenced the nature of consumption in the home and the position of women in the production process, and created paradoxical situations for women. Prior to mass production, household consumption was creative, transforming most market goods into final goods. With the arrival of mass production, household consumption has become less creative, directed toward finished goods that come with instructions and standards for their appropriate use.

As a number of researchers have suggested, mass production in Western industrialized countries forced women out of the public labor force (e.g., in the decades following World War II) and into the private home to consume the fruits of an expanding market. Once in the home, women faced paradox and tensions. Women's expertise in consumer activities was trivialized and ridiculed, while excessive frugality was condemned since low consumption could hurt the economy. With more time- and labor-saving devices women's household labor was expected to be more productive; however, more of these products were consumed with the end result that little if any time was actually saved.

Consumption and Gender in Postmodernity

Recently the producer role has lost its privileged status as the primary source of meaning; increasingly, both men and women tend to represent themselves through consumption, rather than define themselves through their occupation. Consumption is no longer exclusively feminine or a passive activity.

> It is not yet possible, however, to state that gender categories are lost, or that significations of feminine and masculine are completely changed. Modern significations of gender categories are still very strong. It is just that males and females are encountering a culture that is much more tolerant of both sexes participating in roles and meanings attached to both gender categories. That is, increasingly, we find both males and females representing the feminine and the masculine during different moments in their lives (males participating in housework, taking on more nurturing roles with children, and increasingly consuming fashion products, cosmetics, and so on, while women are becoming part of the workforce, managers, politicians, and representing masculine qualities in their participation in production in the public domain).[217]

Increasing tolerance for gay and lesbian lifestyles is suggestive that traditional gender categories of male and female may eventually become obsolete.

As the public and private domains are increasingly fragmented into separate spheres (such as home life, work life, shopping life, neighborhood life, recreational life), successful participation in each requires a distinct persona that can be constructed through consumption. The need to cultivate various images increases dependence on the marketplace, but also allows a measure of control over the means of self-production for both men and women. Consumption becomes an active process of self-construction rather than a passive process of need satisfaction.

Summary of

Meanings of Material Possessions as Reflections of Identity

by Helga Dittmar

[Published in *The Social Psychology of Material Possessions: To Have Is To Be* (Hemel Hempstead: Harvester Wheatsheaf, 1992), 123–154.]

The neoclassical economic model of consumer behavior, with its emphasis on functional use values, has traditionally ignored the value material possessions contribute to a person's sense of self. But in fact, many goods have meanings that are important to the development of identity, especially in industrialized countries. This summary argues that such meanings originate in the social realm and that cultural assumptions about gender, class, and status are reflected in the way individuals relate to their most treasured possessions. It suggests that aspects of gender inequalities may be perpetuated with goods that embody stereotypes which shape self-development.

Personal Identity and the Meanings of Goods

Aside from the instrumental uses of goods, possessions have meanings that help define a sense of personal identity. Goods may have both public and private meanings: symbols that are ascribed to goods in the cultural realm and more personal meanings that are attached to goods by individuals. Both types of meaning have a role to play in creating a sense of identity through the ownership of goods. Previous research has exaggerated the significance of private meanings, while underemphasizing the contributions of public meanings.

It is commonly assumed that the meanings attached to an individual's most treasured possessions are highly individualistic and private, reflecting memories and feelings that others may not fully appreciate. This view, however, neglects the connections between private meanings and the meanings attached to these goods by other people and cultural influences. For example, while owning a fancy automobile may carry certain personal meanings (e.g., its receipt as a gift), these vehicles imply a range of qualities that are determined by cultural influences that exist beyond the individual. There is a strong link between how others react to us on the basis of our possessions, the symbols attached to these goods, and self-perceptions.

Gender and social-material position (a term that covers both socioeconomic status and class affiliation) are two of the most important cultural dimensions in which social interactions occur. Given the relationship between other-perception, self-perception, and material symbols, an individual's favorite possessions should reflect cultural assumptions about gender and social-material position. "For example, if female gender identity is characterized by an emphasis on interpersonal relationships, this should be reflected in the meanings women attach to their treasured possessions." [124] Discussed below are the results of a study that examines the question of whether individuals attach to their possessions personal meanings that reflect socially shared beliefs about gender and social-material position. Cultural assumptions are similar to stereotypes that aid in the organization of perceived reality. These "commonsense notions are an integral part of our shared beliefs, as well as of our social practices. They therefore act as organizing principles of identity construction and constitute the powerful frame of reference within which women and men continue to define themselves." [128]

Personal Possessions and Gender Identity

The term "gender identity" reflects both an individual's sense of being female or male and cultural assumptions about gender. There is much less research on how individuals view their own gender identity than on social construction of gender stereotypes. Various studies in Britain and the United States have shown that maleness is associated with individualistic properties, such as being independent, forceful, and self-sufficient. Femaleness is associated with communal characteristics, such as being warm, understanding, and sensitive. Assumptions about gender tend to vary across cultures, and may change even within specific cultures.

A group of 160 British subjects—business commuters, unemployed people, and students—were asked to list their five most treasured possessions and the reasons these goods were important. Although the findings on gender described here are from the student portion of the sample, the older subjects manifest even more pronounced gender differences in how they relate to their possessions. The students, who were in their early twenties and had recently left home, all tended to discuss their possessions in pragmatic terms, suggesting the importance of goods in establishing an adult identity. Their most treasured objects were classified into seven main types: assets (e.g., financial or property), transport (e.g., car), basic utility (e.g., clothes), leisure (e.g., stereo or television), extensions of self (e.g., trophies), sentimental (photos), and other (documents, plants). Gender differences were most pronounced with respect to the reasons why the listed goods were valuable.

> Women gave many more relational than instrumental reasons—in fact, relational reasons were the ones used most often by women, and least by men. Despite their common concern with functional and use-related features of possessions, men's responses refer strongly to instrumental and use-related features of possessions, whereas women's reasons revolve equally around emotion-related features of possessions and their role as symbols for interpersonal relationships. [132]

Men referred to relationships in less than 6 percent of their reasons, while women referred to relationships in nearly 30 percent of their reasons. Women derived a greater sense of personal history from goods that expressed their relationships with others. In contrast, men derived a sense of personal history from their leisure possessions that expressed primarily pragmatic functions. They generally derived a sense of self-continuity and personal history from their leisure goods

These findings support the argument that commodities can perpetuate sex-role definitions and gender inequalities. In industrialized countries, children are socialized with gendered role models and gendered toys that make it difficult to effect changes in the gender status quo in adult society. For example, from an early age boys and girls are urged to relate to different types of clothing in distinctive ways. One result is readily apparent in British culture: It is inappropriate for women to wear to work the dark, plain suits that symbolize male success and authority. Alternatively, if changes in the gender status quo do occur they should be reflected in changing material symbols. Power dressing by women in the United States is an example of just such a change. Shoulder pads and tailored suits with pants are worn by American women to express a look of professional authority previously restricted to men.

Social-Material Status and Possessions

Social psychological research on the relationship between social-material position and identity is relatively sparse, compared with that on gender. Sociological findings indicate that classes differ in their aspirations, concerns, and consumption goals. Working classes orient their consumption to short-term gratification; the most preferred leisure goods are recreational. In contrast, middle- and upper-class people want possessions that serve prestige, status, and self-expressive needs and have a long-term, delayed gratification perspective, centered on self-development. Working-class people describe objects in concrete terms, without much nostalgia, while middle-class accounts emphasize the abstract value of steering one's life. In general, individuals in the "lower classes" tend to emphasize their concern with emotional relationships and are concerned with economic security, whereas people from more affluent strata place more emphasis on autonomy and self-actualization.

In the study mentioned above, business commuters and unemployed responses support the notion that individuals in a "higher" social-material position view their most important possessions in more symbolic terms than their less affluent counterparts. Interestingly, there was little difference in the types of good listed as most important. Everyone in this part of the sample felt that possessions symbolize one's personal history, but they differed with respect to the types of value associated with their goods. Business commuters viewed their goods as contributing to their personal growth (a long-term perspective), whereas unemployed people had a larger concern with the here and now, emphasizing the financial, emotional, and pragmatic aspects of their goods. The latter finding is not surprising given the levels of economic and emotional insecurity in an unemployed person's life.

Taken together these findings suggest that material possessions are not just expressions of self-conceptions, they are also integrally involved in the reproduction of self-definitions, value orientations, and general outlook. The social nature of these meanings calls into question the overly individualistic economic model of individual preferences.

Summary of

Friendship or Commodities? The Road Not Taken: Friendship, Consumerism, and Happiness

by Robert E. Lane

[Published in *Critical Review* (vol. 8, no. 4, 1994), 521–554.]

Since the mid-1960s there has been a dramatic rise in the incidence of clinical depression in economically advanced and rapidly advancing countries. Lack of companionship and social support is one of the principal causes for depression. This summary considers whether and how the "rage to consume" fostered by market economies may be weakening social ties and thus leading to an increase in the cases of clinical depression.

Affluence and Depression

Advanced economies as well as rapidly modernizing countries have been experiencing a rising tide of depression. As demonstrated in a study of nine different countries by Myrha Weissman and a cross-cultural group of scholars, not only are people suffering from depression at an earlier age than previously, as shown in a different study of the United States, but people born after 1945 are ten times more likely to suffer from depression than those born earlier. Each succeeding generation since World War II has shown a greater tendency toward depression; new research suggests that a quarter of the American population now experiences depression at least once over the course of their lives.

The chronic absence or loss of friends, as well as weak social support in general, is one of the crucial explanatory factors in depression. Major depression leads to feelings of hopelessness, helplessness, and worthlessness as well as to physical manifestations such as insomnia, hypertension, and a loss of energy. In addition to these personal effects of depression, there are also wide-ranging societal costs. Not only are unhappy people harder to associate with, they are also less effective at work or school and more susceptible to other disorders. A higher rate of absences from work and the heavy cost of treatment or hospitalization incurred by depression are borne by society in general.

The documented rise of depression in modernized or rapidly modernizing areas of the world has not been seen in the less developed countries, suggesting a relation between modernity and depression, and undermining the doctrine that market economies maximize well-being.

Consumer Culture and Friendship

Although the loss of social networks may be both cause and consequence of depression, increasing consumption-oriented activities at the cost of friendship explains an important portion of the recent growth in clinical depression. Three factors contribute to social isolation within market economies: television viewing, the shopping experience, and the nature of what is consumed. There are various theories that explain why the structure of market economies is directly responsible for the increase in social isolation, but none of them are clearly supported by the evidence. The time and attention that people devote to commodities cannot be proven to crowd out the time and attention they give to affiliation. In fact, in periods when the time spent on market work declined, such as the decade from 1965 to 1975, the newly available time was devoted neither to shopping nor socializing, but to watching television. While this activity may promote certain social feelings, television viewing promotes passivity and social isolation.

Both the increasingly impersonal character of shopping and the increasingly individualized nature of affluent consumption contribute little to social interaction. "The demise of the neighborhood store, the colder relations between shopkeepers and their clients, and the modesty of the growth of husband-wife shopping all suggest an increasingly unsociable climate for consumers." [540] Also, beyond a certain income level, disposable income is more likely to be spent on goods consumed by individuals than on goods consumed collectively by households. For example, recent analyses of household budgets indicate that expenditures on personal care and apparel have risen much faster than other, more communal aspects of household budgets, such as food.

If depression may be cured or avoided by stronger social connections, and if happiness is unaffected by the consumption of material goods above a certain level, why then do people in market economies continue to pursue the acquisition of commodities rather than the cultivation of friendships? There are several possible answers to this central question. In general, perhaps we have been distracted from an effective pursuit of happiness by an ideology of scarcity that has persisted from the times of our hunter-gatherer ancestors. Another major part of the problem lies in the assumption of market economies that people have perfect knowledge of what will lead to their own felicity. People often do not know what makes them happy. Other possible explanations for our unwillingness to replace commodities with friendships are the addictiveness of immediate gratification versus long-term gains; the lack of a way to measure the hedonic yield of friendship; and the direct and indirect effects of advertising that perpetuates the idea that well-being is achieved only through consumption.

Giving Friendship Priority Over Commodities

Giving friendship priority over commodities promises to protect against depression and lead to happiness for five additional reasons. First, the satisfactions of friendship mature slowly whereas the pleasures of consumption are often instantaneous. Second, friendship is a variable-sum game and eternally expandable. Third, self-esteem, the key characteristic associated with happiness and one of the most effective guards against depression, has been shown to be unrelated to income level but closely linked with intimacy. Fourth, in opposition to the system of financial rewards on which market economies work, friendship is based on a reward system of praise, one that is more likely to be interpreted as informational rather than controlling. Finally, in comparison to consumption, friendship is ecologically friendly.

Economic growth has obviously failed to solve the rising deficit of companionship, as it is in the wealthiest and most rapidly modernizing countries that this problem exists. The welfare state, democracy's attempted solution to distress, has worked no better, as it has been proven that unemployment and welfare are isolating experiences, with a much higher rate of depression among public dependents than among the employed. New solutions to the rising tide of depression within market economies urgently need to be found. While a sense of personal control over one's life has been shown to be an effective substitute for social support as antidote to depression, cultivating the bonding instinct natural to the human species is more likely to work as a long-term solution.

Summary of

Playing with Culture: Toys, TV, and Children's Culture in the Age of Marketing

by Stephen Kline

[Published in *Out of the Garden: Toys, TV and Children's Culture in the Age of Marketing* (London, New York: Verso, 1994), 316–352.]

The problems that have been identified in children's marketing are the same as in all marketplaces—it is not a question of "harm done" but, rather, of our failure to find ways to make the marketplace a positive cultural force in contemporary society. For this reason the debates about the limits on children's advertising, the banality and violence in children's programming, and the maintenance of creativity in children's play can all be reduced to the same root issue. The marketplace will never inspire children with high ideals or positive images of the personality, provide stories which help them adjust to life's tribulations or promote play activities that are most helpful to their maturation. [350]

A child's play behavior constitutes an essential part of his or her cognitive development, emotional maturation, and socialization. Since the deregulation of television, the imaginative play of children has been structured increasingly by animated television programming and marketing strategies that target children's emotional investment in toys. This summary argues that the developmental benefit of some toys is compromised by marketing activities that inhibit creativity in play behavior and calls into question the large role that the market plays in the production of children's culture.

Although the effects of television content on children are equivocal, the fact that children spend 80 percent of their spare time fantasizing—while watching television and/or playing with toys—suggests that television has an important influence on children's culture and behavior. The main television fare offered to children is animated fantasy programming that introduces gendered, stereotyped characters who eventually make their way onto toy store shelves and into the homes of young viewers. These shows deliver stories about the background and adventures of characters and specify what is appropriate behavior for each, providing a fictional universe from which children construct their imaginative play.

Character-Toys, Marketing, and Play

Capitalizing on the strong connection between children's emotional investment in character-toys and sales, marketers make use of animated programming and construct lovable, attractive, and heroic characters that facilitate identification and modeling behavior. Effective marketing of character-toys coincides with their successful placement in children's play and conversation.

In light of Piaget's observation that all learning combines creativity and imitation, it is particularly worrisome that play involving character-toys exaggerates the imitative component of play behavior. Animated television programs as well as advertisements tell children what character-toys can do, how they should look, and how to play with them. Children's mimicry of a narrative voice, the brief, aimless, episodic nature of their pretend stories, and the limited resourcefulness in the use of their play areas reflect impoverished creativity. Children rarely mix characters from different fictional discourses, and seldom break or transform rules or alter the perceived narrative context associated with a given toy. "The rehearsal and practice of tactical thinking is the only evidence we saw of complex cognitions being employed in children's character-toy play." [340] For example, in one study, boys employed a great deal of tactical knowledge when playing with toy soldiers—surprise attacks, sabotage, and attacking from the blind side.

Unlike earlier generations in which street play incorporated group-oriented games, modern play is represented by many children as a solitary activity, removed from the experience of parents and involvement with peers. When children are engaged in peer play, most contemporary interactions involve the articulation of rules and the following of rules that are known to accompany toys.

The ultimate threat presented by character-toy play behavior is that play becomes more a source of entertainment and less a source of emotional growth. Many psychologists believe that pretend play advances emotional development by allowing children to gain control over emotional conflicts. But fantasy play with character-toys does not lead toward mastery of emotional conflict, especially in the case of heavy viewers of television violence. One group of researchers indicates that emotional mastery is absent from the fantasy play of viewers who are overexposed to the limited range of emotions that occur in action-adventure programs. Other research indicates that children often represent play with character-toys as a happy time with limited emotional engagement.

Play, Socialization, and Consumerism

Gendered character-toys and television programming feed into play behavior that exaggerates differences between boys and girls.

> Targeting in the toy market . . . gendered the themes of children's television programming and it created a markedly sex-typed image of peer play

in the commercials. Television before deregulation strove for large audiences so producers designed programs for a homogeneous children's audience. Whereas the cartoon characters of the 1950s were either asexual or balanced in their gender appeal, the action-figure animations specifically use characterization and storyline to accommodate known gender preferences and play values. [341]

Children prefer to play with others who are familiar with and share an interest in their favorite toys. Since most character-toys are gendered, play with these toys is also gendered. As a result, boys and girls develop different sets of cognitive, emotional, and social skills through their use of toys.

Gendered toys and television programming feed into play behavior that exaggerates differences between boys and girls. To the extent that play is based on television characters and action figures, children prefer to play with others who are familiar with and share an interest in their favorite toys. Since most character-toys are gendered, boys and girls find it increasingly difficult to play together with certain kinds of toy.

Television and toy marketing socialize children in a much broader way than simply introducing gender stereotypes. The same forces also help develop consumerist attitudes and consumer skills in children by linking the ability to recognize and understand advertising with toy requests and purchases. Commercials tell children of the need for money and the availability of purchasable toys. Parents facilitate the consumer socialization of children by using toys as rewards. Children make judgments about each other based on the type, number, and cost of their toys, explicitly recognizing socioeconomic status through play. Children may also associate short- and long-term aspirations with goods: wanting to take Barbie on vacation or desiring the career of a favorite character-toy.

Psychologists have much to say about the importance of play to a child's understanding of personal, social, and economic issues. Bruno Bettleheim contends that the most important functions of play involve problem resolution, social experimentation, and the accommodation of time pressures. Lita Furby theorizes that children learn from play the concept of property rights, regard for possessions, and an ability to manipulate environments, all of which contribute to a sense of personal autonomy. However, in an era of intensified marketing, children also learn consumer skills and consumerist attitudes.

Conclusion

To contend that marketing to children is a strictly economic venture is to ignore the powerful impact of the marketplace on the socialization of children. To frame the question of whether the market harms children in any measurable or discernible way directs attention away from the problem of whether we want children's culture to be a reflection of adult consumer culture. Marketers, interested primarily in the bottom line, have been granted such an unprecedented influence over the construction of children's culture that we should reconsider this arrangement, bearing in mind the bottom line for children and our future.

> Business interests trying to maximize profits cannot be expected to worry about cultural values or social objectives beyond the consumerist cultural vector that underwrites commercial media. If we value a cultural dimension beyond the domain of the commodity, we must first establish a new framework for the culture industries which recognizes this limitation and ensures that quality and excellence remain criteria for the production of children's culture. [350]

PART IV

The History of Consumer Society

Overview Essay

by Frank Ackerman

When did the consumer society begin, and why? Turn the clock back just a few centuries, and our ancestors, of whatever class and nation, displayed neither the attitudes toward consumption nor the behavior described in the previous sections of this book. But did they awaken gradually to the dawn of mass consumption, or were they roused abruptly in a "consumer revolution"?

The questions about the history of consumer society are so broad that it is necessary to begin by delineating what will not be included in the discussion. A basic distinction must be drawn between the existence of occasional luxuries or goods consumed for symbolic purposes on the one hand, and widespread, nonutilitarian consumption as a way of life on the other. Traces of luxury and symbolic consumption can be found throughout history; anthropological and archeological evidence suggests that such consumption is even older, perhaps as old as human material culture itself.[1] In contrast, consumer society—in which ever-growing consumption becomes the principal aspiration, source of identity, and leisure activity for more and more of the population—is a much newer construct.

Our question is not when consumption beyond subsistence first appeared, but when it took over. This distinction parallels the one made by Karl Polanyi between the quite ancient appearance of markets and the more recent domination of society by the market.[2] Since the rise of markets and of mass consumption are closely related, Polanyi's conclusion that the dominion of the market was finally established in England in the 1830s is potentially relevant to the history of consumerism.

Surveying Perceptions of the Past

Before the 1970s it was possible to complain that very little had been written about the history of consumption. The gap was filled, first by the massive works of Fernand Braudel and soon after by many others. Braudel described the evolution of material culture throughout Europe from the fifteenth through the eighteenth centuries, bringing to light an astonishing amount of provocative detail: For example, while religious paintings of the Last Supper can be found throughout European history, the first time that Jesus and his disciples were shown eating with forks rather than their hands was in 1599.[3]

In an article summarized here, Grant McCracken surveys the literature on the history of consumption, beginning with Braudel and other pioneers of the field. McCracken delineates the multiple contexts within which the history of consumption should be understood, emphasizing the close connections between culture, social change, and patterns of consumption. While offering a rich theoretical perspective, this multifaceted understanding also presents a practical problem, especially for earlier historical research. We would like to discover the attitudes, beliefs, and motivations of past consumers, and the meaning that consumption had for them. Unfortunately, we are often limited to records of what was consumed and when. In many of the cases discussed below, we will see aspects of the rise of consumer society only darkly through the glass of past purchasing patterns.

The expanse of historical research that is now available makes clear the need for a restricted focus both in time and space. Those who want a more detailed guide to historical studies of consumption will find extensive citations in both McCracken's article (the original, not the summary) and the recent literature review by Paul Glennie.[4] The work summarized here is largely restricted to the history of consumption in England and America, the countries in which the consumer society began.

It is natural to locate the rise of the modern consumer society in relation to the Industrial Revolution. After all, contemporary mass-consumption goods are largely mass-produced commodities that were either unavailable or prohibitively expensive prior to industrialization. As a historian of the period put it, "The Englishman of 1750 was closer in material things to Caesar's legionnaires than to his own great-grandchildren." England was transformed in the late eighteenth and early nineteenth centuries: Imports of raw cotton for use in the textile industry rose from less than 3 million pounds in 1760 to more than 360 million pounds in the 1830s, while the price of yarn fell to one-twentieth of its earlier level or less.[5] Nor was the textile industry alone in its expansion, as production of coal, steel, machinery, railroads, and more burst forth. Much the same changes arrived, a few decades later, in the United States and in northern and western Europe.

But to say that the birth of consumer society is linked to the Industrial Revolution does not yet specify which way the causal and temporal sequence runs. Broadly speaking, there are three possible relationships. The spread of modern consumerism could come first, as a foundation on which industrialization could have later been built; or the two could have arisen nearly simultaneously, as part of a single process of rapid change; or the consumer society could have been of a more complex construction, which only became possible well after the consolidation of industrial production. The articles summarized here reflect all three of these views. To some extent they simply disagree with each other, but to a larger extent they emphasize different aspects of the rise of consumer society, for which differing hypotheses may be appropriate.

The contemporary interest in the history of consumption has raised a broader issue concerning the interpretation of industrialization. Accounts of the causes of the Industrial Revolution often mention such factors as capital accumulation, the Protestant ethic and entrepreneurial behavior, patterns of international trade and political institutions, availability of natural resources, and technological innovation. The influence of consumption typically comes far down the list, if it makes it onto the list at all.

But histories of consumer behavior have identified two ways in which consumption could play a leading role in the story of industrialization. First, some historians have revived the formerly obscure analysis by Werner Sombart, who stressed the economic stimulus created by luxury consumption in the early modern period (the two or three centuries before industrialization). In Sombart's view, a new personal freedom and sensuality on the part of both old and new elites created rising demand for luxuries, and brought into existence thoroughly capitalist enterprises to supply that demand. Building the fountains at Versailles, for example, required a French ironworking industry that could produce a lot of pipes.[6] Second, Neil McKendrick has argued that the rise of mass consumption based on emulation of the rich created the demand for the products of new industries; the views of McKendrick and some of his critics will be discussed below.

Early Modern Consumption

Three authors included in this part address, from very different perspectives, the nature of consumption before the Industrial Revolution. Chandra Mukerji, whose work spans a broad range of topics in early modern European consumption, here turns her attention to one of the earliest examples of mass consumption of luxury goods, namely pictorial prints. No one would claim that the market for prints, or even the industry that supplied them, was in itself large enough to be an important part of aggregate supply and demand. But Mukerji traces the ways in which the production and dissemination of prints, made possible by innovations in technology and industrial organization, both reflected and promoted an increasingly modern, secular, cosmopolitan worldview in the fifteenth, sixteenth, and seventeenth centuries. The cultural connection forged among consumers of prints throughout Europe may have laid the groundwork for the national and international markets that became so important in the centuries that followed.

Carole Shammas takes a ruthlessly quantitative look at mass consumption of imported "groceries" in early modern England and its American colonies. Using a plausible standard for when a commodity reaches the level of mass consumption, she finds that tobacco became a mass-consumption good in England by the middle of the seventeenth century, sugar products (including rum and molasses) by the end of the century, and tea early in the eighteenth century; the colonies lagged only slightly behind. Unlike pictorial prints, groceries were economically significant in themselves, accounting for one-third of English imports in 1800. Mass consumption of these luxury goods in the early modern period might have stimulated tastes for other luxuries, and could be a harbinger of the broader spread of consumption in the era just ahead.

In one important way, however, the groceries studied by Shammas are not typical of later consumption goods. Tobacco, rum, and tea are all, to varying extents, physically addictive, providing a different mechanism and meaning for their mass consumption. Tobacco, the most addictive, spread the fastest, with potentially serious health effects. The ample quantity of rum consumed in the colonies is at odds with the latter-day American mythology of sober, hard-working Puritan settlements. The difficulty of generalizing from these to other goods is shown even in Shammas' other area of data analysis, concerning consumer durables, where the patterns and conclusions are less clear-cut. However, a valuable insight that emerges from this second area is her suggestion that physical consumption levels per capita grew rapidly while budgets remained fairly stable, since the growth of commerce was steadily lowering prices. The same expenditure yielded more and more goods as time went on, much as happens today, for example, with personal computers.

A very different side of consumption just before the Industrial Revolution is explored by David Shi, in his analysis of the difficulty that the Quakers of Pennsylvania experienced in maintaining their traditional commitment to simple living. Quakerism began in the turmoil of the English Revolution (1640–1660). Initially it was a politically radical, theologically millenarian, and not particularly pacifist sect. In the much more conservative climate that prevailed after 1660, the Quakers turned abruptly toward pacifism and withdrawal from active politics. Although their radical origins were soon forgotten by Quakers themselves as well as others, Cristopher Hill suggests that it is only in light of this early history that the Quakers' ongoing sense of social separatism and resistance to authority can be understood.[7] They should, therefore, have been ideally prepared, if anyone was, to resist the temptations of a materialist society that offered ever-greater levels of luxury.

Nonetheless, it was soon evident that, as an old saying puts it, the Quakers came to Pennsylvania to do good and ended up doing well. Even in their own colony, founded on strict religious lines, Shi finds that the shared moral commitment to simple living was eroded by material success and its increasingly extravagant display. Consumption, it seems, had become integral to the life of the community, despite strong religious beliefs to the contrary. By the 1740s, only sixty years after the founding of Pennsylvania and a century after the first appearance of Quakers in England, a revival movement was needed to bring back the traditional Quaker commitment to pious simplicity. This experience has important lessons for contemporary advocates of voluntary simplicity (see Part X); it also emphasizes the extent to which a culture of mass consumption had become an irresistible part of colonial life by the middle of the eighteenth century.

By this time, as England was on the eve of industrialization, the American colonies were on the eve of independence. The prevalence of mass consumption could be seen in the movement for independence, as described by T.H. Breen.[8] Resistance to Britain was frequently expressed through refusal to buy British goods; mounting social pressure to buy domestic products and use homespun cloth was a key part of the creation of a shared sense of national identity in the decades immediately before independence. A very similar, and perhaps better known, role was played by the *swadeshi* (home industry) movement in the struggle for India's independence in the first half of the twentieth century.

In short, the evidence for the rise of consumer society prior to the Industrial Revolution is impressively diverse. Throughout Europe people were buying goods that helped to create a common aesthetic and culture. In England and America, a mass public had become regular users of tobacco, sugar and rum, tea, and other imported, nonessential foodstuffs—items that had formerly been available only to the elite, if at all. Purchases of durable consumer goods were evidently on the rise. In the American colonies, waves of prosperity eroded religious traditions of simple living; consumption of imported manufactures was so prevalent that its refusal could become a potent expression of national identity and unity.

Yet the consumer society as we know it today was far from completely established. In eighteenth-century England, side by side with the emerging signs of modern consumer behavior, precapitalist traditions still shaped the popular understanding of the purchase of grain in the towns and countryside. The "moral economy of the English crowd," based on the laws and customs of a much earlier era, called for all grain to be sold locally in open markets on specified days at a publicly agreed-upon "just price," with the poor of the village given slightly preferential treatment. In times of shortage, when farmers, merchants, or millers were suspected of withholding grain from local markets for export or speculative sales outside the community, crowds frequently seized grain and enforced the traditional standards of sale.[9] This militant traditionalism affected the consumption of only one commodity—in fact, the one least likely to be involved in the pursuit of luxury or status. But it suggests the persistence of older perspectives on distributive justice and appropriate patterns of consumption, which had to be eliminated before consumer society could prevail.

Emulation and Industrialization

There is a long road left to travel between village riots to defend medieval notions of a just price for grain, and shopping for bread at a modern supermarket. Moving along that road, we next encounter the second of the three broad hypotheses about the rise of consumer society: Some aspects of mass consumption may have arisen at about the same time as industrialization. On some level this must be true; the appearance of mass production must be accompanied by mass consumption. The new goods have to go somewhere, and someone has to learn to buy them. Two of the articles included here bear directly on this question—and disagree emphatically with each other.

Neil McKendrick's research has played a central role in the evolving history of consumption. As he argues in the article summarized here, a "consumer revolution" in late eighteenth-century England was the demand-side analogue, and essential stimulus, to the Industrial Revolution on the supply side. A century of intellectual debate had overturned traditional moralism and won acceptance of the economic benefits of high and rising consumption, even of luxuries. New fashions in elite consumption spread geographically from London to the provincial gentry, and socially from master to servant to the working classes as a whole; without an expanding desire for novelty in appearance, the new flood of textiles produced by British industry could not have been sold. In this and in other work, McKendrick gives primacy to the historical role of growth in demand, which made it possible to market the growing supply of manufactured goods.

In response, Benjamin Fine and Ellen Leopold contend that it is a mistake to simply give demand, or supply for that matter, a leading role in explaining long-term historical change. While short-run business cycles or events in particular industries may usefully be analyzed in terms of the divergence of supply and demand, a long-run, aggregate analysis must recognize that the same forces tend to cause growth on both sides of the market. Fine and Leopold call for a return to the sweeping scope of the classical economists, who sought to identify the historical causes of growth in both supply and demand. They also offer a detailed response to McKendrick's portrait of emulation in the demand for fashion and clothes. While they do not dispute (or address) the possibility that desire for fashionable attire could spread through emulation, they show that "effective demand"—desire combined with the money to buy the clothes—could not have spread in the manner suggested by McKendrick.

As we move through the period of the Industrial Revolution, the modernization of labor, daily life, and consumption have come a long way. By the 1830s the English countryside had witnessed the last of the enclosures of common lands; the traditional "moral economy" and the notion of a "just price" had vanished from sight. In the same decade, the last of the income subsidies provided under the Poor Laws were eliminated, making urban labor wholly dependent on wages; this was the point at which, in Polanyi's view, the market could finally be said to dominate social and economic life. By that standard, America was not a market-dominated society until the abolition of slavery some thirty years later. For the first time in history, the working population of a society worked entirely for wages, and obtained material necessities and luxuries entirely through purchases in the marketplace. Consumption of purchased goods played a growing part in daily life, expanding as fast as incomes allowed. While this may not have been a sufficient condition for the triumph of modern consumer society, it was undoubtedly a necessary one.

Creating a Lifestyle

The expansion of the American and British economies over the course of the nineteenth century led to further changes that reshaped the consumer experience. Businesses grew in size, sophistication, and market power. This both allowed and depended on the creation of new commercial institutions, new advertising strategies, and finally new ways of life centered on modern consumption. These institutions, strategies, and lifestyles (to use the modern term) constitute three aspects of the transformation in consumption that occurred in the late nineteenth and early twentieth centuries, creating a consumer society that looked increasingly like the one we live in today.

Stores had existed for ages, but nothing quite like the modern department store had been seen before the second half of the nineteenth century. The new interest in the history of consumption has given rise to many studies of department stores in the United States, France, and England (see Glennie's literature survey, cited above), including the article by Rudi Laermans summarized here. For Laermans the rise of the department store represents the intersection of several social and economic trends. While earlier stores typically specialized in only a few lines of merchandise, department stores sought to sell almost everything, consciously designing the store environment to promote a pleasant and prolonged shopping experience. The department store created a new public space in which middle-class women felt comfortable; the tension between the liberating aspects and the commercialized nature of the experience is one that recurs in more recent contexts. In an era before the automobile, the department store was both creation and creator of metropolitan life. Only in a large city with trolleys connecting neighborhoods to downtown was the market large enough to support such a store, and the cosmopolitan styles sold in the department store allowed consumers to define themselves amid the anonymity of urban life.

In America, the rise of the department store transformed popular culture in more ways than we usually realize. To a large extent, contemporary Christmas customs were created by late nineteenth-century marketing efforts, often by department stores.[10] Christmas gift-giving was virtually unknown in the 1840s, to judge from December newspaper advertising; promotion by Macy's and other department stores after the Civil War made Christmas shopping into the seasonal phenomenon it is today. Saint Nicholas only rarely was described as traveling across the sky in a sleigh before that era, and did not acquire his rotund, cheerful, white-bearded appearance until the 1860s. Christmas tree ornaments were all but unknown before 1880, when F.W. Woolworth began to promote them; Christmas cards date from about the same period. "Rudolf the Red-Nosed Reindeer" was written, much later, by an employee in Montgomery Ward's advertising department.

New approaches to marketing in this period were not confined to department stores. The emergence of large corporations around the turn of the century led to the rise of nationally advertised brand names, as Susan Strasser has documented.[11] While commonplace today, the idea of brand names was initially unfamiliar, and advertisers struggled to associate their brands with a reputation for quality; success in this struggle allowed them to charge a substantial premium over the price of generic goods.

The heightened visibility of advertising affected more than the prices of specific brands. As T.J. Jackson Lears explains in the article summarized here, the turn of the century was a time when much of American culture turned from the Protestant ethic of salvation through hard work and self-restraint to a "therapeutic ethos" in which self-realization became the goal.

Jackson Lears traces this change to the growing numbers of people who felt themselves to be adrift in a technologically complex urban world; as identity through work became less compelling, the new urban population sought meaning for their lives in other areas such as consumption. Advertisers were quick to realize the potential of the therapeutic ethos and the quest for self-realization, and soon moved away from narrowly informative ads to ones that played on consumers' emotions. Jackson Lears' discussion of emotionally based advertising anticipates some of the themes that are addressed in more detail in Part VII of this volume.

What kind of life was created by these changes in marketing and consumption practices? The final article summarized here, by Gary Cross, follows his work that was summarized in Part II. In the earlier selection Cross considered the reasons why, after about 1920, workers received the benefits of productivity gains almost entirely in the form of pay increases and higher consumption rather than shorter hours. In the current selection, Cross examines and critiques the interpretations of the turn toward consumerism offered by several of the authors represented in this volume, and then presents his view of what consumerism offered to the working-class household of the early twentieth century. Homeownership brought a combination of status-conscious consumption and creation of private space, a refuge from the world of work; the effort of creating the new household life required the role of housewife as full-time homemaker. Vacations to a commercially developed seaside resort likewise offered a refuge in time, a week of escape from the routine of the work year. As in the home, status-conscious consumption of standard, public vacation experiences was combined with the creation of private experiences and memories.

By the time we reach Cross' working-class household, in the 1920s, many essential aspects of the consumer society we know today have been established. After a lengthy interruption for the depression of the 1930s and World War II, the growth and development of consumer society continued into the postwar era of television and suburbanization—as is described further in Part VII.

Notes

1. See, for example, Colin Renfrew, "Varnu and the Emergence of Wealth in Prehistoric Europe," in Arjun Appadurai, ed., *The Social Life of Things: Commodities in Cultural Perspective* (New York: Cambridge University Press, 1986), 141–169.

2. Karl Polanyi, *The Great Transformation* (New York: Farrar & Rinehart, 1944).

3. Fernand Braudel, *Capitalism and Material Life 1400–1800* (New York: Harper & Row, 1973), 140–141. Other historical evidence presented by Braudel confirms that table utensils first became common at about this time.

4. Paul Glennie, "Consumption Within Historical Studies," in Daniel Miller, ed., *Acknowledging Consumption* (New York: Routledge, 1995), 164–203.

5. David Landes, *The Unbound Prometheus* (New York: Cambridge University Press, 1969), quote from p. 5, cotton statistics from pp. 41–42.

6. Werner Sombart, *Luxury and Capitalism* (Ann Arbor: University of Michigan Press, 1967; first published 1913). See the discussion of Sombart in Arjun Appadurai, "Introduction: Commodities and the Politics of Value," in Appadurai, ed., op. cit., 36–39.

7. Cristopher Hill, *The World Turned Upside Down: Radical Ideas During the English Revolution* (New York: Penguin Books, 1975), especially chapter 10.

8. T.H. Breen, "'Baubles of Britain': The American and Consumer Revolutions of the Eighteenth Century," *Past and Present* 119 (1988), 73–104.

9. E.P. Thompson, "The Moral Economy of the English Crowd in the Eighteenth Century," *Past and Present* 50 (1971), 76–136.

10. See Daniel Boorstin, *The Americans: The Democratic Experience* (New York: Random House, 1973), 157–164.

11. Susan Strasser, *Satisfaction Guaranteed: The Making of the American Mass Market* (New York: Pantheon, 1989).

Summary of

The History of Consumption:
A Literature Review and Consumer Guide

by Grant McCracken

[Published in *Journal of Consumer Policy* 10 (1987): 139–166.]

Changes in consumption have played an important role in the transformation of Western societies. This summary presents the history of consumption in seven different contexts—cultural, sociological, psychological, political, intellectual, marketing, and consumer. The summary offers a brief overview of the history of consumption, issues for future research, and a review and criticism of recent work in the history of consumption.

Historical Precedents: Caveat Emptor

Four recent studies in the history of consumption have attempted a broad sweep of the subject. Fernand Braudel's *Capitalism and Material Life 1400–1800*, published in 1973, was the first work to suggest the contribution of consumption behavior to the development of the West, and to establish the history of consumption as a legitimate field of study. In a volume edited by Neil McKendrick, John Brewer, and J.H. Plumb, entitled *The Birth of a Consumer Society: The Commercialization of Eighteenth-Century England* (1982), McKendrick argues that the consumer revolution was a necessary companion to the industrial revolution in bringing about the great transformation. The other two studies that offer a broad view of the history of consumption are Rosalyn Williams, *Dream Worlds: Mass Consumption in Late Nineteenth Century France* (1982), and Chandra Mukerji, *From Graven Images: Patterns of Modern Materialism* (1983).

These ground-breaking studies, followed by a number of smaller scale detailed studies, have opened up the research field. Two major challenges face the growing field of the history of consumption. The first is to show how culture and consumption are mutually determining. The second is to acknowledge that consumption is not just a reflection of social change, but is a cause of social change as well.

Salient Contexts in the History of Consumption

Cultural Context

Culture creates the categories of "person, time, space, activity, and object" and "supplies the distinctions of class, sex, age, occupation into which the social world is organized." [144] It transforms the world into a shared body of distinct impressions.

A study of the history of consumption can help us understand and define different cultures by seeing changes in fashion and style in clothing, pottery, food, architecture, and the like. For example, Western notions of space determined new kinds and amounts of consumption, especially in housing. Innovations in housing helped realize new ideas of privacy. It is possible that notions of privacy were a product of new attitudes about possession, which were in turn a product of the consumer revolution.

Another important cultural context in the history of consumption is the emergence of the individual from the family or the clan. The use of consumer goods helped the individual define individuality and provided the necessary meaning and definition for individual expression. Consumption has also played a vital role in the transformation of the individual over time. This is seen in Colin Campbell's thesis of the development of the romantic self, which expresses itself through new levels of consumption. Others have seen the consumer revolution as redefining and commodifying the human body.

Finally, culture and consumption are intertwined through goods. The interrelationship between marketing, consumption, and the meaning and symbols attached to goods has profoundly impacted Western culture.

Sociological Context

One of the key issues shaping the sociological context of consumption is the influence of the group (such as family, social class, ethnic group, friendship circle, or occupation) on the individual as a determinant of the level and pattern of consumption. In turn, the aggregate consumption levels of groups are a function of "demographic composition, social location, resource base, status entitlements and ambitions, and concepts of self, society, and world," [148] as well as the influence that groups have on each other.

Historical research on consumption in the sociological context should concentrate on how consumption contributed to and was changed by the transformation of class and family. From the sixteenth to the twentieth century the concept of class was relatively well defined and was an important determinant of consumption patterns. There has been an erosion of the concept of class since the beginning of the twentieth century, and research should concentrate on the declining influence of class and on the increasing role that other reference groups now play in determining consumption. Research should also look into issues surrounding consumption and class mobility, and the relationship between the democratization of consumption and the democratization of society.

Similar to class, the importance of the genealogical family has eroded as a determinant of consumption, and today the individual has emerged as an autonomous consumer. Changes in consumption patterns should be traced from the days when the family was the central social unit through the present. The relationship between family, "the home," and consumption is also a growing area of research. Along with issues surrounding class and family, the sociological context must examine the role of conspicuous and competitive consumption.

Psychological Context

Fundamental psychological changes were needed to bring about the increase in consumption in Western Europe and North America. People's attitudes toward new objects, influences, information sources, and behaviors had to be changed. Advertising and film were employed to change and mold the new attitudes. New brands and products introduced new meanings, and new concepts about self. Information processing underwent radical change. Along with issues of information, questions of sexuality and advertising contribute to the psychological context of consumption. All these changes must have resulted in new skills needed to process information.

Political Context

There are a number of issues in the history of consumption that have a political context. First is the historical appearance of participation in mass consumption. Here we must ask when different social groups became consumers, and what choices they faced. The second is the issue of how consumption was used as an instrument of politics. There is a body of literature that argues that fifteenth-century Italian leaders, Elizabeth I in England, and Louis XIV in France used consumption as a political tool. Research should be done to understand how the consumption strategies of ruling courts helped legitimize their claims to power.

Intellectual Context

The intellectual context of consumption looks into how a society comes to terms intellectually with the social and cultural changes that follow changes in consumption behavior. Over time in all societies intellectuals have commented on the effects of changing consumption. In fact the social sciences can be seen as intellectual attempts to come to terms with the social changes brought about by the industrial and consumer revolutions.

Marketing Context

Marketing and the manipulation of the marketplace have played a key role in the development of consumption. Marketing existed as early as the

1500s and took on a modern form by the eighteenth century, as exemplified by the English entrepreneurs Wedgwood and Boulton. In the nineteenth century the department store was a key marketing innovation. With the advent of film, marketing created fantasies to entice consumers. An historical look into marketing and consumption should examine how producers have perceived consumers and the methods they have employed to persuade them. The creation of *homo economicus* and the shift of exchange activities from social exchange to market exchange are also noteworthy.

Consumer Context

As consumption increased, the nature and opportunities of the consumer changed. Once-a-week market days gave way to being able to shop on any day of the working week. Shopping expanded from the localized, traditional marketplace to venues throughout the city. Laws protecting the consumer against fraud by the producer were enacted and sumptuary laws were removed. Consumption was raised to a new social and cultural activity by the individual. "[C]hanges in consumption are just as important as changes in production and this transformation represents a consumer revolution as well as an industrial revolution." [159]

Summary of

Changes in English and Anglo-American Consumption from 1550 to 1800

by Carole Shammas

[Published in *Consumption and the World of Goods*,
eds. John Brewer and Roy Porter (New York: Routledge, 1993), 177–205.]

Economic historians have usually been more interested in studying production than consumption. This "supply-side orthodoxy" has been challenged by historians of the early modern period (the sixteenth, seventeenth, and eighteenth centuries), many of whom have focused on the role of consumption. For example, some historians suggest that the desire for newly available types of goods may have motivated early modern households to increase production for the market. However, history can only tell us who consumed what, not why.

There were important changes in household consumption patterns in the early modern period. This summary examines two categories of goods: groceries (such as tobacco, sugar, and tea) and consumer durables. It seeks to determine when a mass market arose for these goods, and whether the availability of new products resulted in a structural change in expenditures.

Consumption of Groceries in England and America

"Probably the most striking development in consumer buying during the early modern period was the mass adoption by the English and the colonials of certain non-European groceries." [178] In 1559, groceries accounted for 9 percent of the imports into England and Wales; at that time pepper was the major mass-consumed grocery, while no tobacco, tea, coffee, or chocolate came into London at all. Two centuries later, tobacco, sugar, and tea were widely consumed; by 1800, groceries comprised 35 percent of the imports into England and Wales.

Let us say that a grocery item is mass consumed when sales are sufficient for a quarter of the adult population (about one-sixth of the total population) to use it on a daily basis. One pipeful of tobacco daily adds up to about two pounds per year; likewise a daily cup of tea requires two pounds of tea leaves annually. Daily use of sugar to sweeten food or beverages might add up to twenty-four pounds of unrefined brown sugar annually. So when per capita use reached one-sixth of these levels, the groceries would meet the standard for mass consumption.

Tobacco was the first of the new groceries to reach mass consumption. Large-scale production and shipment of tobacco from the colonies started soon after settlement of the Chesapeake region. Legal imports into England and Wales jumped from 0.02 pounds per capita in 1630–1631 to 0.93 pounds per capita in 1669; in addition, smuggling may have been significant, and tobacco was produced in England itself until the end of the seventeenth century. So it is likely that tobacco became a mass-consumption item sometime in mid-century. English consumption reached two pounds per capita before 1700, and did not rise much higher until the introduction of cigarettes, which were marketed to women as well as men, in the twentieth century.

Tobacco consumption data are scarce for the colonies, but are believed to have averaged between two and five pounds per person per year in the eighteenth century.

Sugar sales had a slower start, but continued to grow throughout the eighteenth century. Sugar imports reached four pounds per capita, the threshold for mass consumption, in the 1690s, and rose steadily to twenty-four pounds per capita a century later. Much of the imported sugar was refined, yielding both white sugar and molasses; the latter could be either directly consumed or turned into rum. The American colonists consumed less sugar, but much more rum and molasses, than the English: In 1770 the colonies imported 1.7 gallons of rum and three gallons of molasses per capita. In that year, England's sugar, molasses, and rum imports totaled 140 calories per capita per day, while the colonies' imports provided 260 calories per capita per day.

Tea imports from China began in the 1660s, but legal imports into England and Wales were still insignificant on a per capita basis at the beginning of the eighteenth century. Mass consumption levels were probably reached in the 1730s; the dates are somewhat in doubt since it appears that at least half of England's tea was smuggled into the country until the 1780s. Tea drinking was slower to spread in the colonies, but may have reached mass consumption levels, again assuming substantial smuggling, by the 1750s or 1760s. Coffee became more accessible to Americans after the break with Britain and the reorientation to trade with the coffee-drinking nations of continental Europe.

As sales expanded, prices dropped rapidly for all of these new groceries. Sugar eventually supplied almost as many calories per penny as meat or beer. So the changes in consumption habits may not have required extensive reallocation of household budgets.

Consumer Durables in England and America

Histories of the early modern period often describe a proliferation of durable consumer goods. However, as with groceries, little change in expenditure patterns was required: Increasing quantities of goods were bought, but at declining prices; household expenditures, corrected for inflation, were remarkably constant.

Most of what we know about personal wealth and consumer goods comes from probate inventories, which were recorded until the 1730s in England, and the nineteenth century in America. In eight of the ten available studies of such inventories, spanning the entire early modern period, consumer goods account for one-fifth to one-third of personal wealth; the exceptions occur in the two wealthiest communities. In nine of the ten studies, the mean value of consumer goods in household inventories was between nineteen and thirty-five pounds sterling (using constant English prices of 1660–1674), with no clear trend over time. More than half of the consumer goods, in every case, consisted of bedding, linen, apparel, pewter and brass, and plate and jewelry.

If, as is sometimes suggested, household production gave way to paid labor outside the home in the early modern period, then there should be visible changes in the composition of household assets: Production goods should decline in importance, and consumer goods should increase. In fact, after the sixteenth century, there is no evidence of such a trend.

In the absence of quantitative trends in ownership, how can we interpret the reports of proliferating ownership of consumer durables? One possibility is that probate inventories, recording only what was owned at the time of death, became increasingly inaccurate evidence of lifetime expenditure. As cloth became cheaper and less durable, for example, clothing and bedding would wear out and be replaced more often during a lifetime. Another possibility, quite compatible with the first, is that roughly constant expenditure nevertheless bought a rapidly increasing quantity of goods, as prices of most durables dropped throughout the early modern period.

Economic and Social Characteristics of Consumers

Data from individual probate inventories within the ten studies cited above can be used for a simple analysis of consumer behavior. A common model of the "traditional" consumer assumes that once basic needs have been met there is no further desire or use for additional consumer goods. "Modern" consumers, in contrast, are assumed to continue accumulating consumer goods as their incomes rise.

Statistical analysis of the ten sets of data on probate inventories shows no support for the traditional model. The wealth-elasticity of early modern consumer goods ownership falls between 0.6 and 0.7 in almost all cases, or between 0.4 and 0.6 if corrected for household size. The latter figures mean that, for every 10 percent increase in household wealth, there was a 4 to 6 percent increase in the value of consumer durables found in the inventories. As wealth rose, so did the household's stock of goods, consistent with the image of "modern" consumer behavior.

Evaluating Consumer Demand in the Early Modern Period

There were demonstrable changes in consumer demand in the early modern period within the two categories of groceries and consumer durables. Yet there is no evidence of a change in the proportion of income or wealth spent on either of these categories. Rather, declining prices allowed an expansion of quantities and types of goods consumed, within the context of roughly constant expenditures in each category. In this respect the early modern changes in consumption differ from the changes in the late nineteenth and early twentieth centuries, when the proportion of household income spent on food declined sharply and consumer durable spending correspondingly increased.

Summary of

Pictorial Prints and the Growth of Consumerism: Class and Cosmopolitanism in Early Modern Culture

by Chandra Mukerji

[Published in *Graven Images, Patterns of Modern Materialism*
(New York: Columbia University Press, 1983), 30–78.]

In the fifteenth and sixteenth centuries, "the increased production and use of consumer commodities was helping to join both rich and poor into similar market relations and gathering together buyers throughout Europe into common patterns of taste. The new patterns of consumption of these novel goods brought to life a cultural system that, because it tapped and bred new levels and types of demand, was particularly suited to and encouraging of capitalist development. . . . The desires of new consumers and the patterns of their purchases stimulated new economic activity in Europe in specific ways: by discouraging hoarding, thus making new surplus a more potent economic force; by creating the broad patterns of taste that would support larger-scale production and trade; and by increasing the general level of demand for goods by making a greater proportion of the population consumers than had been typical in the past." [77–78]

This summary traces the meaning and the impact of early modern consumerism through the example of pictorial prints, one of the first mass consumer goods of purely decorative value.

Culture and Material Culture in Medieval Europe

Before the early modern period medieval European culture had appeared stable and unchanging for centuries. People from all social strata shared in a common popular culture. Strict egalitarianism among peers was often the rule, as in guilds and monasteries. The level of material culture was low. Even in the great medieval households, only the most rudimentary utilitarian furnishings were available. However, despite the appearance of stability, technological innovation continued in areas such as agriculture and warfare. The revival of long-distance trade after about 1100 AD allowed new concentrations of wealth, while the spread of literacy among the upper classes led to the development of new styles and tastes. The trading towns of the late middle ages displayed increased concentrations of wealth and concern for conspicuous consumption, harbingers of the materialist culture that would come to dominate Europe from the early modern period to the present.

Prints and the Growth of Consumerism

Pictorial prints, valued for nothing more than their decorative uses, fit perfectly the definition of consumer goods as expressive artifacts. While Europeans made woodblock prints in the fourteenth century, "the development of the printing press, movable type, and plate engraving during the fifteenth and sixteenth centuries made printing a sophisticated technology for producing a wide variety of marketable goods." [38] Although prints created before the eighteenth century are often displayed in museums today, they were not considered fine art or valuable "collectibles" until the late seventeenth century. Originally, printmaking involved images created for a popular audience in using more conservative styles than the painting of the era. Of course some artists, such as Albrecht Dürer, worked both in painting and in printmaking, but more did not. With the growing cosmopolitanism of the art of the period, and the simultaneous development of a quite different world of popular prints, the distinction between elite and mass culture began to be a visible part of European culture. This differentiation of visual consumer goods both resulted from and stimulated increased consumerism.

Guild Egalitarianism and Capitalism

In the fifteenth and sixteenth centuries, artisans produced a growing variety of goods for both elite and mass consumption. The expansion of and change in the European economy in this period undermined the guild system that had controlled craft production in the middle ages. Guilds held legal monopolies on their trades, protecting their members from competition from outsiders. They also enforced a strict egalitarianism among the guild masters, ensuring that each had the same amount of work and income. Expansion of trade thus tended to increase the power and income of the guild members. This was frustrating to customers who faced high prices and limited supplies, as well as to would-be artisans who faced burdensome apprenticeship requirements and other membership hurdles. Even the most successful guildmasters were held back because they could not expand their businesses faster than that of the guild as a whole, thus losing out on promising new commercial opportunities. All of these factors led to conflict and undermined the strength of the guilds.

Printmaking and publishing arose outside of the guild system, both because they involved new skills and trades and because book publishing in university centers had been outside the guild system in the late middle ages. However, toward the end of sixteenth century printers in England, France, and some parts of Italy established their own guilds to protect their position and to formalize their control over workers in printing shops. By the sixteenth century the increasing division of labor in printing had transformed the industry from craft production of manuscript books to capitalist manufacture of printed ones. As printing expanded there were numerous attempts at political and religious censorship; however these were directed almost entirely at the words rather than the pictures in printing, leaving printmakers substantial freedom of expression.

Dürer and the New Consumer Culture

Few individuals were as important in the articulation of new cultural forms as Albrecht Dürer (1471–1528), the German artist and printmaker. His education included an apprenticeship to a painter, training in printmaking, and travel to Italy to study the work of Renaissance painters. He quickly became successful both as a painter, gaining the support of aristocratic patrons, and as a printmaker, selling his work to a mass audience. He is often described as a transitional figure, using a mixture of medieval and modern elements in his prints. The formula for his commercial success was the use of the skillful naturalist techniques of the Renaissance to depict familiar medieval religious imagery. He helped to codify an aesthetic for prints, emphasizing skillful technique in the production of mass culture and increasing the range of pictures available not only to wealthy patrons of the fine arts, but also to more common consumers.

Cosmopolitan Patterns of Culture

Prints contributed to the geographic spread of consumerism, helping to shape international patterns of taste, by introducing designs across vast areas. Because they were easy to transport and had become easy to read, prints played an important role in creating standardized images that were shared throughout Western Europe.

Mass-produced prints of classical and Renaissance art, spreading throughout Europe in this period, were used to define the classical heritage for Europeans. One hundred years after Dürer, the great painter Peter Paul Rubens (1577–1640) not only sold his paintings but also had reproductions of his own paintings made by engravers and sold under his supervision. In so doing, Rubens increased his wealth and fame by exploiting the new legitimacy of printed reproductions of artworks.

With the spread of Baroque and classical art, regional cultural traditions declined but did not disappear. In fact, books about regional designs, artifacts, and costumes became popular. Dutch prints and books were read throughout Europe, helping to recreate a common culture after the Reformation. Trade in single-sheet prints was extensive and influential in this period: Rembrandt, for instance, was able to develop a cosmopolitan style, in spite of the fact that he did little traveling, because he collected prints reflecting cultural currents that he could not experience directly.

Summary of

The Quaker Ethic: Plain Living and High Thinking in American Culture
by David E. Shi

[Published in *The Simple Life: Plain Living and High Thinking in American Culture* (New York: Oxford University Press, 1985), 28–49.]

Like the Puritan settlers of New England, the Quakers who founded Pennsylvania were intent on establishing a pious society dedicated to plain living and high thinking. However, economic success soon eroded the Quakers' commitment to simplicity and spirituality. A religious revival in the mid-eighteenth century temporarily restored the traditional ethics of the Society of Friends (Quakers), but at the cost of diminished public influence for their beliefs.

Philosophy of the Simple Life

From their founding in the mid-seventeenth century, Quakers were known and sometimes persecuted for their egalitarian, pacifist beliefs. Despite their theological differences, the Quakers shared the Calvinist and Puritan emphasis on the virtues of thrift, sobriety, and hard work. The Friends chose the path of simple living to keep themselves free of greed, and to be able to devote themselves to spiritual pursuits and social service rather than material gain.

George Fox, the founder of the Society of Friends, recognized that some Quakers would grow wealthy, but cautioned that when "Riches do increase, take heed of setting your Hearts upon them, lest they become a Curse and a Plague to you."[1] He urged affluent Quakers to sell their unnecessary possessions and distribute the proceeds to the poor. Quakers did not expect everyone to have the same income, but believed that the gap between rich and poor should be narrowed.

William Penn and His Colony

As persecution of nonconformist sects intensified in late seventeenth-century England, many Quakers emigrated to North America, especially to the colony created by William Penn. The son of an admiral and friend of the king, Penn enjoyed the upbringing of an affluent gentleman, but he experienced an abrupt religious conversion in 1667 at the age of 22, and thereafter he became one of the most influential proponents of the Society of Friends, going to jail several times for his beliefs.

Like other early Quakers, Penn advocated the simple life, but not monastic self-denial. It was important to carry the faith into everyday life, in part to influence the broader society. Wealth alone was not evil, but luxury and avarice were: "Riches serve wise men, but command fools."[2]

Upon founding Philadelphia in 1682, Penn and the other religious authorities in Pennsylvania and West Jersey insisted on strict moral codes of behavior. Wage and price controls were enacted, as were sumptuary laws to prevent needless display of luxury. The Quakers were as strict as the Puritans in prescribing codes of moral behavior.

Doing Good or Doing Well?

In retrospect it is remarkable how rapidly the Quaker commitment to pious simplicity faded away. Migration of other settlers into Pennsylvania soon made Quakers a minority, undermining the political, social, and religious orientation of the original settlement. But even among the Friends themselves, who enjoyed the first access to the colony's fertile lands and promising trade, prosperity often overwhelmed the simple life. Complaints about the extravagant ways of affluent young Quakers in Philadelphia began almost immediately, and only grew in intensity over the years.

Penn himself was shocked, as early as 1697, by the lack of modesty and virtue he saw in Philadelphia. Yet Penn's own life reflected the ambiguity of the Quaker commitment to simplicity. Despite his religious conversion, he never lost his personal taste for aristocratic living, and maintained a magnificent country estate overlooking the Delaware River, with numerous servants and slaves. He told his critics that a certain amount of material display was needed to sustain the power and prestige of his office as head of the colony. Temperance and self-restraint were virtues, Penn felt, in relation to one's social standing. In a similar spirit, one of the wealthy Quakers of the day requested imported furniture from a London merchant, specifying that it should be "*of the best Sort but Plain.*"[3]

John Woolman and the "Great Awakening"

The "Great Awakening," the religious revival that swept through many of the colonies in the middle of the eighteenth century, had its counterpart among the Quakers of Pennsylvania. Beginning in the 1740s and continuing for well over a generation, a reformation occurred among Friends. The reformers criticized the growing worldliness of affluent Quakers and called for a return to the traditional ethic of simple living.

It was in this period that Quakers lost control of the political life of Pennsylvania. With the outbreak of the French and Indian War in 1754, settlements in western Pennsylvania came under attack. While some Quakers supported defensive military action, seven pacifist Friends resigned from the Pennsylvania Assembly over the issue in 1755. They were replaced by supporters of Benjamin Franklin's policy of vigorous military defense. This ended Quaker control of the Assembly.

The loss of political power allowed the Friends, now no more than a quarter of the population of the colony they had founded, to focus on internal renewal of their own faith and relationships. Strict moral codes were again enforced; Friends were expelled for marrying non-Quakers, violating standards of simple living, or supporting military action.

The most prominent leader of the Quaker reformation was John Woolman (1720–1772). He became a successful merchant in the 1740s, yet at the same time began to speak out about the effects of commercial success on religious and family life. He was also an early crusader against slavery, helping to persuade the Philadelphia meeting in 1758 to disown those who continued to buy slaves.

After the Assembly crisis in 1755, when it was clear that Penn's "holy experiment" of a Quaker-controlled colony had failed, Woolman and others worried about what would become of their faith and social ethics. Woolman increasingly devoted himself to writing and speaking about the evils of wealth and the virtues of simplicity. Unable to curtail his growing business, he left it altogether, and instituted a regimen of relentless simplification. His plain appearance, dressed in undyed cloth, startled even Quakers.

Simplicity for Woolman had economic as well as spiritual benefits. Rejecting the argument that lowered consumption would lead to unemployment, he replied that in a simpler society more workers would have the satisfaction of producing staples rather than baubles, and that work days could be reduced, making vocations a source of pride rather than drudgery.

The Quaker ethic, reinvigorated by Woolman and other reformers of his day, survived largely intact through the turbulent revolutionary years and beyond. Yet it survived at the price of withdrawal from social leadership and influence. The Quakers self-consciously embraced their new minority status as a "quiet and peculiar" people set apart from society. Even within that minority, commitment to the simple life proved hard to maintain. The forces opposing pious simplicity included not only personal tastes for luxury, but also traditional hierarchical social values, as in the case of Penn, and the belief in diligent pursuit of one's calling, in a fast-growing economy where many were sure to prosper.

Notes

1. L.V. Hopkin, *A Day-Book of Counsel and Comfort, from the Epistles of George Fox* (London, 1937), 109, 90–91; cited by Shi, 29.
2. William Penn, "No Cross, No Crown," in Society of Friends, *Selected Works of William Penn*, 3 vols. (London, 1825), 1: 333; cited by Shi, 31.
3. Isaac Norris to Joseph Pike, 25 February 1707, in Edward Armstrong, ed., "Correspondence between William Penn and James Logan," *Memoirs of the Historical Society of Pennsylvania* 10 (1872); Tolles, *Quakers and Atlantic Culture* (New York, 1960), 76–77, 79, 86–88; cited by Shi, 36.

Summary of

The Consumer Revolution of Eighteenth-Century England
by Neil McKendrick

[Published in *The Birth of a Consumer Society: The Commercialization of Eighteenth-Century England*, eds. Neil McKendrick, John Brewer, and J.H. Plumb (Bloomington: Indiana University Press, 1982), 9–33.]

A consumer revolution occurred in England in the eighteenth century along with the industrial revolution. The consumer revolution was the demand-side analog to the supply-side industrial revolution. All classes took part in this revolution, characterized by new prosperity, and new production and marketing techniques. The consumer revolution marks a turning point in the history of human experience.

The change was heralded by commentaries that wondered at and complained about the new phenomenon. Change was seen all over, including architecture, pottery, furniture, fabrics, cutlery, and gardening. The wealthy led the way and the masses followed in this consumer boom, which was driven by vertical social mobility, social emulation, the influence of fashion, and unprecedented levels of prosperity. Advertising had reached a feverish pitch and new sales techniques were developed in pursuit of the consumer.

The consumer boom was in the making over a long period of time. The intellectual origins of the revolution can be traced back to new ideas that emerged in the 1690s. In the early 1600s the mercantilist notion that a nation's wealth grew through a favorable balance of payments was widely accepted; this discouraged consumption, especially of foreign goods. Domestic consumption (also called home demand) was seen as a necessary evil, with only the rich expected to consume luxuries. The idea that increased consumption would generate demand, which would in turn increase a nation's wealth, was not grasped at first. However, the introduction of cheap calicoes and muslins from India by the East India Company and the huge demand for them revealed the economic benefits of catering to the power "of envy, emulation, love of luxury, vanity, and vaulting ambition." [14]

By the end of the 1600s the benefits of progressive levels of spending were becoming well recognized, and were challenging the prevailing orthodoxy that disapproved of self-indulgence. Among writers who wrote in favor of the consumption of luxuries were Dudley North, John Houghton, and Nicholas Barbon.

However, in the beginning of the eighteenth century these views were still controversial, as they implied that class distinctions fostered hedonism and were based on little more than purchasing power. The negative reception given to Mandeville's provocative allegory, the *Fable of the Bees* (published in 1714), shows how great the threat of the new ideas about consumption was seen to be. Mandeville argued that national social and economic benefits resulted from luxury, avarice, prodigality, pride, envy, and vanity. He went on to say that lavish consumption resulted in employment for many, and he extolled the virtues of conspicuous consumption and emulative spending. For these unpopular ideas, he "was held to rival Machiavelli and Hobbes as the father of lies." [16]

It was only in the middle of the eighteenth century that consumption and the pursuit of luxury came to be universally accepted as socially beneficial. In 1776 Adam Smith wrote in his *Wealth of Nations* that "Consumption is the sole end and purpose of all production; and the interest of the producer ought to be attended to, only so far as it may be necessary for promoting that of the consumer. The maxim is . . . perfectly self-evident."[1] Socially too, England was ready for a consumer boom. English society was multilayered, with vertical mobility both possible and coveted. Such a mobile social structure was important for the spread of the consumer revolution as each group tried to climb up the social ladder by acquiring possessions, especially clothes that symbolized advancement.

Another factor in the creation of the consumer revolution in England in the eighteenth century was the size and character of its capital city, London. Sixteen percent of the English population lived in, or moved in and out of, London, and were exposed to the city's shops, lifestyles, and fashions. London was the center for forms of conspicuous consumption, which were mimicked elsewhere. The numerous servants in the city emulated their masters and spread the consumer revolution to the lower classes. While none of these factors were unknown in other times and places, the sheer size of eighteenth-century London and the gradual rise in English incomes allowed new levels of commercial activity to take place.

Family incomes rose in part as a result of longer working hours and increased employment of women and children as well as men in industry. With more women employed, there was an increase in demand for goods previously made at home, such as clothes, beer, candles, and other household items. Economic theory gradually caught up with reality, recognizing the importance of the home market. Enjoyment of consumption was no longer seen as the prerogative of the rich. New industries supplying furniture and home furnishings grew rapidly toward the end of the century; and sales of countless commodities soared upward. In the last fifteen years of the eighteenth century, while the population grew by 14 percent, consumption of tea increased by 98 percent and that of printed fabrics by 142 percent.

With so much evidence in favor of a consumer revolution, why have historians been reluctant to recognize its importance? Economic history has traditionally seen market expansion as merely a reflection of and response to increased supply. Preindustrial life is often romanticized as a comfortable, organic, uncorrupted existence (a view that is easily refuted by the evidence of overwhelming preindustrial poverty). Pessimistic interpretations of the industrial revolution, based on the fact that many suffered during industrialization, have prevented some historians from recognizing that there were many who gained. Some economists have argued that home demand could not have risen fast enough to be the source of the period's rapid economic growth. The evidence seems clear, however, that a consumer revolution driven by commercialization and home demand had overtaken eighteenth-century England.

Note

1. Adam Smith, *An Inquiry into the Nature and Cause of the Wealth of Nations,* 1776; cited in McKendrick, 15.

Summary of

Consumerism and the Industrial Revolution

by Ben Fine and Ellen Leopold

[Published in *Social History* 15: 1 (January 1990): 151–179.]

The Industrial Revolution must be understood by reference to a structured explanation of change (rather than as exceptionally large shifts in
supply and/or demand)—one which unites social and economic forces together rather than reducing one to the other. [152]

Traditional economic thinking identifies supply as the most important factor in long-run economic changes. In 1982, Neil McKendrick presented a
forceful, revisionist perspective emphasizing the equally great importance
of demand as a necessary feature of such change.[1] This summary argues
that McKendrick's consumerist emphasis on demand-led growth is inadequate, and that any theoretical approach to economic history that focuses
primarily on the interaction between supply and demand cannot explain
economic trends. Supply and demand are themselves products of historical
and social forces, and these forces must be the analytical starting point for
any adequate theory of economic change.

Is There a Supply and Demand for Industrial Revolution?

A common approach to economic growth, and economic history, assumes
that supply creates its own demand in the long run, even though fluctua-
tions in effective demand may be unrelated to supply changes in the short
run. In contrast, McKendrick argued that the long-term economic changes
that occurred during the industrial revolution owe as much to consumption
(demand) as they do to supply. McKendrick marshaled important evidence
of the significance of demand during the industrial revolution, but there is
no theoretical basis for viewing demand as a decisive factor in long-term
economic progress.

The consumerist approach is based on a causal model that implies that
shifts in demand curves lead to movement along supply curves. For example, McKendrick looked to the success of the pottery industry as well as the
clothing and fashion industries for evidence that a consumer revolution was
a significant driving force behind the industrial revolution. By examining
the entrepreneurial activities of a leading eighteenth-century pottery man-
ufacturer, McKendrick observed that the demand for mass-produced pot-

tery followed a growth in demand for luxury pottery items. He concluded that the lower classes emulated the fashion interests of the upper classes and this stimulated the demand for and supply of less fashionable, less expensive, and more widely available products. However, McKendrick's observations do not support his generalizations about the pottery industry, the industrial revolution, or long-run economic change.

This type of consumerist approach fails primarily because it rests on the false assumption that if consumption in the lower classes chronologically follows that of the upper classes, then it must be a case of status-seeking emulation. But emulation need not be the cause of all such consumption patterns; among other reasons, new consumption patterns might result from changes in lower-class incomes and the availability of goods. For instance, domestic coal consumption rose from one to two million tons in 1700 to five million tons in 1800, but it would be unreasonable to attribute the increase to emulation of the rich. Rather, coal consumption reflected a variety of factors, including transportation costs, the price of coal, its potential substitutes, levels of income, overall population, housing conditions, and weather. This example illustrates the weakness of the argument that a shift in demand based on emulation was primarily responsible for the industrial revolution.

Is an Emphasis on Demand and Supply the Answer?

The objection to demand-led growth leaves open the question of whether a theory that combines demand and supply can provide a satisfactory explanation of the economic roots of the industrial revolution. A model that considers both demand and supply curves might seem to offer a more balanced perspective.

However, such an analysis is still limited in that it ignores the fact that complex major historical events like the English Industrial Revolution cannot be forced into the same analytical framework that is used for individual sectors of the economy. Furthermore, the orthodox model confuses chronology with causality in discussing the relations between shifts in demand and supply. The difference between a chronological history and a causal history represents the difference between a description and an explanation of events.

A more informative analysis of long-run economic change focuses on underlying historical and social forces; these forces give rise to shifts in both the supply and demand curves, but are not reducible to them. This approach takes account of such issues as class conflict, distribution of income, work intensity, market restrictions, and availability of financing. The great writers of classical economics, such as Smith, Malthus, and Marx, all had theories of the underlying conflicts and potentials for development that shape and inform the market. The modern supply-demand framework is impoverished by comparison, both in the traditional supply-oriented approach to growth and in the more recent demand-oriented, consumerist alternative.

The Demand for Fashion in Clothes

McKendrick's treatment of fashion and emulation illustrates some of the limitations of the consumerist approach. In his view, social emulation and emulative spending in the late eighteenth century led to mass-based consumer demand fifty years later. Emulation is manifested above all in the dress of domestic servants; this process was viewed as the transmission of upper-class tastes to the working class.

But the market in which this emulative spending occurred remains obscure. Eighteenth-century servants could not afford the clothing their masters wore, and, in fact, rarely bought their own clothes. Frequently they were given used or outmoded clothing from their masters' wardrobes, or were clothed in uniforms at their employers' expense. Servants were also bequeathed clothing upon the death of their employers, and were sometimes given the right to keep or sell the masters' cast-off clothing as a condition of employment.

Outside of the city, London fashions had little direct influence. A more important influence on the emerging mass market of the nineteenth century was the spread of the Protestant ethic, which emphasized middle-class modesty and conformity. In fact, middle-class professional dress, and even workmen's frock coats, were emulated upward into high society, much like blue jeans in the twentieth century.

Production of Clothing

Before the arrival of the sewing machine in the mid-nineteenth century, all clothing was handmade. The fabric with which a fashionable dress was made was more expensive than the labor or the trimmings (buckles, ribbons, lace, and the like). As such, a single garment would often be altered and restyled several times, with changing fashions reflected in the trimmings. Good fabric was, in effect, a consumer durable; men's coats were passed down from one generation to the next.

Well after the adoption of the sewing machine, luxury clothing was often handmade. The earliest department stores employed hundreds of tailors for this purpose. Emulation of such luxuries bore no relationship to the emergence of a true mass market in inexpensively manufactured fabrics. The new, low-priced calicoes and ginghams were sold almost exclusively to working-class women, whose preferences are absent from McKendrick's tale of London fashions.

> To create the image of a forward-moving society fueled by demand from above, consumerists have to jettison the interests and contributions of at least three-quarters of its members. The incomes and consumption habits of the laboring and middle classes are left out of the picture altogether, obviating the need to measure the relative impact of luxury spending on the economy as a whole. [177]

Note

1. N. McKendrick et al., *The Birth of a Consumer Society: The Commercialization of Eighteenth Century England* (London: Europa Publications, 1982).

Summary of

Learning to Consume: Early Department Stores and the Shaping of the Modern Consumer Culture (1800–1914)

by Rudi Laermans

[Published in *Theory, Culture and Society* (London: Sage, 1993), 79–102.]

The work of sociologists and historians in recent years has aided the understanding of the role of social and commercial institutions in the development of a culture of mass consumption. As this summary explains, early department stores in European and American cities were leading proponents of the modern consumer culture through commercial innovation and the creation of public spheres for middle-class women. Active buying was transformed into passive shopping by the department store.

Shapers of Modern Consumer Culture

Sociological interest in consumption has focused on everyday practices where individual creativity, social resistance, and collective pleasures are expressed. Sociologists have identified within homogeneous mass culture a heterogeneous mass of creative symbolic practices fueled by individual imagination and grounded in everyday social relations. Both recent historians and writers of the late 1800s have recognized the leading role that early department stores played in the development of a mass-consumption culture in the second half of the nineteenth century, particularly in New York, Chicago, and Paris. (In England and Germany department stores were introduced later, around the turn of the century.)

Department Stores as Commercial Innovators

Until the beginning of the nineteenth century local markets and neighborhood stores supplied the daily needs of people, while luxury goods could be found in specialized shops in large cities. In such specialty shops, products were neither advertised nor displayed; prices were not fixed, but were established by bargaining between customers and merchants. Entering a shop was often taken as an implicit agreement to buy something, at a price to be set by bargaining. Exceptions to this mode of commerce were the Quaker merchants (who posted fixed prices as early as the 1600s) and London shopkeepers who displayed merchandise, offered exchanges to dissatisfied customers, and publicized their businesses with cards. These exceptions paved the way for the sense of freedom and choice experienced in department stores, where impersonality made it possible to enter and exit the store without a comment. This, in turn, allowed comparison shopping.

Female Public Spaces and Leisure

Department store managers stimulated the transformation of their stores into distinctly female-oriented public spaces. Department store shopping became a leisure activity, a way of pleasantly passing the time. It also became increasingly time-consuming, as the possibility of collecting a great deal of information about commodities and about bargains created an expectation that this was a major part of the role of the good housewife. Contemporary commentators had both positive and negative reactions to these changes. Newspapers in the 1880s expressed concerns about the new shopping mania among well-to-do women. The transformation of buying into shopping, and the subsequent "leisurization" of shopping, offered middle-class women new opportunities within the public sphere, legitimizing their escape from the home. The stores stressed comfort and convenience, and provided free services such as refreshment and reading rooms. However, the commercial provision of women with a public place of their own came with its own social costs. Traditional sex stereotypes were reproduced: "Keen, cold-blooded males encouraged women to be what they were supposed to be, that is, 'irrational', 'childlike' and 'thoughtless' human beings." [96]

As competition grew between growing numbers of stores, credit facilities were introduced to attract buyers. The continual growth in credit services helped to reinforce the ambiance of leisure.

Advertising Innovations and the Display of Commodities

In the absence of the sales talk that had traditionally accompanied the act of buying and selling, commodities had to sell themselves. Print advertising was reformed by innovations such as enlarged size, catchwords, slogans, and even new printing techniques. Early department stores were among the first to use photogravure and chromolithography. Images transformed commodities into desirable items. "The external rhetoric of advertising had to be continued inside the store through an appealing and eye-catching 'commodity rhetoric.'" [90]

Many display strategies of the early department stores have by now become generally accepted. However, at the time, the stores seemed to be "object theaters" in which commodities were staged, thereby transforming merchandise into a permanent spectacle.

The advertisements and displays of early department stores pioneered the "technocracy of the senses"—an artificially produced fascination of the consumer. The practical value of an item counted for less than its appearance in the sights of gazing shoppers. The luxurious, comfortable, and fashionable way of life was on display for all. The real success of early department stores was partly due to low prices; goods were not handmade but mass-produced. The aura of luxury in which the goods were presented compensated for their actual cheapness.

Conclusion

Modern capitalism created its own culture in the sociological and anthropological sense. It transformed mass-produced products into symbolic goods that convey specific meanings. In this context, the rapid take-off of the new kind of store can be traced to three causes: (1) Early department stores offered middle-class women an opportunity to escape the dullness of domestic life. (2) The stores appealed to the appetite for status symbols of

the rapidly growing urban middle class whose members wanted to distinguish themselves from the lower social strata. The early department stores
fulfilled this need—their merchandise was relatively cheap but possessed
imaginary associations with luxury and comfort. (3) The social conditions
of life in large cities required the invention of new forms of social interaction among individuals who were mostly strangers to each other. By selling
the goods needed for respectable appearance in an anonymous urban setting, the department stores helped to create what has become known to us
as modern culture.

Summary of

From Salvation to Self-Realization: Advertising and the Therapeutic Roots of Consumer Culture

by T.J. Jackson Lears

[Published in *The Culture of Consumption: Critical Essays in American History,
1880–1980,* eds. Richard Wightman Fox and T.J. Jackson Lears
(New York: Pantheon Books, 1983), 1–38.]

The summarized article is made up of three sections—only the first two are
summarized below. The third examines the life of an advertiser and uses the
biography to illustrate the author's argument.

During the nineteenth century the Protestant ethos of salvation and self-
restraint dominated the moral landscape of the United States. In contrast,
modern consumer culture is characterized by the unrestrained pursuit of
goods and services. The significance of Protestantism gradually diminished
with the rise of a therapeutic morality that emphasized self-realization and
a quest for psychological and physical health. This paper argues that the
emergence of a therapeutic ethos provided the moral climate in which consumer culture could flourish. National advertising quickly developed as an
expression of and tool for the dissemination of this ethos.

The Emergence of a Therapeutic Ethos

All people to varying degrees are preoccupied with their own physical and
emotional well-being, but the modern ethos is unique in its secular and ob-
sessive concern with developing a coherent sense of self. It developed primarily as a response to a growing feeling of "unreality" among the educated, urban bourgeoisie who perceived reality as something to be sought,

rather than lived. This feeling of unreality derived essentially from an erosion of individual autonomy that developed within the framework of technological, religious, and economic changes.

> In all, the modern sense of unreality stemmed from extraordinarily various sources and generated complex effects. Technological change isolated the urban bourgeoisie from the hardness of life on the land; an interdependent and increasingly corporate economy circumscribed autonomous will and choice; a softening Protestant theology undermined commitments and blurred ethical distinctions. [10]

Personal isolation from the world bred a historically unique collection of emotional needs that valued bodily vitality, emotional intensity, and a coherent sense of self. The flight from unreality became a quest for self-realization as the ultimate solution to feelings of disconnection.

Two disparate approaches to self-realization developed: one emphasized self-control through the management of personal resources and the other stressed personal growth through intense experience. The "prudential" approach carried some vestige of the Protestant value of restraint, but success in life came to be understood in a moral and spiritual vacuum. The "abundance" approach promoted the impulse to let go and replaced morality with morale. These approaches shared the belief that self-realization is the most significant aim of human existence.

The secular world view of the therapeutic ethos competed with the values of religious institutions. Ministers mistakenly thought that by emphasizing the value of human potential they could maintain interest in traditional religious symbols. For example, in both the Emmanuel movement and liberal Protestantism, ministers redefined religious goals in terms of self-realization and prudence, thereby devaluing ultimate purposes (e.g., God and heaven) and transforming religion into a form of abundance therapy. By supporting the secular worship of personal growth, the therapeutic ethos diminished the values of customs, traditions, and family history.

Advertising Strategies and the Therapeutic Ethos

The advertising industry targeted the American longing for autonomy, authority, and cultural roots, and unintentionally reinforced these emotional needs. Between 1880 and 1930 the national market and urban conditions spawned a group of harried consumers. In response, advertising altered its product messages from descriptions to sensational imagery that caught the attention of the busy consumer. This shift was facilitated by advances in image technology that rendered lexical advertising dull by comparison. By the early 1900s, psychological consultants had developed advertising methods to manipulate the consumer and associate images of physical, psychic, and social well-being with the acquisition of products. The idea that the human mind is malleable, susceptible to suggestion and irrational longings, played an important role in the social control exercised by advertisers. Advertising expressed this control through a developing industrial complex of mass media and mass amusement, which facilitated the proliferation of sensational and confusing advertising messages.

The bewildering array of symbols and images that accompanied the new marketing strategies established a culture of meaningless symbols. Few symbols were rooted in specific customs or clearly referred to anything in particular. Images were divorced from the functional attributes of products, while advertising language spread misleading information.[1] The "corrosion of meaning" was gradual and unintended, as national advertising suggested an alternative set of values that promised well-being and fulfillment. Desires and anxieties were associated increasingly with criteria that were based in the perceptions of others. Fulfilling domestic responsibilities, climbing the corporate ladder, self-improvement, avoiding disease, and confronting social fears all were linked increasingly with consumption and a concern for what other people think.

These advertising strategies had a particularly strong effect on women. Advertising appropriated the role of educator and cultural authority for many women by informing young mothers how to care for their children, educating wives in the etiquette of domestic respectability, and promising youth, social acceptance, and liberation through appropriate consumption. Unfortunately, feminist calls for social equality were muted by the emphasis of the therapeutic ethos on the pursuit of self-realization and intense experiences.

Not all advertising strategies focused on aspirations and fears; some directly addressed feelings of unreality. This advertising promoted "natural" goods as a salvation from the artificiality of modern living. Advertising's emphasis on "natural" states reflected and addressed an urban bourgeois nostalgia for traditional authority by linking many products with the growing prestige of medicine and science. Advertising replaced ancestral cultural authorities with corporate and therapeutic commodified versions.

Thus, the therapeutic ethos developed in response to the demands of urban alienation and was shaped simultaneously by business interests and by the need for emotional stability and a coherent sense of self.

Note

1. For example, Schlitz beer advertised that its beer bottles were steam cleaned, a practice that was common to all beer manufacturers. While the claim was not false, its implication that this practice was unique was misleading.

Summary of

The Consumer's Comfort and Dream
by Gary Cross

[Published in *Time and Money: The Making of Consumer Culture*
(London: Routledge, 1993), 154–183.]

Early in the twentieth century, "the democratization of time and money"—
that is, widespread preference and demands for increasing leisure rather
than increasing income—seemed like a real possibility. Yet in the end mass
consumption won out, not only because it "delivers the goods" but also because it satisfies people's expanding longings. The previous chapter of this
book [summarized in Part II of this volume] examined the economic pressures of the 1920s and 1930s that reinforced consumerism. This summary
reviews other theories of consumerism, and argues that "working people
actively participated in the formation of the consumer society even as they
were being manipulated by it." [155]

Theories of Mass Consumerism

Three widely discussed theories offer overlapping and generally negative
explanations of the rise of the consumer society. The first links mass consumption to the cultural degradation of industrial work. The deskilling of
labor, in settings such as the assembly line, is said to have produced workers who were unable to resist the allure of new consumer goods. The need
for fantasy, ostentation, luxury, and distraction, as expressed by workers
who are detached from traditional ways of life and excluded from new
forms of cultural enrichment, leads to conformist patterns of consumption.
The French sociologist Maurice Halbwachs was an early exponent of this
theory, while authors such as Pierre Bourdieu present more contemporary
variations on the same theme.

A second theory, rooted especially in the American context, identifies
two simultaneous trends as the source of consumer society: an emerging
mass-production economy produced a need for mass markets, while the
erosion of the ascetic Victorian personality created a consumer psychology
susceptible to advertising appeals. Early social theorists like Robert Lynd
believed that consumers were essentially passive objects that were molded
by advertisers. Recently, a more subtle variant of this view has stressed the
decline of the Protestant ethic in the twentieth century and its replacement
with an ethic of adjustment, self-fulfillment, and consumption after working hours. The contradictory longings of the new personality gave meanings to goods, and created scope for advertising.

A third approach stresses the social psychology of spending, as seen in the work of Thorstein Veblen and Georg Simmel. Veblen's analysis of emulation and conspicuous consumption is well known; Simmel came to similar conclusions from an analysis of money, the marketplace, and fashion. For Simmel, fashion reflected humanity's universally imitative character, accentuated by social inequality and mobility: Those who were insecure imitated the fashion of those who were more secure; as a result, the fashion leaders were obliged to create fresh innovations to distance themselves from the crowd. Fred Hirsch presents a modern version of this view and its gloomy implications in his analysis of positional goods.

The third theory is more successful than the first two, recognizing the internal dynamics of consumption and avoiding the assumption of omnipotent manipulation by advertisers. But all three views assume the passivity of consumers and the inferiority of social life constructed around goods. A corrective is provided by a fourth interpretation of mass consumption, recognizing the centrality of goods as positive vehicles of social expression, as seen in the recent work of cultural anthropologists such as Mary Douglas and Baron Isherwood. Likewise, Daniel Miller emphasizes that working people engage in "self-production" when consuming, giving meaning to goods and their uses. However, this anthropological view, like the three earlier perspectives, remains incomplete.

The key to a better understanding of consumption may be found in the linkages between labor productivity, leisure, and consumer needs. In the 1920s, "the productivity of Fordism shifted the motivation to work from fear of impoverishment to the allure of goods. . . . The meaning of inequality was radically changed in the transition from subsistence to Fordism because the locus of dependency shifted from the workplace to free time. To be sure, the 'golden chain' of installment buying had replaced the stick of hunger; in exchange for those goods that equalized and privatized, families sold their future time." [162–163] Free time represented "the realizations of the consumer's comfort and dream: domestic time provided continuity and memory through accumulated goods while holiday time suspended temporal routines and was expressed in the magic of uninhibited spending." [164]

Shaping Consumerism: Nationality, Class, and Gender

The modern Anglo-American consumer's household was a middle-class creation with its origins in the Victorian home. Domestic goods presented a "silent socialization" about the meaning of culture, property, gender, and authority. Working-class culture rigidly defined the rules of domestic consumption, reflecting its aspirations to middle-class respectability. The gender-based division of labor helped to reconcile leisure and spending; few married women worked outside the home in Britain or America in the interwar years.

Because domestic consumption often involved labor rather than leisure for women, the idea of consumption as self-production can be best applied to female homemakers. Time and goods at home hardly had the same association with leisure for many women as they did for working men. In fact, the norm of the eight-hour workday for male workers depended on the existence of women homemakers; without the gender-based division of labor, a more radical transformation of the division of labor and time would have been necessary.

Home, Display, Privacy, and Temporality

Homeownership and suburbanization spread rapidly in interwar Britain and America. Status was conveyed not only by location, but also by the choice and arrangement of household objects, particularly in formal front parlors. The move from old urban neighborhoods to new suburbs created anonymity and a concern for appearance, but also allowed privacy and retreat. Homeowners'wanted space for private family life and longings, with "friendliness but not friends" in the neighborhood.

For working-class families, purchased furnishings were often modest at first, as the cost of the home itself was a financial strain. However, homes provided space for artifacts and souvenirs, ritual objects from the family's past, and objects of current personal significance. The radio, the most important new consumer good of the interwar years, brought a new dimension to family entertainmeni. Although leisure time activities blossomed, it was "real" time at work that gave meaning to domestic time, especially for male breadwinners. For the female homemaker, of course, this dichotomy did not exist; instead, her hours of housework justified her access to her husband's money and her enjoyment of the private time that she created.

Holiday's Dream of Spending and Freedom

Time and money were also reconciled in the rituals of the holiday, which came to England earlier than to the United States or France. The English seaside vacation was a perfect metaphor of the consumer moment, a transcendent experience for modern industrial people. Blackpool, the archetypical holiday mecca, received seven million visitors in 1937.

The summer holiday took over the role once played by religious or seasonal rituals, and the trip to the sea acquired new rituals of its own. People on holidays sought freedom from ordinary, regulated, mechanical time; the resorts were organized to provide novelty, frivolity, and opportunities for spontaneous choices of diversions. Binge-like spending unrestrained by ordinary budget limits was part of the experience, even for many who could ill afford it. Year-round saving and austerity to prepare for the holiday were welcomed by many; the ordinariness of everyday life was relieved in the annual week of luxury.

In holiday spending, domestic life, and elsewhere, consumption fulfilled the combined needs for privacy and sociability, allowing autonomy and group membership at the same time. "Goods prevailed because they reconciled time and money. . . . Goods and 'sacred' time become fused in the cyclic rites and museums of domesticity and in the vacation time of the consuming crowd." [183]

PART V

Foundations of Economic Theories of Consumption

Overview Essay

by Frank Ackerman

The standard economic theory of consumer behavior is a relatively recent creation in historical terms, no older than consumer society itself. That theory, in brief, assumes that consumers come to the market with well-defined, insatiable desires for private goods and services; those desires are not affected by social interactions, economic institutions, or the consumption choices or well-being of others. Only prices, incomes, and personal tastes affect consumption—and since tastes are "exogenous" (that is, determined outside the realm of economics), there is little point in talking about anything but prices and incomes.

The relationship of this theory to the visible facts of economic life is tenuous at best. No other social science accepts this theory, nor holds a similarly narrowed view of the process of consumption. Yet in economics the neoclassical theory, as it is called, has dominated professional discourse throughout the twentieth century. Its abrupt appearance in the last third of the nineteenth century is a central event in the history of economic thought. Parts V and VI examine the foundations of the neoclassical theory of consumption, and the critiques and alternatives that have been proposed. This part focuses on work done before 1960, while Part VI addresses the period since then.

The economics that we know today did not triumph for lack of well-articulated criticisms and alternatives. Indeed, one great mystery of the field is how rapidly and totally its dissenters have vanished. One step beyond the mainstream in economics, evidently, there lies an intellectual Bermuda Triangle where voyages of thought disappear without a trace. Some of the missing have turned up on other shores, leading new lives as influential voices in sociology, history, political debate, and cultural criticism. But word of their survival rarely makes it back to their native discipline.

The goal of this part is twofold: to explore the origins of neoclassical theory and to rediscover some of the lost dissenters of economics, whose criticisms may yet point the way toward a new frontier in economic thought. Of the nine articles presented here, the first four span the period from the beginnings of economics through the nineteenth century. The remaining five include a unique look at the views of John Maynard Keynes and four seminal contributions from the generation of economists who followed him in the 1940s and 1950s.

Materialism, Humanism, and Classical Economics

Modern economics often traces its origins back to Adam Smith. The core ideas go back even farther, to an innovation in philosophical tradition at the dawn of the capitalist era. In the beginning economics was seen as a branch of moral philosophy. However, the lead actor in the standard economic model, the "rational economic man," is an insatiably acquisitive individualist—which is not a personality type that is endorsed by traditional moral philosophies. In the first summary in this section, Joel Kassiola examines the history and meaning of materialism, both as a philosophical doctrine and in the more colloquial sense, as a synonym for acquisitiveness.

Kassiola begins his discussion of modern materialism, in the latter sense, with the thought of Thomas Hobbes. Writing in the seventeenth century in the midst of the English Civil War, Hobbes expounded a competitive individualism: Everyone always wants more power and material goods to protect what they already have, and to satisfy the desires for social recognition, honor, and vanity. "Felicity is a continual progress of the desire from one object to another, the attaining of the former being still but the way to the latter," said Hobbes. "I put for a general inclination of all mankind a perpetual and restless desire of power after power that ceases only in death."[1]

At the time this was as novel and controversial as Hobbes' better-known innovations in political theory. Rousseau was a prominent early critic, arguing that relentless competition and acquisitiveness were not innate in human nature, but rather were created by a particular social system and could be changed by a different system. Kassiola's sympathies are clearly with Rousseau in this disagreement; he traces the criticism of unlimited acquisitiveness back to the ancient Greek philosophers, and forward through a number of the authors whose work is summarized in this volume. But economic theory has taken Hobbes' side of the debate. As competition and acquisitiveness came to play a more important role in the theories of the day, economics detached itself from moral philosophy and became known as "political economy."

A little more than a century separates Hobbes' *Leviathan* from Adam Smith's *Wealth of Nations*. In that interval, as English capitalism advanced from the Civil War toward the Industrial Revolution, economic theory moved toward acceptance of the merits of consumption as an end in itself—as described in the article by McKendrick in Part IV. The prevailing school of economic thought in the seventeenth century was mercantilism, which viewed foreign trade as the key to national prosperity, and saw domestic consumption as an impediment to trade and growth. Moreover, the religious beliefs of the day tended to stigmatize luxury consumption as immoral. But these skeptical views of consumption dissolved in the warm bath of eighteenth-century economic growth. In 1714 Bernard de Mandeville caused a furor with the publication of his satirical *Fable of the Bees,* extolling the virtues of wasteful luxury consumption as a means to create work for the poor. By 1776, however, Smith's classic work could argue confidently that increasing individual consumption was the goal of all economic activity; since his time that goal has often been simply assumed without comment.

The rise of economic theory was not a smooth crescendo from Adam Smith's day to the present. Discordant notes were heard almost at once, as described in the article by Mark Lutz and Kenneth Lux. They explore the history of humanism in economics, by which they mean the explicit concern for the well-being and opportunities for self-development for all individuals. Lutz and Lux quote Smith's cheerful assertion that laissez-faire economics would be good for everyone, leading to almost the same results as equal division of all resources. Smith's successors, in contrast, were less sanguine. Classical economics was often a rather grim affair, weighed down by population pressure, declining wages, crop yields, and the like. Nor, as it turned out, was it a very long-lived school of thought. In the second half of the nineteenth century, according to Lutz and Lux, classical economics split into three branches: humanistic economics, Marxism, and neoclassical economics.

Humanistic economics may be the first of the dissenting traditions to disappear without a trace. In their day, Simonde de Sismondi, John Ruskin, and John Hobson were well-known, influential figures.[2] Their critiques of the social effects of industrialization and mass production, their advocacy of creative work and production for human use, their concern for the aspects of human welfare that transcend material needs and private consumption, all made an impression on their contemporaries. Sismondi's descriptions of early industrialization were quoted extensively by Marx in *Capital;* Ruskin had a significant impact on Gandhi's thinking; Hobson received an uncharacteristically friendly treatment from Lenin, who relied heavily on Hobson's analysis of imperialism. Yet virtually nothing was heard of them in academic economics.

The next branch off the tree of classical economics was not exactly forgotten. In the hands of Karl Marx, the labor theory of value and other elements of classical economics were combined with ideas from history and philosophy to form a sweeping indictment of capitalism. Production, specifically the labor process, was the focus of Marx's economics, and received far more attention than consumption. However, as Martyn Lee explains, a subtle understanding of commodities and consumption played an important role in Marx's analysis. At the beginning of *Capital*, his magnum opus, Marx introduced the idea of commodity fetishism: In a capitalist society commodities acquire meanings and values unrelated to their actual use, and relations between people as producers are concealed in the "fantastic form" of relations between commodities. This idea has a surprisingly modern ring to it, and has been put to creative use, as Lee demonstrates, in a number of contemporary Marxian interpretations of consumer society. But the modern writers discussed by Lee, examining issues such as the cultural definition of the meanings of goods, the role of advertising, and systems of social control, speak a language that is not often heard or understood within the discipline of economics.

The Rise of Neoclassical Theory

By the late nineteenth century, a specter was haunting classical economics. Most economists were not inclined to identify with proletarian revolutionaries who had nothing to lose but their chains. However, Marxism appeared to be an uncomfortably logical consequence of the theoretical apparatus of Smith, Ricardo, and Malthus. The desire to answer or avoid Marxism contributed to the rise of neoclassical economics, as David Hamilton wryly observes (with the concurrence of Lutz and Lux). Political economy was now replaced by economics pure and simple. Any explicit mention of the labor process was banished, replaced by a vision of production as merely a combination of inputs to yield the maximum profit, rather like assembling a jigsaw puzzle. Consumption was interpreted in a precisely analogous manner, as an assemblage of purchases selected to yield the maximum utility. Since production is only profitable if someone buys the output, producers were described as responding to the commands of "sovereign" consumers. Thus the consumer, not the capitalist, was ultimately in control of the market system.

Although neoclassical theory operates at a high level of abstraction, its origins were undoubtedly influenced by the economic conditions of the time. By the late nineteenth century the development of consumer society, as seen in Part IV, was well advanced. The activity of the consumer choosing among myriad options in the marketplace was becoming more important in reality, making it more plausible for economic theory to focus on consumption. A century earlier, when consumer society was less firmly established, an economic theory of consumption would have seemed beside the point.

The scientific developments of the nineteenth century also played a part in shaping neoclassical economics. Rapid progress in physics, expressed in elegant and powerful mathematical formulations, defined the image of a successful science; the pioneers of neoclassical theory borrowed heavily from the physics of their day.[3] Adam Smith's metaphor of the invisible hand fit comfortably into an analogy with thermodynamics, where individual producers and consumers are seen as particles moving toward equilibrium.

In one crucial area, however, neoclassical theory fell well behind the state of the art. In their understanding of human behavior and motivation, the inner forces driving the economic particles, the early neoclassicals looked back even earlier to the utilitarianism of Jeremy Bentham. Utilitarianism was a hedonistic philosophy that assumed that the goal of society was to make individuals as happy as possible; Bentham asserted that the level of satisfaction, or "utility," of each individual could be added to yield a measure of social welfare. Reliance on utilitarianism had its advantages: The notion that all motives can be reduced to the pursuit of individual pleasure (or "maximization of utility") provides a theory of behavior that is easy to formalize in a mathematical model; the assumption that each individual is the sole judge of his/her own satisfaction leads to a subjective theory of value that is above any suspicions of Marxist implications. However, utilitarianism was incompatible with the understanding of human motivations and behavior developed in the emerging fields of psychology and sociology.

Modern critiques of neoclassical economics are presented in Part VI. For now it is enough to note, as Lutz and Lux do, that some of the founders of neoclassical economics held more complex views of human nature and desires. Alfred Marshall, the creator of the familiar graph of intersecting supply and demand curves and many other fundamentals of modern microeconomics, was a former theology student who was deeply concerned about the ethical implications of economic theory. Marshall believed that it was possible to make a distinction between higher and lower desires; indeed, a hierarchy of more and less urgent wants is one possible basis for the declining marginal utility of consumption. Unfortunately, Marshall concluded that such subtleties could not be incorporated into economics, writing that

> Such a discussion of demand, as is possible at this stage of our work, must be confined to an elementary analysis of an almost purely formal kind. The higher study of consumption must come after, and not before, the main body of economic analysis; and, though, it may have its beginning within the proper domain of economics, it cannot find its conclusion there, but must extend far beyond.[4]

Ironically, Marshall is remembered today for what he referred to as elementary and almost purely formal analysis.

More Than Sociology

The behavioral assumptions of neoclassical theory received somewhat harsher treatment from one of Marshall's contemporaries:

> In all the received formulations of economic theory . . . the human material with which the inquiry is concerned is conceived in hedonistic terms; that is to say, in terms of a passive and substantially inert and immutably given human nature. The psychological and anthropological preconceptions of the economists have been those which were accepted by the psychological and social sciences some generations ago. The hedonistic conception of man is that of a lightning calculator of pleasures and pains, who oscillates like a homogeneous globule of desire of happiness under the impulse of stimuli that shift him about the area, but leave him intact.[5]

For Thorstein Veblen, the neoclassical view of the consumer was already "some generations" out of date in 1898. Veblen argued that "it is the characteristic of man to do something, not simply to suffer pleasures and pains . . . . [Human nature is] a coherent structure of propensities and habits which seeks realization and expression in an unfolding activity."[6]

Veblen is of course famous for the idea of conspicuous consumption, which he introduced in *The Theory of the Leisure Class* (although an earlier economist, John Rae, had presented a similar perspective on luxury consumption[7]). Hamilton reminds us that Veblen was developing a theory of consumption, not just presenting social commentary or satire. For Veblen, goods were both ceremonial and instrumental, yielding both status and use value to their consumers. Over time the ceremonial aspect of consumption could expand indefinitely without producing any net increase in satisfaction, as Veblen so effectively and satirically demonstrated; but at any point in time, there was an appropriate level of status-oriented consumption for each group in society.

Conspicuous consumption was not Veblen's only innovation. He created an evolutionary, institutional theory of economics that differed from mainstream views in countless ways. He offered a feminist interpretation of anthropology and the origins of private property; a critique of absentee ownership, bureaucracy, and militarism; and an admiration of the "instinct of workmanship" and the potential of technology. These and other elements combine to create a strikingly original and thought-provoking theory.[8]

Despite his renown in other fields, Veblen is another casualty of the

Bermuda Triangle of economics. All that remained floating on the surface after his disappearance was the comparatively small school of institutional economics (of which Hamilton is a member); this school draws much of its inspiration from Veblen and is almost entirely ignored by the mainstream of the economics profession. From the vantage point of other disciplines, few economists are as important as Veblen in discussions of consumption; more than one recent writer has simply declared him a sociologist, a reasonable inference from the company he (posthumously) keeps. For the record, Veblen was offered the presidency of the American Economic Association in 1925. Bitter at his lifelong rejection by the profession—he was then 68, in his last year of work—he declined the offer.[9]

Keynes and His Successors

A different analysis of consumption was central to the leading twentieth-century innovation in economic theory. Reflecting on the nature and causes of mass unemployment in the depression of the 1930s, John Maynard Keynes created a new approach to macroeconomics that legitimized government intervention to boost employment. His *General Theory of Employment, Interest, and Money* focused attention on the aggregate propensity to consume, devoting a chapter each to the objective and subjective factors influencing consumption. His principal macroeconomic conclusion in this area, the existence of a stable relationship between changes in national income and aggregate consumption, has prompted extensive theoretical and empirical debate. That debate is not reviewed here since it raises complex technical questions but adds little to the analysis of consumer behavior and motivation.

Keynes had little patience with theoretical deduction that ignored common sense, writing that "extraordinary achievement of the classical theory was to overcome the beliefs of the 'natural man' and, at the same time, to be wrong."[10] He based his work on fresh and perceptive observation of the real world rather than on neoclassical theory; a novel understanding of consumer behavior often seems implicit in Keynes' work, but is never quite spelled out. Since his time, economists have produced numerous more or less tortured attempts at reconciliation of Keynesian macroeconomics with neoclassical models of individual behavior, resulting in a thicket of mathematics at which Keynes himself surely would have been horrified.

According to S.A. Drakopoulos, generations of graduate students may have suffered through this mathematical thicket in vain. Carefully examining some of Keynes' less well-known writings, Drakopoulos demonstrates that Keynes quite emphatically rejected the neoclassical model of behavior and its utilitarian foundations. Unfortunately Keynes offered only scattered comments about his preferred alternative; Drakopoulos argues that those comments are consistent with belief in a hierarchy of wants of differing urgency and importance. A formal model based on such a hierarchy provides a neat explanation of one of Keynes' more puzzling observations, the "stickiness" of prices and wages. Thus an alternative model of consumer behavior may be lurking behind the scenes of Keynesian macroeconomics.

The tumultuous events of the depression and World War II, and the success of Keynesian theory, may have created an opening for new approaches to the economics of consumption in the 1940s and 1950s. The last four articles summarized in this section are leading contributions from that era. While older than other selections included in this volume, these mid-twentieth-century works still represent new frontiers where many economists have not yet dared to go.

James Duesenberry is mentioned by Drakopoulos as the later economist who was closest to Keynes' approach to consumption. Duesenberry began with an empirical puzzle: the decline over time in the amount of savings by households at any constant level of real income. Rejecting much of the neoclassical theoretical apparatus, he took it as self-evident that individual preferences are interdependent, in part socially determined, and subject to learning and habit formation. The result of social interdependence was the "demonstration effect": Contact with superior consumption goods and higher standards of living leads to a desire to increase one's own consumption. Although Duesenberry mentioned in passing that the demonstration effect need not depend on conspicuous consumption, most readers will find echoes of Veblen as well as Keynes in his analysis.[11]

The solution to the empirical puzzle was the "relative income hypothesis": Consumption depends not only on an individual household's income, but on its income relative to others. Duesenberry demonstrated that unconventional hypotheses could be modeled in formal mathematical terms (see the original article rather than the summary). Today, however, he is cited primarily by those who are looking for alternative theoretical perspectives; mainstream economics, with only a few exceptions, was quick to critique and then forget him.[12]

Another approach to formal modeling of alternative theories can be seen in the summary of the article by Harvey Leibenstein. His "bandwagon, snob, and Veblen effects" are simplified models, depicted graphically in the illustrations, of three different ways in which social interaction can alter consumer demand for a good. (All three would have made sense to Veblen, despite the fact that his name appears on only one of them.) Each of Leibenstein's models implies a relationship between price and demand that differs from the standard neoclassical model, for in the latter social interactions do not affect demand curves. Taking Leibenstein's models seriously would require complex, far-reaching changes in the neoclassical theory of consumption; instead, they are more often exhibited as classroom curiosities than used for serious analytical work.[13]

Ragnar Nurkse's *Problems of Capital Formation in Underdeveloped Countries* was an early classic in the new field of development economics. His chapter on consumption, summarized here, is the place where Duesenberry's demonstration effect had the greatest impact on economic theory. Just as Duesenberry had argued that a household consumes more when it comes into contact with higher-income households, Nurkse concluded that the same should be true of nations. Like Duesenberry, Nurkse was concerned about the aggregate rate of savings; inadequate savings and investment were crucial impediments to development. The demonstration effect of American consumption patterns, in particular, seemed to promote consumption and discourage savings in lower-income nations. Thus international inequality was inherently bad for development: The greater the inequality, the greater the force of the demonstration effect. In the postwar era of expanded international travel and communications, Nurkse feared that the demonstration effect would make it impossible for other nations to accumulate enough capital to industrialize. Nurkse's ideas are discussed further in Part IX, in connection with the global aspects of consumer society.

Finally, there is the economist who needs no introduction (in fact, we asked him to introduce us, as seen at the front of this book). *The Affluent Society* is one of the best-known books by John Kenneth Galbraith; its chapters on the nature of private consumption are summarized here. The book as a whole is a remarkably readable treatment of the history of economics and the problems of the American economy. Galbraith argues that it is no longer appropriate for affluent societies to place a priority on economic growth and maximization of output. Overemphasis on production for private consumption leads to too little spending on public goods and services, and too little leisure and economic security, among other undesirable consequences.

Galbraith believes it is obvious that increasing affluence makes the growth of private consumption less urgent. Something unnatural had to happen, therefore, to keep people spending. The villain is the all too visible hand of advertising, creating the demand for new products as part of the process of production. Advertising, Galbraith suggests, is too large to ignore in an analysis of business behavior. And it cannot be considered of great social importance to satisfy desires for products if the desires were created solely by their producers' advertising.

Galbraith studied economics with members of the institutional school, and has always focused on the behavior of corporations and other major institutions. His history of economic thought, in the early chapters of *The Affluent Society*, highlights Veblen as perhaps the most important American economist to date. The chapters on consumption cite Keynes' comments on differing types of wants, and Duesenberry's analysis of the demonstration effect. Galbraith's prose style is lively enough that the publisher felt compelled to warn readers, on the book jacket for the first edition, that "while the author uses criticism, irony, ridicule—and humor—to make his case," nonetheless "it is a carefully reasoned economic treatise." The end result has been one more victim of the Bermuda Triangle: Like Veblen before him, Galbraith is a central figure in discussions of consumption outside economics, and all but ignored within the profession from which he came.

The story of the debate about the neoclassical theory of consumption continues with more recent contributions in Part VI.

Notes

1. Thomas Hobbes, *Leviathan* (1651), quoted in Kassiola, 125.

2. For a related discussion of the same economists, see the article by Gerald Alonzo Smith summarized in Krishnan, Goodwin, and Harris, eds., *A Survey of Ecological Economics.*

3. For a thorough but dense presentation of the influence of physics on economics, see Philip Mirowski, *More Heat Than Light* (New York: Cambridge University Press, 1989).

4. Alfred Marshall, *Principles of Economics* (eighth edition, 1920), quoted in Lutz and Lux, 47. See also Neva Goodwin, *Social Economics: An Alternative Theory. Volume 1: Building Anew on Marshall's Principles* (New York: St. Martin's Press, 1991), and A.M. Endres, "Marshall's Analysis of Economizing Behavior with Particular Reference to the Consumer," *European Economic Review* 35 (1991), 333–341.

5. Thorstein Veblen, *The Place of Science in Modern Civilization*, excerpted in Max Lerner, ed., *The Portable Veblen* (New York: Viking Press, 1948), 232.

6. Ibid., 233.

7. Stephen Edgell and Rick Tilman, "John Rae and Thorstein Veblen on Conspicuous Consumption: A Neglected Intellectual Relationship," *History of Political Economy* 23 (1991), 731–743.

8. For a concise exposition of Veblen's economic system, see E.K. Hunt, *History of Economic Thought: A Critical Perspective* (Belmont, California: Wadsworth Publishing, 1979), 299–327.

9. Lerner, ed., op. cit., 19.

10. Keynes, *The General Theory of Employment, Interest, and Money* (1936), Chapter 23.

11. See Ken McCormick, "Duesenberry and Veblen: The Demonstration Effect Revisited," *Journal of Economic Issues* 17 (1983), 1125–1129.

12. The high point of later mathematical modeling based on Duesenberry's work may have been the series of papers by Robert Pollak in the 1970s, including "Interdependent Preferences," *American Economic Review* 66 (June 1976), 309–320; and "Habit Formation and Dynamic Demand Functions," *Journal of Political Economy* 78 (1970), 745–763. See also the more recent empirical work of George Kosicki, "Income Redistribution and Aggregate Consumption: Implications of the Relative Income Model," *The American Economist* 34 (1990), 40–44.

13. Early papers by Robert Pollak are the most prominent applications of Leibenstein's approach, just as with Duesenberry. See Pollak's "Endogenous Tastes in Demand and Welfare Analysis," *American Economic Review* 68 (May 1978), 374–379; "Price Dependent Preferences," *American Economic Review* 67 (March 1977), 64–75; and other articles cited there.

Summary of

Materialism and Modern Political Philosophy
by Joel Jay Kassiola
[Published in *The Death of Industrial Civilization*
(Albany: State University of New York Press, 1990), 125–149.]

Materialism can mean either a philosophical doctrine or an ethic of acquisitiveness. The latter is central to an understanding of consumerism. Debates over materialism in both senses may be traced back to the contrasting views of human nature held by Hobbes and Rousseau. More recent discussion of acquisitiveness involves analogies to the psychopathology of addiction, and the significance that commodities assume in the eyes of consumers. In fact, an anthropological perspective suggests that, in industrial societies, commodities are desired more for the social values they represent than for any inherent physical characteristics.

Hobbesian Versus Rousseauian Conceptions of Man

Thomas Hobbes, one of the founders of modern political philosophy, prescribed a thorough-going materialism in both senses of the word. More important than his philosophical view of materialism was his idea that competition lay at the heart of acquisitive behavior. This included several elements: individualism and competitive social values, and ceaseless striving for more material acquisition and power to defend against threats to one's past achievements. For Hobbes the acquisition process ends not with satisfaction or satiation but with death.

Jean Jacques Rousseau was perhaps the most penetrating early critic of such views of human nature and society. Rousseau accepted as descriptively true, but prescribed against, the Hobbesian vision of society founded on selfishness and competition. For Rousseau, egotistic individualism is a creation of society, not a part of human nature.

The distinction between natural and unnatural traits, between those desires that ought to be fulfilled and those that ought to be rejected, is a theme of political philosophy stretching back to Plato. It forms the basis for normative discourse about social values. Rousseau's conception of human nature underlies his critique of the competitiveness and alienation of modern society.

Adam Smith took for granted the drive for competitive social recognition, about which Hobbes seemed positive and Rousseau negative, and based his economic theory on it. For Smith, "that great purpose of human life which we call *bettering our condition*" [131] inspires economic activity. Noneconomic motives such as the desire for recognition and status are collapsed into pursuit of material advantage. Acquisitiveness and the propensity to trade are viewed as universal human traits.

When economic activity is based on the competitive pursuit of recognition, then there can never be enough. The desire for "goods of the imagination" is unlimited; the wants of the mind are infinite.[1] As modern as this problem may seem, it has been discussed by philosophers since the days of Aristotle. To the ancient Greeks, *pleonexia*, "the insatiable desire to have more," was a moral and political fault that Aristotle sought to redress in his theory of natural and limited acquisition.

On the Psychopathology of Addiction

The conception of human nature and society as based on unlimited acquisitiveness suggests an analogy to the pathology of addiction. The status-seeking consumer, like the addict, requires bigger and bigger doses to produce the same effect. In the words of Gerald Smith, "We get hooked on economic growth." A book on the subject, by Philip Slater, is entitled *Wealth Addiction*. In a similar vein, Tibor Scitovsky points out that "one reason for the persistence of habits is that once they are established, they become painful to stop."[2] He then applies this finding from experimental psychology to status-seeking consumption.

The addictive nature of consumption may explain the pervasive anxiety, noted by analysts from Hobbes onward, of a society characterized by unlimited competitive materialist values. Once one attains competitive success the greatest fear is of loss, in the sense of downward mobility, if others should get ahead. To protect against the withdrawal symptoms that would accompany a loss of relative status even the successful must continually seek more.

When goods are valued in relative or positional terms, there is no benefit to society from unlimited economic growth. More in an absolute sense does not, in fact cannot, mean more in a relative sense, as has been observed by writers ranging from Epicurus in ancient Greece, to Thorstein Veblen a century ago, and Fred Hirsch more recently. An important related perspective is found in the work of Karl Marx, especially his concept of the "fetishism of commodities" and the nature of goods in general within industrial capitalism. For Marx, individuals in a capitalist market make contact with one another solely through the exchange of commodities. Market value appears to be a relationship between commodities, when in fact it is a relationship between people, especially via the labor they expend in production.

The fetishism of commodities emphasizes the importance of material goods rather than social relations as the primary source of individual welfare. All the social values attached to commodities, such as recognition and competitive success, could be deemed fetishes in Marx's sense: human creations that distort or mystify reality. The pursuit of pure luxurious or positional goods, while millions of other human beings go hungry, is not only unproductive of happiness and a threat to the environment—it is unjust.

It is a mistake to confuse material welfare with human welfare, more broadly defined. There are many needs beyond physiological survival and safety requirements; self-actualization should not be defined in terms of material goods alone. Yet beginning with Hobbes, reductionist materialism has denied the possibility—or even desirability—of material saturation. Central to the materialist's denial of saturation and the resulting endless nature of material wants is the (false) claim that the continual increase in material goods will produce a continuous increase in welfare or happiness.

Industrial Values and Commodities

Another treatment of these issues rejects the materialist approach to consumption in favor of what may be called the anthropology of consumption. In this approach, consumption of commodities is viewed as an information system whereby material possessions make visible statements about the owner's hierarchy of values. Implicitly, this establishes a broader, normative, nonmaterial component to the consumption of material goods, namely a representative or symbolic function.

For example, Leiss argues that every human need has a "symbolic correlate" and is mediated through elaborate patterns of social interactions; neither the material nor the symbolic aspects of needs can be reduced or collapsed into the other. Kelvin Lancaster views commodities as groups of traits, and says that "a producer is ultimately selling characteristic collections rather than goods."[3] If this view is correct, what matters to affluent consumers is not the particular commodities they own, but rather the culturally imputed values reflected by these material goods. A black-and-white television set has diminished cultural value (even if it works perfectly) once the neighbors all have color.

The relationship between the consumer's values and the characteristics of commodities is not a purely individual matter. Although experienced individually, the characteristics consumers perceive in material goods reflect the essential values of their society as a whole. If the society's values are competitive and embody endless, insatiable striving for objectives that are neither inherently desirable nor environmentally sustainable, then those values—and the society built on them—are in danger of extinction and do not deserve acceptance.

Notes

1. Adam Smith, *An Inquiry into the Nature and Cause of the Wealth of Nations,* Book I, chapter 12, Modern Library College Editions (New York: Random House, 1985), 15; cited by Kassiola, 131.

2. Tibor Scitovsky, *The Joyless Economy* (New York: Oxford University Press, 1976); cited by Kassiola, 137.

3. Kelvin Lancaster, "Change and Innovation in the Technology of Consumption," *American Economic Review* 56 (May 1966), 14–23; cited by Kassiola, 146.

Summary of

The History of Economics
from a Humanistic Perspective
by Mark A. Lutz and Kenneth Lux

[Published in *The Challenge of Humanistic Economics*
(Menlo Park, California: Benjamin/Cummings, 1979), 25–55.]

There appears to be little room for a human-centered approach in contemporary economics, which focuses on the dilemma of unlimited wants confronting limited resources. But the science of scarcity has not always been the core of economic thought. This summary traces the concern for human well-being and self-development in the history of economics and describes the emergence of a school of "humanistic economics" in the nineteenth century.

Adam Smith, the founder of modern economics, was in a sense narrowly concerned with material values but recognized that what counted was the material interests of the people at large. His original description of the "invisible hand," in his first classic, *The Theory of Moral Sentiments*, was that the rich "are led by an invisible hand to make nearly the same distribution of the necessaries of life which would have been made had the earth been divided into equal portions among all its inhabitants . . ."[1]

Smith recognized the importance of "moral sentiments" in creating a spirit of good will and reciprocity throughout society. *An Inquiry into the Wealth of Nations*, written in 1776, is infused with the themes of optimism and harmony; self-interest, held in check by competition, will lead to increasing wealth for all.

Yet in the hands of Smith's successors, such as Say, Ricardo, and Malthus, classical economics became increasingly preoccupied with the search for "natural laws" governing the distribution of wealth. For Ricardo and Malthus, those laws led inexorably to immiseration for almost everyone.

Simonde de Sismondi, a Swiss aristocrat, was the first well-known critic of classical economics, writing in the early nineteenth century. In Sismondi's view, the invisible hand of competition did not help workers, but instead produced periodic crises of overproduction and unemployment. Sismondi believed in providing material well-being for all as a necessary basis for moral and intellectual development. He advocated reforms such as shorter working days, abolition of child labor, progressive taxation, and support for the unemployed and the elderly.

John Stuart Mill was the last and most humanistic of the great classical economists. Mill distinguished between the laws of production, which he viewed as immutable scientific truths, and the laws of distribution, which depend on the customs and institutions of society. Mill's ideal was a society "in which, while no one is poor, no one desires to be richer, nor has any reason to fear being thrust back, by the efforts of others to push them forward."[2] Similarly, he remained critical of the individualistic, hedonistic form of utilitarianism developed by Jeremy Bentham.

After Mill, economics branched off in three directions: Marx, humanistic, and neoclassical economics. The work of Karl Marx mixes humanistic and nonhumanistic elements. His early, more humanistic writing argued that the process of human self-realization occurred through the formation of, and conflict among, social classes based on economic position. The whole evolution of capitalism becomes a mere step toward a new system that would allow more self-realization and less alienation. *The Economic and Philosophical Manuscripts*, the most important of Marx's early writings, contains the outlines of an economy of human needs, thwarted by the institutions of capitalism.

In later years Marx turned to the development of "scientific," often quantitative, laws of development of capitalism. The earlier concepts of individual alienation and self-realization vanished into the aggregate categories of class and class struggle. Only after "the expropriators are expropriated"—after capitalism is overthrown and replaced by socialism—will fulfillment be possible for the working class. This reduction of individual needs and values into the domain of group economic self-interest undercuts the humanism of the early Marx.

A contemporary of Marx, John Ruskin, was central to the development of humanistic economics. Ruskin maintained that conventional economic theorizing was logical but uninteresting, since it assumed away all the social aspects of life but treated avarice as the essential, constant human characteristic. He compared it to "a science of gymnastics which assumed that men had no skeletons."[3] Ruskin claimed that commodities have value only to the extent that they satisfy basic human needs; market prices and scarcity often represent capricious desires rather than basic needs.

Real wealth, for Ruskin, had two components: the production of useful things, and the production of the capacity to use them. Human capacity to use and appreciate things is, to a large extent, determined by the nature of work. Thus, Ruskin did not advocate machine production, preferring instead creative, imaginative labor that made beautiful things and enriched laborers' capabilities.

John Hobson carried on and extended Ruskin's work. Hobson identified both immediate physical needs and higher values as contributing to human welfare; both, he believed, were important on a biological basis. Since social cooperation plays so large a part in human life, it must have evolutionary survival value. Therefore an ordered economic system, promoting cooperative behavior, will maximize human welfare. Mass production could efficiently satisfy basic physical needs; but other objectives such as meaningful work, participation in decision making, and economic security were key ingredients of Hobson's good society. Like Sismondi and Ruskin before him, Hobson went almost entirely unrecognized by the economics profession.

Modern neoclassical economics was born between 1870 and 1900, pushing aside whatever was left of humanistic values, and developing mathematical formalisms based on utilitarian calculus. The law of diminishing marginal utility was originally based on Karl Menger's concept of a hierarchy of needs, to be satisfied in order of importance. But in the hands of other economists such as Jevons and Edgeworth, the hierarchy of needs gave way to an unspecified variety of wants, allowing the mathematical treatment of marginal utility to proceed. This not only avoided the value judgments that Menger was willing to make about economic behavior and policy but, more important, provided supporters of neoclassical economics with an alternative to Karl Marx's disturbing variant on classical economics.

With all human needs reduced to the common denominator of utility, the neoclassical school could argue that all economic behavior followed the principle of rational, calculating utility maximization. Many other problems were solved by the same framework. For example, the marginal productivity theory sought to explain the shares of income going to wages, rent, and interest as determined by the contribution that labor, land, and capital made to satisfying the consumer at the end of the line.

Alfred Marshall, the British economist who gave these theories their modern form, had some moral qualms and broader insights, but failed to incorporate them into his economic analysis. Originally a theology student, Marshall was well aware of the moral issues raised by Mill and others; he recognized and wrote about the distinction between basic wants and "efforts and activities" of a higher nature, but judged that economic theory was not yet ready to address such issues. Instead, Marshall formalized the theory of "rational economic man" as a utility maximizer, analogous in detail to the theory of the firm as a profit maximizer.

The most effective critic of the emerging neoclassical theory was Thorstein Veblen, who argued that a person "is not simply a bundle of desires that are to be saturated . . . but rather a coherent structure of propensities and habits which seek realization and expression in an unfolding activity."[4] Consumption behavior of the wealthy and even the not-so-wealthy, said Veblen, is based heavily on the behaviors and reactions of others, not on individuals' independently defined preferences. Consumers in thrall to social trends, fashions, and advertising can hardly be the rational economic men described in textbooks. Yet Veblen's critique, influential in the realm of social commentary, had little or no effect on economic theory.

Conclusions

In summary, humanistic economists have traditionally favored a mode of analysis that can be described as organic, historical, social, and institutionally prescriptive. A preoccupation with the social context involves ethical considerations; humanistic economists never believed that advocacy of social reform was in conflict with their scientific endeavors. Finally, a concern with human welfare led humanistic economists to focus on the role of work as a vehicle to satisfy many human needs directly, and to advocate humanization of the workplace.

Notes

1. Adam Smith, *The Theory of Moral Sentiments*, quoted in Lutz and Lux, 28.
2. John Stuart Mill, *The Principles of Political Economy* (1898), quoted in Lutz and Lux, 32.
3. John Ruskin, *Unto This Last*, quoted in Lutz and Lux, 39.
4. Thorstein Veblen, *The Place of Science in Modern Civilization and Other Essays*, quoted in Lutz and Lux, 49.

Summary of

Capital, Labor, and the Commodity Form
by Martyn J. Lee
[Published in *Consumer Culture Reborn: The Cultural Politics of Consumption* (London: Routledge, 1993), 3–24.]

Karl Marx's critique of capitalism included a provocative discussion of the nature of commodities, but did not address the problems of consumer behavior and motivation. This essay summarizes Marx's view of commodities in a capitalist economy, and reviews the work of more recent authors who have applied a Marxian analysis to modern consumerism.

Marx's Analysis of the Commodity

The uniqueness of human nature, in Marx's view, is that we are not chained solely to basic physiological needs, but are capable of adapting the resources of nature far in excess of our needs. Implicit in this formulation is the concept of culture as based in material production. People express and realize themselves through production, both through what they produce and how they produce it. The activity of labor is the process of realizing human consciousness. That is to say, human consciousness is objectified in the material products of labor.

In capitalism the objectification that is inherent in material production occurs under estranged social conditions. Workers do not retain control of the potential that is embodied in their labor, the potential which Marx termed "labor power." Instead labor power has become a commodity to be bought and sold. The workers now see neither the fruits of their labor nor any reason to work other than to obtain wages.

In precapitalist social systems, production was essentially the production of use values for consumption. However, with the advent of markets and private property, the unity between production and consumption breaks down. Through the dominance of exchange value the producer is separated from the product of labor. The product now confronts the producer as an unrecognizable form in the alien sphere of consumption. This experience of estrangement and alienation was the hallmark of capitalist societies for Marx.

The commodity is the form that material products take in capitalist societies. Commodities possess both use value (the capacity to satisfy some human want) and exchange value (the capacity to be exchanged for other commodities). Use value is a qualitative relationship between objects and human needs, while exchange value is a quantitative relationship between commodities. Marx was concerned with rebutting the notion, fundamental to neoclassic economics, that prices derived from the working of supply and demand based simply on use value. For Marx, exchange value bore no intrinsic relation to use value, but was simply a measure of the amount of labor necessary to produce the commodity. If two commodities have the same price and may be exchanged for each other, they need not be equally useful, but they must embody the same amount of labor.

Marx's theory of value seems to present a paradox. If all commodities are exchanged for equivalent values, how is it possible for surplus value, or profits, to arise in production? The resolution of the paradox lies in the unique nature of labor power as a commodity that can generate more than its own cost of reproduction. Workers must be paid wages sufficient to reproduce their daily life—that is, social or physical subsistence—but labor, unlike other commodities, can yield an increased value when applied in production. Machines alone cannot produce; labor alone can. The product of labor beyond the amount necessary for the workers' subsistence can be appropriated by capitalists, based on their control of the conditions of employment. Any social system generates a surplus beyond what is needed for the reproduction of the lives of the workers; under capitalism that surplus is appropriated as private profit.

How is it that this appropriation of surplus value goes unrecognized by those who are exploited? For Marx, the answer lies in the concept of fetishism, by which he means the way in which social relations appear to be impersonal natural forces. This finds its clearest manifestation in the fetishism of commodities. The exchange values of commodities conceal their basis in labor and appear to be natural facts.

> It is nothing but the definite social relations between men which assumes here for them, the fantastic form of a relation between things . . . I call this the fetishism which attaches itself to the products of labor as soon as they are produced as commodities.[1]

Modern Marxist Perspectives on Consumerism

Writing in the nineteenth century, Marx did not anticipate the consumer society of the twentieth century. Yet a number of more recent writers have drawn inspiration from and extended the Marxian analysis to describe contemporary consumerism.

The starting point for the modern Marxian analysis is the recognition that commodities are presented to us solely in terms of exchange values, with their origins in production obscured. They therefore appear to be objects without any overt social meaning. The function of institutions such as advertising is to define those meanings, a function that Sut Jhally has referred to as the theft and reappropriation of meaning: "The function of advertising is to refill the empty commodity with meaning. . . . Advertising would make no sense if objects already had an established meaning."[2]

Not only advertising, but a whole host of cultural activities and industries can be interpreted as attempts to construct an economy of symbolic or cultural goods that supports the successful reproduction of capitalism. This perspective is taken to an extreme by Herbert Marcuse in *One-Dimensional Man*. For Marcuse, affluence is far from liberating. Working-class acceptance of the modes of relaxation, enjoyment, and consumption prescribed by advertising is proof of capitalism's pervasive social control. Rather than the products of labor being a healthy extension of the self, people themselves are now mere extensions of the products they consume. As people come to recognize themselves in their commodities, the mechanism that ties individuals to society changes, and social control is anchored in the new needs it has produced.

Marcuse's work highlights an issue that is central for other critics as well, namely the loss of the idea that goods embody any real use values. In becoming pure exchange values, the cultural meanings of goods have become malleable, and are based on little other than nonmaterial desires and ideological fantasies. John Berger identifies advertising's imagery and language of sexuality, power, guilt, envy, and glamour as fantasies unrelated to the reality of goods and their consumption. Raymond Williams provides an ironic reversal of the common cliché that modern society is too materialistic. "If we were sensibly materialist . . . we should find most advertising to be of insane irrelevance. Beer would be enough for us, without the additional promise that in drinking it we show ourselves to be manly, young at heart, or neighborly."[3]

The triumph of symbolic and cultural meanings supplied by advertising over the use values of goods is explored by W.F. Haug. He emphasizes that desire and fantasy are founded on the artful appearance of the modern commodity. Beautiful packaging and exterior surfaces are designed to accelerate the rate of sales. The ideal of commodity aesthetics for Haug is to deliver a minimum of use value disguised by a maximum of seductive illusion.[4]

Haug and others assume that behind the cultural and symbolic meanings that goods have acquired lies a natural and unequivocal relationship between needs and use values. This relationship is questioned by the French sociologist Jean Baudrillard, who argues that both needs and use values are historically specific and are inevitably socially determined.[5]

In orthodox Marxism, needs and use values exist separate from or prior to class society, and provide the foundation upon which a utopian system of production could someday be established. For Baudrillard, in contrast, the whole network of social relations of modern capitalist society is inscribed within the realm of consumption. Use, utility, and need are culturally determined and cannot exist independent of society. The fetishism created by alienated social relations is thus able to affect use value as well as exchange value.

Baudrillard's analysis highlights the manner in which commodities serve as culturally defined symbols. Even as utilitarian an object as a washing machine may acquire connotations of comfort and prestige as well as providing laundry services. For Baudrillard the logic of sign values represents the final triumph of capitalism, imposing a cultural order compatible with large-scale commodity production. But in the end, by reducing use value and need to mere functions of the manipulation of sign values, Baudrillard, like those who he criticizes, provides only a narrow perspective on a multifaceted subject.

Notes

1. Karl Marx, quoted in Lee, 14.
2. Sut Jhally, quoted in Lee, 17
3. Raymond Williams, quoted in Lee, 20.
4. W.F. Haug
5. Jean Baudrillard

Summary of

Institutional Economics and Consumption
by David B. Hamilton
[Published in *Journal of Economic Issues* 21 (December 1987), 1531–1554.]

This summary reviews the treatment of consumption in classical and neo-classical economics, and presents an institutionalist alternative based on Thorstein Veblen's analysis.

Jeremy Bentham and His Ghost

Classical economics focused on the problem of increasing production and paid little explicit attention to consumption. Both classical and neoclassical economics sought to demonstrate that prices are based on values—derived from embodied labor in the former case or from subjective feeling in the latter. For the neoclassical school, psychological egoism, in the form of the hedonism championed by Jeremy Bentham, provided an alternative approach to value. For the classical school, work was viewed as painful and the products of work were valuable in proportion to the amount of work that went into their construction.

The problem with the classical economists' labor theory of value was that it led directly to Marxism. "If labor is the ultimate author of all things, then it seems only reasonable that the author should also be vested with ownership. This proposition suggests itself even to sluggish minds; those with more nimble minds can do all sorts of things with it." [1535] Neoclassical economics and its treatment of value and consumption were largely a response to Marx and his elaboration of the labor theory of value. By the 1870s, when Stanley Jevons, Carl Menger, and Leon Walras published their works on marginal utility theory, the first volume of Karl Marx's *Capital* was widely available and becoming influential in the socialist movement.

"The psychology that snatched victory from the Red Baron was itself flawed, however. Hedonism was not acceptable in any other area of social inquiry except economics. Rather than rise to the defense of Bentham, an impossible task, some economists began to deny that psychology was relevant to the theory." [1537] This approach, epitomized in Lionel Robbins' much-quoted phrase, "We take wants as given," was later formalized by Paul Samuelson in the mathematics of revealed preference. Although Galbraith and others have made it clear that wants are not "given," but are shaped by social influences, conventional economics views consumption as the final, external end to economic activity, largely outside the realm of analysis by definition.

Goods as Symbols of Status and as Instruments to Achieve Ends

One of the classic works in institutional economics, Thorstein Veblen's *The Theory of the Leisure Class*, was written as a theory of consumption. Although frequently misinterpreted as solely a satirical social commentary or a description of exceptional behavior, Veblen's work in fact presents an alternative to the hedonistic model of behavior underlying conventional theory.

While neoclassical theory assumes that individuals are always striving to reach (and then, presumably, passively remain at) a static, optimal equilibrium, Veblen viewed human beings as active and evolving. Production and consumption are interrelated, ongoing activities, neither of which is simply a means to an end.

Conventional hedonistic theory treats people as isolated individuals with minimal, narrowly defined influences on each other. Economists are fond of alluding to the story of Robinson Crusoe and his isolated plans and calculations as an illustration of economic behavior. However, all behavior is simultaneously individual and social, and assumes culturally conditioned forms. Viewing consumption from this standpoint, Veblen noted that all actions have two dimensions: one ceremonial and the other technological or instrumental. We use consumer goods both as symbols of status and as instruments to achieve some end.

Veblen's treatment of consumption and status is frequently misrepresented as "keeping up with the Joneses," a nonstop race to outspend each other. In fact, he maintained that everyone is expected to spend on a level commensurate with his or her status. Conspicuous consumption demands "adequate" expenditure but also places limits on that expenditure. To exceed what is called for will attract unwanted attention as surely as will inattention to status-defined expectations.

Style and fashion are tangential to this phenomenon. Veblen contended that the leisure class set styles that were then emulated by others. Items of fashion, losing touch with function, could go out of style quite quickly. Emulation by lower-status groups makes yesterday's fashions no longer stylish for the upper strata.

The ceremonial value of any good depends on its authenticity or appropriateness for particular circumstances. A tuxedo or wedding gown would be out of place at a tennis match. Conformity to social standards begets a certain self-satisfaction, seemingly giving credence to a hedonistic interpretation of behavior; but conspicuous consumption should not be interpreted to mean simply that socially approved spending patterns make individuals happy. Such an interpretation of Veblen and the institutional theory of consumption would be faulty for two reasons.

First, individual feelings are prone to change far more often than social norms of consumption and therefore provide an unstable basis for valuation. Conventional economics has responded to this dilemma by moving even farther away from social analysis, adopting an extreme relativism and refusing to express any judgment on anyone's feelings or preferences. This nihilism resembles the cultural relativism of sociologists and anthropologists, although economists go even further in making truth dependent on the individual rather than on culture.

Second, the utilitarian interpretation of Veblen ignores his understanding of the dual function of consumer goods. If goods were used solely as symbols of status, then conspicuous consumption could be viewed as socially induced irrational behavior, as is sometimes suggested. However, Veblen distinguished between the use of goods to satisfy conspicuous consumption and the use of goods to achieve some instrumental objective. Cars, for example, are simultaneously symbols of status and instruments of transportation. A simple problem (such as physical deterioration of the car) may interfere with both its ceremonial and its technological roles.

Veblen's standard of value was ultimately an instrumental one. Society does care about the instrumental efficacy of goods, as shown for example by the existence of consumer testing organizations. But since status considerations also affect consumer decisions, an institutional theory of consumption cannot link price to instrumental value alone.

Aggregate Consumption Expenditure Does Matter

In conventional macroeconomics, savings is a dynamic force that allows for investment and growth, while consumption is a deterrent to savings. In the institutional view, consumption and savings are interdependent and tend to increase together. Indeed, it is sometimes hard to distinguish one from the other; only in the second half of the twentieth century has economics realized that a consumption expenditure such as education can be treated as investment in human capital. The same is true for expenditures on health and nutrition (food), as well as on other necessities of personal and family life. Since consumption is so closely tied to production, investment cannot be expanded in the long run without a concomitant increase in consumption.

Summary of

Keynes' Economic Thought
and the Theory of Consumer Behavior

by S. A. Drakopoulos

[Published in *Scottish Journal of Political Economy* 39 (August 1992), 318–336.]

Although John Maynard Keynes developed a macroeconomic analysis in which aggregate consumption played a central role, he said little about the microeconomic theory of consumer behavior underlying his work. Subsequently, economists have often taken for granted that Keynesian macroeconomics can and should be integrated with the standard utility-maximizing model of individual consumption. This summary, however, argues that there are signs that Keynes rejected the standard theory of consumer behavior, and that an alternative model of consumer choice can help explain important aspects of Keynesian macroeconomics.

Microeconomic Foundations

An extensive body of literature, beginning in the 1940s and continuing up to the present, attempts to combine Keynes' macroeconomics with the neoclassical framework, and in particular to derive Keynes' aggregate consumption function from a model of individual maximization of expected utility. The possibility that Keynes rejected standard microeconomics is rarely discussed. While Keynesian unemployment is clearly incompatible with the automatic market-clearing mechanisms of general equilibrium theory, economists have often tried to confine the disagreement to that single issue.

The most important exception is James Duesenberry, who attempted to take into account other elements of Keynes' work. Duesenberry recognized the importance of learning, habitual behavior, and preference interdependence in consumption, arriving at a formulation that comes closer than most economists to Keynes' original views.

Keynes and the Utility-Maximizing Model

Although Keynes did not formulate an explicit theory of consumer behavior, several points imply that he rejected the standard theory: his disagreements with the philosophical hedonism underlying the neoclassical model, his ideas on probability and uncertainty, and his expansive views of the motivations for consumption.

The neoclassical theory of the utility-maximizing individual was originally derived from Jeremy Bentham's philosophical hedonism—his "calculus of pleasure and pain." Later changes in the theory, such as the switch from cardinal to ordinal utility, and Samuelson's introduction of revealed preference, never entirely eliminated the marginalist, hedonistic basis for the theory of consumer behavior.

Keynes, however, studied with and was influenced by the philosopher G.E. Moore, a prominent critic of hedonism. Moore, and Keynes, believed that the purpose of life was not the pursuit of pleasure, but of the "Good," an approach that was compatible with idealistic approaches such as neo-Platonism. Keynes explicitly attacked Bentham and his theories, referring to the "Benthamite tradition" as "the worm which has been gnawing at the insides of modern civilization and is responsible for its present moral decay," and commenting on early work in microeconomics, "How disappointing are the fruits, now that we have them, of the bright idea of reducing Economics to a mathematical application of the hedonistic calculus of Bentham."[1]

Keynes also wrote about the theory of probability and uncertainty, and criticized the concept of probability as a numerically measurable frequency—at least for economically important events. The probabilities of future wars, major inventions, or even changes in prices and interest rates, he maintained, were numerically indeterminate or undefinable; such events are uncertain on a deeper level than the outcome of a game of roulette. However, the expected utility model of neoclassical economics, and much of the writing on microeconomic foundations of Keynesian analysis, assumes that future economic events are calculably uncertain, in the manner of games of roulette. In a summary of his views on neoclassical microeconomics, Keynes emphasized the expected utility approach as one of his principal disagreements:

> The orthodox theory assumes that we have a knowledge of the future of a kind quite different from that which we actually possess. This false rationalization follows the lines of the Benthamite calculus. The hypothesis of a calculable future leads to a wrong interpretation of the principles of behavior . . . [2]

Since the future was fundamentally uncertain, Keynes believed that much of human behavior was based on spontaneous urges to action rather than on calculation of mathematical expectation. In the *General Theory*, Keynes asserted that consumption depends on both objective and subjective factors; his list of subjective motives includes enjoyment, shortsightedness, generosity, miscalculation, ostentation, and extravagance.[3]

Indications of Alternative Formulations in Keynes

In the few places where Keynes addressed individual consumer behavior, there are indications of an alternative theoretical approach. His discussion of the propensity to consume assigned an important role to habits; a household will first make the purchases needed for its habitual standard of living, and only then adjust—imperfectly, in the short run—to changes in income. Recalling Keynes' theory of probability, habits, and customs may help individuals cope with the irreducible, unquantifiable uncertainties about the future.

In his analysis of the relation between income and savings, Keynes viewed it as obvious that higher incomes led to a greater proportion of savings, since additional consumption became less urgent once immediate, primary needs had been met. This suggests a hierarchical structure of needs, as found in psychological theories such as Maslow's. A hierarchical structure of needs points to a conceptual framework different from standard utility-maximizing theory—as does Keynes' emphasis on spontaneous behavior and the "animal spirits" of investors.

Possible Alternative Models

A formal model, consistent with Keynes' scattered comments on consumer behavior, can explain some aspects of Keynesian macroeconomics. The existence of a hierarchy of needs suggests that there are consumption thresholds: Below a certain level of food consumption, for example, all available income may be spent on food; above the threshold, food and other goods are substitutes, competing for the consumer's next dollar. This implies that the individual's demand curve for food has a "kink," or corner, when the threshold is reached (when the price is such that the consumer's entire income is just adequate to buy the threshold quantity of food).

Significance for Keynesian Macroeconomics

One of the most important reasons for unemployment in the Keynesian system is wage and price rigidity. The idea of price rigidity has been even more difficult to explain than wage rigidity, and a number of economists have criticized this aspect of Keynes' theory. However, the model of hierarchical or threshold consumption provides a novel explanation for price rigidity. Although the model proposed in the preceding discussion applies only to individuals, mathematical investigations suggest that it is likely to yield kinked aggregate demand curves as well. The standard techniques of microeconomic theory show that, with a kinked aggregate demand curve, it is possible for the profit-maximizing price to remain constant even in the face of significant shifts in supply or demand. This rigidity in prices may also be related to the persistence of habitual or customary consumption in the face of short-run changes, and is similar to the ideas of "shopping based on experience" and "information asymmetry" that have been proposed to explain price rigidity.

> The basic idea here is that Keynes' rejection of the . . . expected utility model which ascribes perfectly optimal choices for economic agents, and his inclination toward the ideas that compose the alternative models that we described, can explain the price or quantity inertia that has been viewed as a mystery by many theorists in the Keynesian model. [333]

Notes

1. J.M. Keynes, *Essays in Biography, Collected Writings X* (London, 1972), 445, 184n; cited in Drakopoulos, 322.
2. J.M. Keynes, *The General Theory and After Part II: Defence and Development, Collected Writings XIV* (London, 1972), 122; cited in Drakopoulos, 324.
3. J.M. Keynes, *The General Theory of Employment, Interest and Money* (London: 1936), 108; cited in Drakopoulos, 325.

Summary of

A Reformulation of the Theory of Saving
by James S. Duesenberry
[Published in *Income, Saving and the Theory of Consumer Behavior* (Cambridge: Harvard University Press, 1949), 17–46.]

James Duesenberry's classic work on consumption proposes a model of consumer choice based on social interdependence and habit formation, tests the model against the available macroeconomic evidence, and speculates about the implications of the model for other areas of economics. This is a summary of the third chapter of the book, in which Duesenberry formulates his model of consumer choice. Portions of the chapter dealing with macroeconomic analysis of savings have been omitted.

In the conventional economic analysis of consumer choice, changes in behavior can only be explained in terms of shifts in preferences, a subject about which economists have little to say. The alternative pursued here is to make some definite, though general, assumptions of a psychological and sociological nature in order to model the interdependence of consumer choice.

Nature of Consumption Choices

If we ask why consumers desire the things they buy, the answer on one level is obvious. Some goods and services are purchased to maintain physical comfort, others such as transportation may be necessary for work, or used to maintain social status or to provide pleasure. Nearly all purchases are made ostensibly "either to provide physical comfort or to implement the activities which make up the life of our culture." [20]

The same needs can be met by goods of higher or lower quality. There is widespread agreement about the ranking of different automobiles, houses, and other goods in terms of quality. An improvement in the standard of living often consists of satisfying the same needs with higher quality goods.

The Process of Choice

Consumers do not consider a menu showing the prices of all available goods and services, and make their selections from it, as assumed by marginal utility theory. The principal choice made by consumers is to vary the quality of goods and services they purchase. Such decisions are not made simultaneously from a listing, but rather individually, as the need arises. The connection between different decisions and the budget constraint is conveyed through learning and habit formation. A consumer who spends too much on one item learns that he runs out of money before the end of the pay period, and regrets having made lower-priority purchases earlier in the period. Eventually the consumer achieves a habitual consumption pattern that leads to no regrets. When an individual's income decreases, this process is repeated until a new, lower consumption pattern becomes habitual.

The Drive Toward Higher Consumption

The drive toward continual improvement in the quality of consumption goods leads people to work hard and yet save little of their income. At the same real income level, households saved more in the past than they do today. It is easy to see why consumption increases when income does; but why does consumption increase over time even at a fixed income level?

The habits that govern consumption are a compromise between the desire for higher-quality goods and either the limitations of income or the desire for savings. However, each contact with higher-quality goods "is a demonstration of the superiority of these goods and is a threat to the existence of the current consumption pattern." [26] If other people's consumption levels rise, each household will have more frequent contact with high-quality goods, increasing the strength of the impulse to buy them; the result is an increase in spending at the expense of saving. This can be called the "demonstration effect."

The Social Significance of Consumption

Thus far the impulse to increase expenditure has been based on the perceived superiority of higher-quality goods for fulfilling existing needs. But when the pursuit of a higher standard of living becomes an end in itself, it provides an even stronger drive to increase expenditure. As the attainment of increased standards of living becomes a generally recognized social goal, individuals are socialized into recognizing its importance; a certain degree of success in reaching this goal becomes essential to the maintenance of self-esteem.

While some other societies attach prestige to the acquisition of certain completely useless objects, we gain self-esteem by buying a Buick instead of a Chevrolet. Virtually everyone has contact with people of slightly higher as well as lower status than themselves, and receives frequent reminders of the goods that provide higher status. "Our social goal of a high standard of living, then, converts the drive for self-esteem into a drive to get high quality goods." [31]

It seems quite possible that above some minimum income level, a consumer's satisfaction depends purely on a comparison of his consumption to a weighted average of other people's consumption (with the weights reflecting the degree of contact and other factors), rather than on his absolute level of expenditure.

Interdependence, Savings, and Taxation

How is the decision about savings affected by the social interdependence of consumer choices? The savings decision represents a choice between present and future consumption. All of the factors that make current consumption depend on relative rather than absolute expenditures are equally applicable to future consumption. Thus the entire process of choice between current and future consumption can be recast in terms of relative income. That is, the consumer cares primarily about the ratio of his own consumption and income levels to the weighted average of other people's consumption.

The result is that consumption is proportional to income, and the rate of savings is independent of the absolute level of income. If everyone else's consumption and income increase by a fixed factor, any individual consumer will be induced to increase consumption at the same rate. The rate of savings will be unchanged.

This model of interdependence in consumption would lead to changes in many areas of economic theory. For example, assume that the satisfaction of every consumer is negatively affected by the consumption of those with higher incomes, but unaffected by those with lower incomes. Under this assumption, a progressive income tax is required to achieve efficient allocation of resources, with the optimum tax rates determined by the strength of the dependence effect. Such a tax will decrease the inequality of incomes and consumption, and cause a reduction in paid work and an increase in leisure—changes that are necessary to achieve a welfare optimum in a world of interdependence.[1]

Note

1. Mathematical proof of these assertions is presented in a later chapter of the same book: James Duesenberry, *Income, Saving and the Theory of Consumer Behavior* (Cambridge: Harvard University Press, 1949), 96–102.

Summary of

Bandwagon, Snob, and Veblen Effects in the Theory of Consumers' Demand
by Harvey Leibenstein
[Published in *Quarterly Journal of Economics* 44 no. 2 (1950), 183–207.]

Conventional economic theory assumes that any individual's desires for goods are independent of the actions and desires of others. More formally, individuals' demand curves are assumed to be independent of each other, so that the market demand curve for a commodity can be regarded as a simple sum of individuals' demands at each price. But that assumption is often inappropriate; in many important instances, individual demands interact with each other. This summary presents three instances of such behavior and demonstrates graphically how the theory of consumer demand can be extended to accommodate interactions between individuals.

Demand for a commodity may be either functional, based on qualities inherent in the commodity itself, or nonfunctional, based on other factors. Nonfunctional demand is often a result of external effects on consumers—cases in which the actions of others make a commodity seem more or less desirable. Three types of such external effects may be distinguished: the "bandwagon" effect, in which an individual's desire for a commodity is increased by other people's purchases; the "snob" effect, in which an individual's desire for a commodity is decreased by other people's purchases; and the "Veblen" effect, or conspicuous consumption, which makes a commodity seem more desirable simply because it is more expensive.

The Bandwagon Effect

Some commodities appear more desirable because others are buying them; this is the bandwagon effect. In such cases, an individual demands more of the commodity, at any given price, if she expects that others will buy more of it. The bandwagon effect can be analyzed diagrammatically, as shown in Figure 1.

Prices for a commodity are plotted on the vertical axis and amounts sold on the horizontal. The lines D^a, D^b, D^c are three of the many fixed-expectation demand curves that could be drawn, each based on a different assumption on the part of consumers about what everyone else is buying. D^a shows the amount that could be sold at each price if the consumers on the average believed that a units would be sold in total. Notice that this is only a "virtual" demand curve; the only price on it that can actually be realized is the price at which a units will be sold, indicated here by p^a. At any higher price, sales will be less than a, while at a lower price they will be greater. But in either case, sales will differ from the expected amount, a, leading consumers to revise their expectations; as a result, the D^a demand curve will no longer apply. The other curves, D^b, D^c, and countless others that could be drawn, are interpreted similarly for consumers' expectations of sales of b, c, or other amounts.

The only points on the diagram that can be experienced more than transiently are those such as E^a, E^b, and E^c, for which the expected sales lie on the corresponding demand curve and so can be realized without falsifying the demand curve's expectations. The curve D^b connecting these realizable points is the effective demand curve; it shows all the price-quantity combinations that can actually be realized more than instantaneously.

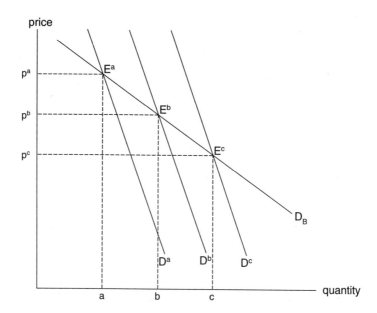

Figure 1. The Bandwagon Effect Demand Curve.

The Snob Effect

Some commodities appear less desirable because others are buying them; this is the snob effect. In such cases an individual demands less of the commodity, at any given price, if he expects that others will buy more of it. The diagrammatic analysis of the snob effect is shown in Figure 2.

The logic of this diagram is almost identical to that of Figure 1 for the bandwagon effect. Again, the fixed-expectation demand curves D^a, D^b, D^c are based on the assumption that total sales will be a, b, or c, respectively. The points E^a, E^b, E^c are the only ones that can be realized more than transiently; hence D_S is the effective demand curve. The difference is that in the case of the bandwagon effect, increases in expectations from a to b to c shift the fixed-expectation demand curve to the right—everyone wants more if they think everyone else is buying more. However, in the case of the snob effect, increases in expectations shift the fixed-expectation demand curve to the left—everyone wants less if they think everyone else is buying more. As a result, the bandwagon effect demand curve, D_B in Figure 1, is flatter than the fixed-expectation curves D^a, D^b, D^c, while the snob effect demand curve, D_S in Figure 2, is steeper than the fixed-expectation curves.

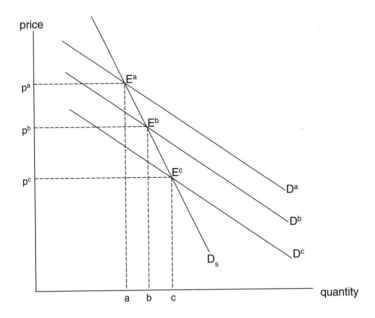

Figure 2. The Snob Effect Demand Curve.

The Veblen Effect

Veblen's theory of conspicuous consumption is a complex and subtle sociological construct, of which only one aspect is addressed here: its effects on the demand curve. Conspicuous consumption implies that the utility derived from a commodity depends not only on the inherent qualities of the good but also on the price paid for it. The higher the price paid, the more desirable the good appears for purposes of conspicuous consumption.

In this case the diagrammatic analysis in Figure 3 again involves fixed-expectation demand curves D^a, D^b, and D^c; but this time they are based on expectations that the price will be p^a, p^b, and p^c, respectively. As the expected price increases, the demand curves shift to the right, reflecting the increased desire for conspicuous consumption of the good at a higher assumed price. However, it is again clear that only one point on each demand curve can be experienced more than transiently, namely the one corresponding to its assumed price. The points E^a, E^b, and E^c thus trace out the Veblen effect demand curve D_V.

Unlike the bandwagon and snob effect demand curves, the Veblen effect demand curve can be either positively sloped (as shown in Figure 3) or negatively sloped, depending on the relative strength of conspicuous con-

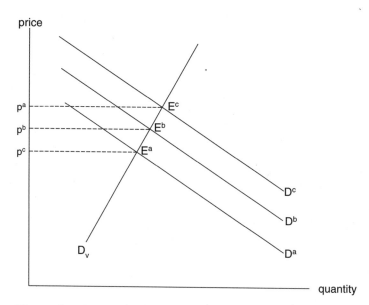

Figure 3. The Veblen Effect Demand Curve.

sumption and ordinary price effects. In fact, it is possible for a single good to have a demand curve that is positively sloped in some regions and negatively sloped in others. The Veblen effect may predominate only at high prices, for example, while other effects may predominate at lower prices.

Summary of

The Standard of Living and the Capacity to Save
by Ragnar Nurkse

[Published in Problems of Capital Formation in Underdeveloped Countries (New York: Oxford University Press, 1953), 57–81.]

Many poor nations face a vicious cycle that prohibits development: A very low income level provides little basis for savings; without savings there is little capital and therefore low productivity; low productivity perpetuates low income. "Outside help" in the form of foreign assistance is often seen as the only viable way to interrupt this cycle. However, both the absolute and the relative level of real income determine the capacity to save; as such, income disparities among nations may create additional problems that can render this option ineffective. This summary applies the economic theory of the "demonstration effect" to explain why many poor nations are not generating the sufficient capital to have productive economies.

A New Theory of Consumption and Saving

James Duesenberry's theory of consumer behavior is relevant in the context of both the individual consumer and international economic relations. Duesenberry states that consumers become dissatisfied with their current goods when they learn about superior modes of consumption. When this dissatisfaction arises, new wants are triggered and the propensity to consume shifts upward. This "demonstration effect" could have a profound effect on the choice between consumption and saving. According to Duesenberry, a consumer's savings is not only a function of his or her absolute income, but also may be dependent on the ratio of personal income to the superior income level of peers. Therefore it can be assumed that greater income inequality may reduce, rather than increase, savings ratios.

Growing Awareness of Advanced Living Standards

The consumption levels of individual countries may be interrelated in a similar way, whereby the demonstration of superior modes of consumption in some countries can lead to the imitation of those modes of consumption in others. Thus, the awareness of new goods and new modes of consumption tends to raise the general propensity to consume. Whether these new goods are imported or produced domestically, they become part of the nation's standard of living.

This phenomenon is most evident in the widespread imitation of American consumption patterns. This could be, at least in part, a function of American advertising ("the art of creating new wants"). America's influence through the demonstration effect is particularly felt in the poorer two-thirds of mankind, but it is also evident in places such as Western Europe.

The international demonstration effect is a product of two factors: the size of the disparities in real income and consumption levels, and the level of awareness of those income disparities and consumption levels. Discrepancies in living standards are vast, but just as important are individuals' increasing awareness of them. American cinema, radio, and travel technology have accelerated this awareness, especially among urban upper-income groups (thanks to mass media and education).

Imitation of American consumption patterns can, however, limit the supply of investable funds—required in order to copy production methods—by curbing people's willingness to save. Some might argue that new wants would motivate people to work harder and produce more, thereby making necessary funds available. However, the demonstration effect suggests that the extra units of output would in fact be used for immediate consumption, rather than saved.

Effects on the Propensity to Save

The international demonstration effect can hinder the development of lower-income nations by adversely affecting both voluntary personal savings rates and an entire nation's ability to utilize taxation as a means of compulsory savings. When both the relative and the absolute level of real income is considered, it is clear that diminishing the income gap between nations, not the injection of foreign aid and investment, may prove to be the best way to aid underdeveloped countries. However, one must also consider the possibility that even if the income gap between nations remains constant, a rise in the living standards of individuals in both poorer and richer countries may increase the level of communication between the two, thus strengthening the demonstration effect.

Saving is made even more difficult in underdeveloped nations because of the international disparities in income that cause individuals to consume immediately (because of the tension, impatience, and restlessness that result from the demonstration effect), rather than postpone that consumption in the form of saving. The conventional economic view of the demonstration effect would be a positive one, implying that the knowledge and imitation of superior modes of consumption would make prosperity spread. For the reasons outlined above, however, "A high income and consumption level in an advanced country can do harm in that it tends to reduce the domestic means of capital formation in the underdeveloped countries; it puts extra pressure on countries with relatively low income to spend a high proportion of it." [68]

Effects on the Balance of Payments

Balance of payments disequilibria are indirectly related to levels of productivity. The demonstration effect suggests that there could be a natural tendency for disequilibrium between countries with wide income differentials. This is not, as might be assumed, because an advanced country's high productivity allows it to export cheaply, thus giving it a comparative advantage; rather it is because the poorer country's propensity to consume (as explained by the demonstration effect) is greater than its ability to produce. International income gaps can therefore have a direct impact on the balance of payments because the demonstration effect in such cases greatly increases the demand for imported goods.

Summary of

The Imperatives of Consumer Demand and the Dependence Effect

by John Kenneth Galbraith

[Published in *The Affluent Society* (Cambridge: The Riverside Press, 1958), 152–160.]

> Were it so that a man on arising each morning was assailed by demons which instilled in him a passion sometimes for silk shirts, sometimes for kitchenware, sometimes for chamber pots, and sometimes for orange squash, there would be every reason to applaud the effort to find the goods, however odd, that quenched this flame. But should it be that his passion was the result of his first having cultivated the demons, and should it also be that his effort to allay it stirred the demons to ever greater and greater effort, there would be question as to how rational was his solution. Unless restrained by conventional attitudes, he might wonder if the solution lay with more goods or fewer demons. [153]

This selection, from one of the classic critiques of consumer society, explains why conventional economic theory has so little to say about the origins and importance of consumer demand. It offers an alternative perspective in which production itself gives rise to demand for the goods that are produced. In recognition of the unique clarity of Galbraith's prose style, most of this summary consists of direct quotes.

The Imperatives of Consumer Demand

A high and rising level of production is widely viewed as desirable. "There remains, however, the task of justifying the resulting flow of goods. Production cannot be an incidental to the mitigation of inequality or the provision of jobs. It must have a *raison d'être* of its own. . . . The rationalization begins with the peculiar urgency of production not to society but to economic science. . . . All existing pedagogy and nearly all research depend on it. . . . Anything that increases the product from given resources increases welfare. It is important that it be done. Here is the anchor. To cast doubt on the importance of production is thus to bring into question the foundation of the entire edifice." [139–141]

"Once students were attracted by the seeming urgency of economic problems and by a sense of their mission to solve them. Now the best come to economics for the opportunity it provides to exercise arcane mathematical skills. Could this mean that society itself is losing the sense of urgency of the economic problem? Does it mean that there is now a subjective realization that increased product is being used to serve rather unimportant ends?" [142–143]

"The theory of consumer demand . . . is based on two broad propositions. . . . The first is that the urgency of wants does not diminish appreciably as more of them are satisfied or, to put the matter more precisely, to the extent that this happens it is not demonstrable and not a matter of any interest to economists or for economic policy. . . . The second proposition is that wants originate in the personality of the consumer or, in any case, that they are given data for the economist. The latter's task is merely to seek their satisfaction. He has no need to inquire how these wants are formed. His function is sufficiently fulfilled by maximizing the goods that supply the wants." [143–144]

Economic theory has long relied on the principle of diminishing marginal utility to explain relative prices: The more you already have of something, the less you will pay for a little more. This appears to imply that, as real incomes rise, the additional wants being satisfied are of diminishing urgency. But economic theory has explicitly rejected this implication, at least since the days of Alfred Marshall. It is taken as axiomatic that only consumer behavior, not states of mind, can be studied, and that intertemporal comparisons of consumer satisfaction are impossible.

"The notion of diminishing utility still serves its indispensable purpose of relating urgency of desire and consequent willingness to pay to quantity. . . . Hence the greater the supply the less the willingness to pay for marginal increments and hence the demand curve familiar to all who have made even the most modest venture into economic theory. But, at the same time, the question of the diminishing urgency of consumption is elided. . . . On the yield of satisfactions from [a growing stock of consumer goods over time] the economist has nothing to say." [149–150]

The Dependence Effect

"The notion that wants do not become less urgent the more amply the individual is supplied is broadly repugnant to common sense." [152] Yet the notion is hard to disprove in the absence of firm grounds for intertemporal comparison of states of mind. However, there is a flaw in the argument that affluence does not reduce the urgency of desires. "If the individual's wants are to be urgent they must be original with himself. They cannot be urgent if they must be contrived for him. And above all they must not be contrived by the process of production by which they are satisfied. . . . One cannot defend production as satisfying wants if that production creates the wants." [152–153]

"That wants are, in fact, the fruit of production will now be denied by few serious scholars." [154] Keynes commented on the existence of needs based purely on the emulation of others while Duesenberry developed a theoretical analysis of such needs. "The even more direct link between production and wants is provided by the institutions of modern advertising and salesmanship. These cannot be reconciled with the notion of independently determined desires, for their central function is to create desires—to bring into being wants that previously did not exist." [155]

Advertising expenditures "must be integrated with the theory of consumer demand. They are too big to be ignored. But such integration means recognizing that wants are dependent on production. . . . It recognizes that production, not only passively through emulation, but actively through advertising and related activities, creates the wants it seeks to satisfy." [156] "A man who is hungry need never be told of his need for food. . . . [Advertising is] effective only with those who are so far removed from physical want that they do not already know what they want. In this state alone men are open to persuasion." [157–158]

Conclusions

In summary, "as a society becomes increasingly affluent, wants are increasingly created by the process by which they are satisfied." This may operate passively through suggestion or emulation, or actively through advertising and salesmanship. "Wants thus come to depend on output. In technical terms it can no longer be assumed that welfare is greater at an all-round higher level of production than at a lower one. . . . There will be frequent occasion to refer to the way wants depend on the process by which they are satisfied. It will be convenient to call it the Dependence Effect." [158]

"Among the many models of the good society no one has urged the squirrel wheel." [159]

PART VI

Critiques and Alternatives in Economic Theory

Overview Essay

by Frank Ackerman

Faith in the market is one of the most powerful forces in the world today. It has succeeded where Napoleon and Hitler failed, in conquering the vast expanse of Russia. In America it is fast sweeping away the remaining icons of an earlier faith in government intervention and social welfare. The central doctrine of the new faith, the creed of the bourgeois jihad, emerges from neoclassical economics and its claims of the "optimality" of market outcomes. The optimality of the market rests squarely on the theory of consumer behavior. That theory in turn is built on a series of debatable assumptions, as suggested by the following catechism:

Why is the market a good thing?
Because it promotes freedom and efficiency.

Freedom and efficiency for what?
Freedom to satisfy consumer desires as efficiently as possible.

What do consumers want?
Individual, marketable goods and services for themselves and their families.

How much do they want?
More. Their desires are insatiable.

Why should these desires be satisfied?
Consumer desires exist prior to and external to the economy; there is no scientific basis for questioning their urgency or validity. Satisfaction of individual consumer desires is what happiness and human well-being consist of; the economy has no other goal.

How can we tell if consumer desires are satisfied?
Consumers are rational and well-informed. Give them the freedom to choose and they will always select the most satisfying available option.

Accept all this on faith, and the rest follows. Indeed, the discipline of economics is amply supplied with consumer researchers who do accept the traditional theory, raising only the most narrowly technical questions and modifications.[1] Yet as seen in Part V, economics also has a long, if often ignored, history of dissent from the dominant view of consumption. That history has continued up through the present. This part summarizes the work of eight authors writing from the 1960s through the present, all seeking in different ways to reform the prevailing economic theory of consumer behavior. The later portions of this essay also address the leading mainstream innovation in consumer theory, Gary Becker's household production model.

Rearranging the Big Picture

The first three articles included here provide critiques of the underlying behavioral assumptions of the neoclassical theory of consumption. Bodies of thought as diverse as marketing studies, feminist theory, and philosophy, as well as economics itself, lead to arguments that basic changes are needed in the standard picture of consumer choice.

Our first critique comes from an unlikely source: the field of marketing studies. Raymond Benton, Jr., begins where Part V ended, with the views of John Kenneth Galbraith. Marketers often share Galbraith's premise that advertising can shape consumer preferences, but object to his conclusion that wants created by advertising are not urgent to satisfy. Logic is on Galbraith's side, says Benton, but it is no surprise that marketers resist a logical argument that undercuts the meaning of their work. Benton's discussion of consumer choice continues with a look at William Leiss (see summaries in Parts I and VII), who suggests that in an ever-expanding market economy consumers do not have the time or ability to learn exactly what they want or how satisfying particular goods will be. Benton concludes with the implications of such critiques for the ethics of marketing: Some things that can be sold should not be; society should be structured to provide other satisfactions such as meaningful work, rather than simply maximizing private consumption.

Another important critique of mainstream economics comes from the small but growing number of feminists in the profession. Economics is overwhelmingly a male profession, a fact that is sometimes attributed to its highly mathematical nature and the well-known gender difference in mathematics training. However, the proportion of women in economics is even lower than in university mathematics departments.[2] Paula England suggests that many basic economic assumptions reflect a male bias. Feminist theory, with roots in and respect for women's traditional roles, would lead to a very different approach to the economics of consumer choice. Those who are used to an empathic, emotionally supportive role would not assume that it is impossible to make interpersonal comparisons, nor that people are unchanged by social influences, nor that perfect selfishness is the rule in public life. Yet these unempathic assumptions, which England ascribes to a traditionally male model of the "separative self," are fundamental to neo-classical theory.

The predominance of stereotypically male, "separative" behavioral assumptions has not led the neoclassical theory of consumption to scientific success. In a brief but perceptive review, Benjamin Fine and Ellen Leopold observe that there is no distinct theoretical model of the consumption process in economics; instead, there is only a clone of the more detailed and fruitful model of production. Consumers are treated as little make-believe firms, combining purchased inputs to maximize utility (profit, in the original) subject to a budget constraint. Yet changes in profit are observable, while changes in utility are not. Issues such as monopoly and oligopoly, barriers to entry, information costs, and the role of advertising therefore are taken up in the analysis of production, but not in the theory of consumption, which retains its pristine abstraction. As in their other contributions summarized in this volume (see Parts IV and VII), Fine and Leopold call for an integrated analysis of production and consumption as a single system, paying attention to the specific social and institutional relationships that shape economic reality.

The impossibility of observing or measuring utility was an awkward feature of neoclassical theory from the start. Economists sought to escape this embarrassment by showing that the same results could be obtained without measurement of utility. For instance, it turns out that no harm is done to the theory by switching from cardinal to ordinal utility; instead of saying that good A yields, for example, 17 utils of satisfaction and good B only 11, it is enough to say that good A yields more satisfaction than good B. Measurement of utility appeared to be banished entirely in the "revealed preference" approach introduced by Paul Samuelson in the 1940s. For Samuelson, no utility function, cardinal or ordinal, was required; it was enough for consumers to reveal their preferences via their actual choices in the marketplace. So long as the choices satisfied a few innocuous-sounding consistency conditions, the standard results of consumer theory could still be derived. Revealed preference remains part of the technical presentation of neoclassical theory to this day, seemingly freeing the theory from its dependence on outmoded utilitarian ideas and unobservable quantities alike.

But as Amartya Sen has demonstrated,[3] Samuelson's sleight of hand conceals, but does not remove, the restrictive and unrealistic assumptions that neoclassical theory makes about the basis for consumer behavior. Since preferences cannot be directly observed, the assertion that behavior reveals preferences cannot be tested; it is either a tautology or a controversial assertion about human motivation, depending on the meaning of "preferences." If preferences are defined as that which behavior reveals, then revealed preference is true by definition, and uninformative. If your preferences are interpreted as "that which makes you more comfortable, all else being equal," as is often suggested in discussion of consumer choice, then Sen's arguments demonstrate that behavior need not reveal preferences. Both the well-known example of the prisoners' dilemma and contemporary questions of environmental policy provide cases of behavior that cannot be understood in the neoclassical framework. Sen suggests that such cases are common enough to require revision of the theory to include the effects of loyalty and beliefs, altruism, and other forms of social interdependence.

The preoccupation with motives of self-interest is often described by economists as a point of realism, an example of positive rather than normative analysis. Sen has shown, however, that there are plenty of other important patterns of behavior available for "positive" analysis. By refusing to include other motives, economists may become creators as well as chroniclers of self-interest. Empirical research has found that studying economics makes college students more selfish and less cooperative.[4]

Inside the Mind of the Consumer

Although the articles discussed thus far provide solid critiques, they only hint at alternatives to neoclassical theory. The next three explore in greater depth the implications of more realistic models of consumer desires and the goods that satisfy them.

Tibor Scitovsky, after a long and successful career in mainstream economics, became increasingly concerned about the failure of economists to incorporate the findings of modern psychology into their theories. His book on the relationship between the two fields, *The Joyless Economy*, is indispensable reading for anyone interested in new approaches to consumption. The first half of the book is summarized here. While economics assumes that there is a single thing called consumer satisfaction, psychology, according to Scitovsky, makes a sharp distinction between two different types of satisfaction—comfort and pleasure. Pain is not, as common figures of speech suggest, the opposite of pleasure; it is more properly speaking the opposite of comfort. There may even be a physiological basis for the distinction between comfort and pleasure: Scitovsky connects comfort to an optimum level of stimulus, and pleasure to changes in the level of stimulus. The complex and sometimes surprising relationship between comfort and pleasure provides a much richer and more specific theory of human wants than is normally seen in economics.

When he turns to the implications for economic theory, Scitovsky asks two principal questions: which desires are insatiable? and which satisfactions are necessarily obtained through purchases in the marketplace? For conventional theory, these questions scarcely arise: Enough wants are insatiable, and enough satisfactions are obtained in the market, to keep economists busy studying them; the nature of desire and of nonmarket activity are said, by definition, to be the subject matter of other disciplines.

For Scitovsky, in contrast, virtually all desires for comfort are satiable. Discomforts are specific things, and it is easy to tell when they have been eliminated. There is a limit to how "not-hungry" you can be. The one exception harks back to Veblen and conspicuous consumption. The comfort of belonging, of winning social acceptance, can require indefinitely rising consumer expenditure as the price of status. In addition, pleasure, which often results from novelty, can and often does absorb ever-increasing expenditures. As yesterday's novel pleasures become today's habits and tomorrow's socially defined necessities, maintaining the same level of pleasure requires new levels of consumption.

If insatiable demand only arises in status-seeking and pleasure-seeking consumption, it seems less urgent to satisfy it with incessant growth in production. This is all the more true since many of life's most important satisfactions, as Scitovsky persuasively argues, come from nonmarket activities or from the process of work rather than from consumption of purchased goods and services. Thus Scitovsky's plaintive concluding question: Whatever made us believe that income yields happiness?

For Scitovsky, examination of the nature of desires led to the conclusion that money cannot always buy happiness. Another underground classic of economic theory from the 1970s came to the same conclusion, based on an analysis of the nature of commodities. In *Social Limits to Growth*, Fred Hirsch introduced the concept of positional consumption and relentlessly spelled out its implications for consumer welfare. One part of Hirsch's book is summarized here, and another in Part II. Positional goods are ones that are desirable because they are scarce; examples include paintings by old masters, antiques, and exclusive access to scenic land. Jobs at the top of a hierarchy have a similar positional value, as do any goods that are desired because others cannot obtain them.

Unlike ordinary goods, the supply of positional goods cannot be increased when demand rises. There is no way to create more Rembrandt originals, beachfront properties, or jobs in the top 10 percent of the labor force. While positional goods quickly become status symbols that play a role in conspicuous consumption, the two categories are not identical:

Some status symbols, such as fashions in cars or clothing, are manufactured goods that can be produced to satisfy rising demand.

Hirsch sees positional consumption as pervasive, affecting many decisions about schools and suburban locations, for example. When demand for positional goods rises, there are three possible responses: congestion or crowding; increased screening and positional competition (greater educational credential requirements for top jobs); or price increases. The result for society is at best a zero-sum game, with one person's loss being another person's gain; nothing of value is created in response to the increased demand.[5] In contrast, increased demand for ordinary goods leads to increased production of things that people want. Hirsch's rather somber conclusion is that measures of aggregate output and growth are flawed or ambiguous if they confuse rising expenditures on positional goods with rising supply and demand for ordinary goods. When income gains are spent on positional goods, there is no reason to believe that there has been a net increase in social welfare.

Robert Frank draws on the work of Hirsch and Duesenberry to create a useful formal model of positional consumption and the demonstration effect. If people engage in positional competition, for example striving to ensure that their children are better educated than anyone else's, the result is more work and less leisure than people would really prefer. A cooperative outcome, which the market alone cannot achieve, would yield greater satisfaction than unfettered competition. However, positional consumption is rational for the individual; in cases of limited information, employers and others may interpret some forms of consumption as a proxy for ability.

The bias in favor of visible, positional expenditures has exactly the same effect on savings as Duesenberry's demonstration effect. Frank argues that economists abandoned Duesenberry's model too quickly, and that empirical evidence supports Duesenberry rather than rival theories of savings.[6] Finally, Frank shows that the existence of positional consumption and the related bias against both savings and leisure imply that people can be made better off by many forms of regulation, including pensions and other forced savings requirements, limits on hours and conditions of work, and taxes on positional expenditures.

Characteristics and Household Production

While the work of Scitovsky, Hirsch, and Frank suggests one approach to developing new economic models of consumption, another new approach has arisen and won far greater recognition within the mainstream of the economics profession. Almost simultaneously, in the mid-1960s, Kelvin Lancaster, Richard Muth, and Gary Becker each proposed similar rethinkings of the theory of consumer behavior. Conventional theory posits a direct relationship between goods and consumer satisfaction; consumers know exactly how much they will enjoy each potential purchase. In contrast, the new approach holds that consumers want something—experiences, satisfactions, characteristics of goods—that is obtained from their purchases. A third term is added to the equation; an intermediate arena of analysis opens up between the consumer and the purchased good.[7]

This approach seems to offer the potential for incorporating many insights from other fields concerning the complexity of the relationship between the consumer and the commodity. Yet the technical, mathematical presentation of the new model may have discouraged dialogue with noneconomists. Both Muth and Becker use the language of a household production process: The household combines purchased inputs (groceries, cooking utensils, fuels) and household labor to produce desired outputs (meals). The image of the consumer as a firm, discussed by Fine and Leopold, is now full-blown, and the extensive mathematical apparatus used to analyze ordinary production can be applied to household production as well. Becker highlights the analogy with a uniquely obscure choice of terminology, referring to the outputs of household production as "commodities" analogous to those produced by businesses. The reader who lacks an English-to-Becker dictionary must remember that what Becker calls commodities are what others would call experiences or satisfactions, while the commodities visible to the rest of us are, for Becker, inputs purchased by households in order to produce commodities.

Although Becker has become the most famous for application of the new approach, Lancaster's version is by far the most accessible. The less technical one of Lancaster's two original articles is summarized here. Lancaster's starting point is his objection to one aspect of standard consumer theory: No one can possibly know exactly how satisfying each available good or combination of goods will be; when new goods appear, as they constantly do, there is no plausible way for consumers to revise their preference rankings to encompass the expanded set of possibilities. The alternative, says Lancaster, is to recognize that consumers want characteristics that they obtain from goods: flavors, textures, and nutrition from food; fuel-efficient transportation, comfortable seating, and visible status from cars.

To complete his model, Lancaster assumes that consumer demand for characteristics resembles the conventional picture of demand for goods—consumers know exactly which characteristics they want, and always want more. The relationship of characteristics to goods, on the other hand, is a simple technical matter. Twice as much of a good always produces twice as much of each of its characteristics. This model turns out to lead to sweeping changes in the theory of consumption.

The best-known implications of the model are shown in the figure reproduced in the summary. If multiple goods can supply the same characteristics, then different bundles of goods may be more or less efficient in yielding the desired characteristics. In terms of the analogy to production, varying combinations of inputs can be more or less efficient in yielding profits. But consumption is different, as Lancaster points out. No competitive process forces consumers to be efficient in producing the desired characteristics; it is possible to go through life as an inefficient consumer. At the very least, this is a strong argument for better consumer information services and product labeling requirements. The efficient pattern of consumption can change when prices shift; a good that was formerly inefficient and chosen by almost no one can, with enough of a price cut, move onto the "consumption efficiency frontier" and become much in demand.

Lancaster's model is in some ways a revolutionary departure from neoclassical theory, but in other ways still closely connected to it. His idea that people consume characteristics rather than goods has been cited in a number of recent studies of consumption (including several presented in this volume), but usually only as an image or metaphor; application of Lancaster's model in any detail is much less common.[8]

A handful of articles by economists have questioned Lancaster's theoretical approach, challenging two assumptions in particular.[9] First, do all characteristics of goods produce positive satisfactions? If some goods have negative characteristics, or if satiation sets in so that some characteristics can switch from positive to negative sources of satisfaction (if one glass of wine with dinner is pleasant, how about five?), the model breaks down. However, the same is true of neoclassical theory, which must assume that all consumers obtain either positive or at worst zero satisfaction from each good. Second, is the satisfaction obtained from characteristics independent of the goods that deliver them or the combinations in which they are experienced? Does one cup of tea with lots of sugar followed by another cup with none produce the same satisfaction as two cups of tea with a little sugar in each? If the satisfactions obtained from goods are inseparable package deals, then there are limits to the usefulness of the characteristics framework. Lancaster's work is more reasonably seen as a provocative starting point for the development of a new theory than as its final form.

On the other hand, if one avoids the specificity of Lancaster's model, the danger is that the new analysis of consumption can become general enough to explain everything and nothing. This danger can be seen in the problematical development of the other variant, the household production model. Of the three founders of the new approach, Muth went on to other pursuits almost immediately, as did Lancaster after a few years. Becker, however, has continued to apply and extend the new approach; he won the Nobel Prize in Economics in 1992 in part for his far-reaching applications of the household production model.[10] In Becker's hands the subject matter of economics has expanded to include education, discrimination, crime, marriage and divorce, childbearing, and much more. He has shown that the theoretical apparatus of selfish, rational maximization can produce explanations of a wide variety of behavior, often through use of the household production model.

The meaning of this model can be seen in an article in which Becker and a co-author argue that it is rarely necessary to assume that consumers' tastes have changed.[11] In cases where preferences appear to have shifted, Becker et al. prefer to say that the technology of household production has changed, while the satisfaction obtained from homemade "commodities" (i.e., experiences) may have remained constant. Thus a growing appreciation of and desire for a particular style of music reflects a change in the technology of production of the commodity "music appreciation." Pursuit of new and changing styles means that a changing technique is needed to produce the commodity "distinction." Advertising, unfairly accused of manipulating consumer preferences by Galbraith and others, actually provides information about new technologies that have become available to produce commodities such as "prestige." Perhaps most remarkable is the discovery that even addiction to harmful drugs does not represent a change in tastes—it is merely a change in the technology that the household uses to produce the commodity "euphoria."

In each case a story can be told about the change in the household production function that produces the apparent change in tastes. The household can then be described as acting rationally, meaning that it is engaging in utility maximization, with unchanging tastes for some hypothetical, unobservable commodities. In effect this is mathematical deconstruction: pick a behavior, tell a story about what it might be maximizing. Recent work along these lines has focused on the problem of addiction, spelling out the argument that this, too, is a rational choice, not a change in tastes. The addict, equipped with high-powered intertemporal maximizing capabilities, recognizes that use of an addictive substance today will make it more enjoyable to continue using the same substance in the future.[12]

If this is still economic theory, as its supporters frequently assert, then economists have emulated the American soldiers in Vietnam who had to destroy a village in order to save it. Not much is left standing of the edifice of neoclassical economics, once Becker's firepower has established that virtually any possible behavior represents utility maximization. The entire

structure of belief in the market rests on results derived from very strict behavioral assumptions: Consumers must act as if their preferences for purchased goods and services are exogenous and independent of social interaction. If, following Becker, a consumer's purchases are influenced by what
others purchase, in the "production" of stylish distinction, or if current
consumption alters one's own future purchasing patterns, in the production of music appreciation or chemical euphoria, then the proof of the optimality of market outcomes has been demolished. All that remains is the
formidable mathematical weaponry, the curious commitment to modeling
the combination of rationality and selfishness, and the attitude of smugness
about what has been accomplished.

One might excuse all this if the household production model achieved
great insights into consumer behavior. However, as Paula England points
out, Becker makes trivial and stereotypical assumptions about the dynamics
within the household. There is a single head of household, repeatedly referred to as male, who is efficient at earning money and completely altruistic about sharing it within the family.[13] England objects that it is unreasonable to expect the same person to be perfectly selfish in the market and
perfectly unselfish at home. Either the external greed should affect family
life, or the internal altruism should affect public life; in fact, spillovers do
occur in both directions. Unfortunately, a model that begins with trivially
stereotypical premises is in danger of ending with conclusions such as

> A person may be well-read (i.e., have read the recent books generally be-
> lieved to be important), but if his time is valuable in the market place, it is
> much more likely that his spouse will be the well-read member of the fam-
> ily.[14]

The Economics of Addiction

Addiction provides an interesting puzzle for a modern theory of consumption. If consumption makes people happy, how do we explain addiction?
Becker's answer is the simplest: Addiction also maximizes happiness. Most
others find this hard to stomach. Some propose drawing a distinction between dangerously addictive substances, which should be prohibited, and
normal substances that are not addictive. However, there is more of a slip-
pery slope than a clear line in the sand. Scitovsky observes that people in
love display many of the characteristics of addiction. Some people act as if
they were addicted to harmless hobbies, favorite performers, television
shows, or video games. Mild addictions to tea and coffee are legal, as are
more dangerous addictions to gambling, alcohol, and tobacco.

Several interesting articles in the *Journal of Consumer Research* have speculated about what might be called the pathology of consumption, including impulse buying, compulsive consumption, and addiction.[15] These articles suggest that there are many self-destructive motives and patterns of consumption, even among those who are not using dangerous substances. Far from being prohibited, self-destructive consumption may be encouraged by some aspects of consumer society.

The quest for alternative explanations of addiction brings up the last article summarized here, by George Akerlof. It is one of the best examples of what might be called "nearly neoclassical" analysis, in which the objective is to relax as few as possible of the constricting assumptions of conventional theory and still obtain more realistic and useful models. Akerlof models the almost universal behavior of procrastination, in which immediate costs and benefits appear just a little more salient than deferred ones. Slight overestimation of immediate impacts can lead to progressively larger deviations from optimal outcomes, as Akerlof demonstrates with several examples.

Akerlof maintains that this leads to a far more plausible story about addiction than Becker's model: Addicts frequently know they should quit, and mean to do so very soon. But the benefits of one more high, and the costs of quitting today rather than tomorrow, loom too large for them, just as the merits of procrastinating about more humdrum affairs do for everyone. In an interesting extension of his analysis (in parts of the article not summarized here), Akerlof proposes that it can explain pressures for social and political conformity, including a number of major political events. For the theory of consumption, Akerlof's model implies that public intervention to override private market choices can be beneficial, not only in cases of dangerous addictions, but also in many other situations where procrastination leads to harmful undervaluation of future outcomes.

Thus there are many critiques and innovations, but not yet a coherent alternative to the neoclassical theory of consumption. Many of the authors discussed here have, like the famous critics of the past, been more widely read outside of economics than inside. No suggestion is being made that the views presented here could be combined into a single alternative; for example, satiation of consumer desires is a normal state of affairs for Scitovsky, but difficult to incorporate in Lancaster's model. Much more remains to be done; the frontier of the economic theory of consumer behavior is far from closing.

Notes

1. See the extensive literature cited in Richard Blundell, "Consumer Behavior: Theory and Empirical Evidence—A Survey," *Economic Journal* 98 (1988), 16–65.

2. Julie Nelson, "The Study of Choice or the Study of Provisioning? Gender and

the Definition of Economics," in Marianne Ferber and Julie Nelson, eds., *Beyond Economic Man: Feminist Theory and Economics* (Chicago: University of Chicago Press, 1993), 23–36.

3. Amartya Sen, "Behavior and the Concept of Preference," *Economica* 40 (August 1973), 241–259.

4. Robert Frank, Thomas Gilovich, and Dennis Regan, "Does Studying Economics Inhibit Cooperation?" *Journal of Economic Perspectives* 7 (1993), 159–171.

5. For this reason, Scitovsky has argued that in terms of macroeconomic effects, positional consumption is more like an unproductive form of savings than like ordinary consumption. See "Growth in the Affluent Society," in Tibor Scitovsky, *Economic Theory and Reality: Selected Essays on Their Disparity and Reconciliation* (Aldershot, UK: Edward Elgar, 1995).

6. See also George Kosicki, "A Note About Savings as a 'Nonpositional Good,'" *Eastern Economic Journal* 14 (1988), 271–276.

7. Richard Muth, "Household Production and Consumer Demand Functions," *Econometrica* 34 (1966), 281–302; Gary Becker, "A Theory of the Allocation of Time," *Economic Journal* 75 (1965), 493–517; and see discussion of Lancaster below.

8. For a relatively recent application of the Lancaster model to technical problems see Larry Jones, "The Characteristics Model, Hedonic Prices, and the Clientele Effect," *Journal of Political Economy* 96 (1988), 551–567.

9. See Reuven Hendler, "Lancaster's New Approach to Consumer Demand and Its Limitations," *American Economic Review* 65 (1975), 194–199; Brian Ratchford, "Operationalizing Economic Models of Demand for Product Characteristics," *Journal of Consumer Research* 6 (1979), 76–85; George Ladd and Martin Zober, "Comment" following Ratchford's article; and sources cited by these authors.

10. See the review articles prompted by the Nobel Prize in *Scandinavian Journal of Economics* 95 (January 1993): Agnar Sandmo, "Gary Becker's Contributions to Economics," and Sherwin Rosen, "Risks and Rewards: Gary Becker's Contributions to Economics."

11. George Stigler and Gary Becker, "De gustibus non est disputandum," *American Economic Review* 67 (1977), 76–90.

12. See Gary Becker, Michael Grossman, and Kevin Murphy, "Rational Addiction and the Effect of Price on Consumption," *American Economic Review* 81 (1991), 237–241, and earlier articles cited there.

13. Several short articles in the May 1994 *American Economic Review* discuss alternative analyses of the economics of family life; none have yet approached the popularity of Becker's model among economists.

14. Stigler and Becker, op. cit., 88.

15. Dennis Rook, "The Buying Impulse," *Journal of Consumer Research* 14 (1987), 189–199; Thomas O'Guinn and Ronald Faber, "Compulsive Buying: A Phenomenological Exploration," *Journal of Consumer Research* 16 (1989), 147–157; Elizabeth Hirschman, "The Consciousness of Addiction: Toward a General Theory of Compulsive Consumption," *Journal of Consumer Research* 19 (1992), 155–179.

Summary of

Alternative Approaches to Consumer Behavior
by Raymond Benton, Jr.

[Published in *Changing the Course of Marketing: Alternative Paradigms for Widening Marketing Theory Research in Marketing* Supplement 2 (1985), 197–218.]

This summary contrasts three distinct paradigms for understanding consumer behavior: the traditional approach of the economics and marketing professions; the critical approach exemplified by the work of Galbraith and Leiss; and an ethical approach that develops norms for the evaluation and reform of current patterns of both consumer and business behavior.

Traditional Approach to Consumer Behavior

The study of consumer behavior has not progressed steadily or continuously. Rather, certain concepts have burst onto the field, each initially arousing great excitement but then subsiding. Such changes in the popularity of individual ideas do not constitute a true paradigm shift, but are variations within an established paradigm. Although the field of consumer behavior is multidisciplinary and more or less fragmented, research is framed in terms of an underlying theoretical model—usually derived from economics.

The assumptions of the economic model, as described by researchers in consumer behavior, include the following seven statements:

(1) Consumers derive satisfaction from consumption.

(2) Consumers seek to maximize satisfaction given their income constraints.

(3) Consumers act rationally.

(4) Consumers are capable of judging their tastes and preferences for all products under consideration.

(5) Consumers use the price of a good as the sole measure of the sacrifice involved in obtaining it, and price plays no other role in the purchase decision.

(6) Consumers develop individual preferences, which are not influenced by other people.

(7) Consumers' wants and needs are unlimited and can never be fully satisfied.

In consumer behavior studies, references to the economists' model are often followed by criticisms, but not by alternatives.

The Critical Approach to Consumer Behavior

The most familiar social critic of our marketing system is John Kenneth Galbraith. Much of Galbraith's criticism is levied against economic theory, especially the theory of demand. Galbraith and marketers agree that it is unrealistic to assume that consumers develop their own tastes and preferences without influence from others. The function of modern marketing activities, Galbraith charges, is to create wants that did not previously exist.

Marketers' reactions to Galbraith have been complex; they agree with his basic premise, but claim that his understanding of needs is inadequate and that he misapplies economic concepts to social and moral issues. One marketing critic argued that Galbraith's distinction between natural and artificial needs was inaccurate, since the means of satisfying even the most basic needs are socially determined by advertising and other socialization processes. However, this is, in fact, an affirmation rather than a rejection of Galbraith's position.

Striking parallels can be found between some of Galbraith's strongest statements and the marketing literature. Yet marketers cannot extol Galbraith too highly without eliminating their own sense of meaning or purpose since his analysis undermines the traditional rationale for capitalism.

William Leiss differs from Galbraith in that he attacks the seventh assumption listed above—the doctrine of human insatiability—which both economics and marketing find to be indispensable; it serves both as an explanation and a justification of business activities. Leiss does not question the idea that needs and wants in the abstract are insatiable. What he examines is the assumption that needs and wants *for material things* are unlimited and insatiable. Leiss begins by rejecting the dichotomy between real and manipulated, or true and false, needs. For him, every need has both a material and a symbolic aspect. Since commodities are intended to satisfy needs, they too embody a duality of material and symbolic meanings—an idea that is familiar to marketers.

Consumers are faced with the problem of matching their needs to the ever-growing number of goods available to satisfy them. Attaining the "craft knowledge" necessary to be a competent consumer is difficult because production processes and products have grown so complex. Consumer decision making becomes an increasingly random process, as the number of decisions increases while the time spent on any one decision decreases. The result is that individuals become confused about the nature of their own needs and about the goods that are supposed to satisfy them.

This state of confusion does not arise because people fall victim to artificial wants. Nor is it a result of advertising, although ambiguous advertising messages about wants and their satisfaction may compound the confusion. The confusion originates in the consumption process itself, compelling people to search more extensively for the commodities that will yield satisfaction. Far from a rational search for information followed by a selection of the product that offers the greatest satisfaction, "the image that emerges is one in which people pursue income to buy more and more things to consume and, feeling dissatisfied but not quite sure why, set out after still more income and consumption." [209]

Ethical Approach to Consumer Behavior

Increasingly, some marketers ask not only "Can it be sold?" but also "Should it be sold?" The latter question implies the existence of ethical criteria by which marketing can be judged.

The traditional ethical stance has been that anything people buy contributes to their well-being, because people know what they, as individuals, want—and because those wants are insatiable. Questioning whether something should be sold, however, implies that under some conditions marketing managers should limit consumers' freedom of choice or redirect purchasing into more socially meaningful areas. This discussion has begun to find its place in the pages of marketing textbooks.

As E.F. Schumacher points out, qualitative, not just quantitative, development is needed in order to choose the direction of society's movement as well as measure its speed. The search for the necessary qualitative concepts can begin with the existing body of social criticism. For example, consumer researchers could respond to Leiss' challenge and analyze the relationship between commodities, health, and human and social well-being. Critical analysis of the formation of consumers' tastes would also be helpful.

Another place to begin is with the presumption, dating back to Adam Smith, that consumption is the sole purpose of production. Work is generally held to have no intrinsic value, and is therefore only a means toward the end of acquiring consumption goods; the possibility of meaningful or satisfying work is therefore impossible. But as Hannah Arendt has shown, every European language has two unrelated words for labor and work. The former connotes pain and trouble; the latter, creativity.

All societies have attempted to eliminate labor; in our era, mechanization of the productive process has all but destroyed work as well.

> If work is a necessary attribute of the human personality while limitless consumption is not, and if the degradation of work is inseparably related

to the economy of high mass consumption, then an increasing awareness of the meaninglessness of consumption may be expected to have its reflection in an increased awareness of the importance of "work". . . . We are dealing with whole people and not split personalities that are at one moment consumers, at another moment citizens, and at still another moment workers. [214]

Summary of

The Separative Self:
Androcentric Bias in Neoclassical Assumptions
by Paula England

[Published in *Beyond Economic Man: Feminist Theory and Economics*, eds. Marianne A. Ferber and Julie A. Nelson (Chicago: University of Chicago Press, 1993), 37–53.]

Neoclassical economic theory rests on explicit assumptions about individual consumer behavior and on implicit assumptions about the nature of families as economic units. This summary examines the androcentric (male-centered) biases in both the explicit and implicit assumptions of the neoclassical model and suggests ways in which a feminist theory of economic behavior would differ from the standard approach.

Three of the basic assumptions of neoclassical economics are that (1) interpersonal utility comparisons are impossible, (2) tastes are exogenous and unchanging, and (3) individuals are selfish (their utility functions are independent) in market interactions. These assumptions flow from a separative model of human nature which presumes that people are autonomous, impervious to social influences, and lacking in emotional connection and empathy. A fourth, usually implicit assumption is that, within their families, individuals are not selfish, but behave altruistically. These assumptions may be called androcentric because they take the existing system of gender relations for granted, and are biased in favor of men's interests within that system.

Feminist Critiques of Theoretical Biases

Virtually all feminist views share the belief that women are subordinated to men to a degree that is morally wrong and unnecessary. But beyond this basic point there are significant differences within feminist theory. One body of thought emphasizes the exclusion of women from traditionally male activities and institutions, calling for equal participation in those areas. A second body of feminist thought emphasizes the devaluation of traditionally female activities and traits, calling for greater recognition and reward for women (and men) in those areas. The two approaches are by no means incompatible, but they disagree on some issues.

The second feminist emphasis leads to a distinction between a "separative" self and a self that is emotionally connected to others. Honoring and maintaining emotional connections is an important factor in the activities traditionally assigned to women; such activities have been deprecated or ignored in the academic theory of many disciplines, including economics.

Applying the Feminist Critique to Neoclassical Economics

The feminist critique of the separative-self model applies to all four of the assumptions of neoclassical economics identified above. The contrast between the assumptions about the market and the family reveals the pervasive gender bias of the standard approach to economics.

The first assumption, the impossibility of interpersonal utility comparisons, rests on the notion that utility is purely subjective, hence unmeasurable. In the absence of interpersonal comparisons, all that can be said is that, if a voluntary exchange occurs, both individuals must be better off as a result (if not, the trade would not occur). But the impossibility of interpersonal comparison is a result of assuming a separative self. If economic theory were to assume the sort of emotional connection that facilitates empathy, then interpersonal comparison of emotional states would be viewed as possible; while practical measurement problems may arise, these do not constitute a theoretical impossibility. The neoclassical rejection of interpersonal comparison is congruent with conservative positions on distributional issues. If it is impossible to say that those at the bottom feel worse than those at the top, then there is no theoretical basis for supporting egalitarian redistribution of resources. This discourages analysis of gender-based and other inequalities.

A second assumption of the neoclassical model is that individuals' tastes or preferences cannot and need not be explained by economists. Rather, tastes are inputs into economic models. Some economists have argued that there is no need to assume much variation in tastes between individuals; others believe that individuals' tastes differ. But, for either group, preferences are assumed to be unchanged by market interactions. The "new home economics," which purports to explain family behavior in market terms, must therefore assume that tastes are exogenous to family interactions as well. But if consumer preferences do not arise at least in part from market or family influences, where do they come from?

The strict assumption of exogenous tastes implies that consumer behavior is not influenced by interactions with coworkers (because the labor market must not affect tastes) or with neighbors (because the housing market must not affect tastes). If economics is to explain family life, then the choice of a spouse in the "marriage market" must also leave consumer preferences unchanged. Such imperviousness to social influence is obviously implausible, ignoring research in fields such as psychology and sociology that have studied the processes of socialization and value formation.

A third neoclassical assumption is that people act in a self-interested way in the market. Self-interest need not imply selfishness; altruists may be seen as maximizing their own utility, which is in part a function of others' happiness. However, the standard formulation of the neoclassical model also assumes independent utility functions—which amounts to selfishness in practice. Altruism would imply that one individual's utility depends on what makes another happy, violating the assumption of independence. The assumption of selfishness flows from the separative-self model. It hardly describes the behavior of anyone who genuinely cares for another.

It is common to assume selfishness between employers and employees in labor markets. But collective action involves selective altruism toward other group members. For example, collusion to maintain gender discrimination in employment involves within-sex altruism on the part of men.

A fourth, often implicit assumption of the neoclassical model is that a family acts as a single unit in the marketplace, with perfectly altruistic internal allocation of resources. This is made explicit in the "new home economics" pioneered by Gary Becker. In Becker's model the head of the household is an altruist who controls the distribution of all family resources. Becker never discusses the effects of differential power within the household, but does analyze the efficiency of a household division of labor in which men are the primary income earners. Thus he explores the advantages but not the disadvantages for women of the traditional division of labor.

While family life is undoubtedly more altruistic than relations with others, the extreme bifurcation of assumptions about the two spheres is not believable. If people are purely altruistic within the family, it should spill over into market behavior. Likewise, if people are purely selfish in the market, this habit is bound to affect their behavior at home. Sociological research has found that, in cases of marital disagreement, men's wishes prevail more often in families where men earn a higher proportion of total household income. Thus selfishness and market inequalities enter the supposedly altruistic inner life of the family. The new home economics ignores the issues of power that arise from the traditional division of labor.

Conclusion

The separative-self model, as used in economics, glorifies men's autonomy outside the family while giving them credit for altruism within the family. Unexamined assumptions about gender roles lead to a disjuncture of views about the household and the market, resulting in an inability to see how conventional arrangements perpetuate women's systematic subordination to men.

> Correcting the biases discussed in this paper will generate models in which separation and connection are variable; this variation needs to be explained within both households and markets. Although these new models may entail a loss of deductive certainty, they will illuminate rather than ignore gender inequality in the social and economic world. [50]

Summary of

Economics, Psychology, and Consumer Behavior
by Ben Fine and Ellen Leopold[1]
[Chapters 4 and 5 of *The World of Consumption* (London: Routledge, 1993), 46–61.]

Neoclassical consumer theory is not only self-contained relative to other social sciences, it is also akin to a sealed unit within economics itself. It is partly for this reason that there has been negligible advance in the economics of consumer behavior over the past century. [51]

The neoclassical theory of consumer behavior is subtle and sophisticated in mathematical technique, but rigid and impoverished in social content. These chapters relate the theory's rigidity to its exact parallel with the much better developed theory of production, and discuss the failure of economics to learn from other disciplines.

The Unchanging Economics of Demand Theory

Consumer theory within economics has remained essentially unchanged since the marginalist revolution of the 1870s. The theory focuses on the rational economic individual who optimizes subject to constraints. It is exactly analogous to the theory of the firm, which assumes that producers maximize profits subject to constraints. Like firms combining inputs to yield outputs, individuals combine purchases to yield utility. The formation of specific tastes, habits, and preferences is usually said to fall "outside economics."

The economic approach to consumer behavior is justified on the grounds that it analyzes the rational, systematic part of demand; deviations from optimizing behavior are often referred to as "irrational." Moreover, modern economic theory formally addresses bundles of commodities, so even individual acts of obtaining and enjoying goods become irrelevant.

The economics of consumer behavior has been concerned with deriving empirical laws and theoretical regularities from demand systems. For example, Engel's Law hypothesizes that the poorer a family, the greater the proportion of income spent on food. Subtle relationships of symmetry and other mathematical patterns have been deduced from abstract systems of demand curves. Yet such analyses ignore behavior other than individual utility maximization, and refuse to explore the origins of changes in preferences. The idea that consumers make decisions independently of one another is taken for granted, and social factors that might influence consumption are frequently ignored.

Not surprisingly, the resulting theory of demand is purely formal. Nothing is said about the specific uses of goods, or even broad categories of goods such as food and clothing. The mathematical parallel to the theory of supply is exact:

> Conceptually, individual consumers can be interpreted as if they were entrepreneurs producing utility, rather than output, as efficiently as possible. The strict parallel highlights the extent to which neoclassical economics lacks a distinct theory of consumption. [51]

Yet there is a greater depth and variety of economic analysis around problems of supply. Issues such as the role of advertising are more at home in industrial economics, as part of the theory of the firm, than in demand theory. Competitive mechanisms that can lead to changes in the number of participants in the market are assumed to be at work in production but not in consumption. There is no analogue on the demand side to the theories of monopoly and oligopoly, or of managerial motivation, which examine important deviations from the pure competitive model on the supply side.

The Isolation of Economics

Developments in the theory of supply, specifically in the theory of advertising, are of potential relevance to consumption. One strand of analysis treats advertising as an accumulated fixed cost of production, which can act as a barrier to entry. Another approach examines the role of information, modeling "rational" behavior under conditions of asymmetric information.

But such models have little contact with analyses of consumer response to information developed in other disciplines.

Theoretical advances in economics have generally had little impact on the understanding of consumption in other disciplines. Sociology and anthropology have examined the influence of social factors such as family, class, status, and lifestyle and considered the ritual and symbolic significance of consumption. Psychology has analyzed a broad range of individual motives for consumption and considered the possible meanings of the consumption experience. Yet virtually all theories of consumer behavior fail to analyze the effect of the system of production on the consumption process. Meanwhile, "the role of economics for the theory of consumer behavior has been to provide an increasingly irrelevant core of rational, optimizing behavior." [54]

Attempts to combine disparate economic and noneconomic approaches have produced the discipline of economic psychology, which focuses on consumer behavior. Yet this hybrid has been unable to advance much beyond its parents' accomplishments. On the one hand economic psychology often retains the narrow focus of economists on the allocation of scarce resources to competing ends. On the other hand, when broader motivational factors are admitted, the theoretical coherence of economics is simply swamped by exhaustive lists of possible influences on demand.

The nature of commodity relations as a social system, and the influence of production on consumption, must be considered in any discipline that seeks to create an adequate analysis of consumer behavior.

Note

1. This summary omits the authors' detailed discussion of psychological theories of consumer behavior.

Summary of

The Psychology and Economics of Motivation
by Tibor Scitovsky
[Part I, Chapters 2–7 in *The Joyless Economy*
(New York: Oxford University Press, 1976).]

These chapters, the first half of Scitovsky's major work on the economics of consumer society, review findings from psychology and present their implications for the economic theory of consumer behavior.

Between Strain and Boredom

Economics and psychology shared a common intellectual ancestry in eighteenth-century philosophy, but have diverged almost totally since then. Examination of what psychologists have learned about human behavior can enrich economic theory.

Early psychological theory assumed that specific drives, such as hunger, provided the motivation for human behavior. This approach has been supplanted by a focus on the general level of arousal or excitement. Physiological indicators such as brain waves (measured with an electroencephalograph), blood pressure, and heart rate provide quantitative evidence of changes in arousal. The efficient performance of any task requires an appropriate level of arousal, often differing by task. Increased arousal leads to greater efficiency up to a point, but too much can lead to stress, anxiety, and consequent decrease in efficiency.

More important for economics is the fact that the level of arousal has much to do with general feelings of well-being, and thus with motivating behavior. Excessive stimulation is unpleasant, but so is a prolonged lack of stimulation. Thus there is an optimum level of total stimulation and arousal, in the sense that it gives rise to a feeling of comfort and well-being. This optimum is not constant; for example, it varies over the course of the day with changing levels of wakefulness. But at any point in time, stimulus below the optimal level gives rise to boredom, while an excess over the optimal level creates strain, fatigue, or anxiety.

Attempts to reduce excessive arousal often, though not always, involve basic biological needs. Pain, hunger, lack of sleep, and other physiological deprivations increase arousal, and the obvious responses to these deprivations lower arousal. Thinking about future deprivation can also cause arousal, motivating such behavior as shopping for food even when one is not hungry, or saving for retirement.

The Pursuit of Novelty

"What does an organism do when all its needs are satisfied, all its discomforts eliminated?. . . . Perfect comfort and lack of stimulation are restful at first, but they soon become boring. . . . While discomfort is usually specific and is fully relieved only by satisfying the particular need causing it, boredom is general and can be escaped through a great variety of activities." [31] Physical exercise is stimulating; so is mental exercise, or even seemingly useless or unmotivated exploration of the environment. A moderate level of novelty is pleasant, but too much can become overwhelming or frightening. Numerous experiments with animals and human subjects show a preference for an intermediate level of novelty and complexity in the environment, with a taste for greater complexity growing over time as novelty wears off.

Similarly, a moderate level of threat or appearance of danger, as in suspense novels, amusement park rides, and so on can be pleasantly stimulating, while a greater actual danger would not be. We continually receive far more sensory information than our brains can process; the arousal caused by threats or dangers helps us focus on what is important in the environment, screening out much of the huge potential overload of information. The combination of familiarity and novelty may play the same role in general; for instance, in a new piece of music, "the melody itself must provide some redundancy by belonging to a familiar musical style, though it must deviate from that style enough to avoid sounding hackneyed." [50] The background of redundancy facilitates the act of focusing on the pleasing component of novelty.

Comfort Versus Pleasure

Pleasure is different from the mere absence of pain or discomfort. It is possible, though not common, to feel pleasure and pain simultaneously. Physiological experiments have shown that feelings of comfort and discomfort have to do with the level of arousal, while pleasure is created by changes in the arousal level.

Pleasure and comfort are often experienced together; relief of discomfort or satisfaction of needs, such as eating when hungry, creates pleasure as well. Thus eating, for example, becomes a source of pleasure, and is enjoyable to continue even after hunger has been relieved. The "rational" individual of economic theory would always eat only until hunger was reduced to the point where another need became more urgent, and then would switch to satisfying the other need. However, this is an unrealistic model of human behavior. In fact, even those who must economize on food, such as members of poor peasant communities, choose to produce great feasts for special occasions, rather than eating slightly more year-round. The pleasure of eating to the point of complete satisfaction at a feast is not the same as the comfort that results from relief of hunger.

Too much comfort can interfere with pleasure; if the level of arousal is already at or near the optimum, there is no opportunity for pleasurable change toward the optimum. Continual snacking can spoil an appetite, preventing enjoyment of the greater satisfaction of a good meal. Age may cause a change in preferences toward comfort over pleasure; affluence may lure us into unwittingly making the same choice.

Enter Economics

Why is it that some satisfactions depend on economic activity while others do not? Many services and satisfactions are outside the market, either because they are produced by solitary individual activity or because they come from reciprocal, unplanned, or otherwise unquantified and unpriced interactions. In the case of production of market goods and services, however, the reciprocal nature of the activity is neither automatic nor simultaneous, and must be guaranteed by payment.

Production for the market is an efficient way to produce some satisfactions, but also can give rise to by-products or externalities experienced by others, such as sounds, sights, and smells, either pleasant or unpleasant, which are difficult to confine to the activity that produced them. Moreover, the process of production gives rise to satisfaction or dissatisfaction from work, an important area that is all but ignored by conventional economics. Professionals and self-employed people, who have some control over their hours of work, regularly work for longer than employees who have no control over their hours. This suggests that, at least for some, there are satisfactions in work.

In all, six categories of satisfactions can be distinguished, of which only one—that produced by market goods and services—is economic and measurable. A second category—nonmarket goods and services, such as household production and preparation of food, or other services within the household—is potentially measurable. Some estimates suggest that the value of nonmarket production is more than half as large as national income. The other four categories—self-sufficient satisfactions, mutual stimulation, externalities, and work satisfaction—are not even potentially quantifiable. The value placed on leisure, which might be taken to include all nonmarket satisfactions outside of work, is sometimes estimated to be greater than national income.

Why, then, is so much importance attached to money income? In addition to the satisfactions obtained from the things money will buy, it may be that economic satisfactions are associated with other, noneconomic ones. For example, many higher-income jobs appear to involve more satisfaction from work than lower-income ones.

Necessities and Comforts

Turning from psychologists' views of human satisfactions to economists' views of goods and services, the variety of products demands some system of classification. The common distinction between necessities and luxuries is problematical, and the dividing line between the two is socially determined, varying widely at different times and places. A better distinction was proposed long ago by Ralph Hawtrey, but ignored by other economists. Hawtrey distinguished defensive products, which prevent pain or distress, from creative products that supply positive gratification. This parallels the distinction between comfort and pleasure, although frequently a single product yields both.

Is the demand for comfort, and comfort-producing goods, satiable? The answer is largely yes, with a few qualifications. To begin with, demand for narrowly defined biological necessities such as food and shelter is certainly satiable. Desires for leisure and for relief from anxiety are surely satiable in principle, if not always satiated in reality even in advanced economies today.

The most important exception is the desire for belonging, that is, for social acceptance and esteem. There is no end to what can be spent on status, since it is a relative concept. The "unchanged desire for respectability must be translated therefore into an ever-rising expenditure on the tokens of respectability." [117] Expenditure on status is a zero-sum game, since the supply of relative status is limited. However, status-seeking activities vary in their external benefits: Commissioning great works of art or architecture has social benefits, while driving an expensive car does not.

Habits also give rise to a category of needs: It is gratifying to fulfill our habits and painful to stop. In the extreme, habits blend into addiction. The behavior of someone who is madly in love with another person bears many similarities to the behavior of an addict "in love" with a drug—both feel pain at even temporary separation and need constant new doses—although society views the two very differently. Satisfying our habits can create ever-increasing needs for goods, especially if each new activity quickly becomes habitual and expected; this is what it means to become spoiled.

Income and Happiness

In human interactions, "market exchange is neither necessary nor sufficient for mutual gain" [133] and satisfaction. Yet economists continue to assume that more income and spending leads to more happiness. This assumption is not supported by public opinion surveys by Easterlin (see Part I of this volume) and others, which show that, as income rose steadily after World War II, Americans reported roughly constant levels of happiness. However, at any point in time those with higher incomes appear much happier than those who have less.

Four explanations for these findings, not at all incompatible with each other, can be proposed. First, the importance of escalating status-seeking expenditures can explain why more income does not produce more happiness over time, as well as why the rich, who have succeeded in gaining status, are happier at any point in time. Second, satisfaction from work may be correlated with relative income, as suggested above, but bear little relationship to gradually rising absolute incomes for the population as a whole. Third, the desire for novelty, a principal source of pleasure for those who are comfortable, clearly can absorb rising expenditures over time. Finally, as new comforts become habitual or addictive, the initial novelty and gratification vanish, while doing without the new habits becomes painful.

Whatever made us believe that income yields happiness? Economics shows us, at most, that under somewhat idealized assumptions the economic welfare gains from market transactions exceed the economic costs incurred. But economic welfare is only a small part of human welfare. More income means more happiness only if all else remains equal—which it rarely does.

Summary of

The Neglected Realm of Social Scarcity
by Fred Hirsch
[Published in *Social Limits to Growth*
(Cambridge: Harvard University Press, 1976), 15–67.]

Economic growth is commonly justified as a means of overcoming scarcity and providing more of the goods and services that people want. But scarcity can have many causes, and some are much easier to eliminate than others. These chapters analyze the increasingly important category of "positional" consumption, in which commodities are valued, directly or indirectly, because they are scarce. No amount of growth can satiate the desires for social distinction, exclusive access, and leadership positions—and as these and other positional motives rise in importance, additional economic output becomes less and less effective in providing the things people want.

A Duality in the Growth Potential

The familiar process of adding up economic activity into a single measure of output has yielded powerful insights, but it has also obscured the limits to the potential benefits of economic growth. The problem is not just that a number of significant technical questions can be raised about the standard measures of output. Even if all the technical questions were resolved, the deeper problem would remain: Some goods that individuals desire, and from which they derive satisfaction, are inherently scarce, making expansion of consumption impossible in principle.

Some desirable consumption goods are absolutely scarce for physical reasons, as in the cases of unique natural landscapes or paintings by a particular famous artist. Far more important are the cases in which scarcity results from social factors. Envy, emulation, or pride may create a psychological basis for scarcity; this occurs if, for instance, the owner of an original painting finds his satisfaction diminished by the existence of good copies. Changes in fashion, and the valuation of antiques, also reflect socially created scarcity. In such examples of pure social scarcity, satisfaction is derived from the scarcity itself.

Scarcity may also be a by-product of social and institutional processes; for example, congestion or crowding limits the enjoyment of many urban and even suburban environments. Leadership positions in any hierarchy are intrinsically scarce, and gain their meaning from scarcity. Unlike material goods, positions at the top do not become more abundant over time as production increases.

References to absolute scarcities in consumption are rare in the economic literature. Philip Wicksteed recognized the concept in 1910, but discussed it only briefly.[1] Roy Harrod addressed the issue in a 1958 essay, drawing a distinction between democratic wealth, which is available to all and rises with the average level of productivity, and oligarchic wealth, which is possible for the few but never for all, regardless of productivity increases.[2] Oligarchic wealth, for Harrod, was defined by: (1) command over other people's labor and (2) access to a disproportionate share of the goods and facilities available to society. Harrod was concerned with the possibility of economic satiety; he argued that economic wants as well as cultural and spiritual values would not be met by economic growth, even if the growth was sustained. However, Harrod did not pursue the analysis beyond his initial essay on the subject.

The Material Economy and the Positional Economy

The material economy embraces production of Harrod's democratic wealth, that is, output amenable to continued increases in productivity without deterioration in quality. The positional economy, the basis of Harrod's oligarchic wealth, includes products and relationships that are either scarce or subject to congestion through extensive use.

As material goods in general increase in availability, while the supply of positional goods remains constant, the price of the latter will rise. This increase in the price of positional goods is reinforced as rising income increases the demand for them compared to material goods; expenditures on education, vacation housing, and personal services are examples of such a phenomenon.

Excess demand for positional goods leads to one of three responses: (1) an increase in prices, in effect auctioning off these goods; (2) congestion or crowding, which reduces the perceived quality of the goods; or (3) increased screening or queuing requirements, such as increases in the credentials needed for a job. Price increases cause no loss of efficiency, but simply transfer claims to resources; the two remaining alternatives absorb resources and thereby involve potential social waste. Three examples will illustrate the three methods of allocating scarce positional goods.

The auction mechanism can be seen in the case of scenic or leisure land. Before the twentieth century, only the very rich could afford second homes. More recently, as incomes have risen, ownership of vacation properties has spread into the upper middle class. Rising demand for leisure land bids up the value of this scarce resource, often benefiting the old rich, who acquired their land many years ago at lower prices. The existing concentration of wealth is thereby reinforced.

Suburbanization is a classic example of rationing by crowding, and of the waste of resources that can result. Suburban locations initially allow enjoyment of certain aspects of both urban and rural living. But as the move to the suburbs continues, the character of a suburb will be changed, sometimes even destroyed. Crowding destroys what brought people there in the first place, and at some point those who can afford to will move on to greener pastures. When suburbs employ zoning regulations to preserve the community's quality of life, they raise the price of suburban land, yielding capital gains for existing landowners and replacing some of the crowding with an auction mechanism.

Leadership jobs in any hierarchy are necessarily scarce, and can be regarded as positional opportunities. They are frequently allocated by increased screening, as the proportion of these positions does not necessarily increase as economic growth continues. The structural shift toward service employment often involves new forms of bureaucratization and routine. Yet over time the labor force as a whole becomes better equipped to occupy superior jobs.

The market model suggests that an excess supply of labor seeking superior jobs should lead to a reduction in pay and fringe benefits for those jobs; this outcome, of course, is rarely observed. Factors inhibiting such a reduction include conventional pay norms, high "transaction" costs involved in filling senior positions, and the ability of incumbents in superior jobs to influence their own pay scales.

In general, positional competition—the struggle for a higher place within an explicit or implicit hierarchy—is at best a zero-sum game in which one participant can win only at another's expense. If resources are wasted through crowding or screening, the competition may actually be a negative-sum game for society as a whole.

The Ambiguity of Economic Output

Positional competition reveals a flaw in the common measures of economic output. Some purchased goods and services are desired not for themselves but as means to other ends. Home heating fuel is desired in order to maintain a warm house; if more fuel is required due to colder weather, the increased purchases do not make households better off; rather, the heating fuel is an intermediate good, and satisfaction of the ultimate objective is made less efficient by the change in weather. The same is true of increased educational costs required to qualify for a job; as a result of positional competition, educational expenditure becomes less efficient in producing the desired credentials.

Such intermediate goods can be thought of as "defensive" goods or "regrettable necessities." Since the lines between categories of goods are not clear-cut, there is a continuum or hierarchy of consumption, with regrettable necessities at the bottom and ultimate goals at the top. Travel to a holiday destination is largely an intermediate good or regrettable necessity, while expenditures of time and money at the beach may be more closely tied to the holiday's ultimate objectives.

This hierarchy of wants forces us to consider questions long banished from economic discussion. The relevant problem is not only how much is the individual willing to spend on an activity or purchase, but for what? Additional expenditures on positional competition create increased needs for defensive expenditures on the part of others. The resulting growth of output leaves no one better off, distorting the usual measures of welfare. The larger the role of positional competition, the more serious the distortion.

The evolution and development of human wants, as part of the process of economic growth, was addressed not only by Marx but also by Alfred Marshall and Frank Knight. Yet although Marshall and Knight formed part of the mainstream of economic liberalism, their philosophical reflections remained essentially asides to their systematic exposition of economics. The mainstay of classical and neoclassical economics has always been market valuation, which assumes "consumer sovereignty" and remains blind to any hierarchy of more or less important wants or needs; established theory can see only the extent to which a given set of wants have been satisfied.

The appearance of more refined wants may increase welfare; this has become a standard response to Galbraith's criticism of the continual production of new wants. But the neoclassical presumption in favor of market choice breaks down as soon as endogenous changes in wants are recognized. In particular, defensive consumption involves new "wants" that are solely a response to the change in the physical or social environment. Once the possibility of defensive consumption is admitted, the signals of market demand become ineffective guides to welfare.

In Adam Smith's analysis of eighteenth-century Britain, conspicuous consumption of "baubles and trinkets" by the rich provided employment for others who supplied these goods. The rich were in this way "led by an invisible hand . . . and thus without intending it, without knowing it . . . advance the interest of society."[3] The exchange was beneficial for both the poor and for society as a whole, as the price for luxuries paid by the rich exceeded their opportunity cost to the rest of society. However, this was true because the positional sector of the economy remained relatively uncrowded; the needs of the poor (who supplied the luxuries) remained concentrated on basic material goods. As standards of living rise and demand for luxuries becomes more extensive, positional competition absorbs more and more resources, with less and less scope for beneficial side effects in the nonpositional sector.

> What the wealthy have today can no longer be delivered to the rest of us tomorrow; yet as we individually grow richer, that is what we expect. The dynamic interaction between material and positional sectors becomes malign. Instead of alleviating the unmet demands on the economic system, material growth at this point exacerbates them. . . . The intensified positional competition involves an increase in needs for the individual, in the sense that additional resources are required to achieve a given level of welfare. [67]

Notes

1. Philip H. Wicksteed, *The Common Sense of Political Economy* (1910) (London: Routledge and Kegan Paul, 1933), II, 657.

2. Roy Harrod, "The Possibility of Economic Satiety—Use of Economic Growth for Improving the Quality of Education and Leisure," in *Problems of United States Economic Development* (New York: Committee for Economic Development, 1958), I, 207–213.

3. Adam Smith, *The Theory of Moral Sentiments* (1759), 65.

Summary of

The Demand for Unobservable and Other Nonpositional Goods

by Robert H. Frank

[Published in *American Economic Review* 75 (March 1985): 101–116.]

The demonstration effect applies more forcefully to some goods than others. We know what kind of cars our acquaintances drive, but not what kind of insurance they buy. This summary analyzes the demand for "positional"[1] and nonpositional goods, develops a formal model of the decision to consume such goods, and examines empirical evidence on savings behavior and on labor compensation and union contracts.

Individual Consumption Decisions

Evolutionary forces saw to it that we place great importance on seeing that our children are launched in life as successfully as possible. Parents' utility functions may be assumed to include an instruction such as: "Feel bad whenever your children are less well provided for than are the children of your peers." Because this objective is defined in relative rather than absolute terms, it motivates parents to compete with each other by working longer hours, or under more dangerous conditions, than is optimal for society as a whole.

Of course, as in any positional competition, the supply of relative standings is fixed, and everyone cannot simultaneously succeed in getting ahead. Because extra income is valued for its relative, as well as absolute, advantages, working harder and longer appears misleadingly attractive to individuals. That is, perceived individual payoffs from additional labor add up to more than the realized aggregate payoff.

Simple Model of the Demand for Nonpositional Goods

Suppose that there are only two types of goods: positional and nonpositional. Assume a population of identical individuals whose utility functions depend on the consumption of both types of goods, and on the individual's percentile ranking in the consumption of positional goods. A mathematical model based on these assumptions allows analysis of both competitive outcomes, in which individuals seek to increase their relative standing via positional consumption, and cooperative outcomes, in which individuals accept their relative standing and do not attempt to get ahead of others.

Three propositions can be easily established in such a model. First, demand will be higher for nonpositional goods and lower for positional goods in the cooperative case than in the corresponding competitive case. Second, an individual's utility will be higher in the cooperative scenario than in the other. Third, the share of household budgets spent on nonpositional goods will grow more rapidly as income increases in the competitive case. The third proposition results from the fact that in the competitive case, low-income households have more to gain than others do through positional consumption, and will tend to favor it over nonpositional spending. In particular, note that savings is a nonpositional "good," since others cannot observe your decisions about savings. Thus the model of competitive status-seeking behavior explains why savings are an increasing function of relative income.

Consumption as a Signal of Ability

The competitive pursuit of status through positional consumption may be functional for the individual, particularly in situations of limited information. Suppose that individuals vary widely in productive ability, but employers cannot observe ability directly. If the labor market is even loosely competitive, there will be a strong correlation between ability and income. Likewise, there is a strong correlation between income and visible, positional consumption. Thus, when ability cannot be observed directly, positional consumption may constitute a signal to others about income, and hence about ability.

In a world of imperfect information, it seems likely that an employee's compensation depends not only on actual ability (or marginal product), but also on the employer's best estimate of the employee's ability at the time of hiring. Under these conditions, increased positional consumption may be rational for the individual, since it may be interpreted as a sign of ability, and thus lead to better job offers. This effect should be stronger in situations where information is more limited. But whatever the advantages of increased observable consumption for the individual, it is clearly suboptimal for society as a whole.

A Survey of Empirical Evidence

In the area of savings behavior, economists have struggled to explain why the average propensity to consume (the ratio of consumption to income) falls with income in cross-section data, but is constant over time. James Duesenberry's solution in 1949 was essentially the same as the one proposed above, namely that demonstration effects weigh more heavily on people with relatively lower incomes, causing them to consume more and save less.[2] Since this effect is based on relative position in society, it is not changed if everyone's absolute income rises over time.

The economics profession prematurely abandoned Duesenberry's hypothesis in favor of explanations offered by the permanent income hypothesis and the life cycle hypothesis. However, these theories, unlike Duesenberry's, imply that people of all income levels save the same fraction of their lifetime incomes. Several major studies of savings and income are in accordance with the findings of Duesenberry, finding a positive relationship between savings rates and lifetime income. There is little if any data supporting the alternative position that savings rates are independent of lifetime income.

Analysis of positional consumption also illuminates the role of unions in determining compensation packages. Union members have higher incomes, on average, than other workers of similar ages and backgrounds, and are therefore more likely to perceive themselves as having achieved high status among their peers. Therefore we would expect union members to place a higher priority on nonpositional consumption. This expectation is fulfilled by the fact that unobservable benefits such as insurance, health care, and paid vacations form a greater fraction of total compensation for union workers than for their non-union counterparts.

If interdependent choice and positional consumption are important, then certain limitations on individual choice can improve social welfare. Social security and other programs that force people to save, laws and regulations that limit excessive hours or unsafe conditions of work, or even a simple tax on positional consumption, all may serve to counteract the consumption externalities that arise from the competitive pursuit of status.

Notes

1. As defined by Fred Hirsch; see Hirsch summary in this part.
2. James Duesenberry, *Income, Saving and the Theory of Consumer Behavior* (Cambridge: Harvard University Press, 1949), 17–46; cited by Frank, 109.

Summary of

Change and Innovation
in the Technology of Consumption

by Kelvin Lancaster

[Published in *American Economic Review* 56 (May 1966): 14–23.]

Conventional economic theory assumes that consumers have desires for goods and that they obtain satisfaction or utility directly from these goods. This article proposes that consumers actually desire certain characteristics provided by goods rather than goods themselves. That seemingly minor modification leads to significant changes in the economic theory of consumer behavior.[1]

Characteristics and the Consumption Frontier

Consumption of a good typically provides a bundle of characteristics that consumers want. The consumer's demand for goods is derived from the fact that goods are required to obtain the desired characteristics. For example, a person who eats an apple enjoys a combination of flavor, texture, and juiciness. A different apple may yield a different mix of the same characteristics—perhaps better flavor but worse texture. To develop a model of consumption, assume that characteristics are intrinsic and objective properties of goods and that twice as much of a good provides twice as much of each of its characteristics. Psychological effects, such as diminishing marginal utility, are assumed to affect the consumer's preferences for characteristics, rather than the technical relationship between goods and characteristics.

There is a partial analogy between this approach and the theory of production. Goods are viewed as inputs into a process that produces characteristics. However, a typical production process has joint inputs and a single output, while consumption activities have one or a few inputs that jointly produce several characteristics. Extending the analogy to production, we may refer to the set of activities (the relationships between available goods and characteristics) as the consumption technology.

It seems likely that in an economy like the United States, with a complex consumption technology, the number of goods exceeds the number of characteristics. This leads to patterns of consumer choice and substitution that cannot arise in standard economic theory, as shown in the example of a consumer choosing among three goods that provide two characteristics (Figure 1).

In the graph, Point A represents the characteristics obtained if the con-

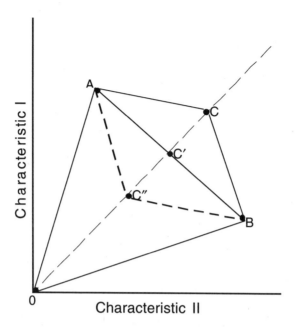

Figure 1. Patterns of Consumer Choice.

sumer's entire budget is spent on the first good; other points on line OA represent smaller purchases of the first good. Point B and line OB are defined similarly for the second good. By spending the budget on a combination of the first two goods, any point on the straight line AB can be reached. This is the consumption efficiency frontier for the first two goods.

Now consider the third good, which yields the combination of characteristics shown on line OC. If the price of the third good is low enough that the consumer can afford to reach point C, then any point on lines AC and CB can also be reached by buying a combination of goods; these two lines have become the consumption frontier. But if the price rises so that the consumer can only afford to reach C", then AB is the consumption frontier and no rational consumer will buy the third good. Thus price changes can lead to substitution between goods solely as a result of consumption efficiency without the conventional assumption of convexity of preferences.

Inefficient Consumption and Technical Change

Can there be innovation and technical progress in consumption technology, as in production? It is hard to identify cases in which the same inputs (goods) are combined more efficiently to yield more output (characteristics), since it is frequently impossible to measure characteristics directly. Nonetheless, technical progress can occur through the introduction of new consumption activities involving either new goods or new characteristics.

Just as technical progress is possible in consumption, so too is inefficiency. Both production and consumption technologies are complex, and ignorance and lack of managerial skill are the principal reasons for inefficiency in both cases. But there is a difference: There is no market in characteristics and hence no market pressure for efficiency in consumption. A consumer who erroneously selects point C" when any point on line AB is attainable is not driven out of the consumption business by competition. Rather than revealing a preference for the third good, such a consumer may simply be revealing ignorance; better information might lead the consumer to make different, more satisfying choices. Inefficiency is most likely to occur when traditional consumption patterns break down under the impact of technical innovations or rapid changes in relative prices—for example, when a society is undergoing a transition from a traditional to a market economy or when it is experiencing rural to urban or other regional migration. Particularly in such cases, there is a valuable role for labeling laws and other consumer product regulations, as well as consumer information and education services. These measures increase knowledge of the available consumption technology, a type of knowledge that is a public good since the efficiency frontier is the same for all consumers.

New Goods and Old Characteristics

> Traditional consumer theory is at its most unenlightening when confronted by the problem of new goods. Introduction of a new good requires either that the preference function defined on n goods is thrown away, and with it all the knowledge of behavior based on it, and replaced by a brand new function defined on $n + 1$ goods, or the fiction that the consumer has a potential preference function for all goods present and future and that a new good can be treated as the fall in that good's price from infinity to its market level. Neither approach gets us very far. [20]

In the case of new goods that possess new characteristics, the theory proposed here does no better. But almost all new goods give rise to existing characteristics in new proportions. A new good of this kind adds a new activity to the consumption technology and should be viewed as an innovation in that technology. Whether the innovation is efficient depends entirely on the price of the good. Even minor product variations may offer slightly different combinations of characteristics and, if priced attractively, may thereby expand the consumption efficiency frontier and increase consumer welfare. However, if a firm withdraws an old product that was still being purchased and replaces it with a different newer one, it is not certain that aggregate welfare has increased.

The mode of analysis suggested here may be applied to problems beyond consumption. If consumers are buying bundles of characteristics rather than goods, then producers are ultimately making and selling bundles of characteristics as well. A theory of the firm could be developed based on production of and competition in marketing of characteristics. The supply of labor is also governed by characteristics of jobs, as suggested by the familiar idea that some jobs have significant nonmonetary advantages. The consumer's sale of labor, like the purchase of commodities, may be a matter of transactions involving bundles of characteristics.

Note

1. For a more rigorous and detailed mathematical presentation see Kelvin Lancaster, "A New Approach to Consumer Theory," *Journal of Political Economy* 74 (April 1966), 132–157.

Summary of

Procrastination and Obedience
by George A. Akerlof
[Published in *American Economic Review* 81 (May 1991), 1–19.]

The rational, utility-maximizing consumer in economic theory would never procrastinate, develop self-destructive habits, or be pressured into unquestioning acceptance of authority. Yet such behaviors occur, and an adequate behavioral theory must be able to account for them. It turns out that repeated small decisions, each of them differing only slightly from utility-maximizing behavior, can cumulatively lead to large deviations from the outcomes predicted by standard textbook economics. This summary presents "nearly neoclassical" models of procrastination and of undue obedience to authority and suggests that such models can explain many important types of behavior, including substance abuse, inadequate savings rates, and membership in cults and gangs, among others.[1]

Salience, Decisions, and Procrastination

Psychologists have found that individuals attach too much weight to salient, vivid, or recent events, and too little weight to nonsalient events and background knowledge. Even after carefully researching different makes of cars in *Consumer Reports*, a potential buyer may be unduly influenced by an acquaintance's individual experience—although the new information only increases the *Consumer Reports* sample by one, likely a statistically insignificant change.

Procrastination may be understood as a tendency to slightly exaggerate the costs of salient, immediate effort in comparison to future effort. If a given task must be done either today or in the future, and salience leads to a slight increase in the perceived cost of performing the task today, then it is easy to construct a model in which it always appears optimal to perform the task tomorrow. In the absence of deadlines, doing the task tomorrow can remain attractive indefinitely.

This model of procrastination may help us understand substance abuse. Interviews and ethnographies of drug abusers make it clear that the majority intend to stop—tomorrow. Many addicts recognize that the long-run costs of addiction exceed the benefits. Yet the immediate costs of quitting are exaggerated by salience, as are the immediate benefits of one more high. This is more plausible than the theory offered by Gary Becker and his coworkers, in which addicts are rational, forward-looking consumers who know that their consumption today will increase their future enjoyment of their chosen drugs, and plan accordingly.[2]

Likewise, procrastination is relevant to lifetime savings behavior. Many households save little or nothing for their retirement. In the absence of procrastination, the life-cycle model implies that an additional dollar of pension savings should lead to a one-dollar reduction in other savings (since households presumably had already selected the optimum level of lifetime savings). However, empirical studies find that this is not the case: One study found no relationship between pensions and private savings, while another found that $1 of pension contribution led to only 62 cents of reduction in other savings among men approaching retirement.

Indoctrination and Obedience

A similar model can be developed of irrational obedience to authority. First assume that there is some cost to disobedience; then we might expect individuals to procrastinate, planning to express their disobedience later rather than at once. Then assume as well that once people have taken an action, especially for reasons they do not fully understand, they find reasons to justify the action after the fact. The latter assumption is consistent with the psychological theory of cognitive dissonance. With these two assumptions it is easy to show that a gradual escalation of unreasonable demands from an authority may be obeyed, overcoming initial resistance and developing commitment to the authority's actions after the fact.

This can explain the classic Milgram experiment in psychology, in which participants believed that they were teachers administering electric shocks to subjects in a learning experiment. Not realizing that the setup was faked and that the "subjects" were actors, most participants followed orders and gave shocks of increasing voltage even when the subjects screamed in pain and begged to be released from the experiment. Other experiments have shown that group pressure is extremely effective in enforcing such irrational obedience, but that the presence of even one or a few dissenters greatly raises the likelihood of disobedience.

Cults, Crime, and Drugs

Membership in cults involves isolation from outsiders combined with escalating sequences of unreasonable demands by authority figures. Those who most strongly disagree tend to drop out, so that at each stage of increasing commitment there is a consensus supporting the leaders.

Crime, like drug addiction, has been described by Becker and his associates as a matter of rational, forward-looking calculation. But not everyone is "rational" in the economists' sense of the term. It is inconceivable that the participants in the Milgram experiment were forward-looking. Nor does it seem likely that new recruits to cult groups always anticipate the personal transformations in their future.

A better explanation of crime is that it is encouraged and supported by group pressure within teenage gangs. That is, street gangs operate like cult groups, enforcing obedience to the leadership and the prevailing group norms—including crime in this case. Ethnographies of gangs describe recurrent internal criticism of deviant individual behavior, parallel to the practices of cult groups. "Such gangs provide a perfect social environment for regrettable decisions. Gang members find the costs of nonacquiescence especially salient, since such nonacquiescence leads to isolation from the social group to which they are committed." [13] Reducing crime, then, requires alternative social networks that can engage actual or potential gang members.

In all of the areas examined here, standard economic theory assumes that individual preferences do not change in any systematic or predictable manner. Becker et al. suggest that preferences do change but that individuals are forward looking and foresee the changes that will occur. This article has proposed an alternative view based on twentieth-century psychology and sociology: Individual preferences do change in ways that are not fully anticipated or even sometimes recognized after the fact. The theory of procrastination and obedience has applications to numerous important areas of behavior that cannot be explained by conventional economic theory.

Notes

1. The author's applications of the same models to bureaucratic indecision and antidemocratic politics are omitted from this summary.

2. Gary Becker and Kevin Murphy, "A Theory of Rational Addiction," *Journal of Political Economy* 96 (August 1988), 675–700; George Stigler and Gary Becker, "De Gustibus Non Est Disputandum," *American Economic Review* 67 (March 1977), 76–90.

PART VII

Perpetuating Consumer Culture: Media, Advertising, and Wants Creation

Overview Essay

David Kiron

On any given day, 18 billion display ads appear in magazines and daily newspapers across the United States.[1] In consumer cultures like the United States the urge to buy is sanctioned, reinforced, and exaggerated in ways so numerous, so enticing, so subtle that ignoring them is not an easy option. The sales message is perhaps nowhere more vivid and insistent than on television. And with credit more widely available, buying is easy, its consequences distant. The cumulative impact on the psyche of all this urging and buying is never fixed. Dissatisfaction recurs with each reminder that the goods we have are not good enough. On one level, this part addresses the cycle of dissatisfaction-satisfaction promoted by the media and advertising. At a deeper level, there is a focus on what happens in a market-oriented society when visions of the good life are structured by commercial images.

When broadcast advertising, television, and modern forms of consumer credit were introduced, each could claim to be services that would further the public good. In the mid-1920s, commercial sponsorship of entire radio programs was widely accepted as a public service. During this period even the advertising industry argued that the dignity of the radio medium should not be debased by advertisements for specific products.[2] In 1940 David Sarnoff, president of the Radio Corporation of America (RCA, then owner of NBC, the National Broadcasting Company), predicted that mass distribution of commercial television would unify the nation and contribute to the greater development of the individual. In the late 1950s Bank of America promoted credit cards as a service that would permit upstanding middle-class citizens to achieve the American Dream.[3] Today, however, the voices extolling the public virtues of credit and commercial broadcasting are difficult to hear above the din of their critics.

Part of the explanation for this transition is that broadcasting, advertising, and credit have become crucial elements of consumer culture, more than just goods and services within it. Instead of merely facilitating cultural goals, they have become cultural entities themselves. For instance, the sheer scale of advertising makes it a cultural force. The 148 billion dollars spent on advertising in the United States in 1994 was greater than the GDP of all but the top twenty economies in the world in 1990. Per capita advertising expenditures in 1994 were four times what they were in 1935.[4] In the United States there are more shopping centers than high schools.[5] The content of advertising also legitimizes consumerist tendencies by associating images of life, liberty, and the pursuit of happiness with consumption. It links success and well-being to consumer behavior, embodies aspirations, and models materialistic ways of appearing and being in the world.

Advertising and Television

The development of marketing strategies takes place within the intersection of cultural trends and technological improvements. Advertising practice, for example, has incorporated commercialized images from a long list of cultural trends including the desire for status within a growing middle class, social movements like feminism, and the agenda of environmentalists. With respect to technology, changes in video and graphics production have altered the medium of advertising. Mass marketing, in particular, has flourished with the evolution of computers and a variety of information technologies. The annual mailing of 14 billion catalogs across the United States would not be possible without the technical ability to track consumers.[6] Sophistication in marketing technique has led advertisers to target the sales message to consumer emotions and beliefs at least as much as to the uses of goods.

If advertising plays such a large role in connecting consumption with happiness, is it possible to be satisfied with the view of economic theory that advertising is simply a cost in the circulation of goods and that it provides information to consumers about the uses of a good or service? Ben Fine and Ellen Leopold (in work summarized here) reject these interpretations, pointing out that economic approaches to advertising fail to appreciate the connections between types of advertising, kinds of goods, and methods of production. They argue that advertising is part of a system of provision, in which production, distribution, and retailing all impact on advertising strategies and techniques.

The extent to which advertising shapes consumerist tendencies and culture is the subject of a debate that has traditionally centered on the issue of whether advertising merely reflects or actively creates wants. In an important respect, this debate has ignored the possibility that the two points of view are compatible. As Richard Pollay suggests in the next article summarized, the themes of advertising emphasize and exaggerate certain values and, in doing so, marginalize others. Pollay is not the first to make this point; indeed his article is based on a survey of the writings of numerous cultural critics of advertising. However, his critique illuminates an important reason why this debate has appeared so intractable. Consider, for example, the oft-cited claim that 90 percent of all new products fail. This shows, critics say, that producers are not responsive to consumer desires; defenders of advertising, on the other hand, argue that it shows that advertising has little influence in shaping tastes.

Just as advertising can simultaneously mirror and distort cultural trends, so too can the content of television programs. For instance, some television programs such as family sitcoms and talk shows are successful because they reflect familiar aspects of culture in an entertaining way. As a result of competitive pressures to be distinctive, there is a tendency for programs of the same format to dramatize extremes, which tends to drive away viewer interest as the content of shows ceases to be familiar. These pressures stem from market forces that make attempts at developing innovative new genres into unacceptable financial risks. The operative principle seems to be that it is better to carve a slice from a successful pie than try to make a different dessert. One result is less program diversity, which may explain why between 1953 and 1988 the top rated network television programs drew smaller and smaller audiences.[7]

Interest in network television as a whole has declined with the rise of cable television and video cassette recorders. Nielson surveys found that time spent viewing network television has decreased since 1950, from 4.5 hours to 4.2 hours a day in 1991.[8] With more options, viewers can now see more of what they want when they want. J. Fred MacDonald, in a historical analysis of the decline of interest in network television, argues that its early and continued dependence on sponsors who demand access to the largest possible audiences guaranteed that programs would focus on what was most acceptable to, rather than what was most preferred by, individual viewers. He extends the debate over consumer sovereignty from the domain of advertising to the area of media content. Lack of program diversity implies lack of choice, not in the number of available shows but in the quality of available choices.

The centrality of television viewing in daily living is suggested by the fact that "more time is spent watching television than doing anything else besides working and sleeping."[9] In an article summarized below, Robert Kubey and Mihaly Csikzentmihalyi found that the average individual watches television four hours a day.

A huge literature has struggled to identify the effects of television viewing. Our research indicates that the most interesting and credible observations come from studies that look at differences between heavy and light viewers. George Gerbner found that people who watch more television than the average exaggerate the amount of wealth and luxuries that others have. Kubey and Csikzentmihalyi found that excessive and indiscriminate television viewing induces a passive state of mind that endures even after the viewing experience. The appeal of this kind of experience is suggested by Schor in Part II: After long hours at draining jobs there may be little energy left over for activities that require more mental effort than television viewing. Others, more recently Robert Putnam, have found evidence that television is responsible for civic disengagement and an erosion of social connections.[10] Whether or not passivity, distorted perceptions of social reality, and civic disengagement all derive from excess television viewing, it is cause for concern that these characteristics are consistently found together.

From the standpoint of economic theory, televisions, like other media technologies that are sold in the market, are no different than appliances. This view was captured by Mark Fowler, one of the chairmen of the Federal Communications Commission during the Reagan administration, who once described televisions as "toasters with pictures." Unlike toasters, however, televisions offer windows into as well as direct access to the market. Recent innovations in communication and information technologies are transforming and strengthening the bonds that tie consumer behavior to consumer culture. The linkages between the home, where most television viewing occurs, and the marketplace have become strengthened in recent years with the introduction of instant credit and instant market access through programs that sell directly to audiences. Increasingly the home is becoming yet another extension of the marketplace. David Morley's article extends the view that the media promotes consumer culture through its institutions, content, and advertising, adding that innovations in communication technologies permit a wider range of expression of gendered power relations within the home. These relations may be strengthened as leisure, consumption, household management, and work are brought together in the high-technology home of the future.

The linkages between television viewing and consumerism can be direct or indirect, through content that sells or through content that reinforces consumerist imagery. The content of an increasing number of television shows are advertisements themselves, for example, infomercials and home shopping networks. Video news releases, which are advertisements that resemble actual news releases, sometimes employ real anchorpersons. Product placement (the commercial sponsorship of brand name goods that appear in films and television programs) is a budding multimillion dollar business. More indirect is the role that regular television programs play in displaying wealth and legitimizing consumerist lifestyles.

Limitless Desire and the Good Life

Consumer culture has evolved along with the neoclassical assumption that wants are limitless, desire insatiable. This view of human nature is crucial to a vision of the good life that, over the course of the twentieth century, has been increasingly formulated by the media and advertising. The vision of the good life that is elaborated by the themes of advertising has become increasingly oriented toward more luxurious and comfortable lifestyles.[11] The assumed limitlessness of desire has traditionally been analyzed in terms of the ephemeral satisfactions that are generated by contemporary goods and promoted by marketing practices. However, recent analyses have focused on the possibility that insatiability follows from problems with satisfying particular desires. Colin Campbell, Marsha Richins, and William Leiss contribute important additions to this discourse, each arguing that the pursuit of wants that are difficult, if not impossible, to satisfy creates the appearance of insatiability.

Campbell views much of modern consumption as directed toward the construction of day-dreams: Individuals build in their imaginations a product-filled world informed by the images and stories of both media and advertising. Consumers revel in anticipation of consuming their constructions, but are inevitably disappointed when their actual consumption experiences fail to meet expectations. Marsha Richins identifies the psychological mechanism behind comparisons with unattainable media and advertising images, and outlines the dangers of continuous and frequent exposure to them. For many, increasing consumption to achieve the idealized image or compensate for the feelings of inadequacy conjured by these images appears to be the best response, especially when the media and advertising persistently inform you that it is the right thing to do. In a point begun in Part II of this book and explored more thoroughly in the summarized article in this part, William Leiss contends that in a high-intensity market setting it is difficult to make judgments of how best to satisfy needs with goods, since it is not always clear which desires are to be satisfied by a given commodity.

The article by Leiss, Kline, and Jhally is perhaps the clearest discussion of how modern consumer culture imbues goods with meaning and the reasons why consumers so avidly consume. Instead of targeting the goods themselves, the strategy is to create a brand image with which consumers identify. Images, icons, and symbols have become essential to contemporary advertising practices. By associating mass-produced goods with a continuous flow of ambiguous displays of happiness, advertising encourages people with diverse preferences to be interested in the same group of goods without having to cater to the lowest common denominator of tastes.

Every one of the authors who focus on advertising in this part points to the environmental impact of economic growth as a reason for his or her critique. Jackson Lears, in a provocative cultural history of advertising, develops an interpretation of advertising that differs from his earlier work, summarized in Part IV. In this part, Lears argues that advertising, beyond stirring hedonistic desires, cultivates an indifference to nature with its commercial fables of how to realize self through market participation. With few exceptions, goods are presented to the consumer without reference to their origins in nature, nor is attention drawn to the environmental consequences of consumption. Even when such concerns are raised, they are co-opted by advertisers, sometimes when representing the worst offenders.

Credit

"The rise of the consumer society, in particular, would not have been possible without a widespread willingness to take on personal debt."[12] And personal debt would not have become as easy and appealing as it is today without the development of the credit card. Until the late 1950s, the ability to acquire consumer debt was determined primarily by bank fiat.[13] Consumers had to prove that they were good risks in face-to-face confrontations with loan officers, and were forced to wait for banks to process their applications each time they wanted a loan. After World War II, sporadic efforts were undertaken to introduce credit cards, which would allow consumers to have more control over the lending process. The first major initiative, which was a major financial fiasco, was undertaken in 1958 by the Bank of America in Fresno, California, before the bank was technically equipped to monitor credit use and avoid abuses. The ultimate success of the credit card, as an institution, awaited successful adaptation of technological innovations such as the computer to the specific requirements of credit card banking.

Between 1958 and 1970, 100 million credit cards were dispersed across the United States.[14] With its mass distribution, the feel of the card and the spontaneity of credit transactions have become commonplace. As consumption levels have risen, so has the number of personal bankruptcies, which tripled between 1985 and 1994 in the United States. Greater accessibility to credit is certainly a factor in this trend. It is easy to confuse the use of credit with greater purchasing power; flexibility in payback schedules offers the illusion of immediate ownership. Compulsive consumption and ignorance concerning the implications of finance charges have resulted in many instances of poor debt management.

In traditional economic explanations, credit becomes a problem when a debt burden is exacerbated by economic downturns, catastrophes, or poor planning. A novel alternative analysis is offered by Samuel Cameron in the final article of this part. He argues that there are structural economic constraints that explain household debt problems, and that these problems may lead toward national and international problems. His basic point is that when consumption is tied to self-esteem, as it is in affluent societies, people are less responsive to borrowing costs and can become problem debtors if they pursue unrealistic images of their comparison group.[15] (The international implications of this perspective will be explored in Part IX.)

As Martin Davidson suggests, consumerism is a phenomenon that has worked itself into the very core of society. Its replacement will require an alternative that is no less central to the modern way of life;[16] consumer culture will continue to reproduce itself until the motivations for consuming more and more are dislodged. We have seen that the multiplication of desires is as much a function of unrequited desire as of ephemeral satisfactions. Both the media and advertising prompt the individual to ask: Is what I have good enough? Unfortunately the answers returned by many consumers prompt environmentalists and other critics to ask: How much is enough? That question is discussed in more detail in Part VIII.

Notes

1. Michael Jacobson and Laurie Ann Mazur, *Marketing Madness: A Survival Guide for a Consumer Society* (Boulder: Westview Press, 1994), 18.

2. Roland Marchand, *Advertising the American Dream: Making Way for Modernity, 1920–1940* (Berkeley and Los Angeles: University of California Press, 1985).

3. Joseph Nocera, *A Piece of the Action: How the Middle Class Joined the Money Class* (New York: Simon and Schuster, 1994).

4. *Marketing Madness* 15 (adjusted for inflation, 1994 dollars).

5. Alan Thein Durning, *How Much Is Enough* (New York: Norton, 1992).

6. Durning, op. cit.

7. Study cited in J. Fred MacDonald's *One Nation Under Television: The Rise and Decline of Network TV.* See book for full explanation.

8. Margaret S. Andreasen, "Patterns of Family Life and Television Consumption: From 1945 to the 1990s," in *Media, Children, and the Family: Social Scientific, Psy-*

chodynamic, and Clinical Perspectives, eds. Dolf Zillmann, Jennings Bryant, and Aletha C. Huston (Hillsdale: Lawrence Erlbaum Associates), 19–36.

9. Michael Morgan and Nancy Signorielli, "Cultivation Analysis: Conceptualization and Methodology," in *Cultivation Analysis: New Directions in Media Effects Research,* eds. Nancy Signorielli and Michael Morgan (Newbury Park, London, New Delhi: Sage Publications, 1990), 14.

10. See Part III.

11. Russell Belk and Richard Pollay, "Images of Ourselves: The Good Life in Twentieth Century Advertising," *Journal of Consumer Research* vol. 11, March 1985, 887–897.

12. Nocera, ibid., 20.

13. Of course, many purchases were and continue to be available through other forms of financing, such as installment loans from institutions other than banks, including manufacturers, money lenders, families, and friends.

14. Nocera, op. cit.

15. An interesting connection between media and credit is made by O'Guinn and Faber (1987), "Mass Mediated Compulsive Consumption: Non-Utilitarian and Dysfunctional Outcomes," in M. Wallendorf and P. Anderson, eds., *Advances in Consumer Research* vol. 14, 473–477. They combined Gerbner's research discussed earlier with their finding that compulsive consumers are envious of others and hypothesized that certain of these individuals will become credit abusers over time given excessive exposure to idealized images in the mass media.

16. Martin Davidson, *The Consumerist Manifesto: Advertising in Postmodern Times* (New York and London: Routledge, 1992).

Summary of

The Distorted Mirror: Reflections on the Unintended Consequences of Advertising
by Richard Pollay

[Published in *Journal of Marketing* vol. 50 (April 1986), 18–36.]

Advertising selects from society's palate of values those believed to be most effective in promoting sales. The nature of this selection process has raised concern among leading scholars over the social effects of advertising. This summary presents a critique of advertising that is based on a survey of the writings of significant scholars in the humanities and social sciences, including "all North American authors known to have written on the cultural character of advertising." [19]

The great power of advertising to infiltrate modes of thought, values, social roles, language, and human goals is both overt and subtle. Overtly, advertising helps articulate a vision of the good life, fostering connections between the search for happiness and the pursuit of goods and services through its omnipresent imagery. More subtle is the scientific nature of its messages: Research methods and visual technologies are used by advertisers to design the most marketable message possible. Perhaps most hidden is the way in which advertising obscures the environmental impact of its incentives to buy. Inducing higher levels of consumption requires increasing production levels; however, advertising rarely discusses the consequences of greater production on water, land, and air pollution.

Advertising's power also consists of its pervasiveness and contact with all aspects of culture. It reinforces stereotypes and produces idealized images that cultivate a sense of dissatisfaction and lack. Advertising sells its goods by modeling unattainable images and fostering insecurities, anxieties, fears, ambitions, greed, and lust that ultimately generate self-doubt and feelings of inadequacy. These effects are particularly acute with respect to women and the elderly. For women, advertising idealizes and promotes the desirability of unrealistic body images that focus attention on "deficiencies" in their appearance. Similarly, advertising corrodes the self-esteem of the elderly when it repeatedly equates happiness with youthfulness. Of course, not all advertising has these effects, and much of advertising associates images with goods to suggest obtainable pleasures; however, its overall purpose is less to promote goods as satisfiers of needs than to create feelings of dissatisfaction and needs for goods.

Advertising's most profound effect is that it "induces people to keep productive in order to keep consuming, to work in order to buy." [25] Advertising perpetuates the need to consume by constantly suggesting and reinforcing the values of buying behavior. However, by romanticizing goods advertising exaggerates the value of consumption at the expense of social relations. The more emotionally involved with objects, the less individuals are involved with each other, thus diminishing the quality of human relations. In addition, advertising's encouragement of self-interest contributes to a political climate in which individual priorities seem to reflect private economic goals rather than a greater concern for economic justice. Ostensibly positive aspects of advertising, such as facilitating marketplace efficiencies, do not compensate for its high cost in terms of displacing affect from social relations among individuals to the asocial relation between persons and goods.

Advertising has also precipitated certain social problems. In the home, advertising has created a new role for parents as intermediaries between their children and the market, sometimes instigating parent/child conflict when a child's demand for goods is in opposition to parental interests. Children are especially susceptible to exhortations and jingles that extol the values of immediate gratification and self-indulgence. Advertising messages that validate conspicuous consumption may contribute to violent behavior by those who are shown the need for goods as a means to respectability but are too poor to buy them.

Advertising's vision of how life ought to be led competes with the views of other socializing agents, including families and religions. In a culture increasingly bereft of traditional authority, advertising wields its influence over a populace susceptible to images of purchasable solutions to life's problems. When cultural or religious symbols (for example, Jesus) are extensively connected to brand name goods (as with Christmas items), their meanings are distorted, leading to a general cynicism toward cultural leaders who can no longer rely on unadulterated or uncommercialized icons.

Taken together, these observations constitute a serious indictment of advertising's social effects. One defense against such criticism is to claim that successful advertising must reflect cultural values and behaviors that are understood and accepted by consumers, otherwise it would fail. This response ignores the fact that advertising picks out just a few of the many values that constitute culture and, in virtue of its frequent, repetitive, and limited selections, disregards others. It would be interesting to examine the value profile of advertising and compare the extent to which it promotes the seven deadly sins of greed, lust, sloth, pride, envy, gluttony, and anger with its promotion of the seven cardinal virtues of wisdom, justice, temperance, courage, faith, hope, and love.

Summary of

Modern Consumerism and Imaginative Hedonism
by Colin Campbell
[Chapters 3 and 5 of *The Romantic Ethic and the Spirit of Modern Consumerism* (Cambridge, MA: Blackwell, 1987) 36–57 and 77–95.]

The "puzzle of modern consumerism" lies in its combination of insatiable desires and constant pursuit of novelty. These summarized chapters review and criticize the explanations of consumerism offered by economists such as Galbraith, and propose an alternative theory of consumption as a process of imaginative hedonism.

The Puzzle of Modern Consumerism

The mystery of modern consumer behavior is the apparent insatiability of wants in general. This differs from traditional patterns of greed or addiction, which focused on a single object of desire. Today, no sooner is one need satisfied than another takes its place, typically involving novel products or services. Mainstream economics cannot explain this insatiability since it does not attempt to account for the origins of needs. Nor can economics explain the pursuit of novelty: Since old goods produce known satisfactions while new ones have uncertain benefits, it is puzzling to see consumers constantly abandoning the old in favor of the new.

John Kenneth Galbraith is a well-known critic of conventional economics who has offered an alternative explanation of consumer behavior. He argues that increased production is desirable only if it satisfies wants that originate within the individual. It cannot be urgent to fulfill wants contrived by the same process of production that satisfies them. In developing this argument, Galbraith employs three main strands of thought on the origins of consumer wants: the instinctivist tradition, which identifies some wants as inherent biological needs; an emphasis on deliberate manufacture of wants through advertising and marketing; and the Veblenesque perspective on wants arising from imitation or emulation of others. None of these approaches, however, provide a completely satisfactory account of modern consumerism.

Instinctivism

The instinctivist perspective is built into the language of economics, as seen in references to "latent demand" for new goods or the "unleashing of acquisitive instincts" due to changes in the marketplace. This view gains plausibility from the obvious fact that human behavior does have a biological basis. However, the behavior motivated by biological needs for food and shelter, for example, is unspecific and does not define wants for individual products. It is impossible to identify any particular consumer behaviors that are instinctual in form, as opposed to underlying motivation. The existence of instincts cannot explain interpersonal variation or change over time in consumer desires.

The related idea of a hierarchy of higher and lower needs is also problematical. It is simply not true that needs are always satisfied in sequence, beginning with basic biological requirements. There is plenty of evidence to show that people will override biological imperatives for the sake of needs such as love or self-respect.

Manipulation

At the opposite extreme from instinctivism lies what has been called the "hypodermic" model of consumers and the mass media. This theory holds that, lacking any preformed desires, individuals are inactive as consumers until they are injected with advertising messages. Some versions of this theory suggest that consumers are persuaded or forced to act against their own inclinations or contrary to their own best interests, for the benefit of producers.

Criticisms of the hypodermic model include the observations that advertisements are only one among many cultural influences at work on consumers; that the audience for advertising is not homogeneous and individuals do not all react identically to commercial messages; and finally that evidence shows consumers respond to advertising in a selective and purposeful manner. Manipulation can only succeed when there is something there to manipulate—which explains why advertisers spend money studying consumer motivation. Through advertising, producers directly manipulate the symbolic meanings attached to products; this process may exploit consumer dreams and desires, but does not create them.

The widespread concern about manipulation of consumers by advertisers rests on two utilitarian assumptions: First, that the only genuine gratification provided by goods stems from their intrinsic utility rather than their symbolic meanings; and second, that whenever emotion and imagination enter the process of consumer choice, manipulation or exploitation must be involved. Yet goods are consumed for symbolic as well as intrinsic values, and emotion as well as calculation is a pervasive part of consumer motivation.

The Veblenesque Perspective

A third approach sees consumers as actively engaged in the creation of their own wants as a by-product of the pursuit of status. This perspective derives almost entirely from the writings of Thorstein Veblen. Unfortunately, Veblen was too single-minded in his consideration of the possible social meanings of consumption. The further collapse of Veblen's analysis into Leibenstein's "bandwagon, snob, and Veblen effects" is notable for its extreme simplicity, failing to grasp the range of symbolic meanings of goods or the social dimensions of the act of consumption.

There is an ambiguity at the core of Veblen's account of conspicuous consumption. The same term, emulation, at times refers to competitive striving for status and attempts to outdo one's peers; at other times it refers to aspiration to the ideal way of life exemplified by the leisure class. Veblen reconciles the two meanings by assuming that each class tries to imitate the one just above itself, so that upper-class standards are conveyed downward throughout society. However, this account neglects the fact that many people are satisfied with their standing relative to their peers. And it overlooks the possibility that status can be obtained through innovation, or even through contesting the criteria that define status.

Many specific objections can be raised to Veblen's analysis of status. Wealth is not the only source of status; modern societies do not have monolithic status hierarchies; the very rich may have less influence on styles than professionals such as architects and fashion designers. Most important for our purposes, Veblen does not distinguish traditional from modern consumer behavior. In fact, his theory of conspicuous consumption was inspired by analysis of traditional rituals. Ultimately Veblen explains insatiable consumption only by assuming insatiable competitive status-seeking, which is no more useful or convincing than the older assumption of insatiable greed.

Modern Autonomous Imaginative Hedonism

Imagination has a part to play in the hedonism that has always characterized consumption. In traditional hedonism, images from memory create effective anticipation of the expected pleasure of consumption. But these images are seldom crafted self-consciously by the individual; the hallmark of tradition is that anticipatory images are taken from the past and employed as they are. In contrast, modern self-illusory hedonism involves the individual as an artist of the imagination, taking images from memory or the environment and rearranging them in a more pleasing manner.

We may distinguish pure fantasy, which involves imagination unrestrained by reality, from daydreams involving imaginative elaboration of possible, even if highly improbable, outcomes. In this sense the modern hedonism of consumption rests on daydreams of desire. Novel products provide new material for the imagination; the experience of desire itself becomes pleasurable. Contrary to popular wisdom, pleasure-seeking is not in opposition to deferred gratification, for it is the deferral that allows the imagined pleasure to develop. The act of purchase, attaining the object of desire, replaces the anticipatory daydream with the real satisfaction provided by the good—which may not measure up to the perfected pleasure of the imagination. The consumer who is dissatisfied with reality may then transfer the daydream to a new object of desire, creating a continual longing for the new and the unknown.

The Spirit of Modern Consumerism

The view of consumption as based on modern hedonism provides a clear explanation of both insatiability and the pursuit of novelty. The consumer is always vaguely dissatisfied with reality and yearning for something better. Wish-directed daydreaming turns the future into a perfectly illusioned present. The illusion is always better than the reality, the promise more interesting than actuality. Window-shopping becomes understandable from this perspective, as does the widespread consumption of cultural products that serve as aids to the construction of daydreams, such as novels, paintings, records, films, and television programs. Portrayal of consumer goods, not only in advertising but also in magazines, posters, and even works of art, serves to entertain as well as to advertise; in fact, the two objectives are barely distinguishable. The importance of daydreaming and novelty provides an explanation of consumer acceptance of ever-changing fashions, since the only fixed standard is the desire for change.

> The inexhaustibility of wants which characterizes the behavior of modern consumers has to be understood as deriving from their permanent desiring mode, something which, in turn, stems from the inevitable gap between the perfected pleasures of the dream and the imperfect joys of reality. No matter what the nature of the dream or, indeed, of reality, the discrepancy between them gives rise to a continuing longing, from which specific desires repeatedly spring. [95]

Summary of

Social Comparison, Advertising, and Consumer Discontent

by Marsha Richins

[Published in *American Behavioral Scientist* 38, no. 4 (February 1995), 593–607.]

Frequent exposure to images of wealthy, beautiful, and happy people generates a false reality in which the uncommon and ideal become mundane and attainable. In our daily unconscious assessments of our lives, we continually fall short. For some, the result is a continual striving and a desire for more, accompanied by a feeling of missing out, of having less than what ought to be.

Striving for more may or may not be inherent in the human character, but modern advertising has been carefully designed to increase consumer desire. It does so in part by inducing social comparison with idealized images and by raising consumers' expectations about what ought to be in their own lives, particularly with respect to consumer goods. For many, the result of these processes is dissatisfaction and a desire for increased consumption. [603]

Many observers of consumer culture hold the view that consumer desires are vulnerable to the influences of advertising and marketing institutions. This summary argues that the idealized images found in advertising drive the desire for more goods by prompting frequent comparisons that leave the consumer dissatisfied and continually raising expectations for acceptable standards of living.

Idealized Images, Satisfaction, and Striving

Social comparison theory, a widely accepted psychological view, assumes that one important way to obtain self-knowledge is through comparisons with others. Comparisons provide information about the social acceptability of one's views and physical characteristics, as well as one's standing relative to others.

Few consumers can avoid comparing themselves with the idealized images of individuals and lifestyles depicted in advertisements. However, comparisons with these images may provide misleading information about oneself, since idealized images depict affluent lifestyles and beauty standards that are unattainable by most of the population. The power of these images lies, in part, in the suggestion of fantasies as objects of aspiration, while the physical imperfections of actors and actresses are hidden, and boring details of life that inevitably accompany advertised circumstances are omitted.

Although individuals look to a variety of sources other than advertising for information about themselves, comparisons involving wealth, living standards, and material possessions are especially important to individuals living in a consumer society. Self-comparison with idealized images is driven by the prevalence of such advertising; the impact of these images is to increase consumer desire for higher standards of living.

The comparisons with others can be either deliberate or unconscious. Individuals may deliberately compare themselves with persons worse-off than themselves in order to feel better about their current situations, or with persons better-off than themselves in order to generate hope and motivation. However, often people do not control or choose with whom or what they compare themselves. The most frequent comparison that individuals make is with media images that are characteristically idealized. Comparisons with idealized media images lead to feelings of inadequacy only if an individual cares about what is represented by the images. For example, a person committed to status consumption will tend to feel more inadequate than an aescetic monk when exposed to repeated images of affluence.

Individuals may attempt to attenuate or prevent these feelings of inadequacy by (1) acquiring more products, thereby reducing the discrepancy between themselves and the comparison standard; (2) diminishing the importance of the comparison domain; and/or (3) refusing to compare themselves with such images. The last option is less appealing in practice since consumerist lifestyles are so important to the identity of individuals in a consumer society.

Idealized Images and "What Ought to Be"

Everyone has an idea of what his or her life should be like, including views on what standard of living and lifestyle to expect given a particular set of talents, motivation, skills, and job opportunities. Adults unconsciously derive their expectations from peers, aspiration groups (such as parents or upper-echelon fellow employees), the media, and various socializing agents (religion and family, for example).

Information integration theory, a psychological model that explains the formation of expectations based, in part, on the processing of a set of psychological models, provides a framework for analyzing the effects of advertising and other media imagery on the formation of expectations concerning the good life. The theory implies that repeated exposure to social stimuli consistently above (or below) personal expectation levels will raise (or lower) individual expectations. "Because advertising images tend to be idealized—that is, they show people who are very well-off in terms of possessions—exposure to large amounts of advertising will raise people's expectations of what ought to be." [509]

The vividness of advertising images—with their high-tech combinations of color, music, and photography—captivates viewers. Such seemingly realistic advertising blurs the distinction between commercials and real life. "MCI, as part of its 'Gramercy Press' serial advertising campaign, has made it possible for consumers to send internet messages to their favorite 'Gramercy Press' characters, who, in turn, will answer them." [600] The pervasiveness of advertising increases the likelihood that idealized images, rather than more realistic images, will influence people's perception of what ought to be.

Advertising influences perceptions of what ought to be only insofar as its imagery is considered relevant to a consumer's life. Relevant images consist of circumstances that appear possible and desirable. In their efforts to gain the widest possible audience, advertisers deliberately provide little objective information about occupation and income levels in order to allow viewers to see themselves as the characters in advertisements.

This lack of context serves to obscure the potential irrelevance of idealized advertising images to many consumers, increases the likelihood that the images will be placed in the zone of possibility, and increases the chances that they will be integrated into perceptions of what ought to be, thus raising expectations about the level of material circumstances one deserves and might expect to obtain. [602]

Consumer Discontent

Although advertisements with idealized images may make a cumulative long-term contribution to consumer discontent, many consumers like such advertising. From a public policy point of view, it may be possible that negative impacts of advertising can be addressed without banishing idealized imagery from advertisements. Consumers could be taught to understand the negative implications of idealized advertising images. Media programming could do more to de-emphasize buying things as a route to happiness.

Summary of

Limits to Satisfaction: Diagnosis
by William Leiss

[Published in *The Limits to Satisfaction: An Essay on the Problem of Needs and Commodities* (University of Toronto Press: Toronto and Buffalo, 1976), 49–94.]

This summary argues that the fast pace of commodity circulation in the modern marketplace inhibits personal striving by making it difficult for individuals to form judgments concerning how to satisfy their needs with goods and services.

In advanced economies, consumption becomes important to the pursuit of well-being as the marketplace systematically orients all needs toward an increasingly complex commodity realm. In a setting where advertising arouses dissatisfaction with existing products, while urging the consumption of the newest products as the best path to happiness, both perceptions of need and judgments concerning the means to their satisfaction become confused. As the consumer looks to the market to satisfy perceived needs, messages that are associated with goods change rapidly as marketers seek the most persuasive advertising strategies. The marketplace requires the consumer to perform a grand experiment in choosing among its wares and services, equipping the consumer with little information about the products themselves while providing vivid descriptions of how mundane goods are supposed to satisfy complex desires. For example, consider an advertisement that associates the taste of menthol in cigarettes with the taste of spring: Is the cigarette purchase supposed to satisfy one's desire for nature?

The tendency of advanced economies to direct the satisfaction of all needs through the market poses two important problems: (1) It diminishes, by neglect, the role of nonmarket routes to satisfaction of needs; and (2) the rapid turnover of goods and their associated symbols intensifies the ambiguous character of both human needs and commodities. Judgments relating perceptions of needs and how best to satisfy them in the market become more difficult as the material and symbolic aspects of both needs and commodities become increasingly complex.

Needs

All human needs are culturally mediated impulses that are influenced by social and environmental factors. Needs have material and symbolic components that are irreducible to one another. In traditional, preindustrial societies material scarcity and rigid norms (such as myths, legends, taboos) structured the expression of needs and determined the significance of objects, creating stable categories of need. There once was a tight linkage between a given need, its cultural expression, and particular goods. In contrast, advanced market economies afford individuals free play in interpreting their needs and how to meet these needs with goods, thereby destabilizing need categories. For example, advertising that links the purchase of an automobile with the acquisition of a new personality takes an ambiguous need or desire and creates an illusory connection between it and a product.

Some critiques of modernity object that inducing wants for more and more goods leads to the ephemeral satisfaction of inauthentic needs. This type of criticism, however, begs more questions than it answers. Focus on the distinction between either true and false needs or needs and desires tends to exaggerate the importance of the quantitative aspects of need (as for shelter or nutrients), and detracts attention from the qualitative or cultural dimension of needs (shelter with which qualities?, nutrients in which forms?).

Recent advances in the human ability to transform the planet and effect global environmental changes introduce an historically novel basic human need: to understand and manage the relationship between humanity and the natural environment. Efforts to categorize basic needs have failed to accommodate the ecological dimension of human needing.

To conceptualize human needs simply with reference to the individual and social dimensions of their formation, in abstraction from their grounding in an orientation to the environment that is unique among all living species, is to obscure one of their most significant aspects. [70]

Commodities

In preindustrial cultures, the types of available goods remained relatively stable over time. Correspondingly, classical economic theory presumed the existence of objective standards that assessed the appropriateness of a good for an individual's needs. In contrast, modern industrial settings are characterized by a furious pace of exchange, which puts into constant flux both types and meanings of goods. Correspondingly, modern economic theory accommodated the growing complexity of the relationship between commodities and needs by asserting that only an individual could judge the suitability of commodities for the satisfaction of his or her needs.

Kelvin Lancaster improved on early marginalist theories, claiming that individuals have a direct interest in the characteristics of goods and only a secondary interest in any particular commodity. Individuals "order their preferences directly in relation to collections of characteristics and indirectly in relation to the goods that possess those characteristics." [80] According to Lancaster, any characteristic might be obtained from any good. So, for any commodity there are two relationships, between goods and their characteristics and between individuals and such characteristics. The first relationship consists of objective information, while the second consists of imputed characteristics.

Individuals formulate beliefs about imputed characteristics based on a variety of sources, many of which send unstable, temporary, and ambiguous messages—a prominent example is advertising. In an advanced market setting, the number of messages in the social environment is staggering. For example, individuals are exposed to hundreds of thousands of television commercials before the age of twenty. Individuals necessarily become less familiar with the symbolic and material characteristics of objects as commodities are linked with an endless stream of associations. The consumer is faced with the problem of interpreting which needs are supposed to be met by any particular ensemble of goods. "When goods become rapidly changing collections of characteristics, the individual's judgments about the suitability of particular objects for particular needs are destabilized." [88]

Summary of

Goods as Satisfiers

by William Leiss, Stephen Kline, and Sut Jhally

[Published in *Social Communication in Advertising*
(London: Methuen, 1986), 237–258.]

For a consumer society the key question is, To what extent are the types
of wants generated in a market-oriented context satisfied by the types of
goods produced there? [251]

In preindustrial societies, traditional norms provided guidance in how to
use scarce goods to satisfy a limited set of wants. In modern industrialized
countries, advertising institutions suggest meanings for an abundance of
products, relating goods to images of personal success and happiness. This
summary argues that in a consumer society, consumption activity is less
about satisfying wants than about interpreting the meaning of satisfaction
in the lives of individuals.

Image and Metaphor

The social function of goods has been transformed "from being primarily
satisfiers of wants to being primarily communicators of meanings." [238]
This transformation is the result of several factors including (1) the identification of consumption as a valid means for personal self-realization; (2)
the realization by the marketing and advertising professions that the individual and social realms of the consumer, rather than the actual characteristics of goods, are at the root of merchandising; and (3) the rapid introduction of mass communication technologies that have given rise to the
visual or iconic imagery of advertising formats.

This social transformation acknowledges that consumption can be a
means to personal and social success; that the consumer is not bound by
traditional norms but instead can respond to social cues that encourage experimentation in achieving satisfaction; and that television offers guidance
in relating commercial goods to the achievement of happiness and success.
Satisfaction and well-being are not functions of the accumulation of goods,
but rather are determined by where an individual stands in society in relation to others and the importance he or she attaches to specific values.

Modern advertising relies on the metaphorical power of images, symbols,
and icons to induce new wants and suggest interpretations of how best to
satisfy them.

> The consumer society does not set up its own fixed models of behavior to replace traditional ones but rather constructs through marketing and advertising successive waves of associations between persons, products and images of well-being in an endless series of suggestions about the possible routes to happiness and success. [239]

These associations create a market-oriented reconstruction of reality by connecting nonmarket elements of daily life with products. The individual and firm both contribute to the production of these associations. Business targets the interpretative predilections of consumers with a vast array of symbols, images, and icons, while consumers develop preferences for certain images from a variety of social cues.

Icons of the Marketplace

Modern advertising focuses primarily on the consumer mind-set, rather than the characteristics of a given product. Contemporary advertising produces symbolic connections between products and psychological states, targeting consumer expectations and feelings about status, peer group pressures, roles, social mobility, and lifestyles. Advertising provides more than functional information about a product; it envelops a product with images that lend themselves to diverse preferences.

Advertisers appeal to human psychological processes either by constructing these images and symbols for mass markets or by catering to specific types of individuals. A single product type (e.g., shampoo) may be associated with an array of images, depending on the targeted market. For instance, one shampoo may be associated with images of youth and excitement, while a different shampoo may be linked with symbols of nature. Consumers can choose among shampoos based on their preferences for the associated symbols.

Goods represent a way people can communicate and place themselves within social structures, transforming the personal meaning of the everyday use of products as a whole. On the surface, advertising may influence specific consumer decisions through attention-getting icons, but a deeper consequence is that the marketplace immerses the realm of needing in a domain of social communication that is strongly influenced by the mass media, marketers, and advertising.

The importance of icons to modern advertising is difficult to overstate. In a consumer society, vast arrays of goods are bundled with symbols and images through product design, packaging, store displays, and fashion trend changes. Advertising images have three essential characteristics: (1) Most important, they redescribe reality, selling happiness by associating scenes from everyday life with the purchase of goods; (2) they convey a level of ambiguity that allows various interests to be linked with them; and (3) they are fluid, constantly shifting the paths to contentment.

Relative Standing

Comparative judgment, a key element in individual consumer decisions, is also important to perceptions of well-being and success that derive from comparisons with some reference group. Unlike traditional societies, a hallmark of the consumer society is that there are no fixed or stable standards of success. Advertising ensures that most tangible forms of wealth represent ephemeral signs of success. Thorstein Veblen, Tibor Scitovsky, and Fred Hirsch have all pointed out the importance and perils of the social context of consumption.

For Veblen, creating social distance through wealth accumulation inevitably leads to dissatisfaction. As soon as a person rises to a new material standard, it ceases to provide any more satisfaction than earlier, lower standards did. Those who are below average for their reference groups are chronically dissatisfied until they catch up; but once the average is reached, a restless striving to exceed and distinguish oneself from the average takes over.

Scitovsky critiques the mainstream economic view that people become more satisfied as their real income increases. He argues that the social forces that influence tastes also change the ability to be satisfied by the things that cater to our tastes. He points out that elevating real income levels fails to achieve higher levels of satisfaction because: (1) much of the satisfaction derived at all income levels is from status; (2) satisfaction is also related to the nature of work; (3) satisfaction is strongly associated with "genuine novelty"—something that is missing in consumer societies; and (4) we quickly adapt to and take for granted the comforts of greater material advantage.

Fred Hirsch distinguishes between goods that meet our material needs and positional goods, those that have value because others do not have them. Hirsch argues that as the wealth of a society increases, the proportion of positional goods in the economy also rises. However, since high-status goods are inherently scarce (fame is for the few), competition for them is ever increasing, absorbing greater material resources with little net benefit.

Both Scitovsky and Hirsch recognize the importance of status consumption, but they differ in their views on the importance of advertising. For Scitovsky, advertising is of little importance, merely influencing the selection of goods that satisfy mass tastes. Alternatively, Hirsch argues that advertising plays an important role by exaggerating the desirability of positional goods and concealing their negative social effects.

Quality of Life

Research on the sources of overall life satisfaction (for example, Robert Lane, Hadley Cantril, Richard Easterlin, and Ed Diener) suggests relative standing, interpersonal relations, and nonmaterial goods (such as love, friendship, a sense of autonomy, and self-esteem) as the most significant. These studies raise important questions concerning the large role of the marketplace in our daily lives.

> If what happens in the marketplace itself has little direct bearing on the deep sources of life satisfaction, too great an emphasis on the ambiguous associations between products and images of contentment may mislead consumers and actually diminish the possibilities for satisfaction. [252]

In a consumer society, are wants satisfied by the goods that society produces? How is satisfaction defined in a consumer society and what is the correlation between satisfaction and the purchase of goods? Is the link between goods and happiness in a consumer society decreasing rather than increasing a sense of satisfaction, even as social wealth rises?

Summary of

Introduction to Fables of Abundance
by T.J. Jackson Lears
[Published in *Fables of Abundance: A Cultural History of Advertising in America* (New York: Basic Books, 1994), 1–13.]

> What do advertisements mean? Many things. They urge people to buy goods, but they also signify a certain vision of the good life; they validate a way of being in the world. [1]

The Protestant ethic gave way to a therapeutic ethos in early twentieth-century America, but has persisted in a subtle, influential form, encouraging personal growth through the management of desire. Advertising embodied this transition, ordering its various themes through the icons of self-realization. This summary argues that the agenda of advertising institutions, in connection with other cultural forces, has been organized around a rhetoric of control, rather than of hedonistic release. Advertising promotes visions of personal striving isolated from or antagonistic to the environment, contributing to "an unexamined commitment to economic growth despite worldwide depletion of nonrenewable resources; [and] preoccupation with an empty pursuit of efficiency that impoverishes personal as well as public life." [11]

Early Advertising Critics and the Productivist Ethos

Early advertising critics, notably Thorstein Veblen, John Kenneth Galbraith, Stuart Chase, and Vance Packard, analyzed the cultural significance of advertising in secular terms that drew inspiration from the Protestant plain speech tradition as well as from fears that the marketplace reduces personal liberties. Together they embraced a "productivist" ethos that exaggerated the producer's ability to influence preferences while underestimating the cultural and personal significance of consumption.

A productivist ethos cannot sustain a critique of advertising, especially in light of the environmental consequences of continuing increases in production. An alternative critique can be grounded in the recognition that advertising is one of the cultural forces that actively disconnect human beings from the material world. Marxist theory offers partial support for such a view. On the one hand, Marxist theory implies that with the rise of industrialized capitalism, production is divorced from consumption, things are isolated from their origins, and desire is directed toward the acquisition of things but not their leisurely enjoyment. Capitalism "underwrote a Cartesian vision of an isolated self in an inert world of objects." [5] On the other hand, the Marxist view relies on the productivist ethos by asserting that work is the most significant way of connecting with the world.

Productivism: Critiques and Alternatives

A common theme among critics of the productivist view is that increasing production has not met its early promises of greater leisure. American antimodernists from Henry Adams to Lewis Mumford attacked faith in progress. The Frankfurt School theorists, including Theodor Adorno, Max Horkheimer, and Herbert Marcuse, maintained that the performance principle that governs the markets of industrial capitalism also constrains the enjoyment of leisure.

Alternatives to the productivist view of the meaning of consumption include ideas inspired by anthropology on gift exchange, and Hannah Arendt's discussion of craftsmanship. George Bataille, Jean Baudrillard, and the poet Lewis have contrasted the prudence of commodity exchange with the energetic release of gift-giving. Hyde argued that gift-giving can create feelings of abundance amid poverty just as commodity exchange can reinforce a sense of scarcity amid material abundance.

Arendt, in distinguishing work from labor, argued that the consumer society promotes indifference to the material world through the production and consumption of throw-away goods. Individuals labor to make a living rather than work to create goods that stabilize human life through their durability. Her opposition to modern consumption stemmed less from a concern over materialism than from the contemporary failure to fabricate, maintain, and care for a durable world of things.

At the heart of Arendt's critique lies an animistic sensibility that values the connections among self, goods, and the world. The collector, either the connoisseur of rarities or the devotee of kitsch or camp, represents one idealized version of the kind of person Arendt envisioned as craftsperson—one who constructs meaning from his or her work, creating permanence through collection. Similarly, creative play and artistic expression permit the construction of meaningful connections with the material world, but are stigmatized as frivolous with the collapse of work into labor. "This animistic sensibility poses fundamental challenges to the subject-object dualism at the heart of Western culture—including the culture promoted by advertising. [8] Through its secular idioms of desire management, advertising conjures and sustains health and personal growth in a worldview that isolates personal striving from the environment.

Advertising and the Rhetoric of Control

A Protestant-inspired rhetoric of control modulated the agenda of national advertising as it developed in the twentieth century. To be sure, advertising stirred desires and elevated pleasure and its symbolic expression, but in general the managerial values of self-realization and health, both individual and national, structured and constrained the more hedonistic icons. This view contrasts with the common assumption (one the author himself once espoused—see summary in Part V) that advertising contributed to the development of a hedonistic consumer culture.

> Consumer culture there was, from the 1910s to the 1970s , but it was less a riot of hedonism than a new way of ordering the existing balance of tensions between control and release. During its heyday, the post–World War II decades, consumer culture was based on an unusual set of institutional

circumstances: a system of tradeoffs between labor and management (labor discipline in exchange for steady, high wages), and the temporary global ascendancy of the U.S. economy. As capital became more mobile and management began looking overseas for cheap labor, consumer culture lost its institutional base. Without a well-paid working population, mass consumption could no longer serve as the integrative glue of civil society. Americans could no longer count on a steady increase in their standard of living. [10–11]

In more recent times, advertising has grown more flashy and pervasive, but has maintained the same underlying themes. "Despite their sensuous surfaces, most brand-name advertisements remain dominated by the ethos of personal efficiency. They continue to construct a separate self in a world of fascinating but forgettable goods." [11]

However, there exists a countertendency among advertising themes, embracing an animistic sensibility expressed through magical and carnivalesque symbols. This sensibility captures the mystery of the cosmos, transcendence, and a feeling for the human organism connected to the world. It suggests an alternative to the values of efficiency that dominate the marketplace and personal striving.

Summary of

Advertising

by Ben Fine and Ellen Leopold

[Published in *The World of Consumption*
(London and New York: Routledge, 1990), 194–218.]

Contemporary analyses of advertising focus either on the meanings associated with commodities (use values) or on economic functions (exchange values). This summary argues that neither of these approaches fully appreciates the role of production in advertising and that this neglect is particularly glaring as concern intensifies over the environmental costs of global industrialization.

Advertising and Value

Use-value approaches to advertising emphasize the relation among consumers, products, and their associated messages, whereas exchange-value approaches emphasize the relation among consumers, producers, and other economic factors. Each approach begins with the notion that advertising differentiates materially similar products through the use of illusions and fantasy.

According to the use-value approach, advertising often produces an aesthetic illusion by concealing a commodity's actual physical properties from the consumer. Since many products have the same functional design and differ only slightly in composition, competition among firms often depends on advertising rather than product quality. For example, since cigarettes differ very little in taste and function, all cigarette advertising involves product differentiation based on image and message. But by focusing on product imagery and the consumer, use-value approaches fail to account for the economic effects of advertising. In general, this approach examines the cultural meaning of commodities at the expense of the role played by production. At the extreme (as in the work of Jean Baudrillard), such approaches hold that the use value of a commodity is entirely independent of its physical properties. In this view, only the images or signs are consumed, not commodities.

In contrast, a variety of exchange-value approaches emphasize advertising's economic functions. In the Keynesian tradition, Kaldor views advertising as promoting consumption in competitive markets and creating jobs in both sales and production. Institutionalists such as John Kenneth Galbraith view advertising as a creator of ever-expanding, unwanted needs. According to the Fordist perspective (represented by Stuart Ewen and Christopher Lasch), advertising is essential both to mass production and to a mass-consumption society. In these views, insufficient consideration is paid to a commodity's use value, and the important role of production is missing.

> The exchange value approach, despite its economic orientation, tends to set production aside since advertising is perceived to be an activity and cost within circulation. Within this framework, it really does not matter what has been produced and how . . . as long as it can be sold as soon and as cheaply as possible. [214]

Advertising and Society

Of all the fields of social science, only economics ignores the social construction of a commodity's use value. In any broader social theory, it is clear that advertising addresses the perception of what is consumed. Various social science theories emphasize the importance of advertising's effects on the consumer's psychology, ritual behavior, and the elaboration of social roles.

Advertising more often reflects, rather than creates, the material culture in which it occurs. Today, the exclusion of blacks from most advertising and the continued use of sexist imagery provide strong evidence that advertising is not a cultural leader. At least with respect to women, advertising cannot be said to be among the cultural vanguard since it has contributed to the ideological obstruction of progressive changes in social roles for women. This is especially true since it has been found that more realistic portrayals of women effectively promote sales.

More generally, advertising is not always effective in its sales pitch: 90 percent of new products fail in the United States. It is important to note that advertising is neither the only nor the most important part of the process of selling. Sales techniques, and retail environments such as supermarkets, retail chains, shopping centers, and specialty stores, have a pivotal role to play in selling commodities. While some critiques suggest that advertising technique is unchanging (and irresistible), in fact advertisers are well aware of their limitations and failures, and constantly innovate in pursuit of greater persuasiveness.

The absence of production from contemporary analyses of advertising is striking given the environmental hazards of increasing economic growth. Advertising involves production in three ways: Production is the source of advertised objects; innovation in production technologies may be the focus of advertising messages and images; and production and sales efforts are interdependent.

With respect to production, advertising theory may assume a horizontal perspective in which advertising is consecutively linked to factors such as culture, demand, and, occasionally, production. Alternatively, in a vertical perspective, the nature of advertising for a product corresponds to the system of provision. The more comprehensive vertical approach implies that the mode of production, distribution, and retailing for an individual product all have an effect on the advertising strategies and techniques that are used to sell it.

Summary of

The Emergence of American
Television: The Formative Years
and
Toward a New Video Order: The 1980s

by J. Fred MacDonald[1]

[Published in *One Nation Under Television: The Rise and Decline of Network Television* (New York and Toronto: Random House, 1990), 3–62 and 221–287.]

In ceding the airwaves to merchandisers who used them to make a living, Americans guaranteed that the utilitarian potential of radio and television would never be fully realized. With transmission initially limited to the few channels possible on the VHF band, competition was stifled and the potential of the medium to serve many audiences was restricted. Allowing a few similarly structured networks to program for such a richly diverse nation ensured the triumph of formula over invention, simplicity over the profound. As impressive as some network fare would be—and, indeed, much network programming was enormously popular with viewers and well received by critics—national broadcasting would always be driven by the propensity to satisfy mass tastes while disappointing the legitimate expectations of audiences with narrower interests. [58]

Daily, [TV] has bombarded an already materialistic society with countless advertisements urging the purchase of specific products, needed or not, affordable or not; but it has been a crucial vehicle for creating popular demand within an economy greatly dependent on mass consumption for its viability. [55]

In the early twentieth century, cultural leaders heralded the arrival of free television as public educator and entertainer, facilitator of an enlightened era. This summary argues that network television has failed to deliver on its early promise, promoting mass-oriented commercial entertainment at the expense of satisfying individual preferences. The growing popularity of cable television and video cassette recorders threatens the networks where they are weakest, offering more autonomy, more choice, and diverse programming that appeal to wider range of tastes.

The success of television programming has always depended on its ability to reach mass audiences. Sponsors' interests in having their products seen by as many people as possible made it less profitable for networks to appeal to diverse preferences. This programming orientation was motivated by the interests of national advertising sponsors, who quickly discovered that television was a much more effective sales medium than radio, albeit more expensive. By 1952, just 13 years after the first TV broadcasts, television had captured more than 50 percent of all broadcast advertising revenue.

While the profit incentive to create mass audiences has led to one nation under television, the inability of network television to satisfy diverse interests lies behind the recent exodus to pay television. The commercialization of television required that successful programming be measured by market share instead of quality. Consequently, network television has traditionally offered what was most acceptable to the largest numbers of people, rather than what was most preferred by individual consumers.

The television industry's tendency to market to the masses was exaggerated by federal regulations in 1945 that restricted early video transmissions to the Very High Frequency (VHF) bandwidth. The decision delayed until 1953 the opening of the Ultra High Frequency (UHF) bandwidth, which could have accommodated more stations and appealed to a diversity of tastes. In the brief VHF-only era, the Big Three networks National Broadcast Company (NBC), American Broadcast Company (ABC), and Columbia Broadcast System (CBS) consolidated their advertising base and created barriers to entry for potential challengers. Development of UHF was effectively crippled by high start-up costs, monopolization of national advertising dollars and big-name entertainers by the major networks, limited transmission range, and small audiences. Early UHF stations were relegated to broadcasting reruns of programs that had already aired on the big networks.

The major networks remained unchallenged until the 1980s, when the cable industry rose to prominence and an alternative network, Fox, began to attract viewers and advertising dollars. The success of cable television was due to its ability to satisfy individual demand without having to rely on national advertising, which requires access to the largest possible audiences. Freed from the constraints of least-common-denominator taste, cable flourished as consumers willingly paid for choice and diversity in programming. The success of Fox also owed much to consumer dissatisfaction with traditional network fare, as well as to the willingness of its owner, Rupert Murdoch, to sink billions of dollars into start-up and promotional expenses.

The original intention that television be a trustee of the public airwaves was compromised by regulatory concessions to corporate interests. The cultural potential of television was undermined by two regulatory events: the early failure of the Wagner-Hatfield Amendment to the 1934 Communications Act and the more recent decision by the Federal Communication Commission (FCC) to "unregulate" television in the early 1980s.

The Wagner-Hatfield Amendment, prior to the advent of television, would have required that one quarter of all radio licenses be reserved for educational and cultural interests. Without this amendment, the Communications Act laid the groundwork for the eventual commercialization of television as well as radio. "Unregulation" meant that television was no longer to be viewed as trustee of public airwaves and should be treated no differently from any other part of the market. Even the modest surviving public interest provisions were gutted under the Reagan Administration. According to the head of the FCC in 1982, a television was just like any other appliance, no more than "a toaster with pictures."

In an important respect "free" television is just like any other service offered by the market: It costs money. Television advertisements cost the average American household an extra $24 a month in 1988 for purchased goods and services.

Network television was neither free nor addressed to a nation's diverse interests. Between 1953 and 1988, the top-rated network programs drew fewer and fewer viewers, as ratings for the most popular shows dropped 54 percent. Consumers became bored with the limited range of programming offered by the major networks.

The rise of cable and development of electronic accessories like video cassette recorders (VCRs) added to the malaise of the big three networks but also gave consumers more choice, more autonomy, and the ability to see what they wanted when they wanted it. Increasingly, the television medium became more personalized with the variety offered by cable narrowcasting and VCRs.

With the imminent arrival of interactive television, the television medium offers the intriguing possibility of facilitating town-meeting style democracy through electronic voting on pressing civic issues as well as the opportunity for advertisers to market to the needs of individual consumers rather than mass audiences. General Motors is currently researching interactive advertising using televisions, personal computers, telephones, and facsimile machines. In the future national advertisers may achieve the ultimate in market segmentation, addressing individual consumers through interactive electronic media.

Note

1. These chapters illuminate the history of network television. This summary emphasizes those parts that address television advertising, television as public utility, and the potential transformation of television into a personalized medium.

Summary of

Television and the Structuring of Experience

by Robert Kubey and Mihaly Csikszentmihalyi

[Published in Chapter 10 of *Television and the Quality of Life:
How Viewing Shapes Everyday Experience* (New Jersey and London:
Lawrence Erlbaum Associates, 1990), 181–222.]

[B]ecause consciousness is necessarily formed by exposure to information,
media fare helps define what our most important and salient goals should
be. Being an intimate part of the consumer society, television tells us that
a worthwhile life is measured in terms of how many desirable material objects we get to own, and how many pleasures we get to feel. To achieve
such goals complex skills are unnecessary. Even though some people spend
a great deal of attention in trying to find bargains, in monitoring prices
and sales, in developing culinary taste and fashion sense, in keeping abreast
of new models and new gadgets, for the most part consumption does not
require much disciplined effort and therefore does not produce psychological growth. [199]

There is little doubt that television plays an important role in the reproduction of consumer culture. On average, individuals spend up to four
hours a day in contact with televised information. This summary argues
that the indiscriminate viewing of television is harmful to personal growth,
and explains why people spend so much time being around televisions; it
also describes the differential effects of this behavior on personal development, and offers possible strategies for making television viewing a better
experience.

Although everyone needs a sense of order in their lives, individuals vary
in how they meet this need. Typically, order is achieved by seeking out or
creating information about the world to reassure people that it conforms to
individual images of it. Redundant information, for example, reassures us
that things are the way we expect them to be. Television is an exemplary
source of redundant information; the predictability of shows, the repetitive
use of familiar genres and circumstances, and the familiarity of characters all
have a reassuring effect. "Many viewers with less structure in their lives,
such as retired persons and the unemployed, use television to give shape to
the day and to demarcate time." [184] Some shows are even named after
the time of day that they come on—for example, The Eleven O'clock
News—to remind viewers and increase ratings. In some ways, television has
co-opted the role that casual conversation once played in telling people the
obvious and recounting the familiar.

Television Content and the Existing Social Order

Although television viewing facilitates a sense of order, its effects on individuals and culture vary depending on cognitive and life circumstances, viewing habits, and the commercial interests of television sponsors. Television content promotes the status quo by packaging messages in comforting, easily digestible segments that require little mental effort to enjoy, and by supporting familiar beliefs. The commercial interests of sponsors, which shape content to a certain extent, have less of an effect on consumer demand than the tens of thousands of hours that individuals spend in front of the television. This large investment of time induces an acceptance of an attraction for televised lifestyles as well as the products of television's commercial sponsors.

Advertising promotes a fictitious connection between consumption and self-development when it suggests that the keys to happiness have the shape of its new and improved goods and services. With few exceptions, achieving the pleasures depicted in, or removing the evil pains described by, advertising requires less the mental discipline that underlies personal growth than consumer skills that contribute little to self-development. Ultimately, the relationship between consumption, television viewing, and self-development is weak, especially for less happy individuals.

> The irony is that television may benefit most those who least need it. People who are already reasonably happy and in control of their lives will be more inclined to find useful information on television and will be less inclined to become dependent on the medium. Those who are less happy and less able or skilled in creating order in their experience are more likely to become dependent, and yet derive less enjoyment from their viewing. [187]

The Crisis of Meaning

Excessive and indiscriminate television viewing reflects both a general pattern of short-term pleasure-seeking behavior and a tendency for meaningful information to be structured by sources outside traditional socializing agents. As the mass media has grown, it has become easier for viewers to allow their attention to be structured by outside factors, thus inhibiting more active personal development.

> Perhaps no better proof could be offered of how television has come to absorb a significant proportion of the authority and power that the church, family, and school once held than the fact that television celebri-

ties are now among those people most talked about, admired, and emulated in our culture. Television and its celebrities now compete with church leaders, parents, and teachers for the attention of children and are important sources of information for how one should live. [197]

Television messages may describe happy situations but, in fact, television viewing induces relaxation much more than it does happiness. That individuals choose to pacify themselves should be at the crux of all critiques of television. Any explanation for why individuals indiscriminately watch television must address the reasons why individuals need to escape from life beyond the television.

> Those who find fault with the viewing experience must also take seriously the aim of trying to make life as a whole a deeper, more complex, more coherent and enjoyable experience for as many people as possible. Otherwise we set television up as a scapegoat blaming the most popular form of escape instead of examining why people need to escape, or recognizing that the need for escape is part of the human condition. Indeed the need for escape has long shaped television programs, and will surely influence future programming regardless of technological change. [207]

Viewing television can be an active process that engenders growth through mental effort. Better television experiences may be achieved either by teaching the audience how to view shows or by improving content. Viewer skills cannot be improved without changing the reasons why individuals watch television.

Summary of

Theories of Consumption in Media Studies
by David Morley
[Published in *Acknowledging Consumption*, ed. Daniel Miller (London: Routledge, 1995), 296–328.]

In the early 1930s, leading cultural analysts believed that media institutions had the ability to influence consumer behaviors and induce passivity among audiences. In contrast, contemporary researchers in the field of media studies conceive audiences as more active, choosing and interpreting a greater range of media products. This summary discusses the major themes and debates of media consumption research since the rise of television and film, illustrating the importance of gender to recent media studies.

Are Audiences Passive or Active?

Media research has oscillated between perspectives that stress the power of the media to dominate audiences and perspectives that view media consumption as an active, creative process. The Frankfurt School of Social Research set the terms of this debate as fascism rose to prominence during the 1930s. Led by Theodore Adorno, Herbert Marcuse, and Max Horkheimer, the Frankfurt School developed the idea that mass culture weakens social ties, creates widespread isolation, and leaves individuals vulnerable to whoever controls the media. Media institutions act as culture industries that inject their messages, like hypodermic needles, directly into the minds of passive individuals who collectively constitute the mass audience.

Each aspect of this view has come under attack in subsequent media research. Unlike the theoretical approach of the Germans, American researchers in the 1940s adopted an empirical research agenda that qualified the notion of media power, demonstrating that media's social effects were complex, indirect, and mediated by audiences. In the 1960s, British researchers rejected the then common view that mass audiences are homogeneous, arguing that individuals respond differently to media messages based on their psychological make-up. This approach, however, neglected the role of cultural influences by exaggerating the importance of psychological factors.

Stuart Hall in 1973 argued that media content must be decoded before it has an effect on the audience. A dialectic exists between media institutions that encode media messages and audiences that interpret or decode them. In his view, media institutions encourage a preferred reading of the media text, but individuals will vary in how they understand its content given cultural differences arising from their social background. The 1970s also gave rise to Screen Theory, which focused on the analysis of films and media texts—the messages displayed in films (principally) and television programs. Influenced by both feminism and psychoanalytic discourses, Screen Theory revived the hypodermic model by assuming that it was possible to deduce audience reactions from analyses of media texts. Its sophisticated analyses of the ways in which film texts attempt to "position" their viewers, however, rely too much on a psychoanalytic model of human development and understates the role of social and historical influences.

More current research has recognized that technological advances are empowering consumers as never before. For instance, video technologies allow greater choice and control over when and what programs will be viewed. Some researchers caution that there is a difference between having power over a text (when and what will be watched) and power over the agenda within which the text is produced. Being active with a remote control is different from being powerful. Others have criticized recent advances, arguing that some cultural studies, in their rush to analyze the active consumer, have lost their critical perspective, becoming apologists for mass culture.

> If the problem with the Frankfurt School was that its members were too elitist, too far outside the culture they examined, many cultural studies writers today have the opposite problem—they are so concerned not to be 'elitist' that they fall into a mode of populism—immersed in popular culture themselves, half in love with their own subject, they seem unable to achieve the proper critical distance from it, and end up writing apologies for mass culture.[1]

Media Consumption

Changes in media technologies influence the nature of consumption as well as gender and class relations. Historically, commercial support of television has influenced consumption by sponsoring the programs that are consumed by audiences and promoting consumption of its products. However, the recent innovation of home shopping networks has linked these types of consumption in an unprecedented way. With the possibility that more shopping, banking, working, and leisure will be done at home through computers and interactive media, gender relations in the domestic setting will be increasingly affected by media technologies. Also, increasing privatization of television access through cable and pay-per-view options tends to diminish effective citizen participation by members of society who lack the resources to buy the new technologies.

Media and Gender

In recent years, media studies has shifted some of its focus from the debate over audience activity/passivity to the domestic context of media consumption. A growing literature is examining the use of particular media technologies in families within specific cultural domains. This approach was initiated by the work of Hobson (1982) and Radway (1984), who raised questions about the home as a gendered space and the significance of gender relations in the consumption of television and other media. Hobson discussed the use of media by housewives to counter isolation in the home, while Radway explored how housewives combated domestic pressures by reading romantic fiction.

Their work is extended by the author in two studies. The *Family Television Study* (1986) examined how gender influences the consumption of television.

> The "Family Television" study was designed to explore, through interviews with family members, the issues arising once one takes the family (or household), rather than the individual viewer in isolation, as the effective "unit of consumption" of television. . . . Once one considers TV viewing in the context of domestic relations, one inevitably raises the question of power relations, and within the domestic sphere these power relations are principally constructed by gender. [321]

The study was conducted in an urban white, lower-middle-class to affluent working-class culture in Britain. It found that men had more control than women over program choice; men planned their viewing in advance, while women tended to have more ambivalent attitudes toward television; and men viewed programs more attentively, more often than women, who would often only watch programs while doing some other activity.

The second study, directed by Roger Silverstone at Brunel University between 1987 and 1990, was called *Household Uses of Information and Communication Technology*. It investigated how gender affects the incorporation of new technologies into the home. The rationale for this project was that there exist gendered domains of competence in the home, just like math and science are defined as primarily male domains in the public sphere, and that these domains will affect how media technologies are used in the home. "The central issue is how different technologies are incorporated into particular, gender-designated domains of culture competence—according to cultural roles defining their appropriateness for individuals . . . " [323] This study as well as others have found that media technologies become gendered upon introduction to the home. For instance, research has shown that in certain cultures the video cassette recorder, the computer, as well as computer games are viewed as technologies requiring male competency.

Note

1. Cited on page 308 of Morley. The passage is from T. Modleski, ed., *Studies in Entertainment* (Bloomington: Indiana University Press, 1986), xi.

Summary of

Household Debt Problems:
Toward a Micro-Macro Linkage
by Samuel Cameron

[Published in *Review of Political Economy* 6 (1994), 205–220.]

In economic theory the borrower is modeled as an individual who chooses a lifetime pattern of consumption, taking on debt to adjust the flow of goods over time. In practice, modern borrowers increasingly engage in problem debt behavior, diminishing their potential lifetime consumption opportunities. This summary argues that the individualistic orientation of the economic model fails to account for macro influences on debt behavior caused by economic growth fueled by high-status consumption.

Problem Debt

Economists and psychologists agree that excessive debt is a problem for individuals. Economists believe that problem debt arises only when unforeseen circumstances interrupt the consumption patterns that individuals choose over the course of their lives. Alternatively, psychologists believe that problem debt arises from personality traits or is caused by compensation for past experiences. Although problem debt is commonly associated with an inability to repay loans, this situation may not be perceived to be a problem by the debtor. Problem debt is characterized by lack of self-control, overindulgence, or difficult circumstances. Ignorance of the implications of credit borrowing is the primary cause of debt problems; other causes include unwarranted risk taking, a failure to come to terms with unfortunate consequences, or a deliberate flaunting of the limits of one's purchasing power.

Standard economic explanations view problem debt through the overly narrow lens of individual preferences. The mainstream approach looks to dual preference models that analyze problem debt as a competition between desires for immediate gratification and desires for long-term good. When applied to the use of credit cards, this approach shows that credit-financed consumption by weak-willed consumers appears to generate increased purchasing power but actually diminishes it over the long run when repayment is not prompt.

Arguments for the dual preference model are unable to explain why long-run preferences do not prevail over short-run preference sets. Problem debt behavior is supposed to reflect a temporary disequilibrium that is necessarily untenable given the unsustainability of problem debt behavior. But the dual preference model cannot assume that a rational consumer will dig him- or herself out of this disequilibrium by measuring costs and acting consistently. The assumption of rationality begs the question when it comes to explaining why profligate behavior must come to an end.

In dynamic settings, psychological models conceptualize debt behavior as arising from loss of self-control due to overstimulation of either income or lure of goods. Maintenance of long-run equilibrium can be upset by sudden changes of income (as with lottery winners), changes in attitude, or inappropriately regulated impulses. Since impulses are influenced by social factors, behavioral or cognitive models should incorporate the importance of social context.

Possible Macro-Micro Linkages

Debt behavior can be examined in an environment without economic growth (static) or with growth (dynamic). The general equilibrium model provides a useful framework for analyzing the relationship between debt behavior and economic sectors in both environments. In a static context,

> Household consumption is financed out of income, earned in the other sectors, plus credit from the retail and financial sectors. If the retail sector provides credit it will be acting as an agent for a financial institution as stores do not make the loans themselves. For the financial sector, credit/debt is a product from which it seeks to extract profit. The essential problem of macroeconomics is the co-ordination of individual plans into a mutually consistent whole. In a general equilibrium model this is achieved through price signals. For credit/debt the interest rate serves this function. [211]

If there are too many overspenders and not enough lenders, the usual corrective is an increase in interest rates, raising the costs of incurring debt. Creditors then attempt to minimize their risks, attempting to distinguish borrowers who pose good and bad risks. This effort leaves a fringe of rejected borrowers-to-be, creating a market for creditors interested in providing high-interest loans to high-risk borrowers. Higher interest rates, in turn, increase the probability of default for higher-risk borrowers.

In a dynamic setting, aspiration levels are determined by social comparison. Following Duesenberry's view that interdependent preferences generate demand for social status goods, consumption of certain kinds of goods become essential to the maintenance of self-esteem. In part this may be based on an unrealistic picture of one's reference group: People systematically overestimate others' consumption of high-status goods, an error which rises with the amount of television watched. Since individuals cannot determine whether their comparison group's growing consumption pattern is based on current income or on borrowing (or even whether it exists beyond the TV screen, in some cases), aspirations may drive a credit explosion. Individuals who pursue externally driven aspirations while overlooking borrowing costs inevitably wind up caught in a cycle of dissatisfaction, resisting the disincentives of higher interest rates as they increase borrowing to fund the consumption dictated by higher and higher aspiration levels.

PART VIII

Consumption and the Environment

Overview Essay

by Jonathan Harris

The consumption of the average U.S. citizen requires eighteen tons of natural resources per person per year and generates an even higher volume of wastes (including household, industrial, mining, and agricultural wastes). Some of these wastes are released to the atmosphere, rivers, and oceans; others are landfilled or incinerated; a small proportion are recycled. The standard conception of economic development envisions the rest of the world's population as moving steadily up the ladder of mass consumption, eventually achieving levels similar to those achieved by the United States and some European economies. Clearly, the environmental implications of the global spread of mass consumption for resource use and environmental waste absorption are staggering. Should not this promote some rethinking of economic theories of consumption, which for the most part have ignored resource and environmental implications?

The articles in Part VIII address both theoretical and practical aspects of this question. We have already become familiar with critiques of the simple economic theory of utility maximization through consumption of goods. The hypothetical consumer at the center of this theory is devoid of social relationships, ethical principles, or any relationship to the natural world. His or her satisfaction is measured only in terms of quantities of goods and services consumed, and the science of utility maximization is concerned primarily with the choice of how to balance consumption among various alternatives offered in the marketplace. The individual's role as consumer is independent of involvement in the productive process, in which capacity his or her labor is sold in the market for the best possible wage. The only link between the two activities is that the money earned through work provides a budget for consumption. Income may also be saved, but savings serve ultimately to support future consumption via the increased production that results from investment.

The limitations of this abstract perspective in explaining the real-world growth of mass consumption have been extensively explored in earlier parts of this volume. In this part we will find that there is a significant overlap between the socially oriented critique of consumption theory and the ecologically oriented analysis of the impact of mass consumption on the natural world.

One of the few economists to draw attention to this overlap at an early stage was John Kenneth Galbraith, whose prescient article "How Much Should a Country Consume?" appeared in 1958. Galbraith called for an investigation into resource and environmental problems that might be posed by ever-growing consumption; he argued for a reorientation from consumption patterns "which have a high materials requirement to those which have a much lower requirement [such as] education, health services, sanitary services, good parks and playgrounds, orchestras, effective local government, a clean countryside." He deplored the economic forces that promote "an inordinate concentration of our consumption on what may loosely be termed consumer hardware."[1] In this short article, Galbraith prefigured by several decades themes that have more recently been developed in detail, motivated by a sharper awareness that the resource and environmental problems of consumption are now not hypothetical but well advanced and continuing to grow exponentially.

The Social and Environmental Implications of Market Consumption

The initial article summarized here, by Mark Sagoff, focuses on one such essential theme in the overlap between social and ecological critiques of consumption theory. Sagoff distinguishes between the individual as consumer and the individual as citizen. In the arena of public policy, we may make choices that are significantly different from those related to individual consumption. In particular, Sagoff envisions an individual who participates in mass-consumption patterns while supporting an environmentally oriented public policy. At one level, this might be taken simply as evidence of hypocrisy—being prepared to advocate collective sacrifice in a good cause, but at the same time being unwilling to give up personal comforts. But this would be to oversimplify, ignoring the essential role of institutional change. Faced with a crumbling public transit system and highways unsafe for bicycling, people will naturally drive. Given a well-run and convenient public transit system, and safe bicycle paths, many more "individual" choices will be made in favor of nonautomotive transportation. (U.S. citizens who believe that "a well-run and efficient public transportation system" is an oxymoron might consider the systems of many European cities.)

This brings up the issue of what we mean by an "individual" choice. Almost any seemingly "individual" decision to purchase a good is tied to a web of public policy choices. An economic textbook example might present the consumer making a choice to purchase a pound of butter. But behind that simple choice lie many institutional factors. Is the butter local or has it been shipped from a long distance? That may depend on whether the state has a policy of preserving farmland, taking into account environmental and aesthetic externalities. It also depends on whether the national government taxes or subsidizes energy production, affecting long-distance hauling costs. Is the butter produced with artificial chemicals and hormones? This depends on agricultural and environmental policies. Does the consumer know whether or not artificial chemicals and hormones are used in production? That depends on food labeling laws. Will a cholesterol-conscious consumer aim at cutting down butter consumption? This may depend on public health policies and information. Has the butter been produced under humane conditions on the farm? That will depend on agricultural regulations and public sentiment. Has the butter been adequately refrigerated and is it free from contaminants? Those will depend on food inspection laws. In even the simplest consumption decision, a multitude of factors are involved; only a small portion of the information relating to these issues can be conveyed to the consumer through the economic "information carrier" of market price.

The economic doctrine of "consumer sovereignty" is thus put in a different light. Consumers can exercise their power through the market by selecting purchases based on price and other information easily available to them. But to affect the multitude of other factors shaping the market itself, they must be involved in public policy issues. This reality is especially evident in the area of environmental policy, as Sagoff emphasizes. The environmental issue is thus linked to a broader critique of the economist's concept of a "utility function," which somehow balances all of an individual's needs and desires. It has been well established in economic theory that it is impossible to derive a "social welfare function" that somehow adds up all of the individual preferences of consumers.[2] The area of social relations and public policy has, so to speak, a life of its own, which cannot be reduced to individual preference functions. The ethical values that provide the basis for social cohesion cannot, therefore, be excluded from any theory of consumption in the pursuit of a "value-free" science. Sagoff clearly makes this point by using examples concerning consumption and the environment, but its implications must extend to all aspects of consumption theory and of economic theory in general. Once the myth of the sovereign individual consumer falls to the ground, the many "free market" policies that it serves to justify are thrown into question.

This line of thought is developed further by Mario Cogoy. He introduces the idea of a "boundary" between market and nonmarket aspects of consumption that can be generalized to apply to the boundary between market and nonmarket elements of human life. The overextension of the market sphere, he argues, has negative implications both for social life and for the environment. But it is very difficult for the individual to resist the institutional forces promoting excessive marketization. Thus the individual purchases and relies on an automobile for transportation, depends on the utility company to deliver home energy, and relies on prepackaged foods from the supermarket. The implications of these choices (such as excessive fuel use, generation of carbon emissions or nuclear waste, energy used in processing, and increased waste from packaging material) are remote from the individual purchasing the products. Were he or she instead to walk or bicycle, spend time insulating the house, and cook meals from basic ingredients, the environmental impacts would be lessened—but the time pressures of work make such a lifestyle impossible for many people.

In accepting increasing marketization as normal, and recommending it strongly to developing nations as a route out of poverty, we tend to ignore such negative correlates. Again, the effects on resource consumption and the environment are especially evident, but the insidious effects of the shifting boundary are more general. The undermining of community and family, as well as the replacement of spiritual values with commercial ones (effects discussed extensively in other parts of this volume) are now joined by the distancing of the individual from the natural world, with attendant environmental degradation.

It is, of course, possible to think of counter examples, in which increased marketization benefits the environment through the spread of resource-saving technology. Most such examples, however, involve the replacement of one set of environmental problems with another. "Modernized" agriculture may help limit conversion of forest and savannah by making possible higher yields on existing acreage, but the trade-off involves increased fertilizer and pesticide pollution. Modern sawmills waste less wood, but may increase overall timber exports by raising their profitability. The replacement of wood and dung fuels with oil-based fuels limits pressure on agro-ecosystems, but increases carbon emissions. Overall, the more common tendency is for marketization to promote increased resource use.

Macroeconomic Perspectives on Consumption

Herman Daly puts the microeconomic rethinking of consumption into a macroeconomic perspective. He draws on Alfred Marshall, who unlike most modern economic theorists emphasized the physical nature of the process of production and consumption. This provides a link to the ecological approach to economics, which Daly has pioneered.[3] Rather than focusing only on the value added to matter or energy by human labor and the use of human-made capital, he emphasizes the inherent limits on low-entropy matter or energy resources to which value is added in the economic process. This suggests that some limits to consumption are advisable and eventually inescapable. If, as Daly argues, the scale of the macroeconomy has expanded to the point where natural resources and environmental waste absorption, rather than human-made capital, are the scarce factors, then consumption itself needs to be rethought.[4] Rather than maximize consumption in the pursuit of welfare, we need to seek ways to maximize welfare with minimum consumption. Hitherto the market system has been better at the former goal than the latter, and economic theory has measured success primarily in terms of greater consumption (or greater investment today in the cause of increased consumption tomorrow). This does not mean that the market system is not up to the new challenges; but it does suggest that it needs new direction. Daly proposes a shift to resource and energy taxes, rather than taxes on labor and capital, to encourage resource-conserving development. He also clearly agrees with Cogoy's warning about overextension of the market system; Daly is particularly wary of calls to extend the market system globally through untrammeled free trade.[5]

These theoretical perspectives suggest, then, that consumption must be seen in its social and ecological context, and that it should be subject to limits in relation to its destructive effects in either context. This provides an interesting contrast to the current efforts by many economists to extend market valuation to the environment. Through techniques of "contingent valuation," economists seek to transform aspects of the environment into quasi-goods, which potential consumers are then asked to value. This is recommended for cases in which the environment cannot actually be transformed into goods through privatization. In effect, this takes a theory that is primarily suited to the consumption of economic goods under conditions of institutional stability and resource abundance and attempts to apply it to problems that have arisen for exactly the reason Daly identifies—the environmental stress caused by an expanding macroeconomy. The alternative approach is to look to the physical laws of the ecosystem and to higher social values for guidance in reforming and limiting consumption.

Consumption and Economic Development

These contrasting theoretical perspectives give rise to different interpretations of economic development. Clive Ponting's *Green History of the World* offers an application of the environmentalist's perspective on economic history. Here we can see some of the practical realities that give rise to the theoretical issues discussed in the first three articles. We are accustomed to hearing the industrial revolution of the nineteenth century and the economic modernization of the twentieth discussed primarily in terms of technological progress and rising living standards; Ponting emphasizes the massive increase in resource use that accompanied economic growth. This inevitably means that impacts on ecosystems have multiplied, but Ponting also suggests that the momentum of economic growth makes it difficult for industrialized nations to step off the path of ever-growing resource use.

In a finite world, inequality of resource use may actually increase with economic growth. Economic power implies command over resources; greater power for some means less power for others. (Consider the issue of carbon emissions, where a global emissions limit would only permit developing nations to increase fossil fuel use if advanced nations actually decrease emissions.) Ponting cites the dramatic inequalities between "developed" and "less developed" economies, but would surely reject the implication of these terms—that eventually all will reach high levels of "development" and resource use. He suggests rather that the evolution of an affluent global consumer class has locked in inequalities of resource control, constraining the economic futures of most of the world's people.

This theme is picked up in Alan Durning's article, which further indicts the global "consumer class" (roughly, the richest fifth of the world's population) as the source of most environmental problems. While some aspects of economic development are seen as environmentally positive—in particular the shift toward improved technologies and services in developed economies—these effects are not enough to reduce overall environmental impacts, merely to limit their growth. Durning's primary point is the impossibility of global "development" as conceived by economic theory. The resource and environmental demands of bringing all the world's people up to "consumer class" standards of living would be catastrophic. This is all the more true in the context of planetary population growth up to an eventual eight or ten billion,[6] which would nearly double resource and environmental requirements even with *no* increase in living standards.

Lest one might think that Ponting and Durning are overgeneralizing or exaggerating the problem, the World Resources Institute biennial report provides a wealth of specific detail to support these assertions. The problem is not, as originally conceived in the Club of Rome's 1972 *Limits to Growth* report,[7] foreseeable shortages of specific nonrenewable resources— at least for the next fifty years or so. Rather, it is the impacts of industrial growth on renewable natural resource systems, including the atmosphere, that pose the greatest dangers. Global inequality accentuates environmental impacts at both ends of the scale: The rich damage the environment through their high consumption levels, and the poor damage the environment by being forced to utilize marginal and fragile ecosystems. If indeed it is impossible for all to ride the escalator up to mass consumption, then some form of development that will reduce inequality while lessening environmental impacts seems essential.

Consumption, Resource Efficiency, and Social Priorities

Some suggestions of how greater sustainability in consumption might be achieved emerge from the article by Young and Sachs. They address only the technical feasibility issue in their discussion of sustainable materials use, but their vision of improved industrial ecology is an essential component of a global alternative to rising consumption of resources. It is difficult, if not impossible, to imagine any scenario in which goods consumption does not rise, if only to keep pace with rising population. Young and Sachs suggest, however, that the environmental impacts of consumption might be dramatically reduced by extensive recycling and use of secondary rather than virgin materials.

A partial solution to the "addiction" to growth is offered by the labor-intensive nature of a recycling economy. Recycled materials generally use less energy and have less environmental impact, but require more labor. This higher labor cost is one reason why such systems are not more widely adopted—it is cheaper to exploit virgin resources and externalize environmental costs. Daly's proposal for a tax shift from labor and capital to resources would greatly expedite the transition to the kind of materials- and energy-efficient economy that Young and Sachs propose.

However, this can be at best only a part of the solution. The most resource-efficient economy will eventually be overwhelmed by the high material demands of a world population growing toward eight or ten billion people, unless more sweeping alternatives to the mass consumer lifestyle evolve. Paul Ekins points out, for example, that technological progress would need to reduce the environmental impact of consumption by a factor of sixteen over the next fifty years to offer any significant environmental improvement in the face of projected population and consumption growth.[8] Environmentally sound technology is undoubtedly crucial. But as Sagoff, Cogoy, and Daly have argued, the forces that drive markets toward ever-higher levels of consumption will have to be tamed if the underlying conflict between consumer desires and biophysical realities is ever to be resolved. This can come about only by redrawing the boundary between market consumption and community life, between the individual as consumer and the individual as participant in the social and natural world. Individual motivations toward greater goods consumption will have to shift in favor of deriving fulfillment from community and nature. This inner shift in priorities is the greater challenge. In Parts IX and X of this volume we will explore the forces driving consumerism worldwide, and the possible alternatives to an insatiable consumer society.

Notes

1. John Kenneth Galbraith, "How Much Should a Country Consume?" in Henry Jarrett, ed. *Perspectives on Conservation: Essays on America's Natural Resources,* (Johns Hopkins Press, 1958), 89–99.

2. The classic demonstration of this is the "Impossibility Theorem" developed in Kenneth J. Arrow, *Social Choice and Individual Values* 2nd ed. (New York: Wiley, 1963).

3. See selections by Herman Daly in Volume I of this series: Krishnan, Harris, and Goodwin, eds., *A Survey of Ecological Economics* (Washington, DC: Island Press, 1995).

4. A biological perspective on the issue of macroeconomic scale is provided by Vitousek et al. in the article "Human Appropriation of the Products of Photosynthesis," which estimates that "nearly 40 percent of potential terrestrial net primary productivity is used directly, co-opted, or foregone because of human activities" (Vitousek et al., in *Bioscience* vol. 36, no. 6, June 1986).

5. See Herman E. Daly, "The Perils of Free Trade," *Scientific American* 269 (November 1993), 50–57, summarized in Krishnan et al., eds., op. cit.

6. This figure is consistent with U.N. low to median estimates (*United Nations Long Range World Population Projections: 1950–2150,* United Nations, 1992). If fertility levels do not fall rapidly, ultimate world population levels could be much higher, above 12 billion.

7. Donnella H. Meadows et al., *The Limits to Growth* (New York: Universe Books, 1972).

8. See Paul Ekins, "The Sustainable Consumer Society: A Contradiction in Terms?" (*International Environmental Affairs,* Fall 1991). Ekins uses the famous $I = P \times A \times T$ equation introduced by Paul Ehrlich, which states that environmental impact equals population (P) times per capita consumption (A) times environmental impact per unit of consumption (T). If population doubles and per capita consumption grows at 3 percent for fifty years, P x A increases by a factor of eight. T must then decrease by a factor of eight to keep environmental impacts unchanged, and by a factor of sixteen to achieve a "sustainable" lower-environmental-impact global economy.

Summary of

The Allocation and Distribution of Resources

by Mark Sagoff

[Published in *The Economy of the Earth*
(Cambridge: Cambridge University Press, 1988), 50–73.]

This summary argues that individuals hold inherently contradictory views on questions of consumption and the environment, that policy debate cannot be confined to the economists' familiar framework of equity versus efficiency considerations, and that we cannot put a price on things, such as the natural environment, that we value the most.

Consumer and Citizen Preferences

An individual often has different preferences as a consumer and as a citizen. Proposals to open national parks to commercial ski resort development can be (and are) opposed by citizens who would nonetheless enjoy skiing at such a place if development occurred.

> I love my car; I hate the bus. Yet I vote for candidates who promise to tax gasoline to pay for public transportation. I send my dues to the Sierra Club to protect areas in Alaska I shall never visit. . . . I have an "Ecology Now" sticker on a car that drips oil everywhere it's parked. [53]

The distinction between consumer and citizen preferences has long been noted by economists in the field of public finance. Recognition of the existence of distinct public policy preferences does not imply rejection of individual preferences, but requires awareness that the two are different and often inconsistent.

Attempts to find a combined preference ordering are bound to fail; individuals have incompatible beliefs, and do not rank them in a single hierarchy in the manner of the "rational man" of economic theory. Citizen preferences are judgments about what *we* should do, while consumer preferences are expressions of what *I* want. No single preference map combines these two very different kinds of statements. Indeed, statements about what we should do as a nation express judgments, which may be true or false, about our shared or common intentions. These objective beliefs must be judged on their merits through legitimate processes of collective deliberation and choice; they cannot be "priced" at the margin.

Allocation and Distribution

There is also an important distinction between the allocation and the distribution of resources. As a matter of allocation, a mountain can be used for either a ski resort or a wilderness; as a matter of distribution, some people gain while others lose from whatever allocational choice is made. Economic theory often suggests that allocational decisions should be made purely on the basis of efficiency, to maximize wealth; distributive choices can then be made separately on a political or ethical basis if desired.

Analysis along these lines tends to break down the discussion of policy into questions concerning efficiency on the one hand and equity on the other. Not all policy proposals allow for a distinct separation between the issues of efficiency and equity; some writers discuss a trade-off between these two goals. Yet efficiency and equity are complementary objectives. Some writers propose placing a greater weight on efficiency, others on equity; but both share a common vocabulary and conceptual framework. They agree that any claim on resources must be based either on rights and fairness or on preferences and productivity. The debate between the two perspectives has become an academic exercise and does not provide useful guidance to public policy and social regulation.

The Rights of Future Generations

Some writers suggest that we need to balance our consumer interests with those of future generations. Yet

> [T]here are few decisions favorable to our wishes that cannot be justified by a likely story about future preferences. Even a nasty strip mine or a hazardous-waste dump produces energy that will strengthen the industrial base left to future generations. [60–61]

In fact, the preferences of future generations will likely depend on education or advertising, and on what is available to them. Citizens of the future depend on the decisions we make today. If we destroy our environmental or cultural heritage, our descendants will be illiterate in those areas, unable to appreciate what they have lost.

Our obligation to provide a future consistent with our ideals is an obligation not to the future generation, but to our ideals. It is morally good to preserve our environmental and cultural heritage, not for the good *of* individuals, but to allow the development of *good individuals*. Although political liberalism has traditionally called for an avoidance of acts of authoritarian paternalism, we cannot avoid paternalism with respect to future generations. "What is worth saving is not merely what can be consumed later; it is what we can take pride in and, indeed, love." [65]

The Conflict Within Us

The conflict between citizen and consumer preferences occurs within each of us; it is an inescapable ethical dilemma. Moreover, it is a conflict that could never arise in a society whose only goals were efficiency and equity in the satisfaction of consumer demand. Yet environmentalists shy away from the presentation of ethical issues, frequently seeking to calculate costs and benefits rather than discuss moral arguments for popular environmental policies. It is tempting to retreat into the "neutral" theories and criteria of economics for evaluating policy problems. "It's scary to think about problems on their own terms; it's easier to apply a methodology. . . . As a result, public officials often discuss the meaning of magnificent environments using a vocabulary that is appropriate to measure the degree to which consumers may exploit them." [68]

Money and Meaning

The worth of things that matter most to us, such as love and religion, are measured not by our willingness to pay for them, but by our unwillingness to pay. Neither true love nor eternal salvation is available for purchase at any price. Such things have a dignity rather than a price. Things that have dignity are those that help us define our relationships with one another. Our common natural and cultural heritage, including the environment we share, has such a dignity. It is dignity, not the calculation of costs and benefits, that ultimately explains why even avid skiers often oppose opening national parks to commercial ski resort development.

Environmental policy may be rational in one of two ways: It may be economically rational in terms of the calculation of costs and benefits, corrected for market failures and environmental externalities whenever possible, or it may be rational in a deliberative sense, based on cogent collective debate about the principles and ideals that we stand for and respect as a nation. The latter approach assumes that the values on which we base policy are objects of public inquiry, and are not derived either from exogenous preferences and market mechanisms or from metaphysical truths about human nature and rights.

Compromise and Community

Although the conflict between citizen and consumer interests is inevitable, compromise can reconcile the desires of individuals and communities. If every mountain were preserved as a wilderness, there would be no place to ski. The judgment that national parks should be preserved, even if commercialization would be profitable (and, in a narrow market sense, "efficient"), rests in part on the belief that there are already many opportunities for skiing and other commercial recreation, but comparatively few wildernesses.

If the stakes were reversed and enormous financial sacrifice was required to protect an environmentally insignificant landscape or to achieve only marginal reductions in pollution, these same people might reach the opposite conclusion. Just as we can reject the dogma of the perfect market, we can also reject the dogma of the perfect environment. Entering the realm of compromise and debate over public policy does not require abandonment of the ideals we hold as citizens, only evaluation of those ideals in the context of the means available to achieve them.

Summary of

Market and Nonmarket Determinants of Private Consumption and Their Impacts on the Environment

by Mario Cogoy

[Published in *Ecological Economics* 13 (1995), 169–180.]

Consumption is an activity that combines market and nonmarket elements. The environmental impacts of consumption depend not only on the physical requirements of market production, but also on the social and institutional frameworks that determine the boundary between market and nonmarket aspects of consumption. This summary argues that environmental degradation results from a bias in the consumption process toward a predominance of market relations and an excess of paid labor in industrial society.

In a modern society, market relations constantly invade and reshape nonmarket sectors of life. The industrialization of formerly nonmarket activity is likely to imply more intensive use of energy and materials, and centralization of skills and process control. Little attention has been paid to the permanently shifting border between market and nonmarket activity as a possible source of environmental degradation. Traditional economic theory considers only market demand for goods and leisure, ignoring the social infrastructure in which consumption is embedded, and the consumption labor and consumption skills that are combined with goods to produce the desired enjoyment of life. Consumption labor includes household work, shopping, traveling, and waiting in lines; consumption skills include the defensive skills of "protecting the brains of consumers from the negative effects of advertising," as well as planning skills and technical knowledge. [171]

Since "economic labor" (working for wages), consumption labor, and consumption skills are all inputs into the production of enjoyment, they are potential substitutes for each other. That is, increased consumption labor and/or skills may be substituted for paid labor time. If taken to the extreme, this substitution would lead either to a market utopia in which all consumption labor and skills are replaced by market relations, or to a "do-it-yourself" utopia in which the largest portion of social labor is performed outside the market. Neither extreme is necessarily efficient or desirable.

Modern society has a strong bias in favor of the market sector, as has been described in great detail by Juliet Schor. Her analysis of the "insidious cycle of work-and-spend" explains a significant source of environmental degradation. In addition, the satisfaction of basic needs such as heating and transportation is organized in a way that gives an inefficiently large role to the market sector, and also leads to unnecessary environmental damage.

The Consumption Process

A formal model can illuminate some aspects of the process of consumer choice. Assuming a fixed-coefficient input-output model, it is easy to calculate the material and labor requirements for delivery of one unit of each type of commodity to final demand. With the further assumptions of constant wage and profit rates throughout the economy it is possible to calculate the paid labor time required to earn enough to buy a unit of each commodity. The consumer combines this economic labor requirement with consumption labor to yield enjoyment. If individuals were free to vary their hours of work at will, it might be assumed that the optimum combination of economic labor and consumption labor would be chosen. However, as Schor has shown, institutional constraints in the labor market prevent such flexibility.

Innovation in consumption can involve a reduction in market inputs and an increase in consumption labor, a change in the mix of market inputs, or an increase in purchases at the expense of consumption labor. Market-expanding innovation increases total profits and paid labor time, but is not always worse for the environment. If a commercial firm introduces innovations that consumers could not have done on their own, the environmental result may be positive—as in the case of some utility-sponsored energy conservation programs. But if consumers utilize the resulting gains for increased consumption with high environmental impacts (using home-energy savings to finance a holiday flight), the global result may still be negative.

Two examples—household energy conservation and transportation—illustrate how environmental damage can be interpreted in terms of the shifting border between market and nonmarket activity.

Household Energy Conservation

The consumption goal of a comfortable dwelling can be attained by using enough heat in a poorly insulated house, or alternatively by using less heat and more insulation. The latter alternative requires more skill and investment planning on the part of the consumer, and possibly more consumption labor, but less economic labor in the long run. The scope of market activities is reduced, as reduced fuel purchases are only partly replaced by increased insulation purchases.

Studies of home energy consumption have repeatedly found a high potential for energy conservation that would produce net financial savings. But home energy conservation programs have had disappointing results, for several reasons. Households are reluctant to engage in investments with long break-even times, energy sales promotions and rate structures often encourage wasteful consumption, and institutional barriers discourage conservation investment in rental housing.

Solutions may be sought in either of two opposed directions. One is to strengthen the consumer's role in planning and investing in energy conservation, thus increasing the importance of nonmarket skills and labor inputs. The other is to expand the market for household energy conservation services, thus making consumption skills and labor less essential by selling the goal of a "comfortable dwelling" directly to consumers. Either alternative would reduce the fuel requirements and environmental impacts of reaching current levels of comfort.

Private Transportation

Desires for mobility result from complex social processes that have important environmental implications. But even if mobility targets are accepted as given, existing consumption patterns are quite inefficient.

Transportation options depend heavily on an inherited infrastructure that poses problems for current mobility needs. Even if the costs of infrastructure were fully charged to users, problems of externalities would remain: Making a highway more useful for cars, for example, can make it less attractive for bicycles or pedestrians.

To envision unbiased choices between modes of transportation, consider the assumption that users are charged the full costs of infrastructure as well as operating costs for each mode, and can lease any transportation option at its full cost per kilometer. The economic labor needed to pay for a mode of transportation plus the consumption labor for that mode (travel time, repair time, etc.) would add up to the total time requirement. Consumers could then choose the time-minimizing mode for each travel route. In reality, the prevalence of traffic jams, in which it would be faster to bicycle or even walk, provides evidence that time-minimizing choices are not being made.

The system of private ownership of automobiles itself is a cause of inefficiency. Once a car has been purchased, many of its costs are fixed and independent of the distance driven, encouraging excessive use. The alternative of full-cost car leasing would charge for all costs on a per-kilometer basis. This would allow consumers to buy automobile services as needed, while preserving the freedom to use cheaper transportation systems whenever appropriate. Since leased cars would spend much less time idle than privately owned cars do, the total number of vehicles could be reduced. For the same reason, depreciation would be accelerated and replacement by new, improved models would be easier and faster. Of course, private car ownership has acquired a symbolic and ideological meaning that goes far beyond its technological qualities as a means of transportation.

Conclusion

Ecological economists have often pointed out that the economy is embedded in a natural environment; but it is also embedded in a social one. The shifting boundary between the economy and its social environment has a significant effect on the relationship between economic activity and the natural environment. In the examples discussed above, consumers spend too much time in the economic system, resulting in too little capital investment in conservation and too much in automobiles. Thus, the impact of the market system on nonmarket aspects of life is interrelated with its impact on the environment.

Summary of

Consumption: Value Added, Physical Transformation, and Welfare

by Herman Daly

[Published in *Getting Down to Earth: Practical Applications of Ecological Economics,* eds. R. Costanza, O. Segura, and J. Martinez-Alier (Washington, DC: Island Press, 1996).]

Economic theory typically neglects the importance of natural resources for production and consumption. This summary argues that the economy has exceeded the optimum scale relative to the carrying capacity of natural ecosystems, and that resource constraints on consumption will become increasingly binding.

Resource consumption is inherently limited by the extent of the earth's ecosystem, a limit that we are fast approaching. Total consumption, which is the product of population and per capita consumption, can be limited or reduced by controlling either of these factors. While the South needs to focus more on population, the North should focus on per capita consumption. Toward the latter goal, this article reconsiders the meaning of consumption.

Consumption and Value Added

Alfred Marshall's view that production of goods is a rearrangement of matter that creates utility and consumption is a rearrangement of matter that destroys utility incorporates the physical laws of matter conservation. Matter and energy cannot be created in production; rather, useful structure is added to matter/energy by the agency of labor and capital. The value of this useful structure is referred to as "value added" and is used up in consumption. Economists have studied the creation and destruction of value added in great detail but have paid little attention to that to which value is added.

Lester Thurow has argued that there is no reason to fear that growing worldwide consumption will cause resource exhaustion, since it is "algebraically impossible" for the rest of the world to reach American consumption standards without also reaching American productivity levels.[1] William Nordhaus believes that global warming would have only a small effect on the U.S. economy because only agriculture, accounting for a mere 3 percent of gross national product (GNP), is sensitive to climate. The entire extractive sector of the economy represents only 5 to 6 percent of GNP, yet it provides the resource base on which the other 95 percent rests. Even the widely used Cobb-Douglas production function suggests that other inputs (e.g., man-made capital and labor) can be substituted indefinitely for natural resources. Ever-growing output can be achieved with ever-diminishing resource inputs if sufficient quantities of other inputs are available.

Consumption and the Physical Transformation

Although matter/energy cannot be created or destroyed, there are still physical limits to our ability to add and subtract value repeatedly from the same natural resources. The second law of thermodynamics states that entropy (randomness or disorganization) is always increasing, that each re-arrangement and recycling of matter leads to both energy and material dissipation beyond recall. To replenish value added that is worn out or consumed, new low-entropy inputs are continually required. Thus we consume not only the value we add to matter but also the value of the preexisting low-entropy arrangement of resources created by nature. The scale of the economy is important: The rate of use of low-entropy resources must be consistent with the workings of the ecosystem that creates them.

Natural value added is just as important as value added by labor or capital. But we tend to treat natural value added as a free gift of nature. The greater the natural value added to a resource, the lower the human effort required to exploit it, and hence the lower the price we put on it.

The basic pattern of scarcity has been changed by economic growth. In the past value added was limited by the supply of labor and capital; now it is also limited by the availability of natural resources. Turning a tree into a table provides net benefits when there are many trees and few tables, but today much of the world has many tables and dwindling numbers of trees. Eventually the economy must reach an optimal scale relative to ecosystem capacity, at which point production should be geared toward maintenance rather than growth. Our goal should be to minimize maintenance costs— to minimize rather than maximize production. As Kenneth Boulding said long ago, "Any discovery which renders consumption less necessary to the pursuit of living is as much an economic gain as a discovery which improves our skills of production."[2]

Consumption and Welfare

As the economy reaches its optimal scale, the shift from maximizing production efficiency to maximizing maintenance efficiency can be interpreted as a shift from economic growth to sustainable development. Growth can be defined as increasing the provision of economic services by increasing material throughput, holding efficiency constant. Development, in contrast, can be defined as increasing the provision of economic services by increasing efficiency, holding material throughput constant. Sustainable development is simply development without growth, with throughput held at an environmentally sustainable level.

Empirical measures of the value of natural capital services are virtually nonexistent; even measures of the value of services of man-made capital are problematical and incomplete. Thus we cannot provide a firm, empirically based answer to the question of whether the economy is above or below the optimal scale; commonsense judgments must be used instead. What judgments can we make about the marginal benefits of growth in human-made capital versus the marginal costs of consumption of natural capital?

In wealthy countries the marginal benefit of growth is surely low. Expensive advertising is required to cajole people into buying more. Deaths from stress and overconsumption are more common than from starvation. For the poor, for whom higher consumption remains important, gains could be made either through redistribution or through additional consumption of natural resources; the economic system has a strong bias toward the latter alternative, to the extent that it makes any provision for the poor.

The marginal costs of growth include the familiar litany of environmental problems. A large part of GNP is spent on defensive expenditures to protect ourselves from the side effects of growth, including pollution control, some aspects of health care, commuting time, and so on. In addition, capital and labor mobility tears communities apart in the name of growth. It is time to redirect our economy away from growth and toward development.

Policy Implications

If natural and human-made resources were good substitutes, then neither factor could be a limit to growth. If, on the other hand, they are imperfect substitutes, or even complements, either one can be limiting. Today natural capital is the limiting factor: The worldwide fish catch is limited, not by the number of fishing boats, but by the remaining population of fish in the sea. We need to economize on natural capital, which means its relative price should rise. Since much of natural capital is outside the market, public policy changes are needed. Instead of taxing value added (labor and human-made capital), natural resource use and pollutant emissions could be taxed.

All taxes are "distortionary" relative to a perfect market; resource taxes would induce desirable distortions.

Different countries will employ different policies to limit total consumption, some emphasizing population and others focusing on per capita consumption. The faddish advocacy of global economic integration will not solve our problems; indeed, national policies cannot be pursued effectively under a regime of completely free trade and capital mobility. This need not imply autarky, but does require some backing away from global integration toward relative self-sufficiency.

Notes

1. Lester Thurow, *The Zero-Sum Society* (New York: Penguin Books, 1980) 118; cited by Daly, 6.

2. Kenneth Boulding, "The Consumption Concept in Economic Theory," *American Economic Review* (May 1945), 2; cited by Daly, 17.

Summary of

Creating the Affluent Society

by Clive Ponting

[Published in *A Green History of the World*
(New York: Penguin Books, 1993), 315–345.]

In the last two centuries a sizeable minority of the world's population has achieved a standard of living that would have been unimaginable for previous generations. But this improvement has been obtained at a price—a vast increase in the consumption of energy resources and raw materials, widespread pollution from industry, and a variety of social problems. In addition it has raised questions of equity regarding the distribution of wealth, both within individual countries and between the industrialized world and the Third World. This summary reviews the history of the emergence of the affluent society and examines the environmental and social implications of its unprecedented levels of resource use.

In the Beginning

Hunting and gathering societies traditionally kept few possessions, as mobility was valued more highly than most material goods. The accumulation of goods, then, could only begin in earnest eight to ten thousand years ago with the rise of agriculture and settled societies.

Until the last two centuries, all societies were primarily agricultural, and average incomes were very low. With limited long-distance trade and transport, regional economic self-sufficiency was vitally important. In medieval and early modern Europe, about 80 percent of most households' expenditures were on food, half of that for bread alone.

The first sustained rise in European standards of living began in the seventeenth century as agricultural productivity improved and trade and manufacturing expanded; however, the gains during this period were small and uneven, and largely confined to the Netherlands, England, and France. More widespread increases in standards of living did not occur until after the Industrial Revolution.

However, large-scale industrialization required a substantial increase in capital investment; accumulation of this capital led to an initial deterioration in the standard of living for the majority of the population. In England, although industrialization began in the last decades of the eighteenth century, living standards did not rise for most of the population until the late 1840s. In the second half of the nineteenth century, living conditions slowly improved but much of the population existed in a state of permanent want and in substandard housing.

In the Soviet Union, the industrialization of the 1930s led to immense increases in the output of basic industries and doubled the industrial labor force in just five years. But the accompanying forced collectivization of farms led to millions of people starving to death in the countryside; concurrently, urban living standards fell sharply, not recovering to the levels of the late 1920s until the mid-1950s.

Impacts of Industrialization

Industrialization altered the patterns of work more quickly than the standard of living by enforcing a strict labor discipline and drawing increasing numbers of women and children into work outside the home. This allowed unprecedented increases in labor productivity and output, leading to a succession of new technologies and industries that have changed the quantity and types of available goods. World industrial output is now fifty times greater than in the 1890s, with most of the increase occurring since 1950. At the heart of this industrial growth have been vast increases in the consumption of energy and metals.

Although iron has been used for weapons and agricultural implements throughout the last three thousand years, total world production was less than 100,000 tons in 1400 and 300,000 tons in 1700. With the onset of industrialization, world iron output rose to 12 million tons a year in the mid-nineteenth century, and 1.2 billion tons in 1980. Similarly, explosive increases have occurred in the use of other metals. The mining required to produce metals on this scale has had a major impact on the environment, including the destruction of topsoil and the creation of large waste piles that often give rise to toxic runoff. The exploitation of increasingly lower grades of ore, as the best deposits are exhausted, produces growing amounts of waste and consumes increasing quantities of energy per ton of metal.

With the rise in affluence has come the emergence of new industries to supply automobiles and other consumer durables. Auto production, barely under way at the beginning of the twentieth century, has reached 33 million vehicles annually, consuming 20 percent of the world's steel, 10 percent of the aluminum, and one-half of all lead production. More than one-third of all oil consumption is accounted for by cars. The rise in automobile ownership has also allowed for the emergence of many related activities. Vacation travel, for example, was made affordable for many people as a result of cars, fueling the twentieth-century take-off in tourism (later boosted further by the rise of commercial airlines).

Pavement in Paradise

Although inequalities in income and areas of poverty persist in industrialized countries, the basic needs of the majority of citizens have been met. Yet the complex economic system that has developed must be sustained by continuing economic growth. Competition forces companies to expand in order to survive; elected governments promise and encourage growth in order to retain popularity; rising expectations and conspicuous consumption propel an ever-expanding consumer market. The expansion of affluence itself creates social and environmental problems.

When automobiles first appeared, it was hoped that they would ease the urban congestion of horse-drawn traffic and reduce the cost of road maintenance associated with cleaning up after the horses. But soon it was apparent that cars created new levels of congestion. Since this time, cities have been rebuilt, at great expense, around the needs of automobile traffic. In the United States, public transportation use reached a peak in 1945 and then fell rapidly as car ownership increased; this has had important environmental effects. Compared to railways, highways require four times as much land, and almost four times as much energy to make the steel and cement needed for construction. Overall railways are six times more energy-

efficient than roads in carrying freight and passengers. Yet in most industrialized countries today, cars—the majority of which are occupied by only
one person—account for 80 percent of all passenger miles.

The rise of tourism has brought with it a blend of opportunity and
blight. Waves of visitors threaten to overwhelm and destroy the original attraction of the places they came to see. Hawaii received 15,000 tourists in
1964, and three million a decade later. Spain accommodates 54 million
tourists annually. In some Mediterranean resorts, crowding has resulted in
water quality problems; dumping sewage—usually untreated—into the sea
has made many beaches unfit for bathing. Third World tourism often involves the construction of luxury hotels, isolated from the country in which
they are situated, and providing few benefits to the local economy.

Affluence and the World Economy

Until a few centuries ago, there was little difference in wealth among major
European and Asian societies. Medieval Europe, India, and China were at
similar stages of development; China was perhaps the wealthiest country in
the world in the eleventh and twelfth centuries. After 1500, the distribution of wealth became increasingly unequal as Europe extended its control
over other regions and began to industrialize. Today an average Rwandan
has 1 percent as much income as an American, while Sweden has almost
100 times as many hospital beds per capita as Nepal. In recent times only a
handful of poor countries have made much progress along the road to industrialization and affluence.

Development aid, despite official rhetoric to the contrary, has been modest and is frequently tied to the commercial interests of the donor country.
Multilateral development agencies such as the World Bank have often supported projects that have caused major social and economic damage; massive hydroelectric dams that have flooded agricultural land and displaced
huge numbers of people are just one example. Economic necessity leads
many Third World countries to concentrate on the production of crops and
minerals for export, even when these export industries interfere with local
food production and damage the environment.

Economic growth since the second World War has increased the gap between the industrialized world and poorer countries. During most of the
1980s, the Third World transferred more money to the industrialized world
in debt interest than it received in new loans and aid. Austerity programs
imposed on debtor nations by the International Monetary Fund have
placed the heaviest burdens on the poorest people. The World Bank offi-
cially estimates that 800 million people worldwide (excluding China) exist

in conditions of absolute poverty, including 20 percent of the world's children.

The emergence of an affluent society has thus been accompanied by a huge shift in the pattern of wealth distribution worldwide. The industrialized countries utilize the vast majority of the world's resources to support unprecedented high levels of consumption. Internal inequity has persisted, but international inequality has greatly increased, together with a large increase in the worldwide impact of pollutants.

Summary of

Natural Resource Consumption
by World Resources Institute
[Published in *World Resources 1994–95*
(Washington, DC: World Resources Institute, 1995), 3–26.]

Global consumption of natural resources has reached unsustainable levels. Yet, a majority of the world's population remains impoverished and requires additional resources for future development. This summary reviews recent trends in natural resource use and the associated environmental impacts in an international context, and contrasts resource use in the United States and India.

Resource Consumption and Development

Consumption in the affluent Northern countries accounts for a vastly disproportionate share of world resources, and includes expenditures that may appear self-indulgent to Southern countries still struggling to meet basic needs. U.S. expenditures on lawn care or on video games, for example, are roughly comparable to the nation's total contribution to foreign development assistance. But in recent decades natural resource use, together with its associated environmental impacts, has been growing more rapidly in developing countries than in the already industrialized nations.

Nonrenewable resources are, by definition, finite and hence will run out someday. However, physical shortages of most materials are not imminent. Reserves of major metals and fuels range from about 20 times larger than current annual production (for zinc, lead, and mercury) to well over 100 times larger (for iron, aluminum, and coal). As shortages become a threat, price increases often stimulate technological innovation, which makes use of more abundant substitutes—as in the replacement of copper telephone wires with glass optical fibers. Recycling metals also reduces the demand for new resources. Yet, although global shortages are unlikely to check development in the early decades of the next century, current rates of use of most nonrenewable resources are not indefinitely sustainable.

Renewable resources are too often treated as free gifts of nature, but it is these very resources that are most in danger of severe degradation and depletion. Clean air is becoming an increasingly scarce resource for much of the world's urban population. More than one billion people lack access to clean water. More than 10 percent of the earth's fertile soil has been eroded or otherwise degraded; in Mexico and Central America, 25 percent of vegetated land has been degraded. Biodiversity is being lost at an alarming rate as tropical forests and other ecosystems are destroyed by development. The emerging shortages of renewable resources are concentrated especially, although not exclusively, in developing countries.

Resources and Environmental Degradation

The consumption of many types of resources gives rise to environmental degradation. Fossil fuel use results in land degradation from coal mining, freshwater pollution from mine drainage and oil refinery operations, marine pollution from oil spills and tanker operations, and air pollution from all forms of combustion. Air pollution from fuel combustion has local effects on public health, regional impacts such as acid precipitation, and globally contributes to greenhouse gas emissions that may lead to climate change. Industrialized countries now account for just under half of all fossil fuel use, with about a quarter in developing countries (including China), and a quarter in the formerly planned economies of the ex-Soviet Union and Eastern Europe.

Metal mining degrades vast amounts of land: In 1991, more than one billion metric tons of copper ore were dug up worldwide to obtain nine million tons of metal. Other effects include air pollution, leachings from mine tailings or abandoned mines, disposal of chemicals used in mining, and dispersion of toxic trace metals found in many ores.

Consumption of forest resources can lead to environmental problems as well as the loss of critical habitat and species. In many parts of Africa and Asia, fuelwood consumption exceeds forest growth, contributing to forest degradation. In principle, logging for timber can be sustainable, but often in practice it is not. Clearcutting in North America and similarly destructive practices in many tropical forests have contributed to habitat loss, soil erosion, and watershed degradation. Commercial tree plantations—which are increasing in number—can supply wood on a sustainable basis and prevent erosion, but do not support the same level of biodiversity as natural forests.

There are 1.3 billion cattle in the world, and their numbers are growing much faster than the human population. More than half of the grain consumed in industrialized countries and in some developing countries is fed to livestock. In addition to the magnitude of grain consumption, problems associated with raising livestock include overgrazing of arid lands and conversion of forest and other lands to pasture. On feedlots in industrialized countries, manure disposal and water pollution are also problems.

Resource Consumption Patterns and Implications: United States

The United States consumed 4.5 billion metric tons, or 18 tons per person, of natural resources in 1989. Construction materials and fuels accounted for more than 75 percent of the total, but significant amounts of many other materials were included as well. The intensity of resource consumption, either per capita or per dollar of GNP, is declining for some commodities but not all. Consumption of paper, plastics, and many chemical products is still growing rapidly.

U.S. per capita consumption of selected ores and basic materials ranges from 1.5 to 7 times the world average. Resources consumed in the United States are largely from domestic sources, with a few important exceptions (such as aluminum, petroleum, and iron). Thus, the local environmental impacts of U.S. resource use are felt primarily within the country. However, as the leading producer of greenhouse gas emissions, the United States also contributes to global warming. U.S. emissions of carbon dioxide (the most significant greenhouse gas), largely from fuel combustion, are still growing, although not as fast as GNP. The United States has an obligation to the rest of the world to take a leadership role in seeking technologies and policies to protect the environment, and specifically to reduce and stabilize greenhouse gas emissions.

Resource Consumption Patterns and Implications: India

In 1990, the wealthiest 1.5 percent of India's population had incomes equivalent, on a purchasing power parity basis, to (U.S.)$6,200 per capita—well below the U.S. average income of $19,300 per person for that year. At the same time, 59 percent of India's population (495 million people) had incomes equivalent to $600 per person on average. Much of this group cannot rely on meeting basic needs for food, clothing, and shelter; as such, they depend directly on the environment—particularly the common property resources of forest, ponds, and rivers—to meet many of their survival needs.

Not surprisingly, reported consumption by low-income groups is negligible for most goods other than basic food crops and clothing. On a per capita basis, the poorest half of Indians consume only 8 to 10 percent as much minerals and fuels as do the richest 10 percent. However, there are still important environmental impacts of resource use by the poor. Overuse of wells, ponds, and rivers for household water needs has contaminated water supplies; scavenging wood, crop residue, and animal dung for cooking fuel not only exposes households (particularly women and children) to risks of disease from burning these fuels, but also contributes to forest and soil degradation. Sanitation services are available to 37 percent of urban and 8 percent of rural India; improper disposal of human waste spreads pathogens via the air, water supplies, and direct contact. Thus, the poor are both agents and victims of environmental degradation.

The environmental consequences of resource consumption in India include not only growing industrial pollution, but also the resource degradation that results from poverty and population growth. Development and environmental goals are inextricably linked in countries such as India: Development must alleviate poverty if renewable resources are to be preserved for current and future use.

Summary of

The Environmental Costs of Consumption

by Alan Durning

[Published in *How Much Is Enough?* (New York: W.W. Norton, 1992), 49–61.]

The high consumption levels of the global upper-income "consumer class" account for a vastly disproportionate share of worldwide environmental impacts. This summary documents the environmental consequences of consumer class resource use and considers the implications for the future growth of lower- and middle-income living standards.

Per capita use of virtually every natural resource varies dramatically with income. Fossil fuel use by the poorest one-fifth of the world's population releases a tenth of a ton of carbon dioxide per person per year, compared to half a ton for the middle-income majority and 3.5 tons for the top fifth, or consumer class. Industrial countries, with one-fourth of the world's population, consume 40 to 86 percent of various natural resources. The average resident of an industrial country consumes three times as much fresh water, ten times as much energy, and nineteen times as much aluminum as someone in a developing country. Not surprisingly, industrial countries account for almost all industrial pollution, including emissions of hazardous chemicals and nuclear wastes.

International comparison of consumption patterns shows that as income rises, consumption of ecologically less damaging products such as grains rises slowly, while purchases of energy, metals, and other more ecologically damaging products multiply rapidly. The components of a consumer lifestyle, such as automobiles, throw-away goods and packaging, high-fat foods, and air conditioning, can only be provided at great environmental cost.

Fortunately, once people join the consumer class, their impact ceases to grow as quickly. Per capita use of chemicals, energy, metals, and paper have been stable in industrial countries since the mid-1970s. This is due in part to higher energy prices, but also reflects a long-run shift toward consumption of technology and services. But the high levels of per capita consumer class resource use is far too high for the entire world to reach without devastating the planet: Bringing everyone up to current consumer class standards would triple greenhouse gas emissions, mining, and logging, for example.

Consumer class environmental impacts are felt worldwide as developing nations export resources and resource-intensive products to the industrial world. Japan imports more than 50 percent of its wood, much of it from the rapidly vanishing rain forests of Borneo. The Netherlands imports an agricultural output equal to three times its own area, much of it from deforested and pesticide-doused tropical regions. In 1989 the European Community, Japan, and North America had combined net imports of primary commodities (crops and natural resources) of $136 billion.

Shifting tastes among the consumer class have, in years past, fueled commodity booms in the tropics, for products such as sugar, tea, coffee, and rubber. Today the illegal trade in exotic and endangered wildlife continues that pattern, as does the production of illegal drugs for American and European consumers. What was once the untouched cloud forest of the Peruvian Amazon is now the herbicide-poisoned heartland of the world's cocaine industry.

Upper-income consumption is too often ignored as a cause of environmental decline. While other factors such as technology and population growth are important, consumption levels play a key role as well. As such, technological change and population stabilization alone cannot save the planet; a complementary reduction of material wants is also required. A study of the international potential for reduction in fossil fuel consumption concluded that the entire world's population could live at the level of West Europeans in the mid-1970s. This includes modest but comfortable homes, refrigeration for food, clothes washers, hot water, and ready access to public transit plus limited auto use.[1] It does not include, nor could the world support, American lifestyles for all, with their larger homes, numerous electrical appliances, and auto-centered transportation. Even the European standard of the 1970s, if projected worldwide, may not achieve the global reduction in carbon emissions that is believed to be necessary to stabilize the world's climate.

"Even assuming rapid progress in stabilizing human numbers and great strides in employing clean and efficient technologies, human wants will overrun the biosphere unless they shift from material to nonmaterial ends. The ability of the earth to support billions of human beings depends on whether we continue to equate consumption with fulfillment." [60–61]

Note

1. José Goldenberg et al., *Energy for a Sustainable World* (Washington, DC: World Resources Institute, 1987).

Summary of

Creating a Sustainable Materials Economy
by John E. Young and Aaron Sachs
[Published in *State of the World 1995*, Worldwatch Institute (New York: W.W. Norton, 1995), 76–94.]

Current patterns of consumption in industrial countries involve unsustainable levels of virgin raw material use. This summary examines the requirements and prospects for a transition to a sustainable economy based on the reduced use, reuse, and recycling of materials.

Society's Consuming Passion

Industrial countries account for about 20 percent of the global population, but consume about 80 percent of many vital materials. Although technological advances have kept material prices low, growth has exacted an increasing environmental cost in both extraction and disposal of these materials. Around the world, mining moves an estimated 28 billion tons of soil and rock annually, ruining whole mountains, valleys, and rivers. Four primary materials industries—paper, plastics, chemicals, and metals—account for 71 percent of toxic emissions from U.S. manufacturing. Cutting wood for paper and other materials plays a major role in deforestation; since 1950 nearly one-fifth of the world's forested area has been cleared. The impacts of chemical and plastics production include hazardous waste dump sites and industrial accidents that have resulted in released toxic chemicals. Raw materials industries are also among the world's largest energy consumers, with mining and smelting alone taking an estimated 5 to 10 percent of global energy use.

Extractive industries have caused environmental problems at a local level for many centuries, but the scale of the problems has expanded with the rapid economic growth of recent years. U.S. consumption of virgin raw materials was fourteen times larger in 1991 than in 1900, while the population only tripled. Much of the growth in per capita resource use occurred in the 1950s and 1960s. Demand for raw materials now appears to be leveling off in industrial countries, but is still rising worldwide. The continuing increase is a result of both population growth and increasing per-person use of materials in newly industrializing countries.

Materials use occurs within an antiquated legal and regulatory framework that often subsidizes and promotes consumption. Some U.S. policies date back to the frontier era; the 1872 General Mining Act, for example, still gives miners the right to purchase mineral-bearing government lands for $5 an acre or less, and does not require royalty payments or reclamation expenditures. Former colonial powers often provide development assistance for primary commodity exports from the countries they once controlled. World Bank and International Monetary Fund planners generally advocate heavy investment in commodity exports. Public agencies, at the other end of the materials cycle, have often subsidized landfills and incinerators far more extensively than recycling facilities.

Building a Secondary Materials Economy

Sustainability requires a shift from today's throw-away culture of convenience and planned obsolescence to an approach that designs products to reduce material use and seeks value in reusable goods. Bottles and containers could be reused dozens of times before being recycled and remanufactured; composted organic wastes could be plowed back into gardens and farms; recycled paper mills and metal smelters could come to outnumber their virgin material counterparts. Cities, where secondary resources are found, would then become a more important source of materials than mines or forests.

This transition will require a mobilization of capital, skill, and commitment on a scale usually seen only in wartime. An obvious starting point would be to eliminate the current subsidies for virgin materials extraction and to tax polluting industries to cover the full environmental cost of their activities. This would raise virgin material prices to more realistic levels, providing market incentives for materials efficiency. Other initiatives could include making households and businesses pay the full cost of disposing of their waste, and developing the infrastructure needed to support recycling and reuse on a broader scale.

It will ultimately be necessary to go beyond recycling, to make basic design changes that reduce overall material throughput by eliminating waste and inefficiency at the source. Since the energy crisis of the 1970s, new technologies have made it possible to cut energy use by 75 percent or more in many applications; the same can be done for materials use. For example, wood consumption could be cut in half by a combination of technologies already available, ranging from improved sawmill and housing construction techniques to two-sided photocopying in offices.

As recycling programs expand in both North America and Europe, policies are needed to create markets for the materials that are collected. Secondary content requirements and procurement standards are among the quickest and most effective market stimulation measures. Economic and community development financing programs can be oriented toward secondary materials industries. Commodity markets for recycled materials, in their infancy today, must be strengthened at a national level.

Economic Opportunity

The transition to a sustainable materials economy may initially be difficult, but will eventually create many opportunities for employment. Recycling rather than landfilling one million tons of waste creates a thousand new jobs, and many additional jobs in related activities will open up in an economy dedicated to reuse and recycling. While labor costs will rise, capital costs will fall, making secondary industries a good investment even by conventional measures.

The jobs lost in extractive industries and related sectors are comparatively small in number, and are unstable in the best of times. Logging and mining towns are often little more than quickly constructed frontier outposts, becoming virtual ghost towns when the nearby resources (hence jobs as well) are exhausted. Today, for example, metal mining employs only 0.1

percent of the workers in the American West. Tourism, which depends on a healthy landscape unscarred by industrial waste, is now much more important to the economies of all of the U.S. western states.

Recycling, reprocessing, and repair services have in fact been among the world's most reliable "growth industries" in recent decades. Supplies of recycled metal, paper, and other materials have grown rapidly in the United States and other nations, becoming an important part of existing industrial processes. Secondary industries are generally far less polluting than their virgin raw materials counterparts, contributing environmental as well as economic benefits.

The current materials economy is a worldwide system; as a result, change in that system must be global as well. Improvement in materials efficiency is most urgent in the industrial nations, but is important in poorer countries as well. Developing nations will need new technologies and assistance from wealthier countries, particularly since virgin material exporters will be hit hard by a reduction in worldwide materials use. Money that now goes toward funding virgin materials projects could be redirected toward retraining displaced workers and shifting them into growing industries.

PART IX

Globalization and Consumer Culture

Overview Essay

Kevin Gallagher

By 1990, 34 percent of people in developing countries were living in cities where daily exposure to global products through television, radio and billboards was inescapable. Even in rural areas of the Philippines any city of over 20,000 will have at least one supermarket, usually a one-room affair about the size of an old New Hampshire general store. In the fishing and rice-farming town of Balanga, Bataan, the San Jose supermarket offers Philip Morris's Tang and Cheez Whiz, Procter and Gamble's Pringles potato chips, Hormel's Spam, Hershey's Kisses, RJR Nabisco's Chips Ahoy, Del Monte's tomato juice, Planter's Cheez Curls, and Colgate-Palmolive's toothpaste. Above the cash register is a large poster celebrating "Sweet Land of Liberty" with a picture of the American Flag.[1]

While globalization and consumerism are important trends, each with its own wealth of literature, there has been little academic attention given to the interaction of the two phenomena. The articles summarized in this part represent the frontier of the small but emerging literature that address these issues together. They suggest that the interrelationships between globalization and consumerism have a profound impact on consumer behavior and development. The myth of the autonomous consumer with exogenously determined tastes and preferences, a staple of economic theory that has been criticized in this volume, is even less appropriate in the global context.

Globalization, Inequality, and Consumerism

In the industrialized world it is difficult to get through a day without hearing about the trend toward globalization. Rarely does a year go by without world leaders signing yet another major trade pact that opens global markets to easy entry by the world's corporations. We have recently witnessed the strengthening of the common market in Europe with the Maastricht Treaty, the North American Free Trade Agreement, a new round of the General Agreement on Tariffs and Trade, and plans for an Asian Pacific Economic Community. These agreements have arisen as the economies of the industrialized world lag, and a new class rapidly emerges in newly industrialized nations with spending patterns relatively similar to those in the industrialized world.

It is important to note that while volumes of buying and selling—and the rising incomes that follow—increase around the world, the bulk of this activity occurs largely among the richest fifth of the world's people. This is vividly revealed by the United Nations Human Development Report's much-discussed "champagne glass" (Figure 1). This top fifth accounts for roughly 85 percent of global income, world trade, and domestic savings. Conversely, the poorest fifth earns 1.4 percent of GNP, 0.9 percent of

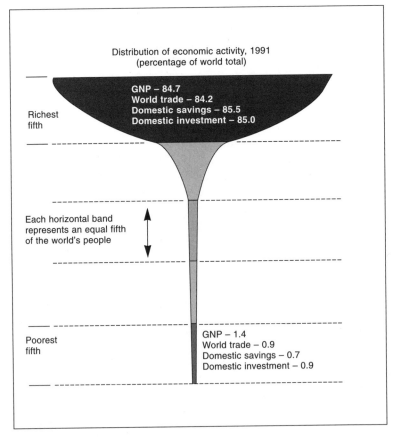

Figure 1. Global Economic Disparities.

world trade, and 0.7 percent of domestic savings.[2] In Part I of this volume, Alan Durning characterizes the top fifth as the global consumer class—traveling by car and plane; eating high-fat, high-calorie, meat-based diets; drinking bottled water and soft drinks; using throw-away products; and living in spacious, climate-controlled, single-family residences where they maintain an image-conscious wardrobe.

Today, while only a few Third World societies earn annual incomes in the UN's top fifth, for the purposes of this part and from the perspective of global marketers, what is significant is the rapidly expanding second 20 percent. In this quintile one can find portions of almost every South American nation, including most of Venezuela and three-fifths of Brazil and Costa Rica. Also included are the rapidly developing East Asian nations, much of Eastern Europe, and a small part of Africa. Interestingly, these nations overlap with the poorest in France, the United Kingdom, Denmark, Spain, and the United States.[3]

In 1953 global income inequality served as the point of departure for the economist Ragnar Nurkse's classic book, *Problems of Capital Formation in Underdeveloped Countries* (a chapter of which is summarized in Part V of this volume). Nurkse's work is the earliest attempt to assess the links between global inequality, globalization, consumerism, and development. Nurkse draws on James Duesenberry's concept of a demonstration effect (also summarized in Part V), asserting that when consumers learn about superior modes of consumption new wants are triggered and the propensity to consume shifts upward. To Nurkse, the demonstration effect is useful in explaining why consumption is favored over saving by individuals of the Third World when they see the affluent lifestyles and consumption patterns of individuals in the First World. Nurkse further claims that such choices hinder Third World capital formation and investment, perpetuating low productivity and underdevelopment.

One can argue that Nurkse's analysis is more relevant now than ever before. However, as Nathan Keyfitz observes in his article summarized in this part, the demonstration effect has had little influence on the world of economic theory. Keyfitz finds the demonstration effect to be important in reality, claiming that "a kind of standard package is emerging in everyone's mind—including a home, automobile, and the means to travel; within the house must be electric lighting, a refrigerator and a television set. One can imagine people being satisfied to slow down their progress once they have these facilities and allow the rest of a country to catch up, but not before."[4] Articles by both Nathan Keyfitz and Russell Belk document the emergence and nature of consumer culture in developing countries. These authors argue that the spread of American and other Western cultures through films, advertising, and other media has taught the Third World consumer to want a "standard package" similar to the one just described.

As to the origins of these desires, Russell Belk points out that while there are a great many similarities in the consumer cultures found in rich and poor nations, their historical emergence is a result of a different path. As suggested in Part IV of this volume, aspects of consumer culture in industrialized countries may date back as early as the sixteenth century;[5] Third World consumer culture has emerged much more recently. In addition, while historians of consumer culture in the industrialized world cite its development as occurring largely *after* the majority of those societies had met their basic needs, Belk points out that the Third World consumer culture has arisen *before* basic needs have been met. The Costa Rican philosopher Luis Camacho adds that consumer culture may not deliver these basic needs:

> [T]he fact that international trade may lead to more consumption in the South does not necessarily mean that poverty will be reduced. For millions of destitute persons in the world, consumption is primarily something that a few inhabitants of their countries can engage in as a privilege; with respect to the majority, it is denied or severely restricted—either because of rampant unemployment or because of great discrepancies between wages and prices. From a Southern perspective, then, what is of primary interest is not so much the distinction between good and bad consumption, but the distinction between consumption as a real option for some and as an unfulfilled desire for most.[6]

Vivid documentation that individual items in the standard package, or the desire for them, can be found throughout the world today is Peter Menzel's *Material World*, a collection of photographs and statistics of the average family's possessions in thirty nations around the globe. China and Vietnam, for example, have average per capita incomes of US$ 364 and US$ 215, respectively. When asked what their most prized possession is, the Chinese family indicated their television. When asked what their wishes for the future were, the Vietnamese family responded, television and radio.[7] In an academic setting, similar questions have been asked systematically in the form of regional case studies that attempt to determine the nature of the emergence of consumer cultures around the world.[8] In this part we have included one such case study on China.

Consumer Behavior and Third World Consumer Culture

A common conclusion of the authors summarized in this part is that the issues discussed throughout the rest of this volume are just as much, if not more, relevant to the developing world.

The economist Jeffrey James has further developed the Duesenberry/ Nurkse behavioral hypotheses by combining them with many of the theories of consumer behavior that are summarized in Parts V and VI of this volume. By developing the work of Veblen, Galbraith, Lancaster, Hirsch, Scitovsky, and Frank in the global context, James argues that consumer choice is at least in part a function of the consumption of others. Thus, the relative income of Third World consumers compared to those in the First World, the status-oriented lifestyles displayed by film, advertising, and other institutions, and the industrialized world's colonial legacy, all cause Third World consumers to remap their indifference curves and seek out the lifestyle that is so vividly presented to them. The welfare effects of this phenomenon can be profound. First, James argues that the opportunity cost of the nonpositional goods foregone to buy positional goods that were designed by and made for First World countries is very high. In addition to the financial costs, Belk and Janus argue that this results in the substitution of high-prestige items for basic nutrition. Finally, James notes that the more the poor spend on positional goods, the more the rich spend to stay ahead, continually exacerbating the problem.

Particular attention has been given to the question of how advertising and media present the modes of consumption practiced by individuals in industrialized countries. James notes that many Third World nations lack strong (if any) consumer protection laws or advertising standards. Thus these ads are less than truthful. Noreene Janus claims that this sets the stage for the practice of "projective advertising," commercializing all aspects of social life, including culture, values, and lifestyle. Such an approach has been most successful for transnational corporations in markets with high advertising-to-sales ratios, such as soap, tobacco, drugs, perfumes, deodorants, toothpaste, prepared foods, beer, and soft drinks. Finally, to many of the authors in this part, the film industry, indirectly, is a form of advertising that works in a similar fashion; the goods and services depicted on films and television become increasingly desirable to the Third World consumer.

Rhys Jenkins sees advertising as a transnational industry of significant importance and consequence. He notes that in the late 1970s, two-thirds of advertising industry revenues in the Third World went to foreign agencies, and foreign billings accounted for one-half of the total for U.S. agencies. By 1989, the simultaneous rise in global markets for consumer goods and global mass communications for their promotion resulted in corporations spending over $240 billion on advertising and $380 billion on packaging and catchy designs that include the logos of the First World's most famous films and cartoons. This averages to $120 for every person on earth, an amount higher than the annual income of the average citizen of Mozambique.[9] In addition to the great rise in advertising expenditures, global advertisers have also shifted their approach. Where it was once commonplace for an international advertiser to cater to the host country's culture to promote its products, firms are now presenting universal themes in their advertising that appeal everywhere. Coca-Cola, whose global advertising campaign theme is to portray "joy, laughter, sport, and music," aired a commercial during the 1992 Winter Olympics that is said to have reached 3.8 billion viewers in 131 countries.[10]

Consumer Culture and Development

A topic that has received only brief attention in this volume, but that does deserve note, is the effect of consumerism on culture and politics. The anthropologist Helena Norberg-Hodge has claimed that the spread of consumerism not only changes consumer tastes in the Third World marketplace, it is also a carrier of deep cultural values that run contrary to and potentially erode the traditional values held by the host societies.[11] In the course of a famous early discussion on education, the philosopher Ivan Illich suggested that consumer culture in developing countries causes underdevelopment as a state of mind, where individuals feel inferior because many of the goods and ideas that they are surrounded by have originated and are produced outside of their culture.[12] Belk credits traditional culture as one of the strongest barriers to the development of the consumerist ethos.

Consumer culture has also been seen to have both adverse and positive effects on Third World politics. Noreene Janus' analysis of advertising in peripheral societies concludes that advertising which presents the lavish consumption styles of the industrialized world to Third World consumers is also imbued with idealized political undertones implying that Western-brand democracy must go hand in hand with such consumer lifestyles. Another study revealed that Western goods embodied notions of freedom for Eastern European youth prior to the collapse of the Soviet presence in that region.[13] On a similar note, Nathan Keyfitz points out that the new consumer class in the Third World resides chiefly in urban areas and wields a disproportionate amount of political power; the resulting urban bias in public policy perpetuates poverty and inequality while exacerbating Third World migration to cities. Jenkins mentions yet another bias: Transnational corporations receive special treatment by host governments that favor government spending to support the transnationals rather than the nations' citizens. A political aspect not touched on at any length in the literature is the reaction of those members of society who cannot fulfill the new desires created by consumerism.

The macroeconomic ramifications that Nurkse outlined are developed further in contemporary terms by Leslie Sklair, Noreene Janus, and Rhys Jenkins. Sklair, a sociologist, argues that many of the industrial societies that consume at high rates also have a significant amount of capital and therefore produce a great deal. This does not present major economic imbalances because high consumption fuels high production (or vice versa), creating productivity and jobs. Sklair points out that in some Third World countries rates of consumption are rising without the rise in national productivity that occurs in the industrialized world. He sees this as part of a global system in which a "transnational capitalist class," through film, media, and advertising, forces a "culture-ideology of consumerism" onto the Third World. Sklair says the result is not only in productivity losses, but also in a Third World dependence on the industrialized world.

Since World War II, nations that cannot mobilize the internal resources to fund development have usually had the option of borrowing. Thomas Walz and Edward Canda assert that this option is becoming more and more difficult. Among other factors, they cite the massive borrowing by the United States since the early 1980s; its perceived creditworthiness makes the United States the preferred borrower, thereby crowding out the Third World demand for loans. To add to this dismal picture, in separate articles Noreene Janus and Rhys Jenkins argue that the long history of multinational corporations in the Third World has given rise to a virtual monopoly in many markets, creating barriers to entry that would further inhibit Third World development even if suitable savings could occur or more loans were made available.

As has been discussed in Part VIII, these emerging trends can be disastrous from an environmental perspective. Alan Durning has suggested that the standard of living that many of the middle three-fifths (see the champagne glass) are capable of attaining is the sustainable one. Therefore, Durning argues that it is in the interests of the populations in the top and bottom fifth of the champagne glass to mimic the lifestyles of the middle three-fifths, whom he calls the "global middle class." These families travel by bicycle and public transportation, eat healthy diets of grains, vegetables, and some meat, drink clean water plus some tea and coffee, use unpackaged goods and durables, and recycle wastes, live in modest, naturally ventilated homes with extended/multiple families, and wear functional clothing. Clearly, the articles summarized here indicate that development is proceeding in the opposite direction of that favored by Durning. People in the second fifth actively emulate the consumption styles of the top fifth, and many in the bottom three-fifths are eager to follow the same path. Consumerist imperatives are winning out over environmental sustainabilty.

The articles summarized in this part make a convincing case that the questions surrounding consumerism should enter the discourse on international economic relations and development. But while these authors offer an array of critiques of consumer culture in the developing world, we must recall that many of the societies analyzed do in fact need an increase in material goods. Thus one of the most important questions at hand is how to sustainably raise the material living standards and the productivity of the world's poorer nations without the negative effect of the consumer society that seems to be coupled with current models of development.

Notes

1. Richard Barnett and John Cavanagh, *Global Dreams: Imperial Corporations and the New World Order* (New York: Simon and Schuster, 1994), 166.

2. United Nations Development Programme, *Human Development Report 1994* (Oxford: Oxford University Press, 1994), 63.

3. United Nations Human Development Report (1992), 99.

4. Nathan Keyfitz, "Development and the Elimination of Poverty," *Economic Development and Cultural Change* 30 (1982), 649–670.

5. Nurkse believed that there was no international demonstration effect in those times because the absolute income gap was smaller and the visibility of lifestyles of other nations was far less than it was in his day.

6. Luis Camacho, "Consumption as a Theme for North–South Dialogue," in special issue of *Philosophy and Public Policy* titled "Ethics and Consumption" (College Park, University of Maryland), vol. 15, no. 4, Fall 1995.

7. Peter Menzel, *Material World: A Global Family Portrait* (San Francisco: Sierra Club Books, 1994).

8. Clifford Shultz, Russell Belk, and Ger Guliz, *Research in Consumer Behavior* (Greenwich and London: JAI Press Inc., 1994).

9. Richard Barnet and John Cavanagh, *Global Dreams: Imperial Corporations and the New World Order* (New York: Simon and Schuster, 1994), 171–172.

10. Ibid.

11. Helena Norberg Hodge, *Ancient Futures: Learning From Ladakh* (London: Rider, 1991).

12. Ivan Illich, "Outwitting Developed Nations," in *Toward a History of Needs* (New York: Pantheon, 1977), 54–68.

13. Gabriel Bar-Haim, "The Meaning of Western Commercial Artifacts for Eastern European Youth," in *Journal of Contemporary Ethnography* vol. 16, no. 2 (July 1987), 205–226.

Summary of

Development and the Elimination of Poverty
by Nathan Keyfitz

[Published in *Economic Development and Cultural Change* 30 (1982), 649–670.]

This summary examines the rise of a middle-class or consumerist lifestyle in developing countries and argues that it can help to explain the persistence of inequality, the urban bias in many development efforts, and the economic neglect of the needs of the rural majority.

A middle-class lifestyle has been taught to the Third World by the United States and Europe. It includes central heating, television, refrigerators, automobiles, supermarkets, paved streets, newspapers, and magazines. The differences in middle-class life from one country to another are much less significant than the similarities.

There are many other forms that our wealth could assume—leisure for contemplation, a simple life focused on athletics or science, involvement in the performance and enjoyment of chamber music, elaborate formal gardening, or other pursuits. None of these alternatives have entered the mainstream of consumer or middle-class culture.

American culture is spreading worldwide, as people learn from films and other media to want a level of consumption that is for the moment beyond their means. But economics has paid too little attention to this demonstration effect, either for its negative impact on saving and investment or for its positive role as a motor of development.

Measuring the Poor and the Middle Class

How large is the world's middle class—the population that drives automobiles, has refrigerators, and watches television? A variety of rough estimates, based on automobile ownership, energy consumption, and per capita income, suggest that there may have been 800 million members of the middle class in 1980; one-fourth of them were in the United States, and more than half of them were in the top seven industrial countries. A similar calculation gives only 200 million people in the middle class in 1950.

In those thirty years, therefore, an average of twenty million people joined the middle class annually. But in the same three decades the world's population grew from 2.5 billion to 4.4 billion, an annual increase of more than sixty million. As a result, there must have been more than forty million new poor people each year, more than twice the number of entrants to the middle class.

Inequality and Development

The spread of the middle class is part of an inegalitarian pattern of development. This is true both because only a minority gains entry to the middle class, and because the middle class consumes large quantities of goods and services that are not produced by the kinds of jobs that the middle class is willing to perform. Income inequality between urban and rural dwellers, of course, is not a new phenomenon; it has been discussed in economics at least as far back as Adam Smith.

A more egalitarian pattern of development is possible, oriented to provision of basic needs for all rather than cosmopolitan lifestyles for a few. Many developing countries have sufficient national income to provide adequate food, clothing, medical services, and education to all their inhabitants, if that were their priority. But this egalitarian model, perhaps most often associated with the Mao Ze Dong era of Chinese communism, has rarely been put into practice. Among the important factors resisting an equitable development path are the attitudes of the middle class and those who are on the threshold of middle-class status.

> Middle-class living is a rounded entity, a lump that seems unstable piecemeal. Those who obtain some part of it want the rest quickly; they are not willing to be held back by the slow pace that making all of their fellow citizens middle class at the same time would require. Each element brings a demand for the next. One who obtains a transistor radio wants to move up to a television set. A kind of standard package is in everyone's mind—including a home, automobile, and the means to do some traveling; within the house must be electric lighting, a refrigerator, and a television set. . . . For those who are well started on this path a bicycle or even a motor scooter will not do for transport, nor will the services of a barefoot doctor be acceptable. [661]

Incentives to Rural-Urban Migration

Although the rural poor are a majority in most developing countries, city dwellers and the middle class are more likely to be active and effective in politics. Thus even in democracies, subways and new urban housing often come ahead of irrigation and services for rural communities. This makes life relatively easier for city people, encouraging additional migration. The same is true of the frequent policies that fix basic food prices well below market rates, making it more attractive to be an urban food consumer and less attractive to be a rural food producer. Millions of people crowd into the capital cities in the hopes of ultimately landing in middle-class jobs. They benefit, in the meantime, from the urban amenities that the elites and the middle class have introduced for themselves.

Holding the price of grain down is not the way to increase food supplies. Nor is differential subsidy to urban life necessarily the best route to development. Returns on investment are often much higher in agriculture than in industry, since industry has received so much more attention from investors in the past. Some of these points are now being recognized, but the results of a potential new emphasis on rural areas remain in doubt. If new styles of scientific management and high-technology investment are simply brought to agriculture, the flight of the poor into the cities will continue.

Conclusion

It is conceivable that creating a middle-class enclave and then allowing it to gradually spread could still be an efficient way to eliminate poverty. Within the enclave, the demographic transition to lower birth rates would occur, savings and the accumulation of capital would become possible, and resources would be conserved by not trying to provide development for everyone at once. Such a view fits well with the strategy of tariff and other regulatory protection for infant industries in a developing country, a strategy that was important in the rise of both Germany and Japan.

But while the growth of the world's middle class after World War II has threatened to be so rapid as to strain natural resources, from the viewpoint of those waiting to join the middle class the growth has been much too slow. Citizens of poor countries understand development to mean access to the goods needed for a modern style of life. The desire for middle-class status is an engine of development; it is not a readily manipulated policy variable, but rather an explanatory variable around which analysis and policy must be developed.

Summary of

Third World Consumer Culture

by Russell W. Belk

[Published in *Research in Marketing, Supplement 4, Marketing and Development: Toward Broader Dimensions* (Greenwich: JAI Press, 1988), 103–127.]

The basic premise of this article is that, quite unlike the evolution of consumption patterns in Europe and North America, Third World consumers are often attracted to and indulge in aspects of conspicuous consumption before they have secured adequate food, clothing, and shelter. The most dramatic instance of such "premature" consumer culture involves sacrificing nutrition for what might well be regarded as the superficial luxury of Western consumption items. The reasons for such a unique development involve the visibility of dramatically different consumption lifestyles to Third World consumers, and various factors such as urbanization that bring about altered interpersonal attitudes in the Third World. [103–104]

Consumer Culture: Definitions and Origins

Definitions of consumer culture have often seemed to rule out the possibility that consumer cultures could exist in Third World countries. For instance, some analysts suggest that consumer cultures can exist only where a large majority of a population consumes above basic subsistence levels. But, the notion that consumer cultures may develop only after basic needs are met is based on the problematic assumption that all consumer cultures follow the European and U.S. models of development. An alternative definition with truly global application states that a consumer culture is one "in which the majority of consumers avidly desire (and some noticeable portion pursue, acquire, and display) goods and services that are valued for nonutilitarian reasons, such as status seeking, envy provocation, and novelty seeking."[105]

The description of the rise of consumer culture as a linear progression from poverty to ever greater levels of affluence and from societies preoccupied with necessities to increased indulgence in luxuries is driven by the desire of affluent countries to justify their own consumption patterns. This self-serving history of affluence masks the disturbing growth of consumer cultures in societies in which luxury consumption may occur at the expense of acquiring basic nutritional needs. It also overlooks the historical presence of cultures that had few goods and wants. For example, the nomadic Bushmen of the Kalahari desert lived well in difficult environments by wanting less and working relatively few hours to secure their basic material needs.

The consumption patterns that are characteristic of contemporary affluent societies are typically measured quantitatively in terms of income, hours worked, education level, life expectancy, and other indicators. In a consumer culture, consumers tend to aspire to a standard of living they have not yet achieved; it is the gap between what is desired and what is achieved that constitutes consumer want. While the desired standard of living changes over time and across cultures, Keyfitz has provocatively suggested the impending emergence of a global standard package that includes a home, electric lighting, a refrigerator, a television, and an automobile.

There are two types of barriers to the export of consumer culture to the

Third World: economic and cultural. The greatest barrier is economic; many Third World countries do not have large cash economies and simply do not have enough income to support a consumer culture. The strongest cultural barrier is fear of envy, a psychological condition that embraces many small-scale societies.

The spread of Western media promotes social comparisons that fuel the development of a hedonistic ethic, especially in large cities. The anonymity fostered by urbanization breaks down traditional attitudes of fearing envy by one's neighbors and, in fact, promotes a "modern" desire to elicit envy from others. Traditionally, envy was to be avoided because it was believed that increases in an individual's welfare occur at the expense of his neighbors. In the modern alternative, envy is acceptable or desirable because it is believed that a community's total wealth expands with the increased wealth of each individual.

Evidence of Third World Consumer Culture

Examples from around the Third World demonstrate the widespread influence of Western consumer culture. In Africa, traditional indicators of wealth and status are increasingly replaced by Western goods. For instance, in Ghana high-status commercial footwear has become a substitute for ceremonial wear among low-income consumers. The formerly nomadic Dobe Bushmen of the Kalahari Desert in southern Africa have become sedentary and less communal as rising consumption levels have led to more possessions, fences, and locked doors. In Central and South America, television sets are coveted by many poor, some of whom will spend as much on a television as they do on the rest of their household goods combined. In China, the most desired types of goods are rapidly escalating and changing to accommodate the most recent innovations from nearby countries and the West.

The problems that accompany current economic development in the Third World should not be considered an indictment of development in general. However, the spread of consumer culture in poor countries may cause inappropriate consumption sacrifices and choices of technology, disdain for local goods, and a breakdown of feelings of community. Consumption priorities become skewed, as in low-income communities in Brazil where refrigerators are purchased by incurring debt and reducing consumption of food. Automobiles that are owned or desired by a small elite incur public expenses such as expensive road networks that involve the sacrifice of valuable resources for the benefit of a privileged few. Local products become less desirable even when they are lower priced and of higher quality. Community sensibility is destroyed as consumption becomes a more individualized activity.

A different model of consumption is needed to secure the benefits of economic development without the costs of consumer culture for the Third World.

Summary of

Positional Goods, Conspicuous Consumption, and the International Demonstration Effect Reconsidered
by Jeffrey James

[Published in *Consumption and Development*
(New York: St. Martin's Press, 1993), 111–136.]

Ragnar Nurkse's hypothesis of an international demonstration effect— namely, that industrial countries' consumption standards exert a powerful attraction on poorer countries—is frequently cited in development literature. This summary argues that Nurkse framed the issue too narrowly, particularly in his attempt to disassociate the demonstration effect from Thorstein Veblen's analysis of conspicuous consumption. A broader understanding is needed, drawing on the work of a number of economists to show that the related issues raised by Veblen and Nurkse have important implications for developing economies.

Nurkse's Formulation

Nurkse argued that contact with superior consumption goods leads to restlessness, dissatisfaction, and the arousal of new desires. He stressed that this was not the same as conspicuous consumption, but merely depended on "demonstration leading to imitation."

Why does this distinction matter? Consider a consumer in a poor country who is exposed to modern consumer goods from an industrial country and shifts his consumption pattern toward those goods. This may happen, as Galbraith might suggest, because the consumer's tastes have changed, perhaps as a result of advertising. Or it may happen because, although tastes are unchanged, the information available to the consumer has changed, as Gary Becker would suggest. In the former case, there is no way to know whether the consumer is better off; in the latter case, the new information presumably improves the consumer's welfare.

Fred Hirsch, in his analysis of positional goods, points out that competition for higher positions in a hierarchy is collectively self-defeating because one person can win only if others lose. Likewise, Veblen believed that much of consumption is driven by the desire to emulate or outdo a peer group. For both Veblen and Hirsch the outcome of emulative behavior (or positional competition) was a shift toward visible, positional goods. If the visible, positional goods are those that appear more modern, in the context of a developing country, then Veblen and Hirsch provide an explanation for Nurkse's demonstration effect.

However, Nurkse's formulation is inadequate because it ignores the manner in which individuals develop a taste for, and become responsive to knowledge about, developed countries products. An understanding of these issues requires consideration of the findings of sociologists who have studied the process of modernization.

The sociological approach identifies several causal factors including urbanization, industrial employment, education, and exposure to mass media; together these factors give rise to a "modernity syndrome," which includes changes in values, openness to new ideas, ambition, and a taste for modern consumer goods. Individuals may become more "modern" through social learning—that is, internalizing the values embedded in the institutions in which they work and live. However, the transmission of values through schools, factories, and offices may represent either the internal processes of these institutions (with, as Nurkse suggested, no need for conspicuous consumption), or increased exposure to Western values and lifestyles (in which case conspicuous consumption plays a central role).

An Alternative Interpretation of the Demonstration Effect

Following Maslow's concept of a hierarchy of needs, status competition should become dominant only after more basic needs are satisfied. Conspicuous consumption, or positional competition, is a high-income taste but is transferred to the poor countries of the Third World via the demonstration effect.

Several instruments and mechanisms are involved in the transfer of positional values to developing countries. Education instills European and American values, often obliquely, as the standards of right and wrong, and directs youthful hopes and ambitions—all too often toward unattainable ends. As employers, foreign-owned enterprises impose standards of dress and behavior, and thus define a "respectable" outlook on life and business.

Advertising, as Hirsch points out, strengthens self-regarding individual objectives at the expense of socially oriented objectives, and often appeals to positional objectives, linking a product to "getting ahead." In develop-

ing countries, advertising is frequently essentially unaltered from its original, host country form, further contributing to pressures to emulate well-
to-do foreign and local elites.

Finally, beginning in the colonial era, direct contact with Europeans and
their consumption patterns has had a pervasive influence on the urban population of many developing countries. Expenditures on traditional rituals
such as weddings may be slighted in favor of everyday display of conspicuous Western consumer goods.

The Welfare Consequences of Positional Taste Transfer

While visibility is part of the definition of positional consumption, it is not
alone sufficient. As Veblen noted, superfluousness is also essential for consumption to convey status: "No merit would accrue from the consumption
of the bare necessities of life."[1] What are the effects of the transfer of tastes
for positional consumption to developing countries?

New goods are developed almost entirely in and for advanced countries,
whose consumers on average enjoy a high and rising standard of living.
Thus new goods have the balance of characteristics desired by high-income
rather than low-income consumers. As a result the consumption of modern
goods becomes an expensive way to obtain other, nonpositional characteristics desired by low-income consumers. For poor countries, positional consumption imposes a high cost in terms of foregone nonpositional characteristics.

The great expense of positional goods leads to efforts to create the appearance of modern consumption without the reality. A ballpoint pen cap
on a pencil placed in a shirt pocket gives the appearance of ownership of an
entire pen. A wall made of brick on the side of the house facing the street
gives the appearance of expensive, modern construction, even if the other,
less visible sides of the house are made of mud. Counterfeiting high-status
brand-name goods plays a similar role in developing countries, where fake
designer sunglasses, watches, and jeans have captured a substantial market
share.

There is a potential squeeze on essential, nonpositional consumption to
the extent that low-income groups in developing countries engage in positional consumption. Veblen noted that even the poorest members of society will engage in some conspicuous consumption, forgoing basic comforts
or necessities as a result. Robert Frank argues that positional consumption
tends to be most intense among the poor, both because they have so little
status that any increase is of great value, and because only moderate expenditure is needed to catch up to the near-poor just above them. Thus
purchases of infant formula and high-prestige packaged foods may come at

the expense of basic nutrition. And, the more that the poor spend on positional consumption, the more the rich will spend to stay ahead—the race never ends.

In conclusion, it has long seemed self-evident that spending patterns in poor countries are influenced by the consumption behavior of richer societies, but how this influence is transmitted has been less clear. In the 1950s Ragnar Nurkse made an important contribution by suggesting that the process works through an "international demonstration effect." However, there are many reasons to doubt his argument that the effect depends solely on the influence of modern goods and is distinct from conspicuous consumption as analyzed by Veblen. Recent economic analyses of consumption in developed countries, combined with the sociology of modernization, suggest that status-seeking, emulative behavior may play an important role at the international level as well as within individual countries.

Note

1. Thorstein Veblen, *The Theory of the Leisure Class* (New York: Macmillan, 1899), 155; cited by James, 127.

Summary of

Advertising in Nonaffluent Societies: Galbraith Revisited

by Jeffrey James and Stephen Lister

[Published in Consumption and Development,
ed. Jeffrey James (London: St. Martin's Press, 1993), 72–89.]

John Kenneth Galbraith has been a leading proponent of the view that advertising can only have a persuasive effect on consumers who have satisfied their basic needs. Galbraith's theory implies that advertising expenditures should be minimal in poor countries and that levels of advertising expenditures ought to correspond to levels of affluence. This summary argues that Galbraith's view is untenable and that transnational advertising practices may create negative welfare effects in less developed countries.

The Galbraithian View

Galbraith's analysis suggests that while producers in affluent societies create wants in order to fulfill them, advertisers in less developed countries

cannot induce wants, since the poor majority are preoccupied with satisfying their basic physical needs. "The further a man is removed from physical need the more open he is to persuasion—or management—as to what
he buys."[1] If Galbraith's premise were true, advertising expenditures
should not be large in poor countries where the majority cannot afford luxuries. However, statistical analysis of data for fifty-seven countries in 1974
shows that the level of development (as measured by per capita GNP) explains some, but far from all, of the variation in advertising expenditures as
a percentage of GNP ($r^2 = 0.31$). Developing countries such as Iran, Ja-
maica, Brazil, Costa Rica, and Peru spent a higher proportion of national
product on advertising than developed countries such as West Germany,
Belgium, and Italy.

Galbraith's error was his failure to see that even the very poor face consumption choices that can be influenced by advertising. Basic needs may be
met by advertised products, and advertising may influence consumer priorities so that psychological needs take precedence over physical needs. Of
course, at the time Galbraith was writing about advertising, in the 1950s
and 1960s, it was difficult to anticipate the more recent explosive growth
of transnational corporations and the powerful influence of globalized
media institutions.

An important source of the strength of transnational corporations is their
marketing expertise. U.S.-based multinationals spend a higher proportion
of sales on advertising than other large American corporations; the greater
the share of business abroad, the greater the company's spending on advertising. Goods such as pharmaceuticals, cosmetics, and soaps are particularly heavily advertised.

Accompanying and facilitating the growth of transnational corporations
has been the increased availability of advertising media in developing countries. A much greater proportion of both radio and TV broadcast hours are
devoted to advertising in less developed countries than in developed ones.
In many countries, international, usually American-owned, ad agencies
dominate the local advertising market and work closely with their transnational clients.

Beyond the specific advertising practices of transnationals, the media flow
to less developed countries represents a form of advertisement all its own.
As media institutions increasingly form larger and larger international con-
glomerates, First World culture is distributed increasingly to developing
countries. For example, Hollywood, a handful of large production and distribution companies that are owned by various global corporations, supplies
films to half the world's cinemas. The goods and services depicted in these
movies become desirable without aid of a formal advertising structure.

Differential Effects of Advertising in LDCs

Consumers in developing countries receive and often perceive different advertising information than their counterparts in industrialized countries. Transnational advertisers often deliver more misleading information to less developed countries (LDCs) where lax regulatory controls predominate. In less developed countries the majority of consumers tend to believe advertising claims more readily than consumers in developed countries since there are fewer, if any, consumer protection laws or advertising standards. In addition, understanding the complexity of mature products marketed in less developed countries requires educational levels attained by few. Less accurate information has a tendency to diminish consumer welfare, since it is often the case that consumers would make different choices if they were better informed.

Galbraith's view that in low-income societies, "all the commercial advantages" lie with the producers of simple goods, is by no means generally true. In fact, multinationals are often able to secure a market for complex, branded goods through heavy advertising.

> [W]hile competition in modern developed societies takes place mainly on the basis of advertising and product differentiation between very large oligopolists, this is not the typical situation in developing countries. Through heavy advertising, multinationals in the latter are relatively easily able to secure market predominance for their particular branded goods. [84]

Since multinationals can outspend their local competition, the market for many goods is no longer open to local producers.

Consumers in less developed countries are exposed to increasingly sophisticated goods that originate in developed countries' markets. In developed countries, brand competition among firms often produces expensive, heavily packaged goods but does not offer the choice of buying only part of the package. Less developed countries will suffer negative welfare effects if transnational advertising reduces savings and investment (and thus constrains future growth) through its promotion of expensive, developed-country patterns of consumption.

Note

1. J.K. Galbraith, *The New Industrial State* (Boston: Hougton Mifflin, 1967), 207; cited by James and Lister, 73.

Summary of

The Culture-Ideology
of Consumerism in the Third World
by Leslie Sklair

[Published in *Sociology of the Global System*
(Baltimore: Johns Hopkins University Press, 1991), 129–169.]

and

The Culture-Ideology of Consumerism in Urban China
by Leslie Sklair

[Published in *Research in Consumer Behavior,* eds. Clifford J. Shultz II, Russell W.
Belk, and Ger Guliz (Greenwich and London: JAI Press Inc., 1994), 259–292.]

The dramatic growth of consumerism in countries where development has
centered on the interests of affluent minorities raises legitimate concerns
over the consequences for poorer majorities. These summaries develop the
thesis that consumerism is spread to the Third World by a global capitalist
class that has followed the expansion of transnational corporations. Utilizing a novel Global System model, the author first illustrates that transnational corporations have spread consumerism worldwide by dominating
Third World media; the author then examines the rise of consumerism in
Shanghai, a relatively affluent city in China.

Global System Model

The global system comprises institutions representing economic, political,
and cultural-ideological spheres of operation. The primary institutional
agent in the economic dimension is the transnational corporation. The primary agent in the political dimension is the transnational capitalist class,
which organizes "the conditions under which its interests and the interests
of the system as a whole can be furthered within particular countries and
regions."[260] This group includes transnational corporate executives,
globalizing state bureaucrats, capitalist-inspired politicians and professionals, and consumerist elites (merchants and media). The primary agents in
the cultural-ideological dimension are transnational mass media institutions
and transnational advertising agencies. These organizations collectively engage in practices that create a culture-ideology of consumerism, defined as
"a coherent set of practices, attitudes and values, based on advertising and
the mass media but permeating the whole social structure, that encourages
ever-expanding consumption of consumer goods."[260]

Consumerism and Producerism

Development models in the 1950s and 1960s were based on the idea that developing countries ought to resemble the economic, political, and value systems of First World countries. In contrast, Global System theory implies that contemporary development in Third World countries invokes the consumerist values of the global capitalist class, rather than the values of First World nation-states. Since the profit-oriented values of a capitalist class may diverge from the values of nation-states, this distinction is important to analyses of development.

The Global System model is consistent with Wells' (1977) analysis of modernization in terms of consumerism (consumption of goods from developed countries) and producerism (increased employment and productivity levels). According to Wells' schema, the most modern societies (e.g., the United States) are high producer–high consumer or overly hedonistic. The least modern, low producer–low consumer countries are ones in which production capacity and purchasing power are both underdeveloped. This model implies that increasing levels of consumerism in underdeveloped countries without effectively increasing production capacity and purchasing power leads to decline and stagnation. The interests of the transnational capitalist class may have just this effect, promoting consumerism in developing countries "with no regard for their ability to produce for themselves, and with only an indirect regard for their ability to pay for what they are consuming."[131]

Cultural Imperialism and Media Imperialism

The Global System model provides an alternative to theories that analyze the relations between countries in terms of state power and exploitation. Typical of the latter view is the "Cultural Imperialism" thesis that powerful societies exploit weaker societies by imposing their values and beliefs on them through the media. This view inaccurately analyzes cultural influences within a state-centrist paradigm—for example, seeing Americanization, rather than consumerism, as the primary force driving cultural and ideological change in the Third World.

It would be an error to identify cultural imperialism exclusively with the United States or even U.S. capitalism, since this falsely implies that without American influence, the spread of capitalist values would cease. Americanization is merely part of a broader consumerist ideology that is disseminated by a global capitalist class, not the U.S. government. For example,

Hollywood (a collection of movie production companies based in the United States, but owned mostly by transnationals) produces a minute portion of films worldwide, but has monopolized distribution to the Third World, thus playing a key role in the globalization of consumerism. That this ethos is often conveyed through American images is peripheral to the main purposes of the global capitalist class; other cultures might have played the U.S. role just as well. "The global capitalist system works through the culture-ideology of consumerism, rather than through a glorification of the American way of life."[144]

A New World Information Order

The central idea behind the much-discussed "New World Information Order" is that there is a global imbalance in communication flows between the First and Third Worlds. A number of researchers in the communications field have argued that transnational media institutions transform the global audience into consumers of transnational commodities through the propagation of a set of self-serving notions of development, communication, organization, daily life, and change.

Transnationals from the United States and Europe have dominated global information flows and have established formidable barriers to entry in broadcasting and entertainment. Imbalances in global information flows are due primarily to the high costs of communications technology, limited Third World government interest in developing a strong public media sector, and the rapidity of technical change. Since First World transnationals can afford technological innovation, adjust to advances in media technology, and offer cost-effective alternatives to indigenous media development, it is not surprising that most Third World media have failed to thrive.

The ethics of some transnational practices evidence a different, perhaps more severe, kind of loss. The celebrated boycott of Nestle, over its marketing of infant formula to customers who lacked the basic resources to prepare the formula safely, highlighted one instance of how transnational practices can cause harm to Third World consumers. Similarly, Searle continues to market an antidiarrheal drug that is an expensive and sometimes dangerous alternative to a simple remedy of boiled water, sugar, and salt. The latter can be prepared by people in substantial deprivation and is recognized by health professionals as usually providing the best treatment. These examples point out that, in its extremes, a consumerist ideology can have devastating or even fatal effects on the uninformed consumer.

Consumerism in Shanghai

The Global System model provides a conceptual framework for analyzing the development of consumerist ideologies in developing countries. Shanghai represents a good test site for research on the subject because transnational corporations, while not currently dominant in China, have grown in influence since economic reforms began in 1978. Shanghai ranks fourth in per capita income among Chinese cities, is exposed to foreign advertising, and has a high per capita ownership of consumer durables. Chinese researchers have concluded that a broad-based consumer mind-set has followed exposure to the outside world despite government threats to control imports more strictly.

In contrast to many Third World countries that experienced negative growth rates in the 1980s, material consumption per capita more than doubled between 1978 and 1990 in China. According to conventional per capita GDP measures, China is one of the poorest countries in the world, but it has rates of ownership of consumer durables that compare favorably with countries that have three times China's per capita income. In urban areas, households are increasing their consumption of luxury goods; the most commonly aspired to basket of goods has changed from bicycles, sewing machines, watches, and radios to refrigerators, washing machines, black-and-white televisions, and other luxury goods. The rapid influx of "Western-style" fast foods, soft drinks, and consumer durables have facilitated changes in the physical marketing system (decreasing the availability of transitional or nonconventional retail outlets) and transformed the symbolic marketing system (giving rise to new media and advertising expenditures as well as types of marketing strategies).

China's 1978 economic reforms engendered a number of radical changes in its rural and suburban distribution systems: extraordinary growth in the numbers of traders, a growing demand for higher quality goods, and increasing numbers of goods suppliers. Collective and private stores increased while state-run stores declined in number. Historically, strict government control over market entry led to an inadequate supply of high-quality consumer goods relative to demand and the presence of very few transnational manufacturing facilities. These restrictions have been relaxed in recent years and many global consumer products are now available in China.

In the late 1970s, government policies experimented with paying higher wages to small segments of the population (especially among coastal residents) to increase their standard of living. Correspondingly, the early 1980s witnessed an exponential growth in foreign advertising, which delivered foreign currency to the government, incentives for Chinese businesses to form alliances with transnationals, and desirable images of the good life to selected citizens.

Although transnational products are becoming increasingly important to growing numbers of Chinese, the state's attitude toward transnational advertising has not been entirely welcoming. A study of Chinese managers' perceptions suggest a positive attitude toward advertising although most felt that Western style advertising was intrusive and should be limited. Younger managers are suspicious of the motives underlying the promotion of inessential goods. A sense of wariness affects government officials who sporadically condemn the polluting influence of Western capitalist values while encouraging the values of a socialist and spiritual civilization. The government often treads a fine line between openness to foreign imports and skepticism concerning its effects on Chinese culture.

Measuring the Culture-Ideology of Consumerism

To analyze the spread of the culture-ideology of consumerism, a survey was administered to almost 600 people in Shanghai workplaces and universities. Consisting almost entirely of young and middle-aged adults, the sample was younger and better-educated than the adult population of Shanghai as a whole. Most of the survey questionnaire's sixty-nine questions concerned knowledge, acceptance, and purchases of ten global brands of consumer goods. Other questions explored attitudes toward advertising and foreign companies, and possession of consumer durables.

The survey results largely confirmed the author's expectations: Those who gave the "consumerist" answers to fifty-two or more questions, roughly one-sixth of the sample, were more likely to be male, single, under thirty-five, above the sample average in income and education, and were self-employed, students, or professionals. However, none of these correlations were perfect. For example, the richest one-sixth and the most consumerist one-sixth of the sample had only a one-third overlap. Significant numbers of lower- and middle-income people were found in the most consumerist group, illustrating the rapid expansion of the culture-ideology of consumerism throughout the population.

Summary of

Transnational Advertising: Some Considerations of the Impact on Peripheral Societies

by Noreene Janus

[Published in *Communications and Latin American Society: Trends in Critical Research, 1960–1985,* eds. Rita Atwood and Emile G. McAnany (Madison: University of Wisconsin Press, 1986), 127–142.]

The social, cultural, political and economic consequences associated with the growth of transnational advertising are profoundly different in Third World countries and require a separate analysis. The consumption patterns promoted by advertising, if excessive in industrialized countries, are inaccessible in poor countries. Transnational strategies of needlessly differentiated products and costly packaging often make these products exorbitantly expensive. Moreover, they often replace local products that are cheaper, more durable, and more nutritious. Furthermore, the lifestyles promoted in advertising include implicit and explicit agendas for social relations, political action, and cultural change. [128]

The explosive growth of transnational advertising began in the 1960s and 1970s as competition forced U.S. corporations to seek out foreign markets. Recently, high rates of income growth in Latin America have attracted the attention of transnational agencies. The resulting flood of advertising has produced a variety of changes in Latin America's economic, social, cultural, and political domains.

The Economic Context

The globalization of U.S. advertising agencies has supported conditions of monopoly capitalism in Latin America by (1) promoting competition at the level of marketing rather than at the level of production; (2) yielding higher profits by accelerating capital turnover; and (3) artificially stimulating demand. Transnational advertising tends to encourage consumption of highly profitable but nonessential products and discourage competition by raising barriers to entry.

Monopoly conditions allow transnationals to limit the range of goods they offer in peripheral countries. Transnationals deliberately choose to market goods that require high advertising-to-sales ratios, which national firms often cannot afford. Leading examples of products favored by transnationals are soaps, tobacco, drugs, perfumes, deodorants, toothpaste, prepared foods, beer, and soft drinks. Prohibitive marketing costs (such as expensive television advertising time) drive away indigenous firms, allowing transnationals to dominate certain markets involving goods with high profit margins. "[R]ather than expressing the level of development in a given Third World country, the production, marketing, and sales of these product types express the kind of development model it has chosen."[129]

Transnational firms sometimes promote consumption habits or lifestyles that are incompatible with traditional cultures. A defense of transnational advertising is that it benefits consumers by teaching novel consumption behaviors and bringing local cultures into the modern world. However, transnational firms often must employ sophisticated and expensive marketing strategies to overcome individual and cultural resistance to new products. For example, Kelloggs struggled for many years to change the Japanese breakfast preference for rice, fish, and seaweed, with some signs of success appearing by the end of the 1970s. Rather than responding to consumer preferences, transnational advertising frequently is designed to overcome them.

Social, Political, and Cultural Changes

Current transnational advertising techniques attempt to commercialize all aspects of social discourse, including culture, values, and lifestyles all over the world. This modern approach to marketing, called *projective advertising*, has become the preferred marketing strategy of transnational advertising agencies. The earliest advertising techniques, consisting of informative and mechanistically repetitive messages, first gave way to psychologically suggestive advertising; but all these approaches addressed the consumer as a single individual making decisions independently of the social environment. The newer style of projective advertising differs radically in assuming that the individual makes consumption-related decisions as a social being embedded in a social environment, and seeks to inscribe commercial messages into that environment.

Utilizing this view of the consumer, transnational advertisers target group attitudes, social norms, and individual preferences through the worldwide promotion of a standardized global culture and lifestyle. A global advertising campaign involves the creation of a common theme or message that is applied in all countries where a particular product is distributed. Transnationals prefer the universal appeal of the U.S. lifestyle that originated during the postwar era of seemingly unlimited growth. "The dissemination of a lifestyle specific to advanced capitalism in the United States is significant because it occurred at the precise historical moment that it became possible to propose a 'lifestyle' for Third World consumers that was unconnected to concrete economic realities."[136]

The political ramifications of transnational advertising in the Third World are dramatized by a Pepsi-Cola advertising campaign in Brazil. Pepsi used the theme phrase "Pepsi Revolution" rather than its traditional "Pepsi Generation" theme to take advantage of the Brazilian desire for change that had been repressed by government for years. This example illustrates how advertisers can undermine social protest by co-opting terms charged with political meaning. As traditional religious and political values disintegrate, advertising helps to create a new social consensus around an ideology of consumerism.

Summary of

Transnational Corporations and Third World Consumption: Implications of Competitive Strategies

by Rhys Jenkins

[Published in *World Development* 16 (November 1988), 1363–1370.]

This summary discusses the ways in which competitive strategies of transnational corporations (TNCs) affect consumption patterns in Third World countries. The impacts of TNC strategies on the Third World include the creation and introduction of new products, advertising expenditure, and influence on the amount and nature of investment in infrastructure. Critics argue that TNCs respond only to local elites and to their own "bottom lines," while supporters claim that TNCs respond to market demand and local conditions.

The Historical Development of TNC Strategy

The development of capitalism in the twentieth century has been characterized by "capital deepening"—that is, by increases in the amount of capital per worker. This has been associated with the continuous innovation and introduction of new consumer goods. The increase in the number of specialized advertising agencies, the consolidation of oligopolistic industrial firms, and the promotion of brand names can all be traced back to the late nineteenth and early twentieth centuries.

However, a different pattern of development has appeared in the Third World, involving (among many other changes) extensive advertising at a much earlier stage in the history of less developed countries; this is largely a result of TNC activity.

New Products in the Third World

TNCs have adopted the same strategy of introducing new products into the Third World as into their countries of origin. Much of technology transfer to the Third World occurs with the objective of introducing new products. Critics view TNC product development as increasingly oriented toward a high-income, luxury market in advanced capitalist countries; in less developed countries (LDCs), the same products are introduced, with a time lag that appears to be gradually decreasing. Little has been done to create products more suitable to Third World income levels and needs. If new products replace more appropriate, less luxury-oriented traditional goods, then consumer welfare may actually decline. However, if new products increase consumer choice, then the welfare implications are more ambiguous, especially since TNCs may affect the formation of tastes for the new products they sell.

Advertising and Trademarks

TNCs spend heavily on advertising to support product differentiation through brand names and trademarks. Such expenditures are substantial in Third World countries as well as in more industrial countries. By the 1970s, more than one-quarter of all trademarks were registered in the Third World, and almost one-half of those were held by foreigners. Advertising as a percentage of gross national product was between 0.6 percent and 1.4 percent in both developing countries and European countries. (The United States was an exception, with 2.0 percent of GNP spent on advertising.) Advertising itself has become an international industry: In the Third World, more than two-thirds of advertising agency revenues go to foreign agencies; for U.S. advertising agencies, foreign billings account for almost one-half of the total.

What are the implications of the international expansion of advertising? "The claim that advertising is a major channel for consumer information is even less plausible in LDCs than in the advanced capitalist countries." [1366] A comparison of prescription drugs marketed to doctors in the United States and Latin America found that in the United States the same drugs were recommended for fewer diseases, while the contraindications, warnings, and potential adverse reactions were given in much greater detail.[1] Cigarette advertising, a generally uninformative category, has expanded in the Third World following health scares and market stagnation in the United States. Advertising may result in an increase in total consumption at the expense of savings, and certainly it creates entry barriers for new firms, protecting the profits of existing companies.

Proliferation of Products

The competitive strategies of TNCs include the proliferation of similar products, with little more than cosmetic differences. By the 1970s more than 10,000 pharmaceutical brand names were registered in each of several Latin American countries; however, 50 to 60 basic drugs could meet 80 to 90 percent of total health needs in the Third World. Likewise, proliferation of automobile models and frequent model changes result in small production runs and high costs for developing-country auto plants.

Demand and Income Distribution

Critics suggest that TNCs produce only for the wealthy elite in LDCs and thus have a vested interest in the preservation of income inequality. However, a more equal distribution of income could also expand the market for some TNC products. "Far from merely serving the rich, the most serious effects associated with the activities of TNCs are a result of their ability to create a demand for their products amongst low-income groups."[1368] The marketing of infant formula is a well-known example. In Brazil, working-class expenditure on appliances at the expense of food purchases has led to deterioration in nutrition levels.

Thus redistribution of income does not challenge TNC domination of Third World markets. A more serious threat would arise from a decision to meet basic needs at the lowest possible cost; this would undermine TNC marketing advantages and require controls on their operations.

Conclusion

TNC activities should not be viewed in isolation; rather they are part of the worldwide process of economic integration. Films, television programs, and tourists also promote Western consumption patterns; without these influences it is unlikely that TNC advertising would be so effective. As part of the internationalization of capital, consumption patterns have become standardized around the world. Controls on specific TNC practices such as advertising cannot significantly alter the situation, since "integration into the capitalist world economy leaves a country exposed to so many other forces which tend to structure consumption in favor of the patterns which prevail in the advanced capitalist countries."[1368]

Note

1. M. Silverman, *The Drugging of the Americas* (Berkeley: University of California Press, 1976); cited by Jenkins, 1366.

Summary of

Gross National Consumption in the United States: Implications for Third World Development

by Thomas Walz and Edward Canda

[Published in *International Journal of Contemporary Sociology* 25 (July–October 1988), 165–175.]

U.S. consumption levels have a systematic, largely negative impact on Third World development. The connection is not merely that a gross disparity exists between U.S. and Third World standards of living, with average American leisure spending, for example, exceeding average African per capita income. This summary argues that there are, on a deeper level, four structural reasons why U.S. consumption patterns act as a barrier to Third World development: the effects of U.S. international debt, competition for scarce resources, influence of the evolution of technology, and promotion and export of military equipment.

During the 1980s, the United States shifted from being the world's largest creditor nation to being the largest debtor. Increases in aggregate consumption since about 1980 have resulted, to an unprecedented extent, from decreases in investment and increases in foreign borrowing rather than from growth in production. In international lending markets, the United States is a preferred borrower and is first in line for available loans. This makes it difficult for Third World nations to borrow, and drives up the interest rates they must pay on the loans they do receive.

The United States is a voracious consumer of scarce resources such as petroleum. The American transportation system, for example, consumes a huge share of the world's oil output. U.S. demand drives up world prices;

in the case of oil, the OPEC cartel was able to raise prices dramatically in the 1970s because it could rely on American demand. Much of the current indebtedness of Third World countries can be traced back to the years of high oil prices, when they were forced to pay, in borrowed dollars, for oil imports. With a lower U.S. consumption level, oil and other natural resource prices would be lower, imposing less of a burden on other resource-using economies.

The evolution of technology in today's First World is geared toward increasingly efficient, labor-saving mass production, producing the consumer goods desired by affluent households. Such technology is increasingly part of an integrated global economy that is no longer confined to individual countries. The Third World is essential to the global economy as a source of natural resources and labor, and as a market for high-technology exports. As Third World elites seek to modernize along the lines of the North, their societies become indebted, and hence vulnerable to intrusions into domestic policy by creditors such as the International Monetary Fund and the World Bank. Often, creditors impose austerity plans, lowering living standards for the poor but promoting the growth of an educated middle class, which expands the market for developed-country consumer goods.

Defense spending, which clearly diverts needed funds from domestic investment, has been growing much faster in the Third World than in industrialized countries. Third World arms purchases exacerbate the international debt crisis, and yield no capital return. Arms sales by the United States and other leaders in high-technology weaponry create profits for the producers, but provide no benefit for the purchasers. In fact, real threats such as terrorism cannot be stopped by technology, but will be solved only through improved distributive and political justice throughout the world.

"A sane and just society must pursue moderation in consumption, embracing at least in spirit Gandhi's call for 'non-possession' (material simplicity). . . . This would, of course, require a momentous paradigm shift in the American way."[172] Gandhi argued for an economy based on ethics rather than profits, based on the spiritual value of material simplicity as well as a concern for exhausting the finite resources of the world.

A move toward a materially simpler life in the United States would free resources for Third World development. But could such a move occur without causing crisis in the United States? Although there is modest evidence of a changing perspective on consumption and the environment, there is not yet the necessary commitment to an ethic of worldwide social justice.

> To enable the Third World to achieve guaranteed subsistence for all, the First World must be willing to reduce the gross exaggeration of consumption patterns and levels. . . . [This] could benefit all people by affirming their right to subsistence and enhancing their spiritual integrity through a morally grounded approach to consumption. [174]

PART X
Visions of an Alternative

Overview Essay
by Neva R. Goodwin

A Revolution in Values

The articles summarized in this part assume that the values of the consumer society are far from ideal—they are values whose impact should be much reduced if society is to change in ways that these authors (and, by and large, the editors of this volume) see as desirable.

A fundamental value shift is likely to have an effect on a society that is at least as great as the most transformative material changes. Truly fundamental value shifts occur rarely, and in modern times they have normally coincided, as both cause and effect, with a concatenation of changes in technical possibilities, basic resource availabilities, and/or social relations. One such shift was the validation of self-interest in the late eighteenth century, supported by the productive possibilities of increased division of labor and new mechanical inventions, and confirmed by the development of economic theory. This was primarily a shift in the mind-set of producers and in the attitudes taken toward producers. It still rested on a comfortable assumption of religious and moral foundations, of the sort that permitted Adam Smith to write about "The Wealth of Nations" in a context of such "Moral Sentiments" as the self-respect that depends on viewing oneself as a decent and honorable person.

In the ensuing two centuries of industrialization a shift to the values of consumerism was enabled and necessitated by the productive revolution. Again self-interest was validated and even exalted, this time on the demand side, by the convergent messages of commercial advertising and neoclassical consumer theory. These forces have combined (with, of course, the commercial sector having a far greater weight than the voice of theory) to preach a powerfully attractive lesson. Neoclassical economics methodologically supports its assumption of "consumer sovereignty" by defining social

333

welfare in terms of preferences revealed by purchasing decisions. This is the theoretical sanction for the commercial message that the prime human motivator not only *is* but *should be* the gratification of any and all personal desires.

There may now be some reason to believe that the continued development of the consumer mentality contains the seeds of the next revolution, essentially for two reasons. Summarizing what we have seen in previous parts, the first reason why consumerist values may not be viable in the future is the set of environmental realities that require a reduction in the throughput of materials and energy in industrialized economies. The second reason relates to the competition between consumerist values and many of the other values that humans hold dear—such as integrity, honor, responsibility, trust, caring, or sharing.

When basic human values have been trampled too far by commercial values, the stage is set for a moral rebellion. The best-publicized forms in which such a rebellion seems to be growing—religious fundamentalism and cultural intolerance—do not necessarily focus on the consumer society as a cause. These reactions may be variously interpreted, as a kind of guerrilla resistance to the materialistic values of consumerism, or as representing a broader rejection of moral, cultural, or spiritual characteristics of modernity. However, such reactions suggest that the consumer societies that have developed during the twentieth century do not necessarily show the way for the dominant patterns of the twenty-first century.

To state this possibility is to point to a great contemporary global drama. Depending on how the drama is resolved, and given the common observation that history is written by the winners, we could imagine the history of this millennial period being written from any of several points of view. Future historians might proclaim the worldwide triumph of the values and lifestyle associated with the United States of America. They may describe the emergence of a new, global, cultural diversity that accepts some of the premises of consumer sovereignty, but combines them (rather than swamping) with a variety of value systems—so that the next century discovers, not one consumer society, but many consumer societies. Or future histories may, instead, celebrate the opening of the twenty-first century as the beginning of a profound change in direction, fueled by a combination of environmental constraints, dissatisfaction with growing inequalities in material possibilities, and a preference for a different set of standards by which to live and to judge oneself and others.

We do not, of course, know which of these histories is most likely to be written. Nor do we know which groups will take the lead in deciding this question. The authors summarized in this part are writing, for the most part, about the developed nations, in particular the United States. The rest of this overview will, therefore, focus especially on visions of an alternative that have been explored in this context. The reader should be aware, however, that this is only a part of what will determine future options and directions, for all regions of the world.

Macroeconomic Alternatives: Uses of the Growth Dividend

As the Frontiers research group began work on this volume, our initial title for the final part was "If Not Consumerism, Then What?" If consumerism is not the driving force, sustaining the current forward motion of the U.S. and the global economies, what will take its place? What aspects of the system might falter or fail if this force were withdrawn?

There are large economic implications to such questions. As we seek a conceptual framework for addressing them we must begin with an understanding of the technological and managerial innovations that gave rise to the dramatic growth in labor productivity since the beginning of the industrial revolution. These processes appear to have slowed somewhat in the nations that were earliest to industrialize (the United States and Western Europe), but by most measures they have not ceased. In most economies we may therefore continue to expect some kind of a growth dividend—that is, an annual increase in the value of the output that can be produced by each hour of work. Accordingly, one way of considering alternatives to the consumer society is to ask: *To what future uses should we devote the growth dividend?*

Possible answers include a reduction in poverty and/or in extreme disparities in wealth; a change in the ways that work is rewarded; a move toward more collective consumption (relatively more expenditure on public goods); a reduction in working hours (because we are more productive, we can afford to work less); a change in the composition of what is produced; or a change in the character of work. Any of these changes could be compatible with an absolute reduction in per capita or total consumption; however none of them logically require such a reduction.

Of the authors summarized in this part, Segal addresses the growth dividend question most directly. He notes that technological advances and an emphasis on efficiency to enhance labor productivity will continue to be important—regardless of whether our focus is on the positive aspects of work, or the need for a better balance of leisure and work, or the need for consumption to be differently oriented or reduced.

Another way of erecting a theoretical framework for understanding "if not consumerism, then what?" is to look at the assumptions now in force and to consider the consequences of some different assumptions. Some of the basic assumptions implicit in a consumer society line up neatly with the way consumption and work are understood in neoclassical economic models: Consumption is the goal, while work is a "bad"—something we do only to earn money to use for consumption. This is half right. Much work is indeed performed to obtain other things that can be purchased with the income from work. However, there is an error built into even this side of the story, since, as Schor points out, institutional rigidities prevent most people from making a free or optimal choice of how much to work.

Work is, for sure, a "bad" when there is too much of it. Schor notes that we are not actually making our preferred choices when we accept a trade-off that gives people less leisure than they want in return for long work hours associated with relatively high income and a high level of consumption. Under current circumstances it appears that people are frequently going beyond the economists' anticipated equilibrium point, where the marginal disutility of work just equals the marginal utility of the wage. As an exposition of the "less-work" option for how to use the growth dividend, the chapter from Schor's book that is summarized in this part sets out an explicit agenda that would make it possible for workers to have, in reality, the option to fine-tune their working hours that has been assumed in neoclassical economics.

A companion critique, associated especially with Block and Wachtel, notes that there is something essentially flawed about models that, in the limit, assume that an ideal life is one that is all consumption and no work. Apparently missing from the parallel logics of the consumer society and neoclassical economics is any notion of intrinsic value in work. The intrinsically desirable possibilities in the work experience may be being swamped by a modern dynamic that, dashing the optimistic hopes of the early part of this century, has largely used the growth dividend to increase consumption rather than to reduce working hours.

These two critiques lead to two kinds of policy proposals: on the one hand, to use the growth dividend to shorten the work week (or work year) associated with the average job; on the other hand, to improve the quality of the work experience by emphasizing worker empowerment, cooperative rather than competitive aspects of work, work-related education, and so on. Segal notes that, of these two types of policy, the ones that focus on the potential intrinsic values of work are more radical and will require deeper societal change than efforts simply to reduce work requirements.

Block includes both of these types of proposals, along with a third approach, in his emphasis on deploying the growth dividend to improve the *quality of economic output* —using that term sweepingly to include satisfying work, economic security, a safe and clean environment, leisure, and the expansion of democracy (in the workplace and in the rest of society).

Moral/Cultural/Social Evolution

Behind the policy proposals we will see in this part there are a host of what may be called value proposals—overt or implicit statements about what values should be brought into the foreground to contend against the values of consumerism. Keynes, for example, anticipated a change in public morality, away from the materialistic value of purposeful behavior (which looks to future consequences rather than present realities of life), and replacing it with the conviction that "the love of money is detestable" and that life should be devoted to higher things. It is interesting—and a little sad—to look back at this article, which was written in the 1920s. Beyond the snobbish elitism of his time and milieu, Keynes was expressing a more generalized image of what civilization could and should mean. His assumption that greater prosperity would release us from material concerns, opening the way for everyone to explore the highest moral, intellectual, artistic, and social potential of the human race, may be found in many writers, including Karl Marx and J.S. Mill. More recently, however, this hope seems to have died. As the fulfillment of any set of desires only seems to create a new set, this route to satisfaction seems increasingly illusory. However we may envision a move to a more evolved society, it will not come about as the *automatic* result of the satisfaction of everyone's basic needs.

Some writers, seeing the futility of such a hope, turn in an opposite direction and propose that social evolution occurs through the renunciation of material things. Wachtel is an especially forceful advocate for a position, related to this ancient prescription, that may be encountered in a number of modern writings. Diagnosing our society as suffering from "an epidemic of loneliness" (see also Lane in Part III), Wachtel views a retreat from consumerism as an essential first step toward rediscovering the value of a satisfying emotional life, emphasizing connectedness with others and the richness of subjective experience.

Schor, calling on cultural shifts that she senses to be already under way, refers to the postmaterialist values of personal fulfillment, self-expression, and meaning. The "culture of permanence" that Durning proposes anticipates a shift to rewarding pastimes that are less commodified and less material-intensive: family and community gatherings, artistic and athletic pursuits, education and appreciation of nature, and the development of spiritual and intellectual traits—in sum, the pursuit of the now almost embarrassing ideals of goodness, truth, and beauty.

How are such value shifts—or, perhaps more accurately, shifts in value emphasis—to come about? The authors summarized here offer an array of suggestions. Television is a major focus for many writers. Elgin and others suggest that, while we must put our longer-term efforts into curtailing advertising that hypes up the consumer society, in the short run the status quo needs to be challenged through counter-advertisements that show the appeal of different life goals. Meanwhile, entertainment programming needs to be pressured to bring its content into line with environmental and social needs, while informational programs (documentaries, etc.) should be encouraged to educate the public about the negative aspects of consumerism.[1]

The other major place to look for institutional effects on values is in education. Scitovsky is the outstanding spokesperson for the position that, as opportunities for leisure grow, appropriate education is required to ensure that leisure time activities do not degenerate into shallow consumerism. Looking at the education system of the United States with the eye of a European, Scitovsky sees an exaggerated focus on the creation of a productive workforce, with inadequate attention to consumer skills. The system fails to develop and support the skills required for high-level leisure activities, most notably arts appreciation and participation, as well as crafts, athletics, and so on. The result is a population that is ignorant of how to achieve many of life's deeper, more enduring, and more progressive enjoyments (in the sense that the economist Alfred Marshall used the term progressive—referring to what leads people in the direction of developing their higher or better potentials). Instead, American consumers gravitate toward leisure time activities that are passive and require virtually no training (such as watching television, window shopping, hanging out at the mall), or that may be characterized as quick fixes and cheap thrills (the use of mind-altering substances, or movies, videos, and other media presentations of sex and violence).

Change on the Production Side: The Issue of Jobs

A focus on media and education targets the demand side of the economy—the values that are presumably being instilled or enhanced in consumers. On the production side a critical target for change is the nature of corporations, including their underlying goals.[2] Wachtel proposes a realignment of the ownership of corporations toward a situation in which the stakes of the workers, or of society, are increasingly recognized. Block envisions cooperative labor relations, making employees genuine stakeholders, though not necessarily owners, in firms.

There is, in fact, already a dramatic shift under way, in which pension funds and insurance funds—organizations that have a large stake in the ongoing and future health of society—are moving into positions of dominance in American corporate ownership. There are also forces moving toward increased worker ownership (employee stock ownership plans, employee buyout schemes, etc.). It is not yet clear how effective these initiatives will be in giving workers meaningful participation—or, for that matter, whether effective worker ownership will necessarily create enterprises that are more geared to a broadly defined social good. The critical question will be whether such institutional investors and nontraditional owners will be motivated to seek, and able to find, ways to make it attractive to producers to offer affordable, low-throughput leisure activities, including products and services that promote health, education, scientific research, environmental maintenance, arts, and entertainment—instead of using promotional techniques to get people to buy things they don't really want, or that will only give a fleeting satisfaction, or that will quickly wear out.

Another type of policy proposal for lending support to the desired value shifts focuses on design. Durning, for example, considers how to reduce some kinds of personal work, like commuting, and make more time for others, like child care. His proposed solutions are in urban design, emphasizing ways in which automobile use can be diminished by encouraging public transport and the use of bicycles (including, for the latter, covered roads against rain).

Such proposals are often dismissed with the statement that "they would cost too much—we can't afford it." It is worth noting that these arguments run directly counter to the argument that we cannot afford to stop building military equipment, or highways, or even prisons, because to do so would hurt the economy and eliminate jobs. Ironically, it is often the same groups that, while protesting against decreasing public support for a polluting industry because to do so would *decrease* economic activity, also resist efforts to support an industry designed to improve the quality of life, on the grounds that would *increase* economic activity.

The close association of jobs with the health of the macroeconomy, on the one hand, and with the well-being of individuals and families, on the other, is often seen as a justification for a high level of consumption, and makes people understandably nervous about the possible economic impact of anticonsumerist values. In the long run any reduction of consumerist values will probably require a movement to societywide job-sharing, achieved by some reduction in the amount of work that each individual does, shortening the work week and/or increasing vacation time. (This is especially likely if labor productivity does continue to increase.) In the short run, however, a reasonable objective is to shift public and private expenditures, and jobs, out of the areas where they are not socially useful or produce net harm, and into the areas that combine environmental, social, and personal benefits. Again, the barrier to such an obvious idea is the fact that the profitable business activities are not now most often the ones that have the desired social or environmental results.

We have a long way to go before we can realize Block's suggestion of expanding the role of the private firm as an instrument of public purpose. He agrees with Schor in seeing a guaranteed basic income support as essential to make the economy work for human goals. However, there is little reason to expect that the U.S. polity will move in that direction any time soon, while European nations, on the whole, are in retreat from such an approach.

An issue such as basic income raises the question of where society will put its resources. It also raises the issue of whether it is in society's interest to force some people to take unappealing jobs, as poverty now necessitates. Block's position is that, in fact, a major task of a rich society is to get rid of bad jobs as far as possible (by automation or restructuring) and to spread out those that cannot be eliminated among a larger part of the workforce.

Clearly such ideals will not be realized without cost; there may be some win-win solutions to be found, but most of the time gains in one area will be achieved only by giving up something else. The most contentious area of possible gains or losses centers around the issue of freedom. There is more than one meaning of freedom; when emphasis is placed differently among the various kinds of freedom, rather different conclusions may be reached. There is implicit in virtually all of the articles summarized in this part a trade-off in which the *gain* is freer use of that resource which is allocated equally to all people—one's own time—while the *loss* is some of the current freedom of consumer choice. The latter freedom, of course, is only relevant for those who have the money to take advantage of the wide array of consumer goods and services now available.

Value and Policy Links Between Individual and Social Change

Most of the authors represented in this part emphasize the requirement for changes on a societywide level, to enable and support individual lifestyle changes, away from the behaviors associated with a consumer society. Implicit in such proposals is often a large, rarely spelled-out role for government. Beneath this assumption is often another one: In a democracy, such government action may—or should—require a shift in relative values within the population as a whole.

By contrast, Duane Elgin addresses the possibility for people to convert values directly into action (rather than proceeding via any public forum). The means of doing so that he describes is the voluntary simplicity movement, whereby individuals and families reexamine their sources of true satisfaction and eliminate consumption behaviors that do not contribute to those. Another place where such ideas have been promulgated with exceptional effectiveness is the New Road Map Foundation.[3]

There remains a large gap between any theoretical understanding of macroeconomic movements and either the calls for individual action of the "voluntary simplicity" type or proposals such as those of Durning, Block, or Schor for supportive social action. Critical questions to which we have no real answers include the following:

- How large could a voluntary simplicity movement grow within the context of a consumer society before it would create macroeconomic disturbances such as loss of jobs and recession? Is there any way that individual, voluntary reductions in income and expenditures could become large enough to affect GDP *without* creating hardship for many people who have not made such a choice?

- What forces presently exist in an economy such as the United States that might move people toward either voluntary or involuntary behavior changes that will have a similar effect to the voluntary simplicity movement?

- How differently would we understand these forces and their implications if we looked at the economy through a different lens than the GDP? (This is an issue that will be addressed in Volume 3 of the Frontiers series.)

- Two of the dominant ways for a modern individual to confirm his or her identity are through work and through consumption activities. If the trend toward emphasizing the second source of identity were to be reversed, what would this mean for future work—its individual meaning, its social roles, its distribution, and so on? What other sources of personal identity might arise to compete with work and consumption? (We will revisit these questions in Frontiers Volume 4.)

- Even without a retreat from consumerism on the demand side, environmental realities, when they are more accurately conveyed by prices, will inevitably force producers to decrease the throughput associated with each dollar value of output. If this trend accelerates to a point where the total physical throughput in the economy is in decline, what adjustments will be required for monetary policy and macroeconomic accounting to remain relevant to the new realities?

- Suppose economic growth as we now know it ceased to be the norm; aside from the fact that investors would not like it, what would be the ripple effects throughout society from a likely dramatic reduction in average expectations for return on investments?

- Over the last 200 years we have come to take for granted a trend in which the labor inputs to production declined as compared with the material inputs of energy and raw materials. In recent decades, however, this trend has begun to reverse. The labor inputs are increasingly part of a more complex package that includes current skills and information as well as the intelligence of former generations, as that intelligence has been captured in technology. What are the micro- and macroeconomic implications of this trend reversal? What are the implications of the accelerating rise in the ratio of information and knowledge, and their embodiments in technology and skilled "knowledge workers" (the numerator), to material inputs of physical throughput (the denominator)? What are the implications of these trends for the relative wealth of North and South countries?[4] For related issues such as famines, disease, armed conflict, and migration?

- Finally, the broadest and subtlest set of questions (summing up many aspects of the research agenda just outlined): In a market economy, what are the necessary relations, on the one hand between jobs and profits and, on the other hand, between society's values and the money values, that create rewards for work?

Some of the foregoing questions have been raised in different contexts; few have been seriously pursued in the context of understanding the consumer society—where it is heading, where it should head, and what effects might radiate out from changes in the values that support it. The research agenda suggested here is of critical importance for the future ability of human societies to provide meaningful life options for their citizens without destroying the ecological basis for our prosperity, or restricting human goals to the wants that coincide with the producers' need to sell their output.

Notes

1. This point is especially well made in *Marketing Madness [A Survival Guide for a Consumer Society]*, by Michael F. Jacobson and Laurie Ann Mazur (Boulder: Westview Press, 1995).

2. This prescription comes from inside of corporate America as well as from crit-

ical outside observers; see, for example, Michael Porter in *As If The Future Mattered,* ed. N.R. Goodwin (Michigan Press, 1996).

3. Their popular book, *Your Money or Your Life* (by Robbin and Dominquez—the book has been on *The New York Times* best-seller list seven times), is not represented here because it is in essence a "how-to" book. It spells out how people can get off the "work and spend" treadmill, simultaneously reducing expenditures and work hours. A good description of the state of these movements in the United States in the early 1990s may be found in Elisa Blanchard, *Beyond Consumer Culture,* available from the Global Development And Environment Institute at Tufts University.

4. For an analysis of these trend with respect to agriculture, see N.R. Goodwin, "Lessons for the World from U.S. Agriculture: Unbundling Technology," in *World Development* vol. 19, no. 1 (1991), 85–102. In the same issue of *World Development* (pp. 73–84) Schor opened the debate on the North–South question raised here; see J.B. Schor, "Global Equity and Environmental Crisis: An Argument for Reducing Working Hours in the North."

Summary of

Economic Possibilities for Our Grandchildren
by John Maynard Keynes
[Published in *Essays in Persuasion* (New York: W.W. Norton, 1963), 358–373.]

"What can we reasonably expect the level of our economic life to be a hundred years hence? What are the economic possibilities for our grandchildren?"[360] In this classic essay, written in 1930, the author looks forward to the time when growth will have eliminated the problem of scarcity, and speculates about the changes in society, work, morality, and behavior that will be possible in the future world of abundance.

Beyond the Short Run

Although the short-term economic prospects (for Britain in 1930) are pessimistic, the more important long-term outlook will be shaped by the cumulative effects of continuing economic growth. This economic growth is relatively new in historical terms; before the eighteenth century, there was little or no upward movement in average living standards. The accumulation of capital that began in sixteenth-century England led to the great age of science and technical inventions, building to a crescendo in the eighteenth century, and continuous innovation and progress since the beginning of the nineteenth century.

As a result, living standards have risen dramatically in Europe and the United States, despite an enormous growth in population. If growth continues, at 2 percent annually, the world's capital stock will increase more than sevenfold in the next century. Technological change is continuing at a rapid pace: Within our lifetimes, agriculture, mining, and manufacturing may require only a quarter of the labor we are accustomed to. In the short run, the very rapidity of these changes is leading to technological unemployment. But in the long run, the same changes mean that humanity is solving its economic problem.

Life After the Economic Problem

Suppose that a hundred years from now, mankind is seven or eight times better off economically than we are today. How will our lives change? The needs of human beings, although seemingly insatiable, fall into two classes: absolute needs that we feel regardless of the situation of others, and relative needs for things that make us feel superior to others. While the desire for superiority may indeed be insatiable, our absolute needs may soon be satisfied "in the sense that we prefer to devote our further energies to noneconomic purposes."[365] In the absence of major wars or population growth, the economic problem may be within sight of solution within a hundred years. "This means that the economic problem is not—if we look into the future—*the permanent problem of the human race.*"[366]

This is startling because the struggle for subsistence has always been the primary problem for humanity. All our impulses and deepest instincts have evolved for the purpose of solving the economic problem. We may be asked to discard within a few decades the habits and instincts of countless generations. Then, for the first time, we will face our permanent problem—how to use the freedom from pressing economic cares, how to occupy the leisure that science and compound interest will have won, to live wisely and agreeably and well. For many years to come people will need to do some work to be contented; the remaining tasks may be shared as widely as possible, perhaps in 15-hour work weeks.

Few of us have cultivated the art of life itself and know how to make use of abundance when it comes, for we have been trained too long to strive and not to enjoy. The independently wealthy, who already live in a state of abundance, have, for the most part, failed disastrously to occupy themselves meaningfully. With more experience we will use our affluence quite differently than the rich use it today.

Changes are to be expected in public morality: "The love of money as a possession . . . will be recognized for what it is, a somewhat disgusting morbidity, one of those semi-criminal, semi-pathological propensities which one hands over with a shudder to the specialists in mental disease."[369] Of course there will still be people who will blindly pursue wealth, but the rest of us will no longer be under any obligation to applaud and encourage them. We will be free to examine and relax our sense of purposiveness that drives us to value the future over the present. We will be able to return to some of the basic principles of traditional religion: that avarice is a vice, usury is a misdemeanor, love of money is detestable, and those who are most virtuous and wise give the least thought to tomorrow. "We shall once more value ends above means and prefer the good to the useful."[371]

But, for another 100 years we must pretend that fair is foul and foul is fair. Avarice, usury, and precaution must be our gods for a little longer, until they lead us out of the tunnel of economic necessity into daylight. The change will happen gradually, not as a sudden catastrophe; ever larger groups of people will be removed from the realm of economic necessity. Economic obligations to others will remain important longer than needs for oneself. The pace of our progress toward economic bliss will be governed by our success in controlling population, avoiding wars, promoting scientific advances, and accumulating capital—of which the last will be easy, given the first three.

> Do not let us overestimate the importance of the economic problem, or sacrifice to its supposed necessities other matters of greater and more permanent significance. It should be a matter for specialists—like dentistry. If economists could manage to get themselves thought of as humble, competent people, on a level with dentists, that would be splendid! [373]

Summary of

Alternatives to Mass Consumption
by Jerome M. Segal

[Paper delivered at conference on "Consumption, Global Stewardship, and the Good Life," University of Maryland (September 29–October 2, 1994), 276–301.]

This summary examines the economic implications of two alternatives to the mass consumption lifestyle of rich industrial nations: "graceful simplicity" and "creative work."

There are at least three respects in which a society may be consumption-oriented. First, a *nonsustainable* society consumes and pollutes, or otherwise damages the natural environment, so much that it undermines its own survival. Second, a *consumerist* society makes the development of and desire for new consumer goods into a central part of life; an individual's status is tied to his or her level of consumption relative to that of others in the society. Third, a *mass consumption* society is one in which most of the population consumes at high levels, and economic success implies maintenance of those high levels.

These three forms of consumption-oriented life are not mutually exclusive; for example, the United States today might be said to exemplify all three. However, they are also conceptually distinct; any one of them could, at least in theory, exist without the other two.

Changing Consumption Patterns

Some critiques of consumerism emphasize not that we consume too much, but that we consume the wrong things for the wrong reasons. Suppose, for example, that millions of people lost interest in television and turned instead toward performing classical music or engaging in amateur astronomy. Some would see it as a move in the direction of excellence in the expression of human capabilities. But, it would not necessarily represent a decline in the aggregate level of mass consumption; new expenditures on musical instruments, telescopes, and courses and private tutors might simply replace the former spending on television.

Other critiques, however, address this dilemma by posing alternatives to both consumerism and the mass consumption society itself.

Alternatives to Mass Consumption and Consumerism

The mass consumption orientation and its alternatives can be compared along four dimensions. In the mass consumption orientation, the prevailing vision of economic life, it is assumed that (1) the economy contributes to the "good life" primarily through the goods and services it provides; (2) economic performance is assessed primarily by the level and growth of output per person; (3) employment is a means to attaining the income necessary for consumption; and (4) the standard of living is measured solely by per capita GNP.

One recurrent theme among advocates of alternatives to mass consumption is the need for a simpler, less harried form of life. This alternative, which may be called "graceful simplicity" or "simple living," should be distinguished from austerity and self-denial. In contrast to mass consumption, graceful simplicity assumes that (1) the primary role of the economy is to satisfy our basic needs for a healthy and secure existence; beyond meeting these needs, the economy contributes to the good life by reducing work and expanding leisure. (2) The economy's performance is assessed by its success in meeting real material needs and in providing leisure time. (3) Employment is a means to attaining the income required to meet our needs. And (4) the standard of living is measured by success in attaining ample leisure and using it well.

A second alternative may be called the life of "creative work." Along the same four dimensions, creative work assumes that (1) the economy contributes to the good life by providing us with work that brings intrinsic satisfaction and social respect; (2) economic performance is measured primarily by the extent to which most people have intrinsically rewarding, socially respected jobs; (3) employment should be assessed by whether it enhances or stifles human creativity and development; and (4) the standard of living is measured by the quality of the work lives that the economy creates.

Graceful simplicity and creative work are both nonconsumerist, offering alternatives to mass consumption. Neither alternative uses productivity gains to provide ever-increasing output and consumption levels. However, technological advance and productivity growth are just as important to the alternative outlooks as to the mass consumption society. Graceful simplicity demands productivity growth in order to expand leisure time and improve the public services that support simple living while maintaining output. Creative work requires productivity growth in many areas to offset the productivity declines that may result from making some jobs more craft-oriented; the goal is not aggregate productivity growth, but continual improvement in the quality of work.

Either to achieve graceful simplicity or to create work, it is necessary for society to control the increase in the cost of meeting basic needs, and to stop the continual expansion in the definition of those needs. These are done more easily in a growing economy, which can more readily shift resources to public programs in support of new objectives; in a shrinking economy, there is a reluctance to support any new initiative.

Policies for Achieving Graceful Simplicity

Juliet Schor has detailed important elements of a policy agenda for expanding leisure (see Schor summary in Part X of this volume). One could go beyond her suggestions and mandate a four-day work week and a shorter work day. This restriction of personal freedom could make us all better off—to the extent that we are working largely to keep up with each other in the competitive pursuit of status, we all gain if we collectively turn toward more leisure rather than income.

Another approach is to redistribute labor and leisure over a lifetime. Extending labor force participation by another ten years but reducing the time worked in any given year could create a more leisurely society while leaving total labor unchanged over an individual's lifetime.

The most rapidly growing area of labor is unpaid or personal work time—commuting, child care, household chores and maintenance, and the like. As women have entered the paid workforce, the amount of personal work they perform has decreased, though not as fast as their paid hours have increased. Total work effort, paid and personal, has increased for both women and men over the past thirty years. Thus, public policy could, for example, focus on reducing commuting and travel time by redesigning urban environments, educational systems, and workplaces. Labor-saving technologies appear to save time, but their effect is ambiguous, particularly if additional hours must be worked in order to pay for them.

Policies for Achieving a Life of Creative Work

Much greater economic transformation is required for creative work than for graceful simplicity. In a society based on creative work, a good life is an active one, and the central output of the economy is meaningful and rewarding work, rather than goods and services. By this standard, there are no existing economic successes; there is a shortage of "good" jobs virtually everywhere.

A policy framework for moving toward an economy of creative work includes both the elimination of the worst aspects of the worst jobs and the improvement of the quality of all jobs. The former has been a traditional objective of the labor movement, and has faced serious obstacles even in more promising political environments than the 1990s. Progress is not likely to occur in a piecemeal fashion; rather, an inspiring vision of transformation is required. The objectives of such a transformation would be to expand the supply of creative jobs, to reduce or eliminate jobs that cannot be made satisfying, and to ensure that the remaining mundane and arduous work tasks are equitably shared.

The transformation of work requires a transformation in the consumption of the products of work. Consumers must be interested in the quality of goods and services that result from creative work. "The extent to which the labor force contains teachers and artists, poets and potters depends on the magnitude of the demand for what they produce."[301] Valuing work, in the end, requires a new interest in what we consume—a true materialism in which we awaken an aesthetic interest in the things we see, hear, taste, and feel.

Summary of

Exiting the Squirrel Cage

by Juliet Schor

[Published in *The Overworked American* (Basic Books, 1991), 139–165.]

The textbook model of consumption assumes that workers can choose freely between labor and leisure. That assumption is increasingly unrealistic in the United States today. Instead, Americans are forced to work long and growing hours, as the author's analysis has shown (see Schor summary in Part II). In her concluding chapter, she proposes a number of structural changes in labor markets and employment practices that would give workers a real choice about their hours of work, and speculates about the impact of such changes on consumerism, leisure activities, and the environment.

The modern consciousness of time as something to be measured and paid for emerged with the development of a capitalist economy, and was initially resisted by workers who maintained a traditional, "timeless" view of the world. Today, the sale of time for money is taken for granted, its legitimacy beyond question, and its sphere of influence ever expanding. Market pressures continue to encroach on individual's right to free time—a right that is established, to a limited extent, by legal holidays and regulated working hours. A redefinition and expansion of the right to free time is now needed.

Employers are biased toward demanding excessive hours from salaried workers, whose pay is typically independent of the actual number of hours worked. To end this bias, every salaried job should have a standard schedule formally attached to it, and compensatory time off should be required for hours worked beyond this schedule. Such a policy would not be a cure-all for excessive hours: Employers could still set very high standards, and pressures to ignore the standards (as happens in Japan today) could continue to lead to unpaid overtime. However, clearly defined schedules would be an important step forward. A second proposal stipulates that employers pay for overtime with time off rather than money. Companies that ask workers to put in time beyond their scheduled hours should offer an equal amount of "comp" time at a later date, preferably scheduled at the employee's convenience.

Changes are also needed to make part-time work more attractive and feasible. In the absence of a socialized health insurance scheme, one step is to ensure that part-time workers receive a prorated share of health insurance, pension benefits, and other fringe benefits, and are given the option of upgrading to full coverage at their own expense. This would eliminate barriers that keep many people from considering part-time employment. Another option is to institute job sharing, in which two people split one position's work, responsibility, pay, and benefits.

While people are generally unwilling or unable to reduce their current paychecks, polls indicate strong support for trading future income gains for additional time off. If an annual wage increase equal to 2 percent above inflation were entirely converted to reductions in hours, the average American work-year of 1960 hours would decrease to 1600 hours in about a decade, allowing either an additional two months of vacation per year or a 6.5-hour work-day. In this scenario, a shorter work-year would come at the expense of wage increases, with paychecks just keeping up with inflation. Although some would undoubtedly prefer to receive all future gains in the form of wage hikes, a large majority of both men and women tell pollsters that they would like to trade at least some income and career advancement for time off.

Inequalities of Time

Many Americans earn so little that they cannot afford to give up future wage gains for free time. Nearly one-third of U.S. workers earn wages that do not lift them out of poverty even on a full-time schedule. At present, a voluntary choice between leisure and wage gains would leave the poorest third of the nation working oppressively long hours. The solution to this inequality is a reduction in the underlying inequality of income and the guarantee of a living wage for all.

Increased flexibility of working hours could also reproduce inequalities of gender. Although the proposed changes in employment practices are gender-neutral, existing gender roles would lead more women than men to take advantage of them. This would reinforce women's current responsibility for housework and child care. However, if men take increased responsibility in these areas, they too will opt for reduced working hours in many cases. Proposals for flexible work arrangements will help undermine rigid gender roles by making shared parenting and two-career families more feasible.

Claims that competition compels long working hours are more than a century old: In 1830 New York employers complained that a ten-hour day would allow foreign firms to undersell them. Today it is often observed that Japanese and Korean workers put in more hours per year than Americans. However, Western European workers have much shorter hours per year, maintaining high living standards without sacrificing time off from work. It is not the number of hours worked or the absolute level of wages that determines international competitiveness, but rather the relationship between hourly wages and productivity.

In fact, long hours, with the Japanese model for example, may actually lower productivity. Several studies of businesses that have reduced working hours have found that productivity increases as a result; in some cases, a modest reduction in hours leads to no loss of output, or even to a gain. With shorter hours, workers tend to be less exhausted, take fewer breaks, have better morale, and maintain a faster pace of work. Yet, management usually resists reductions in the number of hours worked, basing their decision on a much too narrow understanding of costs.

Overcoming Consumerism

For many Americans, escaping from overwork will require not only economic and social changes, but also cultural and psychological transformation. A change in expectations is necessary in order to understand the function that material goods perform. When the struggle to acquire commodities takes the place of an emotionally satisfying life (for example, when men work long hours to provide for their families and thereby spend little time with them), everyone suffers. Those who succeed in "dropping out of the rat race" generally find themselves happier as a result.

What will people do with the increased leisure time that results from a more flexible work arrangement? Certainly some will seek out second jobs, either out of economic necessity or because of the cultural imperative that states that men with leisure are lazy. But this cultural imperative may be losing its force with the rise of "postmaterialist values"—the desire for personal fulfillment, self-expression, and meaning. People do work hard during their time off, but often at unpaid endeavors such as caring for young, old, or sick family members; volunteer or religious activities; continuing education; or participation in sports or community organizations.

Shorter hours at work will leave people less tired and perhaps less focused on low-energy leisure activities such as television viewing. The ability to use leisure well must be cultivated; too much work makes our "leisure skills" atrophy. Moreover, leisure activities have become increasingly market-oriented, expensive pastimes. Government and community support is needed for affordable, non-commodity-related leisure activities.

Although corporations remain the most significant obstacle to the expansion of leisure, there are enlightened, forward-looking companies whose policies could serve as models for others. The existence of progressive companies, as well as the "greening" of public consciousness, changes in gender roles and expectations, and the small but growing number of people who have voluntarily "downshifted" out of the fast lane, all point toward changes in attitudes toward work, consumption, and leisure. Effective organization will be needed to mobilize this changing public opinion; government must play a major role in facilitating this change.

> Commitment to an expanding material standard of living for everyone— or what Galbraith has called the "vested interest in output"—entails our continuing confinement in the "squirrel cage" of work and holds the potential for ecological disaster. Or, we can redirect our concern with material goods toward redressing the inequalities of their distribution—and realize the promise of free time which lies before us. [165]

Summary of

How to Bring Joy into Economics
by Tibor Scitovsky
[Published in *Human Desire and Economic Satisfaction*
(Sussex, England: WheatSheaf Books, 1986), 183–202.]

Economic theory conventionally views work as an unpleasant activity engaged in only to earn the money required for consumption. However, a significant and perhaps growing number of jobs also provide other satisfactions in addition to income. This summary explores the economic sources and consequences of enjoyable stimulation as a step toward what the author calls "a more general economic theory of human satisfaction."[191]

Economics and Psychology

Both economics and psychology rely on an analysis of the categories of human pleasure and pain, echoing themes that can be found as far back as classical Greek philosophy. But while traditional insights have been tested and expounded upon in psychology, in economics the increasing emphasis on formal models has led to excessive simplification and impoverishment of basic psychological assumptions. The works of three distinguished economists—Alfred Marshall, John Maynard Keynes, and Ralph Hawtrey—provide partial exceptions to this pattern, and include provocative but little-noticed discussions of broader psychological motivations.

Alfred Marshall considered the relationship between wants—satiable desires satisfied by consumption—and activities that may either contribute to producing goods and services for consumption or be themselves pleasurable and desired for their own sake. Initially, human wants gave rise to activities, but later activities like science, literature, art, athletics, and travel were pursued for their own sake. Eventually, these new activities gave rise to new wants, rather than the reverse.

John Maynard Keynes discussed leisure and its dangers in his "Economic Possibilities for Our Grandchildren" (see Keynes summary in Part X of this volume) but, in a well-known passage, also commented on the "animal spirits" of investors. In the latter, he suggests that the profit motive may often be subordinate to the businessman's enthusiasm for risk, daring, and creative exhibition of skill.

Ralph Hawtrey focused on the economics of enjoyable activities much more directly than either Marshall or Keynes. Hawtrey distinguishes between defensive products, intended to prevent or remedy pain or discomfort, and creative products, intended to provide positive gratification or satisfaction. He discusses not only creative products, such as drugs, sports, entertainment, literature, and art, but also the creative aspects of defensive products, such as skilled food preparation and artistic elements in clothing. His work provides many of the building blocks for a general theory of enjoyable stimulation.

Enjoyable Stimulation

The nature of the interpersonal interactions involved in pleasurable activity seems unclear to economists. But, far from being an isolated or solitary pursuit, activity pursued for its own sake frequently involves interactions between performer and spectator resembling those between producer and consumer of goods. The resemblance is close enough to allow the incorporation of enjoyable activities into economic theory.

An active individual's enjoyable activity may provide satisfaction to many people who are only passive spectators, as well as to the participant. Varying levels of activity may be preferred by different people, or by the same person at different times. Music, for example, can be enjoyed by composing, performing, analyzing, and criticizing or just by sitting back and listening. While passive enjoyment generates demand for performances, active enjoyment usually creates supply for others to enjoy as well.

In some activities, such as sex, sports, social games, and gambling, an active participant requires one or more active partners. The supply and demand for partners are often roughly balanced, typically through barter (each wants similar services) rather than by market exchange. The interaction between performers and spectators primarily benefits the spectators, but is not entirely one-sided: Active participants may gain additional satisfaction from their awareness of other people's observation and appreciation. However, because there are more spectators than performers, there is likely to be excess demand for passive enjoyment. Active performers must therefore be paid to increase the supply of their activities beyond the level spontaneously offered through nonmarket channels.

Economic Versus Noneconomic Activities

Analysis of enjoyable stimulation reveals that the primary motivation of many economic activities is not, in fact, economic. This is significant in that it shows the market economy to be more open to such influences as "animal spirits," and less self-equilibrating than is sometimes thought. The more important these nonmarket motives become, the less effective economic incentives will be in governing the economy. The distinction between pleasant and onerous work is not always a clear one; many jobs have significant enjoyable aspects, prompting performance beyond what would be called forth by economic incentives alone. Changes in personal income tax rates often have little or no effect on the amount of work done by lawyers and other professionals, revealing the importance of noneconomic motivation.

The dividing line between economic and noneconomic forms of the same activity is constantly shifting. News as a commodity produced by professional journalists scarcely existed before the eighteenth century, since letter writing and conversation largely satisfied the desire for information; only the spread of literacy, faster communication, and better printing presses allowed the gradual rise of the media. Personal advice is given for free in most communities; only in an affluent, transient, mobile society does the demand exceed the supply so much that psychiatry and social work become paying professions. Similar transitions have occurred in the arts, sports, and music. The trend is usually toward the increasing commercialization of enjoyable activities.

Conflict frequently arises between the economic incentive and the intrinsic motivation to perform an activity. Economic incentives usually reward and result in production of more of the same, while intrinsic motivation may induce striving for qualitative excellence, or the making of more difficult, better, or more original products. Monetary rewards have even been shown to decrease intrinsic satisfaction with work in some cases, because it interjects someone else's preferences into the work process.

In a broader sense, there are not two but three motivations for work: enjoyment of work, monetary reward, and fame or reputation among others in the same field. Intrinsic satisfaction should not simply dominate over other criteria; all three represent important social interests. The balance between them must be struck by each individual worker based on the relative weights he or she gives to intrinsic satisfaction, money, and fame.

Social Wants, Conspicuous Consumption, and Novelty

The conflict between the apparently insatiable desire for more income and the satiability of most human needs has led some economists to focus on the desire for social distinction. The desire for positional goods, the outward manifestation of social distinction, is inherently insatiable. The enjoyment of positional goods requires a passive appreciation of them by others.

As individuals seek to emulate those just above them, the rich correspondingly seek to distinguish themselves—but in ways that continue to be respected by others. To resolve this problem, just the right degree of novelty is required, giving the rich the appearance of being not eccentric or frivolous. Thus, new styles, changing at a measured pace, are continually required and created.

Summary of

Qualitative Growth

by Fred Block

[Published in *Post-Industrial Possibilities: A Critique of Economic Discourse* (Berkeley: University of California Press, 1990), 189–218.]

A consumer society offers a vision of quantitative growth for the future in which success is achieved through an increasing number of commodities. This summary offers an alternative vision of qualitative growth in which success includes development of human capacities, increased supply of non-commodity satisfactions, and expansion of democracy and public participation.

Qualitative growth is not inevitable; it is merely a logical, attractive alternative that can be constructed out of visible tendencies in the world today, one among many possibilities for our economic future. In this summary, qualitative growth is presented in two stages: Qualitative Growth I, embodying a set of principles of economic organization; and Qualitative Growth II, proposing specific institutional arrangements for pursuing these principles.

For more than a century, discussion of economic alternatives has been dominated by debates over the relative merits of capitalism and socialism. Today, however, capitalism has come to refer to an extremely wide range of economic arrangements; private ownership of the means of production can encompass many different approaches to employee participation and representation of the public interest. Socialism, meanwhile, has become problematic due to both the failure of the Soviet model and the implausibility of Marx's vision of a society beyond scarcity (since time will always be scarce, and some people will always be striving for greater status and recognition). Thus, the issue is no longer capitalism versus socialism, but rather how to create economic institutions that give maximum scope to democratic participation.

Qualitative Growth I

The first principle of qualitative growth is the positive feedback between the development of human capacities and future expansion of production. This feedback results from the changing nature of work required by advanced technologies. Labor is increasingly employed to innovate, regulate, and change the production process, rather than to facilitate repetitive use of muscle power. As innovations save labor and create wealth, society can use some of that wealth to expand the pool of people with the skills to develop and use new innovations. But, at present, such positive feedback is often serendipitous; a society organized around qualitative growth would reform institutions to ensure and promote positive feedback.

The second principle of qualitative growth is the importance of the qualitative dimensions of output, and of satisfactions that are not directly tied to commodities, including inherently satisfying work, leisure, economic security, environmental protection, and community and voluntary services. Expansion of noncommodity satisfactions and product quality is not cost-free. But most of the growth dividend from the positive feedback dynamic should be used to increase the quality rather than the quantity of output. Continued growth is compatible with environmental concerns for two reasons: first, because consumption is increasingly focused on services rather than goods; and second, because environmental improvement (such as cleaner air) is one of the ways in which qualitative growth can take place.

The third principle of qualitative growth is that neither the market nor planning is adequate as an exclusive organizing principle for the economy. Both have proved to be incapable of giving sufficient importance to product quality and noncommodity satisfactions. The pursuit of qualitative growth requires a combination of individual choice, social regulation, and state action. Many current experiments with hybrid institutional forms may help create new models for economic organization.

Qualitative Growth II

An institutional framework that could support the principles of qualitative growth includes changes in the organization of the workplace and the labor market, public access to and support for new ideas and technologies, and new mechanisms for economic coordination.

Cooperative labor relations are increasingly important for current production processes, and will become even more essential for the positive feedback envisioned in qualitative growth. Firms must provide employees with career development opportunities, greater employment security, and democratic participation in decision making. These acts must be supported by legislative changes that expand the rights of employees. Such institutional and legal changes, ultimately making employees genuine stakeholders in the firm, are required to evoke full, creative participation and innovation from the workforce.

It is difficult to create a cooperative workplace without corresponding changes in the labor market. The most important change is the establishment of a system of basic income supports available to all members of society. This would encourage continuing education and training, thereby accelerating the diffusion of new ideas and technologies into the workplace. Such a system would make it more difficult to fill the least interesting and worst paid jobs, creating incentives for employers either to automate or to restructure jobs to make them more attractive. A basic income system would reverse the current underproduction of leisure by freeing individuals to reduce their hours. Participation would increase in interesting but currently unpaid or underpaid work, such as community journalism, arts, and child care.

Society's arrangements for the development and utilization of new ideas are of critical importance to qualitative growth. There is a fundamental tension between the privatization of innovations and their diffusion into the economy. Public distribution of new software, research findings, or other advances will get them into circulation quickly, but at the expense of the private rewards and incentives that often motivate innovation. Proprietary use of new ideas preserves monetary incentives at the expense of rapid diffusion.

However, there is a rich variety of incentives that can facilitate innovation. For example, the computer hobbyists who helped spark the early development of personal computers came from an antiestablishment, countercultural background, and were not initially motivated by the pursuit of wealth. The fact that the work of successful artists and architects is frequently imitated by others does not appear to diminish artistic creativity; it is generally the innovator who becomes famous. Our goal should then be to shorten the period of patent and copyright protection for new ideas, and to increase the range of activities that fall under the model of artistic creativity—bringing fame but not exclusive use to authors of important advances. "The academic or government scientist who develops an AIDS vaccine should be rewarded with fame and recognition, but the patent rights should enter the public domain."[211–212]

To meet the goals of qualitative growth, complex coordination of production and investment decisions are required. The best way to do this is to expand the role of the private firm as an instrument of public purpose, as has been done with affirmative action. While regulation is needed, the primary emphasis is on forcing firms to internalize a broadened set of goals. The pursuit of profit is always socially constructed, occurring within a framework of law and custom; it is entirely possible to modify that framework to meet social objectives.

New objectives and improved efficiency are also needed in public sector service delivery. Just as in the private sector, lower level public workers must become stakeholders in the operation of their agencies. Incentives should be created to make agencies more responsive to the public that they serve.

Finally, the role of democratic politics should be expanded in shaping decisions about spending on infrastructure and public goods. Democratic planning mechanisms are needed to include nonelite groups in decision making. "Rather than simply being passive victims of either market processes or elite planning, citizens could begin to address the basic questions of how to live and how the society's resources should be used."[215]

Summary of

The Poverty of Affluence: New Alternatives
by Paul Wachtel

[Published in *The Poverty of Affluence: A Psychological Portrait of the American Way of Life* (Philadelphia: New Society Publishers, 1989), 141–171.]

The consumer way of life is deeply flawed, both psychologically and ecologically. . . . I would like to see less emphasis on the economic dimension of our lives . . . and more on the psychological: the richness of subjective experience and the quality of human relationships. [141]

This summary explores the individual, cultural, and institutional changes needed to create a more psychologically satisfying alternative to the "consumer way of life."

Toward a Psycho-Ecological Point of View

A shift toward psychological goals and values is important both for the direct satisfaction it would yield and for its effects on the environment. Most environmental advocacy is associated with images of austerity and belt-tightening—images that are unlikely to ignite the imagination or encourage change. In contrast, a redefinition of success and the "standard of living" has quite different implications, encouraging us to think of new opportunities rather than what we are giving up.

Psychological development is attainable only to a limited degree through individual efforts. Much more important are the outlooks people hold on their lives, the quality of interactions with others, and the social and institutional structures that shape their experience. Some firms, offices, and neighborhoods make their participants feel much better about themselves than others, revealing the importance of the social context of our lives.

Individual and systemic values have a reciprocal, reinforcing relationship with each other. A competitive system leads to competitive individual behavior, which reinforces the system; the same is true for a cooperative system. Without a change in individual values, political and institutional changes will be superficial and ineffective. To create an alternative to consumer society, a shift away from the profit motive and toward communal ownership will have to occur. But, the Soviet experience demonstrates rather unambiguously that ending private ownership alone is no panacea.

Deployment of Resources

Current uses of resources that would change in a more psycho-ecologically oriented culture include the huge expenditures on advertising and sales promotion, costs attributable to style changes and planned obsolescence in such industries as clothing and automobile production, and the enormous size of the defense budget. In place of these unproductive efforts, resources could be devoted to health, education, scientific research, arts, and entertainment. Greater attention to individual health and the environment could lead to lower medical costs.

It is sometimes claimed that concern with exercise, diet, and health foods represents an individualistic effort to save oneself rather than change the social causes of dangers to our health. But there is nothing to prevent people from both eating health food and working to change the conditions that may make some ordinary food unhealthy. Changing one's diet may be a first step toward questioning the values of affluence.

Some solutions address more than one problem at once. For example, much better facilities for bicycle commuting, perhaps including covered roadways for protection from the rain, would promote exercise and reduce air pollution, as well as reduce traffic congestion for those who still must drive. Another transportation scheme, short-range electric car rentals with hourly charges and numerous convenient drop-off sites, could reduce pollution, congestion, and vehicle ownership costs; individuals could rent the size of car needed for each trip, eliminating the need for commuters to own oversized vehicles year-round. All that is lost is the exclusivity of ownership, one of the psychological features of consumer society most in need of change.

The Meaning and Nature of Work

> [Work] is not just "input," to be manipulated in the service of some higher aim, but a part of life experience in itself, to be examined as an activity that occupies many hours of the day. Any gains in available consumer goods must be weighed against the extra pressures and deprivations undergone during the heart of the day when we are at work. [156]

Economic theory habitually assumes that maximization of output is the be-all and end-all of production. However, increasing numbers of individuals are interested in other values, such as preserving time for family life or working in a relaxed, sociable manner—values that undoubtedly lead toward lower worker output but greater satisfaction.

The goal is neither to work less and get paid less, nor to "go back" to the hypothetical good old days. Rather, it is to incorporate and transform older amenities so that they can be combined with the best of the new, to use modern technology properly with a better appreciation of its relationship to human needs. For many people time is becoming more precious than goods; if we barely have time to use the things we already can afford, we need increased leisure more than increased income. Opting for more leisure rather than more goods would provide both psychological and ecological benefits.

However, as Tibor Scitovsky has noted, it takes certain skills to enjoy some consumer goods, or leisure. Lacking these skills, many people are vaguely dissatisfied and occupy their time seeking more income and goods.

Even more important is the sense of psychological restrictions and inhibitions that reflect both social custom and our prolonged dependency in childhood. Our views of the world are largely shaped when we are young, helpless, and uncomprehending. To escape from the endless accumulation of material goods, we need to overcome the constrictions that derive from childhood fears and fantasies. Trends such as the "human potential" movement, which offers "therapy for the healthy," are a promising step toward change in this area. But, there are limits to what an individual can do alone; widespread psychological change is needed in entire families, networks, and communities.

The Renewal of Community

Restoration of the sense of community and connectedness to others must be at the heart of an alternative to the consumer way of life. When economic growth breaks down formerly tight-knit communities, people often feel adrift and afraid rather than affluent. As a result, our society faces a virtual epidemic of loneliness. The deep-felt need to be part of something is sometimes mentioned as a reason why Japanese businesses, with their strong sense of community, have proved to be so economically successful. Although Japan is also a competitive, capitalist society, it is at the opposite end of the cultural continuum from the United States with regard to communal feelings.

> The kind of community feeling that is suited for our affluent and techno-logically oriented culture will probably be quite different from the ties we nostalgically remember or imagine. Moreover, we are faced with having to learn again about interdependency and the need for rootedness after several centuries of having systematically—and proudly—dismantled our roots. [169]

To make use of technology in a way that enhances our lives, we must account for ecological limits and interdependence, and learn to provide the luxury of time to examine our lives, enjoy ourselves, and enjoy each other.

Summary of

A Culture of Permanence

by Alan Durning

[Published in *How Much Is Enough?* (New York: W. W. Norton, 1992), 136–150.]

> If our grandchildren are to inherit a planet as bounteous and beautiful as we have enjoyed, we in the consumer class must—without surrendering the quest for advanced, clean technology—eat, travel, and use energy and

materials more like those on the middle of the world's economic ladder. If we can learn to do so, we might find ourselves happier as well. [149–150]

This summary explores the prospects for a transition to a "culture of permanence—a way of life that can endure through countless generations." [138]

Today's high-income consumers have an ethical obligation to curb their consumption, both to conserve resources for their own descendants and to create a sustainable model for middle-income and poor people to aspire to. However, lowering consumption need not deprive society of the things that really matter. The bulk of the activities that people name as their most rewarding pastimes are infinitely sustainable: Religion, conversation, family and community gatherings, artistic and athletic pursuits, education, and appreciation of nature all fit readily into a culture of permanence.

Individual consumers, when informed of the environmental impact of their spending patterns, sometimes make personal efforts to simplify their lives. Several million Americans were said to be experimenting with voluntary simplicity in the 1980s. "For these practitioners, the goal is not ascetic self-denial, but a sort of unadorned grace. Some come to feel, for example, that clotheslines, window shades, and bicycles have a functional elegance that clothes dryers, air conditioners, and automobiles lack."[139] While the Seattle-based New Road Map Foundation promotes the idea of voluntary simplicity, most practitioners of voluntary simplicity move to low consumption on their own. Many find that a less hurried, low-cost lifestyle leaves them free to enjoy daily life, develop their talents, and work for causes they care about.

But, however attractive the image of simple living may appear, the majority of people cannot easily make the transition. We are trapped by inflexible work schedules, mortgages, car payments, college tuition, and the sprawling suburban infrastructure of our lives. Voluntary simplicity movements have appeared only on the fringes of society, without achieving a lasting impact on either the American mainstream or other industrial countries.

On the other hand, while consumerism has only shallow historical and philosophical roots, moderation, sufficiency, and the rejection of materialism are endorsed by all of the world's major religious and cultural traditions. The Bible, the scripture recognized by a majority of the world's high-income consumers, asks, "What shall it profit a man if he shall gain the whole world and lose his own soul?", and tells us that it is "easier for a camel to go through the eye of a needle than for a rich man to enter the kingdom of God." Similar views of acquisitiveness, consumption, and materialism can be found in the scriptures and teachings of many other religions.

"Consumerisms roots may be shallow . . . but individual action and voluntary simplicity do not appear capable of uprooting it."[145] A combination of personal and political change will be needed. Slow progress in changing attitudes will be punctuated by occasional rapid advances, as seen in the antismoking movement in the United States and the worldwide effort to ban the use of ivory. The challenge, made urgent by the environmental impacts of consumerism, is to generate organized pressure for more rapid change.

Areas where change is most needed include laws and policies that favor consumption over leisure, and high-impact commodities over low-impact ones; the excesses of advertising and retailing (supported by the cultural dominance of commercial television); the wasteful approaches to providing food, transport, and materials in modern affluent societies; and above all, the aspects of our consumption that are wasted or unwanted in the first place. Few people want to drive long distances to work, throw away vast quantities of packaging, receive junk mail, or live in an ever-expanding suburban sprawl. Despite the ominous scale of the challenge, there are encouraging signs that many people are ready to begin saying, "enough."

The future of humanity depends on whether the richest fifth of the world's people can turn to nonmaterial sources of fulfillment, recreating human-scale settlements, eating wholesome, locally produced food, and making and using objects that endure.

> In the final analysis, accepting and living by sufficiency rather than excess offers a return to what is, culturally speaking, the human home: to the ancient order of family, community, good work and good life; to a reverence for skill, creativity, and creation; to a daily cadence slow enough to let us watch the sunset and stroll by the water's edge; to communities worth spending a lifetime in; and to local places pregnant with the memories of generations. [150]

Summary of

Living More Simply and Civilization Revitalization
by Duane Elgin
[Published in *Voluntary Simplicity*
(New York: William Morrow, 1993), 143–160, 195–218.]

Many critics of consumerism advocate voluntary simplicity as an alternative way of life. This summary examines the relevance of simplicity to consumption and work, and considers the material and cultural requirements for a revitalized, simplified civilization.

Simplicity that is adopted voluntarily has a very different meaning than simplicity that is forced on people by poverty. Although a majority of the human race lives in involuntary material simplicity, this discussion focuses on the voluntary choices available to those who live in relative abundance, in part because much of the solution to poverty lies in the choices made by those who are not poor.

To simplify our consumption, we must avoid the opposite extremes of poverty and excess. Living with either too little or too much diminishes our capacity to realize our potential. Finding the right balance requires us to distinguish between our needs and our wants, satisfying the former but not the latter. "We *need* transportation. We may *want* a new Mercedes."[147] This balanced approach to consumption stands in stark contrast to the view that more consumption always increases happiness. "However, when we equate our identity with that which we consume . . . we become possessed by our possessions."[149]

It is transformative to withdraw voluntarily from the rat race. It is a radical simplification to affirm that happiness cannot be purchased, and to accept our bodies as they are—without the latest clothing styles or cosmetics. Voluntary simplicity does not embody austerity and self-denial; rather, it is an aesthetic process in which each person considers whether his or her consumption fits with grace and integrity into the practical art of daily life.

Lower consumption, some fear, may lead to high unemployment. However, the world is full of purposeful, satisfying jobs waiting to be done in areas such as urban renewal, environmental restoration, education, child care, and health care. In fact, the overwhelming emphasis placed on individual consumption today results in the neglect of the kind of work that promotes public welfare. A simple, needs-oriented economy will be better able to address these urgent concerns.

Satisfying, meaningful work will make a great contribution to our individual and collective well-being, for it is through work that we develop skills, relate to others, and contribute to society. Simplicity will affect the institutional context as well as the purpose of work. Today, many people work within massive bureaucracies in both the private and public sectors. Simplicity implies a change toward more human-sized workplaces, and redesigned organizations of a more comprehensible scale and manageable complexity. This will encourage involvement and personal responsibility, combating alienation and boredom.

An Integrated Path for Living

Voluntary simplicity is neither remote nor unapproachable; for the fortunate minority of the world who live in relative affluence, all that is required is a conscious choice. As people begin to participate in the world in a life-sensing and life-serving manner, a self-reinforcing spiral of growth unfolds. Living more consciously leads to less identification with possessions and allows greater simplicity. A simpler, less divided and distracted life also allows for greater consciousness of individuals' ultimate purposes. Voluntary simplicity fosters a refinement of both the social and material aspects of life, and a development of the spiritual side of existence as well.

To support the evolving consciousness and promise of simpler living, both material and cultural changes will be needed. The material changes that will support an industrial society moving in a more ecological direction include:

- Widespread energy conservation and moves toward a "soft energy path" that emphasizes solar and renewable energy sources

- Contraction in wasteful industries and those oriented to conspicuous consumption, combined with an expansion of the environmental industry and cultural and information-based economic activity

- Taxes on the wealthy, and on luxury goods, gasoline, alcohol, and cigarettes, with revenues used to provide public services and tax cuts for environmentally desirable activities

- Massive investments in cleaning up pollution and developing industries that minimize pollution and maximize recycling

- Rapid growth in crafts, hobbies, and do-it-yourself activities

- Increased civic involvement through both voluntary and mandatory programs, perhaps including a year or more of national service for young people

Breaking the Cultural Hypnosis of Consumerism

Changing consumption levels and patterns will require a new consciousness among millions of people, requiring dramatic changes in the consumerist messages we receive, particularly through television. The average American sees more than 25,000 commercials each year; most people watch four hours of television a day, and get most of their news from the television. Commercial television aggressively promotes high-consumption lifestyles. Television stations make their profits by delivering the largest possible audience of potential customers to corporate advertisers. Hence, they deliberately ignore the views and values of both the poor and the frugal, who spend little by necessity or by choice. By programming television for commercial success, TV broadcasters are also programming our society for ecological failure.

To revitalize our civilization, three major changes are needed in how we use television: (1) ecologically oriented advertising to balance the onslaught of consumerist messages and encourage environmental awareness of the impacts of consumption; (2) entertainment programming that explores ecological concerns, alternative ways of living, and innovative role models; and (3) expanded documentaries and investigative reports describing the global challenges we now face. At present, television ensures that we are entertainment rich and knowledge poor. Yet, television discourages discussion of its role in society; "the last taboo topic on television is television itself."[206]

A revitalized, conscious democracy requires more active communication and participation, perhaps through regular "electronic town meetings" that could allow televised dialogues and rapid feedback. This should not be a vehicle for micromanagement of government, but rather a means for citizens to become involved and discover their widely shared priorities. Just as some grassroots movements have helped to renew the commitment to democracy, we now need a citizen-based "communication rights" movement that seeks fair, ecologically responsible uses of the mass media.

> Just as the individual expression of voluntary simplicity is to be found in the intention of living with balance, so, too, with its social expression. A revitalizing civilization will be characterized by greater balance between material excess and material impoverishment, between huge cities and small communities, between massive corporations and smaller companies, between highly specialized work roles and more generalized work roles, and so on. The challenge is to apply our compassion, ingenuity, and tolerance in finding a middle path through life. [217–218]

Subject Index

Cable television, 257, 259, 264
Capacity
  carrying, 284
  ecosystem, 285
Capital, 62, 287, 327, 329
  cultural, 34, 53
  manmade, 2, 273, 286
  natural, 2, 286
  symbolic, 34
Capital accumulation, 56, 111
  captalism, 19, 140, 152, 166, 356
  English, 150
  industrialized, 161, 252
  institutions of, 164
Capitalist class, transnational, 307, 321
Carrying capacity, 284
Child care, 60
Children, 77, 87, 89, 105
  socialization of, 10, 81–82
Children's
  advertising, 104, 106
  consumption patterns, 75
  culture, 83, 104, 106–107
  marketing, 84–85, 104, 106
  play, 104, 106
  programming, 83, 104, 106
China, 11, 124, 304, 313, 320,
    323–324
Choice
  consumer, 15, 22, 29, 74
  individual, 221, 271
  interdependent, 177–178, 221
Christmas
  customs, 116
  shopping, 116
Class, 53, 87, 98, 126, 133, 136, 264
  capitalist, 307, 321
  conflict, 136
  discrepancies, 92
  lower, 12, 136
  middle, 12, 137, 140, 307, 309
  mobility, 19, 120, 287
  oppression, 57
Cognitive dissonance, 227
Collective bargaining, 36
Commercial broadcasting
  degradation of, 83
  mass-oriented, 258

Commercialization, 68, 70, 73, 77,
    134, 280
Commercials, television, 106, 247
Commodification, 93
Commodities, 15, 22, 164, 166, 169,
    214, 245
  attitudes toward, 3
  characteristics of, 3, 8
  durable, 63
  exchange of, 161
  fetishism of, 161
  high-impact, 363
  mass-produced, 3
  nondurable, 63
Commodity
  bias, 70–71
  rhetoric, 140
  sign, 34
Communication rights movement, 366
Communism, 6, 310
Communities, 80
  barriers to entry, 91
  homogenous, 91
Community enterprises
  household, 14
  local, 14
Comparative advantage, 186
Compensation, 220
  labor, 219
Competition, 32–33, 150, 159, 163,
    289
  assumptions of, 9
  perfect, 9
  positional, 70, 217–218, 315
Conflict, parent/child, 237
Conservation, 283
  household energy, 282
Consumer, 1, 8–9, 15, 22, 30, 74, 133,
    187
  autonomy, 301
  durables, 122, 124–125
  goods, 2, 15
  rational utility maximizing, 225
  revolution, 35, 109, 114, 119–120,
    132–133, 136
  satisfaction, 61, 70
Consumer behavior
  approaches to, 135, 201

Name Index